THE MOUNTAINS OF ROMANIA

ABOUT THE AUTHOR

James Roberts finished work on this guide to Romania just before his untimely death in 2002. Since the revolution he had spent more than half of every year in Romania and had travelled throughout the country. An experienced solo backpacker here, as well as in the Himalaya, the Atlas and other areas, he worked as a leader of mountain-walking and wildlife groups. Married to Elena, a Romanian, James spoke the language and had an unrivalled knowledge of the country, having explored every massif solo on foot. With his detailed knowledge of the human and natural history of the country, he was an expert interpreter of the Romanian scene.

Other books by James Roberts

published by Cicerone

The Reivers Way
The Two Moors Way
Walking in Dorset
Walking in Somerset

published by Burton Expeditions

Romania – A Birdwatching and Wildlife Guide

THE MOUNTAINS OF ROMANIA

by

James Roberts

2 POLICE SQUARE, MILNTHORPE, CUMBRIA, LA7 7PY
www.cicerone.co.uk

Reprinted 2008 and 2013
ISBN-13: 978 1 85284 295 6
ISBN-10: 1 85284 295 4

Printed by KHL Printing, Singapore
A catalogue record for this book is available from the British Library.

ACKNOWLEDGEMENTS

This book may have been entirely researched and written by me alone, but the assistance of a great many has made it possible. Most importantly I wish to thank my wife Elena – the perfect travelling companion in her country – for support whilst midnight oil has been burnt during my incarceration with a word processor in England and in Romania, for being bombarded with questions night and day and for being so effective in furthering research. This book is dedicated to Elena.

I am humbly grateful to Jackie Berry for her saintly forbearance on my first research visit in 1990, also to Dan Burchi and to Barry Smith of Edinburgh for his notes. Thanks are due to Adrian Buracu, who was so nonchalant about having effectively wrecked his Dacia car in 1990 in my quest for greater knowledge of the mountains; more than this he is owed a lifetime's thanks as it was at his birthday party the following year that I met my wife. To Fane Cotinghiu and Tudor Blaj for their enthusiasm, stamina, sense of humour and knowledge of the mountains of their country. Thanks are due to Elena Cotelici, Laura Ionescu and the late Aurel Marin for their help with research and especial thanks to Alec Tarassoff for his expertise in word-processing problems. Thanks are due to Erika Stanciu and Ovidiu Ionescu of Romsilva – the national forest authority, from whom I have learnt much about the ecology of the Carpathians; Ovidiu is the co-founder of the Carpathian Carnivore Project. Great thanks are due to that fine body of people – the cabaniers of the Carpathians – whose company in cabana kitchens I have enjoyed so much over the years and from whom I have learnt a great deal about life in the mountains. In particular I must mention Roly Boltres, Vasile and Marilena Prada of Curmătura, the Adrian Mazilu family of Caraiman, Gabi, Mari, the Blendea family and all the staff of Cristianu Mare and also the meteorologists of the Penteleu and Omu met stations, especially the former who invited me in to stay during bad snowy weather in the mountains in January 1994.

I am indebted to all those from Britain, Australia, New Zealand, Belgium, Sweden, the United States and Canada who have walked Romania's mountains with me, whose company Elena and I both have enjoyed; I ask only that you spread the word of the good times we have had! Lastly to my in-laws, the Hristea family of Bucharest who have welcomed me so warmly in their household, whose car I have borrowed so often, and who have helped in the research for this book; in particular I must mention Doina Paraschiv, crafty sniffer-out of ancient mountain tomes and dog-eared old map sheets in the libraries and bookshops of Bucharest.

Any errors contained in the text below are mine and mine alone, and are not attributable to any other.

James Roberts

Front cover: James Roberts on the main Retezat ridge

Contents

Appendices

List of Maps

Note from the publisher

This guide has had an unusually long gestation. James Roberts started work on it in the 1990's on his many visits to Romania's mountains but he sadly died at a young age when the book was at proof stage. The proofs have been checked by James's widow, Elena, who is Romanian and so particularly well qualified to do so. We would like to thank Elena and others who helped check the work. Under these circumstances readers' comments, amendments and suggestions for improvements will be particularly valuable in helping us keep the guide up to date. Please send them to us at info@cicerone.co.uk or by post to Cicerone Press, 2 Police Square, Milnthorpe, Cumbria, LA7 7PY, United Kingdom.

The maps used in the guide, on James's recommendation, are derived from maps originally published by the now defunct state-run Editure pentru Turism. A wider selection of maps for walking in Romania's mountains is starting to become available.

Warning

Mountaineering can be a dangerous activity carrying a risk of personal injury or death. It should be undertaken only by those with a full understanding of the risks and with the training and experience to evaluate them. Mountaineers should be appropriately equipped for the routes undertaken. Whilst every care and effort has been taken in the preparation of this guide, the user should be aware that conditions, especially in winter, can be highly variable and can change quickly. Holds may become loose or fall off, rockfall can affect the character of a route, snow and avalanche conditions must be carefully considered. These can materially affect the seriousness of a climb, tour or expedition.

Therefore, except for any liability which cannot be excluded by law, neither Cicerone nor the author accepts liability for damage of any nature (including damage to property, personal injury or death) arising directly or indirectly from the information in this guide.

Map Key

	route
	town
	village (*comuna*)
	village
	isolated building
	hotel
	inn (*han*)
	cabana open to public (*mountain hut*)
	camp site
	refuge
	mountain rescue post (*salvamont*)
	forestry hut (*romsilva*)
	tarred road
	untarred road or track
	footpath
	waymarking symbols
	railway
	narrow gauge railway
	cable car
	chair lift
	shepherds' hut (*stâna*)
	fortification
	cave
	crag
	pass
	waterfall
	spring
	water-sink (in limestone area)
	gorge

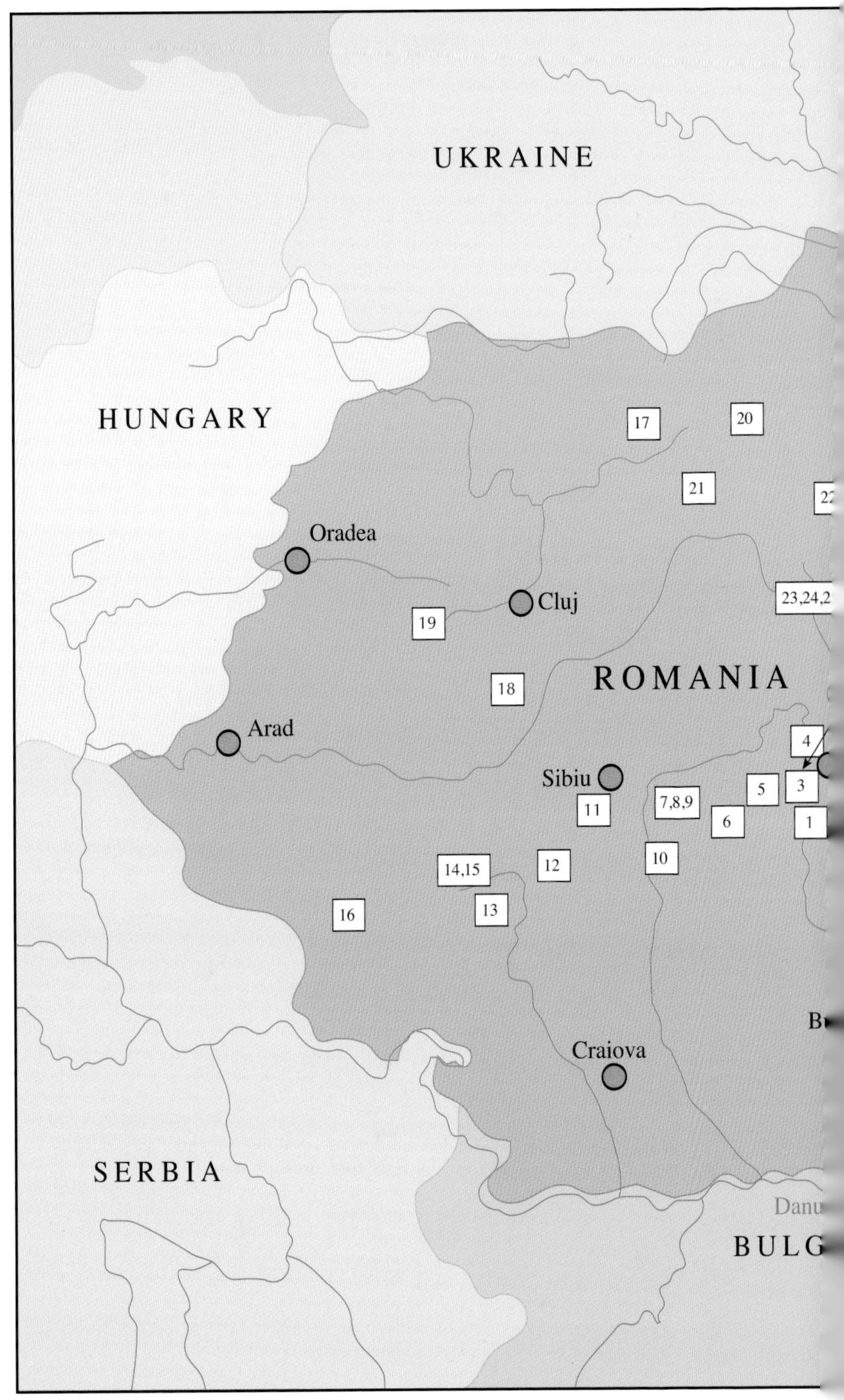

UKRAINE
HUNGARY
17
20
21
Oradea
Cluj
19
23,24,2
ROMANIA
18
Arad
4
Sibiu
3
5
7,8,9
11
6
1
14,15
12
10
16
13
Craiova
SERBIA
Danu
BULG

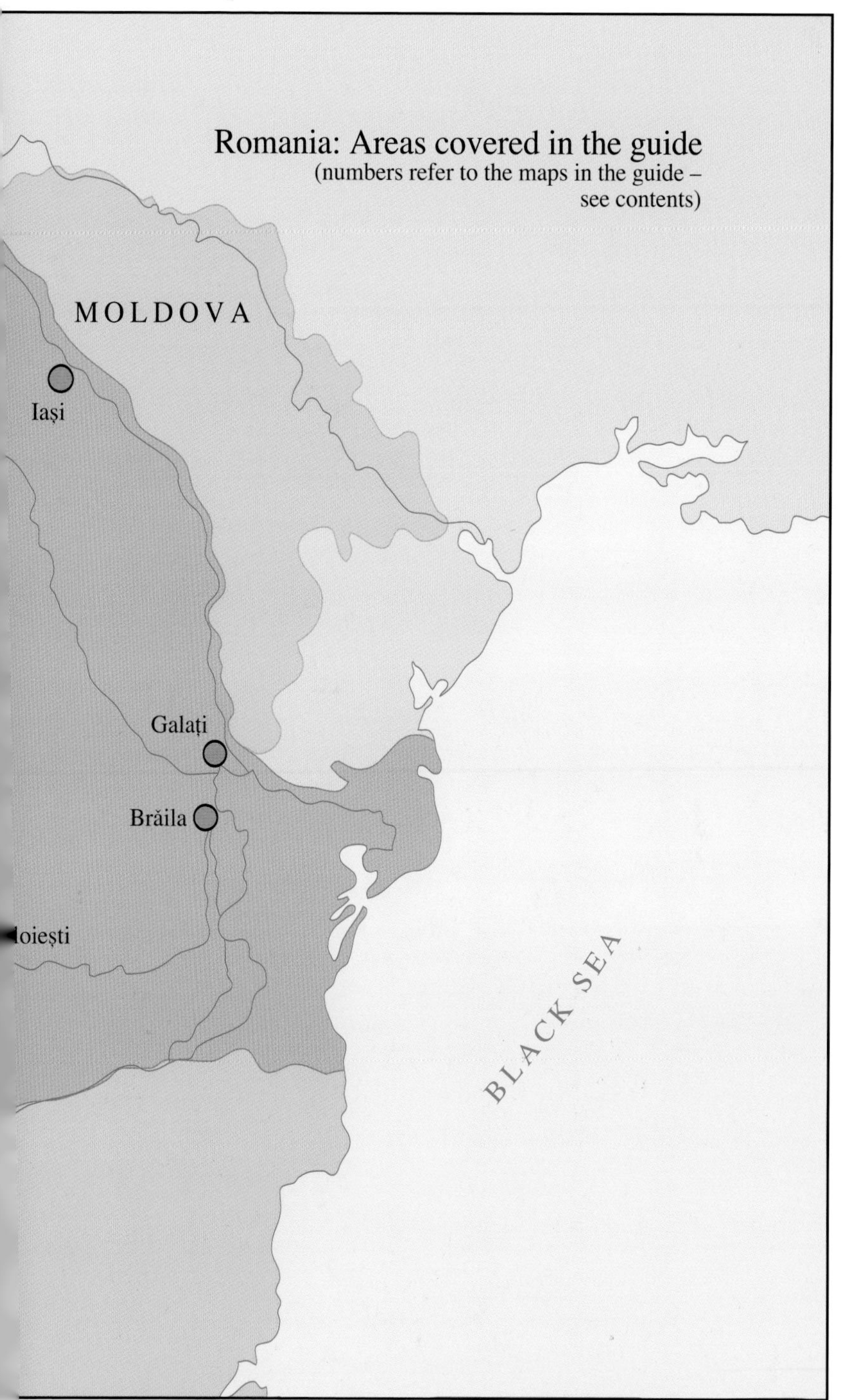
Romania: Areas covered in the guide
(numbers refer to the maps in the guide – see contents)
MOLDOVA
Iași
Galați
Brăila
oiești
BLACK SEA

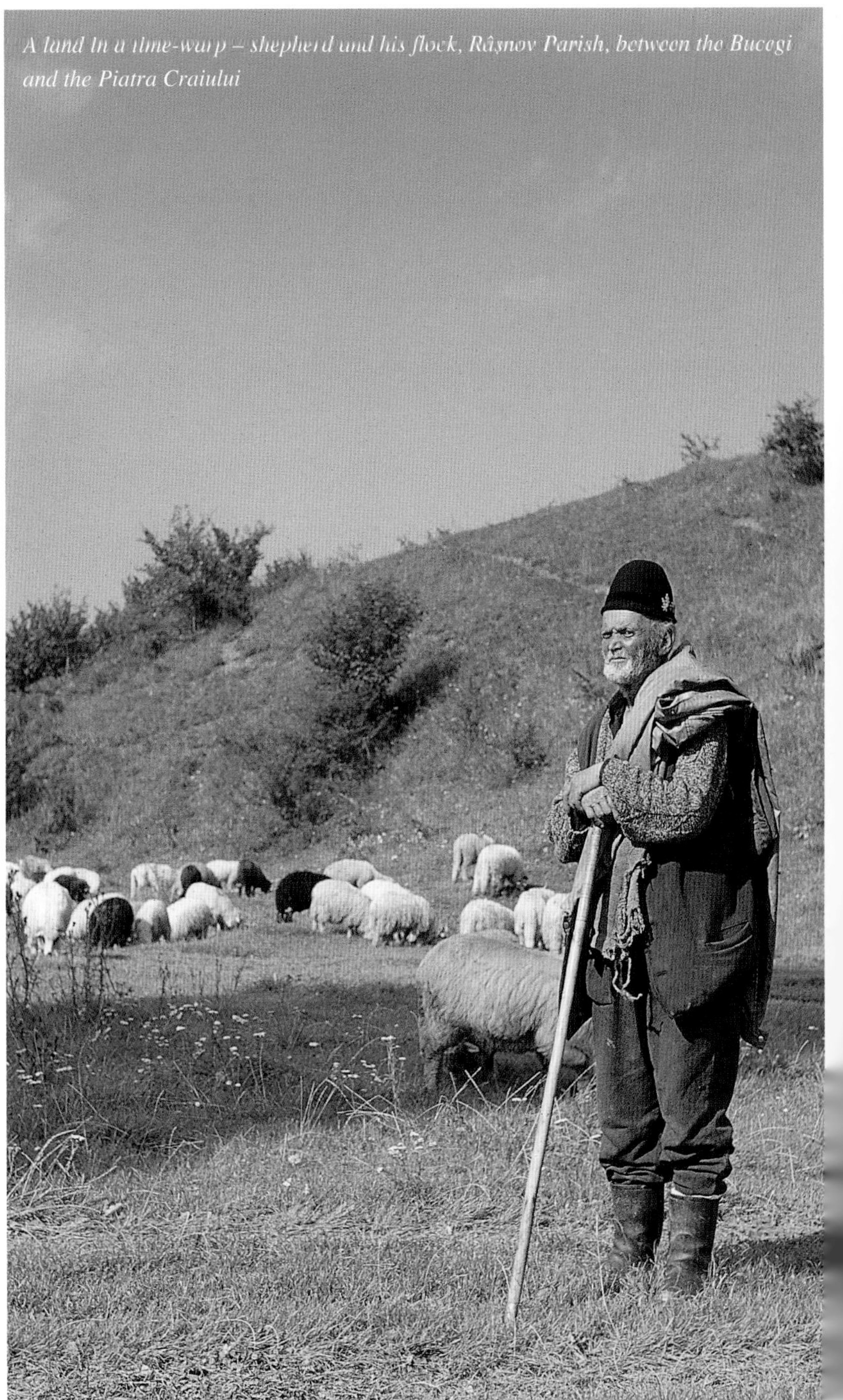

A land in a time-warp – shepherd and his flock, Râşnov Parish, between the Bucegi and the Piatra Craiului

CHAPTER ONE

The Mountains of Romania

'Theirs is not a country you can visit as a detached traveller; their own talent for friendship immediately engages the stranger's sympathy and interest and soon one feels irrationally committed...'

Dervla Murphy, *Transylvania and Beyond*

With excellently waymarked paths through a great sweep of mountains, a number of whose summits rise over 8000ft, a comprehensive system of good mountain huts, an easily-tackled language allied to Italian and French and a low cost of living for western travellers, Romania is by far the most rewarding country in eastern Europe for mountain walkers – and indeed one of the best in Europe as a whole.

More than just beautiful mountain landscapes, a mountain walking holiday or expedition in Romania offers a chance to discover a European scene now disappeared further west. With its wealth of ancient Orthodox monasteries, village festivals and locals in traditional costume, rural Romania offers a European cultural travel experience quite as stimulating as mountain ranges further afield. Romania has become one of the cheaper countries in Europe in which to travel. Combined with its easily-understood language, the extreme friendliness of the local population and the sheer beauty of its wild mountain scenery – all this means that exploring the mountains of Romania can be some of the most enjoyable and rewarding travelling that could ever be undertaken.

Whilst mountain walking is popular in Romania (as is climbing and skiing) the great area of mountains and its low density of population (23 million in a country greater in area than Britain) means that few paths are busy. The unique attraction of Romania is its ability to offer truly wild mountains in close juxtaposition to very civilised life; I have seen wolf in a forest clearing at dawn in the Făgăraş and at lunchtime sat down to a good meal with a bottle of Transylvanian dry white. Many is the time I have dined well in Braşov with a live classical orchestra and, with the music still ringing in my ears, encountered a bear at close quarters in a street in the small hours.

Fully one third of Romania is mountainous; the great sweep of the Carpathians contains some of the few remaining large stretches of wilderness landscape in Europe, the domain of bear, lynx and wolf. The walker can have the choice of a walking holiday in the finest mountain scenery with pleasant mountain huts to stay in, or, taking a tent, depart to the far-flung reaches of the country to discover remote summits with valleys and villages little changed in centuries. Many areas of the Carpathians rise sheer from the plains, giving remarkable views across vast areas of Transylvania. Particularly remarkable in this respect is the western Făgăraş, with views across to Sibiu. This same is true of the Retezat, northern slopes of the Bucegi and the Piatra Craiului ridge; the views you have are of farmland and forest far below, rather than just other mountains.

This book aims to be a complete travel information package to the wilds of

Romania. It is written not only for the dedicated mountain walker, but also for the traveller who wants to discover the wild and hilly provinces of the country, where indigenous folk music can still be heard, and the inhabitants still wear local costume, do their farmwork by hand and travel by horse and cart. It is also aimed at those who find themselves in Romania, perhaps on business or engaged in volunteer work, who wish to spend a few days in the mountains or enjoy a day walk from a railway station or 'cabana' (mountain hut).

This book aims to be a complete information package for a walking expedition in the Carpathians, rather than a comprehensive guide to the country; the Rough, Blue or Lonely Planet Guides best serve the latter purpose, and include information on three of Romania's major cities which the mountain walker is likely to visit: Brașov, Sibiu and Cluj (the access points respectively for the Bucegi/Piatra Craiului/Făgăraș, the Retezat and Cindrel, and the Apuseni). This guidebook does, however, give information on towns and places of interest in the vicinity of the walks, and the Introduction and Appendices provide practical advice and information on visiting the country.

HOW TO USE THIS BOOK

Chapters 2–12 deal with the various regions of the Carpathians and give information on a number of itineraries, ranging from day walks from a settlement or a particular cabana to point-to-point mountain traverses of more than a week. The directions are mostly for well-established paths, with a high standard of waymarking organised by the local Salvamont (mountain rescue) organisations. These waymarked paths were laid out as walks from cabana to cabana, often along ridges. This guide therefore follows this pattern of high ridge walks connecting the major summits. Many of the chapters can be linked together to make a grand tour of Romania's mountains. Each section has information under 'Access' on how to reach the area from Bucharest. This should be read in conjunction with a sheet map of the country.

Chapters 2–8 mostly have itineraries from cabana to cabana (though you may prefer to camp wild). Later chapters deal with wilder regions with much less accommodation available. Here you will need a tent, although you will not have to use it every night. Almost every area covered in the book has some kind of accommodation, as is evident from a glance at Appendix A. It is possible to stay in a cabana overnight and explore these remoter regions in day walks. Most local walkers adhere quite rigidly to itineraries which in any one day start and finish at a cabana, largely because lightweight tents, stoves and dehydrated food are only just becoming available.

Chapters 9–12 are arranged so that a number of separate massifs are covered in each. However, as can be seen from any relief map of Romania, the whole Carpathian area is elevated. In general the Carpathians are densely forested hills, running all the way from Germany, east through Poland, the Czech Republic, Slovakia and Ukraine as well as Romania. Each chapter deals separately with one mountainous section. However, each chapter also has a complete itinerary, linking all the sections together. In some cases it is possible to walk from one massif to another through the forests, along waymarked and signposted paths. Maps for these are not available, and it is difficult to find them in Romania. You may well not want to walk from one massif to another: if it is possible to catch a train or a bus, this is explained in the text. It is possible to explore Romania's mountains by car (see 'Road travel in Romania') but this is probably not as satisfactory as doing a self-contained backpacking expedition.

A welcome in the wilderness – a typical mountain cabana. Paltinu, Făgăras Massif

Chapter 13 covers the monasteries at Bucovina which, although not situated in the Carpathians proper, are none the less in wonderful walking country.

The key to a successful expedition to Romania is preparation. Time spent poring over a map of Romania with this book before you go is well spent, picking the range or ranges you want to walk across. The day stages and walks outlined below are merely suggestions – with a bit of planning you can map out your own itinerary based around what you want to see.

If there is anything in this book that is wrong – no doubt some of my research will soon become out of date – please write to the publishers. Information used in subsequent editions will be acknowledged.

ACCOMMODATION

Hotels

Hotel accommodation in Romania is not as bad as most people expect; every year more and more pleasant small, privately-run small hotels and pensions are opening up, which the proprietors take great pride in, and delight in welcoming foreign guests Outside large cities, all accommodation is very reasonably priced by western European standards; the continuing shabbiness of some older places is compensated by the low price. At the time of writing, many long-established hotels are still part of a local monopoly, the result of former state ownership. It does not necessarily follow that 'privatised means better'; I have experienced some quite acceptable state hotels and a very few revoltingly awful private establishments – attention is drawn to the latter below! In small towns in the provinces of Romania you can expect to pay around 10–30 euros (in lei) per person per night without breakfast. In all respects other than car hire, Romania is a very cheap country in which to travel. If you have a long enough memory to remember when plumbing in France was the butt of British humour, you will find much that is stimulating to the memory in Romania.

Private accommodation

It is easy to find a cheaper alternative to hotel accommodation in many towns. At stations and outside some hotels in most towns (especially mountain resorts) you may be approached as you make your way off the train by someone offering 'Doriți cazare?' or 'Camera?' – a room to stay. In small towns these are generally householders anxious to make some hard currency. They are usually happy to show you the room before agreeing a price. In larger towns a tout may be used, utilising an ability to speak a foreign language, to act as an agent for housewives. This is not a service aimed at foreigners; locals make up the majority of those staying in private houses. If a casual acquaintance asks you into a house as guest then the offer of Scotch whisky (blended or usual brand single malt is fine), or possibly cigarettes is usually appreciated, although euros are easier to carry and will be equally or more gratefully received.

Mountain huts – cabanas

One of the effects of post-war Russian-imposed Stalinist dictatorship was that Romanians could not travel outside their own national borders on holiday. A consequence of this, long overlooked outside eastern Europe, was that good facilities were maintained within the country, especially in the mountains, for skiers and walkers. The county councils, in conjunction with Oficiul Național de Turism Carpați in Bucharest, for many years operated a system of mountain chalets known as cabanas, most of them built between the wars; now they are mostly owned by county councils, leased to their cabaniers. You do not need to be a member of any kind of club or organisation to use all of the facilities in a cabana. However there are some belonging to small private clubs which I have mentioned in the text; it is still possible that in remoter areas your interest value as a foreign walker may be a passport to food and accommodation at these, too. Cabanas give access to some of the finest and highest areas of the country's mountains, especially the Transylvanian Alps.

The word cabana is applied alike to remote mountain huts, high among the crags and far from any road, to roadside halts where in summer the air is full of the sound of children's laughter and the smell of barbecues. What all cabanas share is the time-honoured concept that a traveller can obtain, for very little cost, a hot meal, drink and a bed.

In common with almost everything you find on the far side of what used to be the Iron Curtain, cabanas are scruffy and poorly maintained. However, their saving grace is that, like wayside inns in the Middle Ages, they will not turn away a walker in need of food, drink and overnight shelter. Obviously the higher and more remote the cabana, the more accommodating will be the staff. Even if all the beds are taken, you can sleep inside – somewhere, even if it is on the floor of the bar. Some of the cabanas below mention accommodation in huts – căsuțe – outside. These really are just huts, rather like a child's 'Wendy house', with just enough room to slide yourself in and sleep – a sort of wooden tent. Many cabanas, ostensibly there to serve those walking and skiing in the mountains as a recreation, are in fact used more by local shepherds as a pub – it all adds to the fun of being there.

You may well, as a visiting westerner, find yourself taking part in something of a party in a cabana, possibly with live music. Many of the walkers in the mountains carry instruments: you are quite likely to take part in a musical evening in a cabana or find walkers entertaining themselves with music on the mountainside. If you play a small instrument, take it with you – you will gain instant popularity. It is often the case that the sort of people you come across in the bars and hotels of eastern Europe are perhaps not those that you would wish to meet, commonly wanting to air generally ill-thought out opinions in slightly slurred incomprehensible quasi-English to the visiting foreigner. Generally in the cabanas of Romania's mountains you are likely to encounter more kindred spirits than these. A useful rule of thumb is that the more remote the cabana, the more amenable the crowd in it.

BACKPACKING IN ROMANIA

In common with a mountain walking expedition anywhere, you are left with the choice between carrying a heavier weight and having the flexibility of camping or carrying less and being tied to cabanas. In the Făgăraş, for example, staying at cabanas frequently means long descents in the evening and unavoidable climbing in the morning. I have found that the most satisfactory way to enjoy Romania's mountains is to carry a tent and some dehydrated food, but still staying in the odd cabana when I felt like it. There are plenty of campsites in the country – if you want, you can camp outside most cabanas and eat inside. When in the mountains you are generally free to camp where you like. Most mountain areas abound in spots to put up a tent in splendid isolation. It goes without saying that you should carry out or burn all litter, bury faeces and burn toilet paper. There are areas which for one reason or another are sensitive, such the Retezat National Park, where you are supposed to camp at specific sites; the Gemenele Reserve (boundaries are shown on the relevant map) is closed to walkers altogether.

If you are travelling independently, I consider the best possible way to approach a first visit is to take advantage of the wildness of the area and its innumerable possibilities for camping unseen. Bring a lightweight tent, a stove and a few days' supply of dehydrated food and really get away from it all. Cabanas are marvellous, especially in bad weather, but they are less marvellous if you depend upon them every night.

I have learnt a rough rule of thumb when setting off for research for this book. Each foray into the mountains has been as a self-contained backpacker, carrying tent (or Gore-tex bivvy bag in good weather), stove and food. As a general rule, however many days you pack food for, you will find your supplies lasting three times longer. The cause of this is encountering locals, mainly shepherds who are so shocked to find a foreigner ('Din Anglia?!') that they take you into their stâna and feed you – the meal occasionally washed down with plum brandy. This factor – shepherds' largesse, combined with unexpected refuges and friendly folk in villages, means that you can get to the point where you look forward to your own cooking in your tent. Please don't think I scrounge and sponge my way around the Carpathias, for I don't.

ORGANISED WALKING HOLIDAYS IN ROMANIA

This book is aimed at the walker who wants to travel independently to Romania; I have no doubt, however, that many readers may want to be part of a group. This is a good first way of visiting the country – you will certainly want to return. Whilst independent travel does provide unrivalled flexibility and contact with the local population and is cheaper, it is true that putting your mountain walking into the hands of a specialist company means that your visit ends up as more of a holiday and less of an expedition. You are not likely to experience much of Romania's better cuisine as an independent traveller; as a walker with Kudu Travel or Explore you should do (see Appendix F).

Kudu Travel run walking and sightseeing tours in Bucegi, southern Transylvania and Bucovina. Explore Worldwide also operate holidays that involve a good day hike in the Maramureş mountains, a morning walk up to and along the Rodna ridge and a wonderful walk from Suceviţa monastery to Putna monastery. This is part of an imaginative ten-day tour exploring the churches and village architecture of Maramureş, the monasteries of Bucovina and the Danube Delta. Generally speaking, any group mountain walking holiday will take you to the more popular walking areas (ie for example not Maramureş); if you really want to discover the remotest ranges you will have to pack enough gear to be self-sufficient. As time goes on the walking companies will certainly expand their operation to other areas of the country.

GETTING TO ROMANIA

By air

From Britain, Bucharest is served by daily non-stop flights from London Heathrow on the Romanian national carrier, Tarom and British Airways; a return ticket costs about £260 with either airline at the time of going to press. Both carriers normally use Boeing 737s; BA's are older than Tarom's. Tarom is now a pleasant airline to fly, in fact little different from BA. If you are flying with a mountain bike I recommend BA, with their helpful check-in staff at Heathrow. Bucharest is also well served by other western European airlines, mostly with daily flights by Air France, Lufthansa, Austrian Airlines and SAS. KLM flies from many provincial British cities and offers excellent swift connections via Amsterdam Schiphol to Bucharest; their prices are much the same as non-stop flights from London. If you live in provincial Britain it usually makes much more sense to use KLM or another continental carrier and avoid London.

From the USA, Tarom has direct flights twice a week from New York, also Chicago. Alternatively you can use many of the European carriers mentioned above. From Australia, Bucharest is probably most easily reached by using Lufthansa's offers of cut-price or free onward connections from Frankfurt, having flown from Sydney or Melbourne. This latter also applies to New York as well. Alternatively it can often be as cheap to pick up a cheap ticket to London and buy a cheap ticket to Romania there. See Appendix F – the address list gives details of outlets for tickets and the offices of airlines in Bucharest.

On arrival at Otopeni airport, Bucharest, when you extricate yourself from the customs hall you will find taxi-drivers eager for your euros. Agree the fare to get to your hotel before you go – the driver may want to be paid in euros, not lei. There is a regular bus service from Otopeni airport to Piaţa Unirii in the centre of Bucharest. A step-by-step guide to how to reach your mountain destination is given below.

By train

The rail journey from Britain to Romania takes around two days. A full-price rail ticket costs around twice the return air fare; better to use an Interrail ticket. Backpacking exploration as part of an Interrail journey is an ideal way to discover Romania. A further advantage of an Interrail ticket is that it saves you the hassle of buying a ticket out of Bucharest. Romania has an excellent rail system and an Interrail ticket is probably the perfect way to explore it; if you arrive in the country by other means, you can take advantage of the low prices of Romanian train tickets.

By road

Eurolines (see Appendix F) offer a twice-a-week service from London to Bucharest via Paris, costing £103 for a single and £172 return, but the journey takes 48 hours. Alternatively you can travel by bus to Budapest, from where there are regular trains to Bucharest, Braşov and Cluj, and also buses to Cluj, Sibiu and Braşov. It is possible to drive to Romania from the ports of the Channel coast in two days. Border crossings are not a problem; I have never waited more than fifteen minutes on the only two checked crossings: Austria–Hungary and Hungary–Romania. For information on driving see below – 'Road travel'.

ENTRY INTO ROMANIA

Holders of British passports (and citizens of other EU countries, also the USA) do not need visas to visit Romania for a period of up to 90 days. The requirement for visas was dropped in January 2001.

GETTING TO THE MOUNTAINS

The Carpathians of Romania are surprisingly accessible; several of the walking itineraries given below start around two or three hours' journey from Bucharest. Before leaving home, consult the accommodation guide at Appendix A for hotels in Bucharest. Romanian tourist offices supply free a plan of Bucharest with an address list of hotels, theatres, and various services. When travelling in Romania, always carry your passport. It is quite possible that a policeman may ask you for identification – for a foreigner only a passport is acceptable.

Bucharest

In the morning take a taxi to the Gara de Nord – or if you really want to sample the full Bucharest experience, you can try out the Metro. There are direct trains from Piaţa Victoriei; from other stations in the centre you will have to change (at Piaţa Victoriei). In fact, a taxi called by the hotel to take you to the station will be cheap (settle the price with reception if you are unsure); usually only from the airport are taxi fares over-priced. The reception of your hotel should have a railway timetable.

Train travel in Romania

For most of the time rail travel in Romania is a pleasure; in Western terms ticket prices are absurdly cheap. I suggest you travel first class, for which you will need to reserve a seat. If you are forced to stand in the corridor (unlikely though this is) through not having a reserved seat you are at greater risk of theft. Both in Bucharest and the provinces, first-class reservations are only sold at the station a few hours before departure. If you want to buy a ticket in advance of this (advisable for long-distance trains, though scarcely feasible if you have just arrived in the country and want to depart immediately) you will have to go to an Agenţia de Voiaj CFR. In Bucharest there is one just outside the Gara de Nord and another at Str. Brezoianu. In provincial towns they are usually easily located in the main street. Since most readers will be heading to the nearest mountains, around the Prahova Valley, you can be reassured that there are trains at least every two hours and they are seldom crowded.

Trains are sometimes old and not especially fast, but they do run on time. I suggest you avoid the slow cursa or personal trains, except for scenic rural branch lines where there may be no choice. Booking yourself a sleeper journey is worthwhile, since daytime trains are quite slow and you can save the cost of a hotel. The best are first-class compartments (vagon de dormit – not cuşete), with two berths and their own basin; starched sheets and pillows are provided.

Women travellers in Romania can be reassured that Romanian booking staff and staff on trains are strict in not permitting men to be in a woman's compartment, unless you book it together. Second-class cușete accommodation can be more flexible.

Road travel in Romania – buses, car travel and hitch-hiking

In the provinces of Romania there is a comprehensive public transport system of local buses. The country's long-distance bus network is a post-communist era private enterprise development, much of it in the hands of Turkish companies. Many of these buses depart from outside the Gara de Nord. The public transport system is co-ordinated, so that bus stations and stops are usually near railway stations. Arriving at the terminus station of a branch line in a rural area you will more often than not find a bus waiting. Even remote villages are usually served by one bus (possibly a 'maxi-taxi' minibus per day). Buses can sometimes be crowded.

Hitching a ride with a car or on a truck (or possibly a horse-drawn cart in remote valleys) is easy. It is expected that the passenger pays for the lift (but not in my experience on a cart). Hitch-hiking is widely practised on main roads in Romania; driving on long journeys it has often seemed that if I accepted all the money offered by alighting hitch-hikers, I would have had all my fuel paid for. A prominently displayed flag of your country of origin is a good idea; in many cases you will be invited into the driver's house for something welcoming and generally intoxicating.

If you are driving your own car in Romania you will have to face the drawbacks of the sometimes very potholed state of some rural by-roads and some urban streets; matters are improving considerably. In general, through routes (especially E-roads) are well surfaced and fast and you can keep to 100kph for long stretches. A few rural roads are as bad or worse than any I have seen in India and are at their worst in spring after the thaw and a huge number of villages (even within 50km of the centre of Bucharest) are reached only by dirt roads. Much of the road system is comprehensively old-fashioned, with markings and reflective, night-visible signs rare off the international E-roads. This is a country where, immediately beyond the ring-road around the capital, you can find villages reached only by dirt tracks. I would advise against driving at night in Romania (especially off main roads) because of the rarity of road markings and reflective roadsigns, potholes and craters, combined with the danger of intoxicated, drably-clad peasants (often on bicycles) reeling from the shadows into your path, and other vehicles (especially horse-drawn carts) with no lights or reflectors.

The pleasures of driving in Romania are the utterly empty roads in the provinces and a sense of returning to the heyday of motoring when a car journey was still an adventure. The lack of traffic on rural roads and the open nature of the landsape means that if you see something of interest you can almost always pull off onto the side of the road, with no hedge or fence to stop you. The low price of fuel – one third of its price in Britain – is also an attraction; unleaded petrol is now universally available. Some guides warn of the unreliability of fuel supplies; this is no longer true. There is a tremendous wealth of unsurfaced roads, both in the lowlands and in the mountains. There can be no country in Europe richer in opportunities for self-contained exploring in a Land Rover or similar vehicle; this is probably the best kind of vehicle to take there.

There are few differences to driving regulations in Romania compared to anywhere else; British drivers who are familiar with continental driving will have no

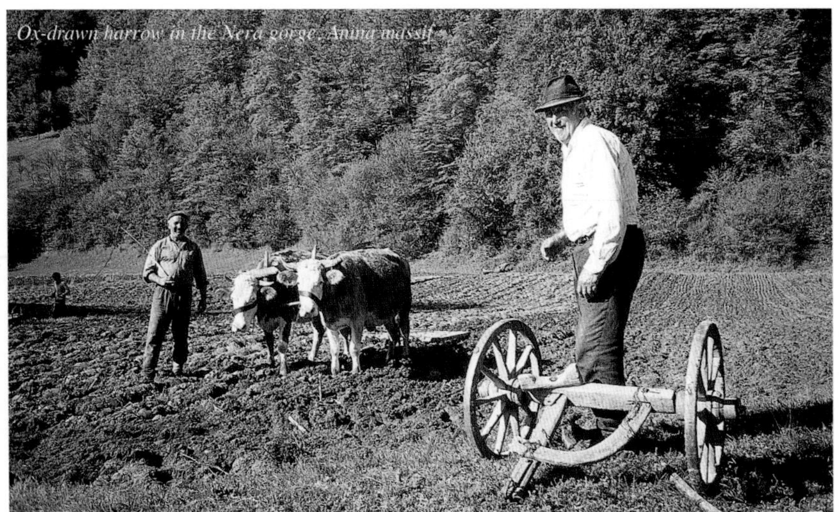

Ox-drawn harrow in the Nera gorge, Anina massif

problems. (Note that DN = Drum Național, equivalent to British A road, and DJ = Drum Județean, county road or minor road.)

Be careful when overtaking as sudden swerves out to the left to avoid a crater are commonplace. You are not allowed to drink at all if at the wheel. Be very careful in towns with trams running along the middle of the streets. When the tram stops for passengers to alight you have to stop and let them reach the side of the road. This is the universal custom in Europe where trams are operating and it is also law. Do not assume that you have the right of way when you are on a roundabout. If you do suffer a breakdown, Romanian mechanics are experienced in making improvised repairs if the right part is not available. Car parts in Romanian are often named in French, so the illustrated booklet given out by the British AA with names in European languages can be useful. Self-drive car hire is available, but in comparison to the general cost of living is very expensive. It is not a time- or cost-efficient way of exploring the mountains, although for those with little time and prepared to spend more money it does offer probably the best way of seeing the monasteries of Bucovina or the villages of Transylvania, combined with some hiking.

MONEY IN ROMANIA

At the time of writing, Romania's banking system is still rudimentary. Credit cards and travellers' cheques are of limited use, although cashpoint machines for credit cards are appearing rapidly; Sinaia now has two (the term is 'bancomat' in Romanian), as do all big cities. Contrary to what is sometimes believed, you cannot spend dollars or euros as cash. These should be changed into lei whenever necessary. The advantage of security provided by travellers' cheques is diminished by the fact that you have to encash them all before leaving town. Banks charge various amounts for this service.

I suggest you change a small amount of currency on arrival at the airport once through into the arrivals hall; the exchange office on the 'air side' before you go through passport control has a poor rate. In fact you will find the best rates at exchange booths in the city – there are plenty. There is nothing in Romania that you will be obliged to pay for in euros. All prices in this book have been quoted in euros: firstly, because euros are the most accepted form of foreign currency (shops selling electrical goods, etc., in rural towns are often happy to change money for you – quite legally), and secondly, because inflation is such that any prices quoted in lei would inevitably be out of date before this book reached the press, let alone the reader. This inflation is, however, approximately matched to devaluation against hard currency, so that prices quoted in euros tend not to rise by very much.

In the Middle Ages, when currency was valued at the weight of gold or silver in the coins, there was no need for the traveller to change any currency as he moved around. In eastern Europe at the start of the twenty-first century the euro has the same universal acceptance. Never, ever change money with anyone who approaches you on the street and move away rapidly if anyone offers you this service. If you have lei left as you leave Romania and need to change it back into hard currency, you will have to show a buletin de schimb (an exchange voucher) to show that you have changed your money officially; exchange houses issue these.

WHEN TO GO

The snow cover in the Carpathians generally lasts from the latter part of October to mid-April or early May, after which it starts to disappear rapidly with the onset of a southern European summer. In June you might find large snowfields above approximately 1800m. In the higher parts, snow can lie in gullies on north facing slopes well into July or indeed right through the summer in the Făgăraş, Bucegi, Parâng, Rodna and Retezat. Above 2000m it can freeze and snow in any month of the year, though this will not last in summer. In common with other mountains, the best time for flowers is during and soon after the spring thaw, altogether one of the best times to explore the Carpathians, given that you will not be able to venture into the higher parts. Ice-axe and crampons are of little help when you are trapped up to your waist in dense soft thawing snow. There are still plenty of flowers in bloom in the mountains in June. Some of the finest fun I have had in the Carpathians is hurtling at some speed down the snow-filled gullies on my ice-numbed bottom – check your exit routes carefully for such exploits.

However the Carpathians are good for flowers at all times when there is no snow cover; there is an abundance and variety of Alpine species every bit as remarkable – or better than – the Alps or Pyrenees. Even more delightful perhaps are the flowers to be found below the tree line, in the hand-scythed hay meadows. Any time between mid-June and the latter part of July is good for this. There is also a crop of crocuses in many hay meadows at the time of the spring thaw in April.

August is the month when most of the country is on holiday. Romanians have a passion for their mountains and whole families set up camp around their Dacia cars parked by mountain streams for days at a time. If you have to visit in August you will find that the more accessible areas are quite crowded. The most popular high ranges are, in order of visitor pressure, the Bucegi, the Făgăraş, the Retezat, the Piatra Craiului; in other areas you simply do not meet large numbers of people out walking. Even in popular areas it is easy to escape the crowds – for example along the western ridge of the Bucegi horseshoe. If the monasteries of Bucovina are your goal, August is the busiest month, and from mid-morning onwards you may find a number of visitors in the area. Early summer is probably the best time to visit this region.

In the heart of the Făgăraş, looking north to Bîlea Valley from Şaua Caprei (351m) towards Bîlea Lake and the TransFăgăraşan road down to Bîlea Cascada

The fact that August is the time for family visits, many with young children, means that, whilst the more accessible cabanas are full, the high paths through the mountains see remarkably light traffic. Nowhere in Romania (with one exception) is the extent of mountain erosion or the size of the crowds comparable to those suffered in England along the Pennine Way long-distance footpath or in the Lake District. The only spot in Romania that is visited to this extent is the area around Babele cabana in the Bucegi, where the existence of a year-round cable car service from a large town on the main road has led to crowding on some days in summer – and the ski season.

Overall, the best time to visit Romania (in common with many other parts of Europe) from the point of view of long daylight hours, few visitors, flowers at their best, and generally the best weather is the months of May and June. What you do miss in June, however, is the great wealth of butterflies which are at their best from mid-July until the end of August.

One method of mountain walking which is ignored by almost all walkers is the possibility of night hiking, the virtues of which were extolled by Robert Graves in his wonderful autobiography *Goodbye to All That*. As he pointed out, it is often much easier to sleep in the warmth of the day in summer and walk in the cool of the night – it means you can carry less gear. In the Carpathians there is a second advantage of night walking. In the summer the bad weather in the region tends to come from thunderstorms resulting from convection currents arising during the day. Night time can offer more stable weather, giving you the opportunity to sleep through the sometimes cloudier days in a tent (next to impossible in a cabana). Paths are so easy to follow and the waymarking so good that the ridge tops of the Carpathians offer superb nocturnal hiking. Of course the best time is around full moon. One useful advantage is that the shepherds move their flocks (and their dogs) down to the sheepfolds along the tree line at night, so that you can walk the high ridges in safety. I do not recommend that you try and walk in the forests at night, largely because of the problems of navigation. At night time you receive a far stronger impression of the spirit of the place, and the views by moonlight can be simply superb.

WHERE TO GO

The question of where to go depends on what it is you want from a mountain walking holiday. If you are after walking well above the tree line in spectacular high mountains, to the exclusion of all else, then you will find that the Făgăraș and the Retezat are exactly what you require. Both of these have the advantage that they are well supplied with cabanas. A similarly high range, smaller in extent and with little in the way of cabanas, is the Parâng; this is much the least frequented of the four ranges that reach 2500m (the Făgăraș, the Retezat, the Bucegi and the Parâng).

Those in search of the highest of the Carpathians, for exciting high-level walking with the grandest of mountain landscapes will head to the Făgăraș, Retezat, Parâng or Rodna ranges. The Făgăraș offer a challenging ridge walk along its east–west crest. The Retezat is a more compact massif with sharper craggy ridges and high mountain tarns; both offer excellent challenging walking.It may be that you want to discover a varied combination of high craggy mountains, wild forests, delightful alpine valleys with hay meadows of more flowers than grass, old-fashioned villages whose ancient walls echo to the sound of horses and carts, plus a day or two's city sightseeing in a delightful old city. In this case I suggest you follow the itinerary given in the Prahova region then walk from Bran into the Piatra Craiului, walk out to Zărnești and return to Bucharest via Brașov. This can easily be fitted into two weeks' holiday from Europe or North America. This holiday, too, can be spent staying only in cabanas, without the need to carry a tent or cooking gear. An excellent alternative would be to travel to Sibiu and spend some time walking in the Cindrel and Retezat.

If you want to wander among remote mountain villages, with plenty of contact with the indigenous population then you should head either for the Apuseni or to the more remote Maramureș county in the far north, with the Rodna mountains. These regions do not have the number of cabanas found further south: you should carry all gear with you although you will not have to use it every night.

If wilderness be your priority, discovering a landscape unaffected by man's activities, then you should head for the Maramureș mountains on the far northern border, combined with a rail journey up the roadless Vaser valley (this is offered with a guide by Explore Worldwide). This could usefully be combined with exploration of the Pietrosul area of the Rodna, followed a walk from Maramureș into the Eastern Carpathians, going off the maps included in this book. This region should be visited with tent, cooking gear, food for several days – it is for someone who has experience of self-contained hiking in remote areas.

If you are after a holiday with mostly moderate walking with excellent variety and delightful views, combined with a dash of culture, then you should head for a few days in Brașov, one of Europe's finest city-centres. When you tire of the churches, organ concerts, galleries, museums and watching the world go by, drink in hand at the town hall square cafes, you can walk from the gate in the city walls at Schei, straight into the mountains on signed paths. I know of no other city in the world whose outskirts are haunted at night by bears.

Whether you are after a spell of gentle rambling with a bed at night or want to tackle some elevated and challenging walking (still with a bed at night), or want to immerse yourself in some of Europe's last remaining wilderness regions, you will find it in the Carpathians in Romania. Wherever you choose for your first mountain walking visit, one thing is certain: you will want to return at the earliest opportunity to discover more.

OUTDOOR EQUIPMENT IN ROMANIA

Over the eleven years of researching this book Romania has changed from being a place where all equipment had to be brought from home, to being a source of good quality low-priced gear, especially boots. For example at the time of writing a pair of Romanian-made Asolo brand boots (£40 new in Bucharest) are providing excellent service in hard use. Major cities also have outdoor gear outlets and the kit you see being worn and carried in the Carpathians by locals is fast catching up with western Europe – at long last.

PHOTOGRAPHY

Kodak, Agfa, Fuji and other main-brand print film is widely available. However slide film can be more difficult to obtain. If you want to take black and white and are in Romania for some time you may care to try (former East) German Orwo film or Romanian Azopan. However you should have them developed and printed here as their emulsion is not properly compatible with western processing methods. The costs of your photography will plummet, using local materials! If you are taking an SLR to the country, a good quality padded dustproof bag is a must. Almost any visit to rural Romania involves vehicle travel on unmade-up roads, exposing it to jolting and dust.

WALKING MAPS

'I was not able to light on any map or work giving the exact locality of the Castle Dracula, as there are no maps of the country as yet to compare with our own Ordnance Survey'

Bram Stoker, *Dracula* – Jonathan Harker's journal

A century later, little has changed from the situation described above. However, finding your way is relatively easy for the mountain walker who is an experienced map-reader. The best way would be to obtain maps before you go. However do not let lack of a good map put you off exploring Romania's mountains on foot. The paths are well signed and waymarked and you may be lucky and buy a map locally.

A consequence of the communist system was that military survey (Ordnance Survey type) remained a closely-guarded military secret. The powers-that-be then had the problem of finding a way to encourage the population to take to the mountains, but to do it without proper maps. The idea of the mountain walker having to study a map to see where his or her path lay is quite alien to many Romanian walkers, who simply follow waymarked trails from cabana to cabana (or, like shepherds, learn mountain topography over long periods of time). I have never seen a Romanian hiker carrying a map in the hand or round the neck in a case or met a walker who knows how to use a compass. In conjunction with the cabanas, what has been developed is a

'Where men have never cared to haunt ... And ghosts then keep their distance'
Brocken Spectre on the main Făgăraş ridge near Vârful Laiţa

system of well waymarked paths, following the usual continental system of coloured symbols, with elaborate signposts indicating which symbol to follow and the number of hours' walk to the next cabana, pass or village. Thus the need for accurate mapping was to an extent done away with.

Walking maps of the principal areas are occasionally available from bookshops (librarie) in towns or roadside kiosks in mountain towns such as Sinaia

Predeal, Bușteni, Zărnești. Stanfords in London and The Map Shop at Upton upon Severn also have a stock of the more popular mountain areas. In Bucharest the best outlet is the excellent Himalaya gear shop at the south end of Calea Moșilor, just behind the Cocor shop. You could also try the bookstalls outside the university at the entrance to the Metro station. The tourist information office in Predeal station and in the centre of Sinaia are both usually well supplied.

The maps of the Carpathians, in a bizarre variety of scales, show the footpaths marked with the symbol used as a waymark on the ground. The maps are very informative: on the reverse of the sheet are detailed itineraries, and symbols, with walking times, and details about the cabanas. However, judged as maps they are poor, with no grid and a contour interval of 100m – they are but one stage better than the sketch maps you might find in any guidebook.

Whilst looking for maps you may find a useful staple-bound booklet of maps and walking instructions entitled *Drumeție în Carpați*; formerly this was issued free by Romanian Tourist Offices abroad in French, German, English and Italian, and was titled *Invitation to the Romanian Carpathians*.

WAYMARKING OF MOUNTAIN PATHS

Marking of paths is maintained by the county councils (usually with the Salvamont mountain rescue), and is often of a higher standard than the Sentiers de Grandes Randonnées in France and Germany's Fernwanderwege. At most path junctions you will find a signpost, giving time to the next summit or cabana, and relevant information, such as whether it involves a difficult descent or if the path is closed in winter.

At first glance, the walking maps of a mountainous area are confusing, being littered with a number of symbols attached to paths. In fact the system is logical and easy to follow; the standard marking is a vertical red stripe in a white square, the same as the standard French Sentier de Grande Randonnée (GR) marker. This mark tends to be used for the route that follows the top of the principal ridge in a range – for most of the Făgăraș traverse you will be following it along the watershed. Stripes in other colours (yellow and blue), and the other symbols – triangle, discs or crosses – are used for other routes. In general, red marks a more strenuous route than yellow or blue, although each itinerary below should be looked at in terms of distance walked and altitude gained in a day, rather than making any assumptions based on the colour of route marking. A route of a particular symbol will start and finish at a noteworthy feature, such as a village, cabana or junction with a road. In fact most of the itineraries given below tend to change symbols part way along – directions for this being given in the text.

At path junctions, passes, in villages and where paths leave roads – and at many other spots – you will in the better-walked areas usually find a signpost telling you where the route goes, what symbol to follow and how long it takes to get there. It may also say that the route is dangerous or forbidden in winter. Sometimes multiple signposts point the way along a number of routes which later divide. Cabanas will have directions on the walls, or a signpost outside; many cabanas have large maps on the wall. Once a signpost has set you on your way you tend to find that every few metres a rock or tree trunk has been painted with the symbol you are following. You rapidly pick up the knack of looking for them to check that you are on your route. A pair of high-quality lightweight binoculars (such as Zeiss, Leica or Swarovski 10x25, 8x30 or 8x20) is invaluable in spotting waymarks in the distance, especially at dawn and dusk.

Times for a given stage tend to be on the generous side on signposts, largely, I suspect because locals tend to be so weighed down with large quantities of equipment. It tends to be that the larger the number of the walking party, the slower it goes.

Whilst the paths along the higher parts of the mountains are used almost exclusively for recreation, those from the populated mountain valleys are used for the same purpose for which they were created – as a means of communication for the local population (in contrast to Britain and much of western Europe, where footpaths are generally used for recreation). The few signs that you see saying 'Keep out' ('Intrarea interzisă') are a recent phenomenon. There is not the same perception of a conflict of interest between those who want to walk across the land and those who farm the land as occasionally occurs in the British Isles. Since there are so many locally-used footpaths, it follows that there are many more paths on the ground (heading from habitation into the mountain meadows) than are shown on the map. The paths shown on the map are well signed and marked, so as to differentiate them from the farm-to-farm and farm-to-pasture paths.

Some of the sections below recommend linking itineraries from one massif to another which are not on the maps in this book: they were not available at the time of publication – nor indeed are they likely to be. You may be able to find maps for these areas in Romania, or meet up with other walkers who are following the route. On the other hand you may be of a disposition to head into these areas armed with what you have. Do so at your own risk. In fact, most of the paths are so

Waymarking is of a high standard

well waymarked that it is perfectly possible to walk from one massif to another on a linking path without mishap. The trick to this is to obtain an overall road map of the country or, better still, the excellent – though contour-less – road atlas from the Direcția de Topografie Militară (the equivalent of the British Ordnance Survey); Stanfords in London usually have supplies of this.

Once off the walking maps, your navigation aids will be a compass, written directions in the text, a contour-less road map and a certain sixth sense born out of experience. If you intend to tackle these ridge-top paths through the forest – a wonderful way to discover what Europe was like centuries ago, before man cleared vast areas of forest – then you may have to navigate with a page cut or photocopied from a road atlas.

INTERNATIONAL LONG-DISTANCE FOOTPATHS

A new development in Romania is the linking of the main ridge routes with the European international footpath network. These are not as well known as they might be in Britain, but are international long-distance paths which cross the whole continent of Europe and are signed as such. An example is the E4

Waymarking in the Postăvaru massif

which starts in southern Spain and crosses the Pyrenees, and southern France to the Jura, across Austria, briefly entering Germany in the Allgäu district, through Vienna to the Hungarian border. There are plans to extend the E8 along the Carpathian chain through Ukraine and across the border into Romania from the north, probably somewhere near the Prislop Pass between Maramureş and Moldavia, from where it would head south towards Braşov. Likewise there are plans to extend the E3 into Transylvania (currently it runs from the Atlantic coast on the extreme west of Spain, up through France to Belgium, across Germany) and eventually to Budapest.

WHAT TO TAKE WITH YOU

This book is intended as a guide for moderately experienced walkers in mountains who want the information necessary to walk in Romania's Carpathians. It is not an instruction book on dos and don'ts in the mountains – such knowledge is in any case not best learnt from books but from personal experience. What is important is that you should be used to living out of your rucksack. Romania then becomes another backpacking expedition. If you are intending to visit the remoter areas of the country where cabanas are thin on the ground, you may anticipate being invited in to private houses, or you may want to ask on arrival in a village in the evening. In this case offer to pay first; it becomes very embarrassing to brandish money next morning when you have sat up all night, becoming firm friends with your hosts whilst representing your country in an international Ţuica-drinking contest. If you are in a situation where money is not an appropriate token then what you want to offer is something attractive that weighs next to nothing in your rucksack. Postcards of your home town are a good idea. Alternatively take some photographs of your hosts, and take down their address and send them the photographs from home. Send no more than three photographs as fat packages are sometimes waylaid by Romanian postal customs.

CLIMBING

Climbing is popular, largely because of the opportunities for it that abound. Competition climbing has been popular there longer than it has in the west. It tends to be combined with mountain orienteering and various quizzes into a multi-activity competition known rather off-puttingly as Turism Sportiv. The Club Alpin Român (for address see Appendix F) has much the same prestige as the British Alpine Club.

A good number of Romania's best climbing sites are very accessible; as well as the mountains there are a number of gorges with some excellent routes. Of the gorges that offer climbing one of the most accessible is the Râşnov gorge just south of Poiana Braşov. To reach it, head east from Râşnov on the DN73A to Pârâul Rece and Predeal and turn left at Cheia cabana. Beware; it is frequented by the army. Prăpăştiile Zărneştilor gorge, in the Piatra Craiului, is the home base for the Torpedo climbing club in Zărneşti, who

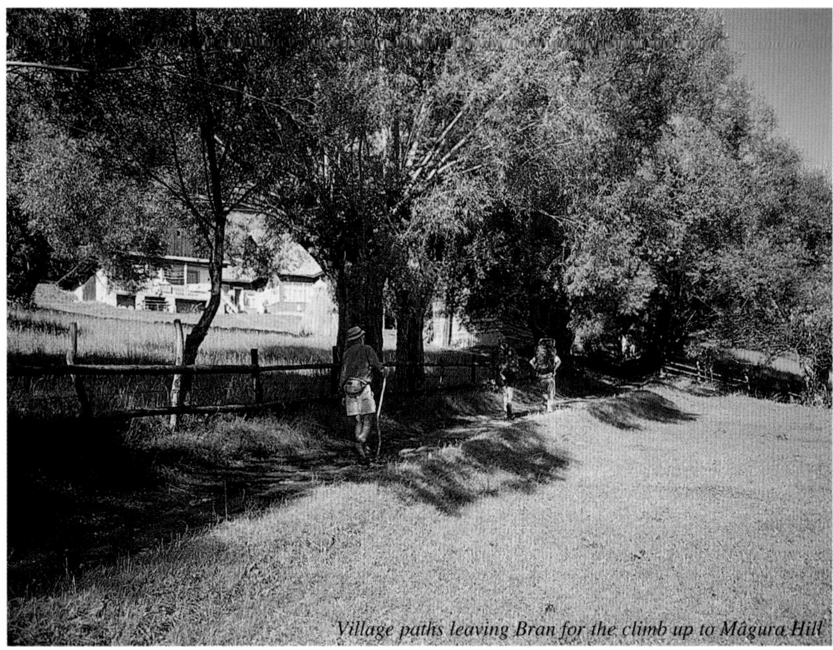

Village paths leaving Bran for the climb up to Măgura Hill

have a climbing hut in the gorge. A similar distance from Braşov to these two sites, but south-east from the city, reached by the DN1A main road, is Gropşoare, the sister massif to the Ciucaş. As well as some challenging walks mentioned in the text below there are a number of climbing routes.

In the Apuseni mountains of central Transylvania, the gorge of Cheile Turzii (see 'The Apuseni Mountains') has some fine climbing routes. Elsewhere in the Apuseni, in the Trascău range, there is climbing in the Râmeţ, Aiud and Întregalde gorges, all with cabanas nearby. Also popular are the Bicaz gorges in the Eastern Carpathians, reached by the DN12C road. In the south-west of Romania, around the Semenic and Almăj mountains, there are three worthwhile gorges: the Cheile Caraşului, just north of Anina and conveniently close to Marghitaş cabana (see Appendix A); Cheile Miniş, just south of Anina on the DN57B road; and, by far the best, the Cheile Nerei, just east of the village of Sasca Montana. In spite of its relative remoteness this gorge is well worth travelling to. In the Banat, sout-east of Aleşd, 40km east of Oradea, are two gorges, near the villages of Vadu Crişului and Şuncuiuş. Vadu Crişului gorge has a cabana at its base (see Appendix A). Climbing sites here are easily reached by train from Cluj or Oradea. The eastern end of the Căpăţân has some climbing in the Cheia gorge, near Băile Olăneşti.

Aside from gorges there is some worthwhile climbing to be had on the crags of the mountains themselves. The most accessible climbing from Bucharest is in the Bucegi, from the town of Buşteni. An hour and a half's walk from the station in Buşteni is the Valea Albă climbing hut belonging to the Club Alpin Român, giving access to the conglomerate cliffs of Valea Alba. The path leads west from Căminul Alpin cabana, signed from the station. A turning off the same path also leads to the same club's Coştila hut, with some fine routes on the flanks of Vârful Coştila. There are a number of other good sites in the Bucegi, for example on the cliffs flanking the western side of Vârful Bătrâna. Access to these is either by walking over Şaua Strungă pass from Padina cabana or by walking from the attractive village of Moieciu de Sus, reached by bus from Bran.

There looks to be good climbing in the Zănoaga gorge, in the south of the Bucegi, although I have not heard of anyone trying it. Climbers from Braşov practise on the crags on the southern side of Postăvarul mountain, reached either by a four-hour walk from the Tâmpa cable car from the old town of Braşov, or by ascending the cable car from Poiana Braşov. The Piatra Craiului offers good climbing, easily accessible from the cabanas at Curmătura, Brusturet and Plaiul Foii, as well as the town of Zărneşti. Two climbers' shelters have been erected at the base of the sites, at Diana and Ciorânga; there is also climbing at a number of other spots in the Piatra Craiului, the location of which can be shown to you by the staff at Curmătura cabana. There are some remote spots for climbing in the Făgăraş range and also around a number of peaks in the Retezat, accessible from Genţiana and Pietrele cabanas. The sites in the Retezat are below the summits of Peleaga, Judele, Bucura and a number of others.

CYCLING

It is not as widely realised as it might be that it is perfectly possible to put a bicycle on an aircraft – it simply requires more preparation than putting it on a train. Romania is very well suited to exploration by bike. If you are used to cycling in Britain, or rather you would like to cycle but are put off by the amount of traffic, you will be delighted by the empty roads of Romania's provinces. The hazards of dense, fast traffic and inconsiderate drivers are replaced by different, perhaps more manageable dangers in Romania – deep potholes and the occasional nasty sheepdog in the mountains.

In the last few years cycling seems to have been taken over by mountain bikes, in spite of them being generally less suitable for on-road use than touring bikes. However because of the potholes in the tarred roads and the wealth of unsurfaced roads in rural areas – lowland as well as mountainous – you are probably better off in Romania with a mountain bike than a road tourer. 'Real' mountain biking – tackling ridge-top routes normally only used by walkers – is possible only in a few areas of the Carpathians. In all others you will end up carrying your bike – with panniers – for an unacceptable amount of time. High ridges that are negotiable by mountain bike are dealt with below. There is adventure aplenty to be had whilst keeping to the rough and tarred roads of the Carpathians.

You should come as self-sufficient as possible in tools and spares. Bicycle repairers are thin on the ground (though are appearing rapidly), with the exception of vulcanizare – repairers of tyres for cars and bicycles alike. Any roadside car workshop can usually fix a bicycle as well.

Otopeni airport is outside Bucharest, exactly on the main DN1 route to the mountains and Braşov. However I strongly suggest that you do not try to cycle along it as it is fast and busy. When you buy your ticket for a train journey, explain that you are with a bike ('cu bicicleta'). You will have to buy a separate ticket and register it at a separate office at the station. It can be difficult to put a bike on an accelerat train. In my experience, in this case the best way is to simply get the bike on the train with you, lock it to the handrail in the corridor, swing the handlebars flush with the frame and then deal with the conductor if he or she objects.

The snag with flying a bicycle is that it is included in your weight allowance, leaving little left over for the panniers and their contents. A Gore-tex bivi bag instead of a tent may well be a good idea if you are travelling solo. If you do fly your bike, pack it in a new bike box, which most cycle shops will happily supply. Alternatively, British Airways check-in staff at Heathrow will happily supply stout polythene sheeting and sticky tape to pack your bike for the flight out. To do this you will have to remove the pedals and turn the handlebar parallel to the frame – take an appropriate Allen key to do this at the airport.

Suggested touring routes

Romania abounds in long empty stretches of road through hill areas through forgotten quaint villages – roads that just cry out to be explored using a mountain bike equipped with panniers to tour. Some of the most enjoyable research for this book has been doing just this. One of the best routes that could be tackled with a bicycle in Romania would be to start at Suceava, in the north of Moldavia, catching the (possibly sleeper) train up there and head generally southwards, visiting some of the monasteries as you go. The best start would be to head up to Rădăuți and take the Putna road from there. Putna is reached by train, but the straight empty road along the Suceava valley is a delight. If you have a mountain bike you will be able to get through the woods to Sucevița and head over from the village of Vicovu de Jos to Marginea. From here you could follow your way generally southwards, the details outlined in the walking itinerary in Chapter Twelve. A tour to the villages of the Someș valley, north-east of Bistrița could be combined with villages of the Iza valley in Maramureș, offering plenty of bad road and rough road cycling and a wealth of village architecture.

Other areas especially worth visiting on a bike are the Apuseni, with many roads snaking along the various valleys. A good start point would be the town of Turda. In the Eastern Carpathians the road west from Dărmănești to Sânmartin is a classic for a mountain bike – see Dervla Murphy's description of it in *Transylvania and Beyond* (see Appendix C). The route from monastery to monastery in Vâlcea county, on the southern side of the Căpățâni, is another excellent area to cycle, as is the road heading south-west from Petroșani, through the towns of the Jiu de Vest valley, all the way to Băile Herculane, and giving access to the massifs of Godeanu, Retezat and Vâlcan on the way. The extreme south-west of the country, with its endless forests and more modest relief than the highest part of the Carpathians is a superb area; I cannot recommend too highly the rough road through the forest from Șopotu Nou (the village at the eastern end of the superb Nera Gorge hiking route), west onto the Cărbunari Plateau and on to Moldova Nouă. The road east along the Danube is also perfect for cycling, with relatively modest traffic and a scenic delight; it has recently been surfaced all the way. However these are just a few recommendations; it is scarcely possible to go wrong with a sheet map of Romania and a touring mountain bike.

MOUNTAIN BIKING

In the visited areas of Romania it is now possible to hire good mountain bikes, for approximately 15 euros per day. This is possible in Sinaia (adjacent to the cable car, tel. 0244 31 18 10) and in Poiana Brașov. There is also a bike shop in Sibiu (SurMont, Str. Avram Iancu 25, tel. 0269 21 83 10) which may be able to hire you a bike to take up into the Cindrel or the Făgărăș. In all cases, the bikes are quality machines and should not be compared to what is usually on offer in Kathmandu, for example. For 'real' mountain biking there are a number of areas that are inviting. Omu, the highest point in the Bucegi and one of the highest peaks in Romania, is unusual in that you can pedal a mountain bike right to its summit – I have done it myself and was not the first. The route there is straightforward; turn west off the main DN1 on the southern outskirts of Sinaia, onto the DN71 to Târgoviște, then right after about 4km, after a series of hairpins, onto a rough road to Cabana Cuibul Dorului. Climbing steadily, you reach a track junction on a grassy col (Șaua Dichiului 1614m, 5295ft). Turn right here and follow the track north from there along the eastern ridge of the Bucegi, past Babele Cabana to the summit of Omu. Cable-car staff in Sinaia or Bușteni are now used to people taking bikes. This offers the best option of all – going up by cable car and descending on the fast rideable track – superb. The top of the western ridge of the Bucegi is also negotiable by mountain bike.

Other areas of the Carpathians that offer 'over the summit' routes are the Sureanu, the Leaota, the Vrancea-Penteleu and the eastern Rodna around the Rotunda Pass and Prislop Pass; the chairlift staff at Stațiunea Borșa seem to be quite amenable to the idea of loading a mountain bike.

Many mountain cabanas are accessible by very rough jeep track, giving access for deliveries of supplies. Generally access further up is by footpath only. An excellent way to explore would therefore be to ask the cabanier to lock your bike in his store whilst you use the cabana as a base from which to explore higher, where a bike cannot go. My suggestions are Poiana Izvoarelor in the Bucegi, Curmătura in the Piatra Craiului, any of the cabanas on the northern flank of the Făgăraș or by the TransFăgărașan road – a mountain-biker's dream road, and Buta and Pietrele in the Retezat (it is possible to explore the western end of the Retezat above Baleia by bike).

SKIING

There can be little advantage in going skiing in Romania as an independent traveller. The National Tourist offices have details of ski companies. During the Ceaușescu years skiing was seen as one way of bringing hard currency into the ailing economy. The result was Poiana Brașov, a spacious modern purpose-built resort (and noteworthy for the tragic self-torching of a student in the winter of 1987–8 in an attempt to draw western attention to his country's plight – and specifically to the uprising in Brașov that had just taken place). I sense that one of the reasons Poiana Brașov was so heavily promoted by the regime that built it is the fact that, tucked against the mountain with just two access roads, at least foreign visitors could easily be monitored, as opposed to Predeal or Sinaia. In fact Romania does offer good cheap skiing; après-ski is a fraction the price of western Europe. The many bars, restaurants and night-clubs, and the low price of drinks and meals, makes Romania very attractive for a value-for-money skiing holiday.

Poiana Brașov is by no means the only ski resort; nearby Predeal offers two black runs and five red (see Appendix D), the same as Poiana Brașov. Furthermore it offers a number of benefits not found at Poiana Brașov; it is a real town with some fine turn-of-the-century villas, in contrast to the (admittedly pleasantly laid-out) modern hotels of Poiana Brașov. There are of course superb views from the slopes – north, out across the plains and forested rolling hills of the Bârsa Land. Predeal has a choice of restaurants and shops and excellent rail connections from the highest station in the country as well as good road connections. There are also

Hikers and shepherd boy. Riding in Romania is for work, not recreation

superb views from the slopes, west across the town to the Bucegi massif. There are other minor ski resorts scattered throughout the Carpathians, at Semenic, Păltiniş near Sibiu, and Cheia. In the Eastern Carpathians there is skiing at Băile Tuşnad, Lacu Roşu, Durău-Ceahlău, Vatra Dornei, Borşa and Izvoarele in Maramureş. All of these are mentioned in the the relevant chapters dealing with walking in the area. Of these, only Sinaia, Predeal and Poiana Braşov offer any black runs. There is full technical information about Romanian ski resorts at Appendix D.

Cross-country skiing is not as developed in Romania as in western Europe and as yet the leading British operator (Kudu Travel, see Appendix F) does not have a programme there. However the landscape lends itself well, particularly the long forest tracks in the Eastern Carpathians. It is possible to cross-country ski on the plateau of the eastern Bucegi from the telecabina top station at Babele; further north and lower down there is a race track at the southern end of Predeal beside the DN73A road. Near Fundata, below Bran-Giuvala Pass on the DN73/E577 road is a rudimentary loipe. The French adventure tour company Terres d'Aventures has attempted to operate snow-shoe trekking in Bucovina.

NARROW-GAUGE FOREST RAILWAYS

The mountains of Romania are well supplied with narrow-gauge railway lines still operating and performing the tasks they were designed for rather than as mere show pieces. Aficionados of these travel from all over Europe to see them in action. The most famous is the Vaser valley steam line, running up to the Ukraine border in Maramureş. Explore Worldwide offer a recommended tour in Romania that involves a ride on the Vaser valley steam train and a stiff hike over a forested ridge back to the Vişeu valley

Some of the suggested walks in Maramureş use this line; those in the Trascău and Muntele Mare in the Apuseni also involve the delightful Arieş valley line from Turda to Câmpeni in the Apuseni.

Less well known, but equally well worth visiting, is the line heading north in the Căliman massif in the Eastern Carpathians, from the town of Rastoliţa. There is another running up the Tazlău valley, west of Bacău in southern Moldavia. Until the 1970s there was a complex of lines running north into the forest from Vatra Moldoviţei in Bucovina, towards the Ukraine border. Incidentally the CFR rail halt at Vatra Moldoviţei, across a hay meadow from the monastery walls, is one of the most exquisite places to catch a train that I know of.

The most accessible of all the narrow-gauge forest lines is the one heading into the Vrancea and Penteleu mountains in the southern part of the Eastern Carpathians. Formerly this line, with its planul inclinat – inclined plane shunting device – went right through the mountains connecting all the way through the Bâsca valley to the standard-gauge network on the south of the mountains at Nehoiu. Nowadays a rump of this network remains, with much of the track made over to roads for unromantic diesel lorries. Some of the above are dealt with more fully in the chapters dealing with each area in detail. There is a German coffee-table book on the subject, complete with maps; see Appendix C.

FOOD AND DRINK

'Sinaia ... possesses ... a restaurant in which the hors d'oeuvre, the white caviar and the crayfish, are in a class by themselves in a land of excellent food.'

Sacheverell Sitwell, *Roumanian Journey*

Food

Predictably, perhaps the most important factor for a visit to Romania that changed beyond all recognition during the 1990s was the quality of food available if eating out. The rate of improvement accelerated in the last three years of the century, so that it is now difficult not to eat extremely well in the country. You will now eat better food on a visit to Romania than most people do in Britain. Tomatoes, for example are ripe and tasty – even in winter, when they are imported from Turkey. Meat is especially good; pork served in the mountains – the pigs having mostly lived on a diet of forest forage and household scraps – has a wonderful flavour. ('Is this pork?' – the uninitiated often ask.) Local cheeses are wonderful, perhaps because the herds graze unimproved pasture with a variety of plants being consumed, rather than sown monoculture leys. Recommended are the hard, golden little smoked cheeses and the burduf, stuffed into a hand-sewn cylinder of spruce bark to mature. In the lowlands, plenty of restaurant menus now attempt an English translation – often with amusing results.

Food served by Romanian wives and mothers to their families is generally very good. The country has a fascinating cuisine, with influences from France, Hungary, the Balkans, Russia and Turkey. Peppers, aubergines, tomatoes and sour cream feature largely in many dishes. Most town-dwelling Romanians are far more knowledgeable than their western counterparts about the relative merits of various species of wild fruit and fungi, also locally-grown herbal infusions. In the summer and autumn there is a great abundance of fruit and nuts available. Like mushrooms in England, local knowledge is essential to the picking of raspberries – you can see forest workers returning to their canton silvic in the evening with buckets of them for their

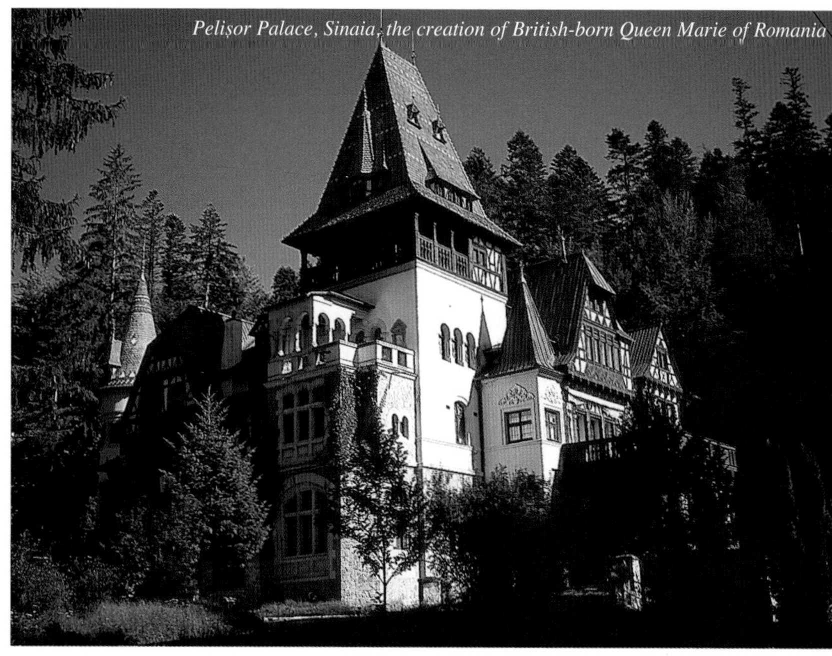

Pelişor Palace, Sinaia, the creation of British-born Queen Marie of Romania

wives to preserve. I recommend a read of Richard Mabey, *Food For Free* (see Bibliography); not all of the species he describes are found in Romania and some of those you will find will not be covered, but nevertheless his book will open up many opportunities for your tastebuds when wandering in the forests and moors of the Carpathians.

Romania's warm summers mean that you can enjoy very cheap and delicious cherries, peaches, apricots, water melons, aubergines and much more – when within reach of produce markets. Imported foods are now common, with bananas, olives, oranges, and so on available even in small rural towns. If invited to stay with a family in the remote areas of Romania you will probably be offered food to take with you – the favourite packed lunch is a cold schnitzel in a sandwich, which tastes a great deal better than it sounds. The type of food likely to be served as a hot midday or evening meal in a cabana is listed at Appendix B.

The key point to bear in mind about the food is that you will almost always be eating very local produce that is in season at the time. Often when you ask what there is for a main course the knee-jerk reaction seems to be to reply 'friptură' – a chunk of (usually tender and tasty) grilled pork, chips and a side-salad in a square china dish. Use appendix B to help you find something different occasionally. It can be difficult to sample the best of Romanian cooking whilst walking independently in the mountains, unless you are invited in to join a family meal; this however is due to language problems rather than any lack of quality or choice. However, with a walking party, you will eat extremely well, given the remote locations. There are some specialities which are extremely good – more details are given at Appendix B. You will probably be surprised by the higher than expected quality of the food served in cabanas. The typical breakfast tends to be omelettes, feta cheese, ham, sausage, bread, accompanied by mugs of sweet fruit tea from an ever-simmering cauldron (if you ask for it unsweetened they will make it especially for you) or strong Turkish coffee (or perhaps instant). If you call into a cabana for lunch you will receive a hot and meaty meal of grilled meat, skinless sausages, goulash or polenta. You can rarely go wrong with soups in mountain huts or anywhere else. Note that if you ask staff what kind of soup they have, the first answer will almost always be that they have tripe soup and only then the other kinds – so highly prized is tripe soup!

Food and drink when backpacking

Water can be drunk from a cabana's supply without purifying. In common with most of Europe, water that drains from grazed areas may contain the giardia virus. Chlorine-based water purification preparations do not kill giardia; use an iodine-based system. This warning applies to surface-flowing streams in the mountains which for this reason I recommend you avoid. Springs are in plentiful supply, generally with a small spout to make the filling of your bottle easier. I have never purified the water from a spring in the Carpathians and have never suffered any gastric problem thereby. One of the great pleasures of wandering in rural Romania is the delicious water from springs and wells. A cheap plastic water bottle can cause disaster inside your pack; an aluminium version, such as the Sigg brand, is much better. Genuine mineral water (normally sparkling) from the country's spa sources is good so there is no need to buy bottled tap water such as Bonaqua – the lamentable product from the Coca-Cola Company.

Food can be found in the mountains even if you are a long way from a cabana or village. All the mountain areas are grazed by flocks looked over by shepherds living high in the mountains for the summer. Cows can often be found quite high up in summer as well. The shepherds are usually extremely friendly and only too pleased to sell you urda, made from the whey left over from caș, the curd cheese itself. They also often have a stock of mămăligă – maize porridge – which is served cold and cut into slices. Urdă and mămăligă together is a traditional shepherd's food and is excellent fare for a hungry hiker, especially when set in the embers of the hut fire to bake and melt the cheese.

The ready availability of mămăligă and cheese high in the mountains means that you can walk for many days carrying only a minimal quantity of food. The shepherds, dressed in their tweeds and with their hats, may look quaint. Do not be misled – they are one of the richer elements in Romanian society and have a tendency to be extremely shrewd.

Stoves: cylinders of propane or butane for camping stoves have become available but need to be bought in gear shops in larger towns (also Sinaia) – I have never found cylinders at filling stations. I recommend that you take a stove that uses petrol – gasoline – as a fuel. Examples are the Coleman Peak stove, the MSR Whisperlite or XGK or Sigg Firejet. In the high forest areas the few vehicles you see use diesel fuel (although you should be able to cadge petrol from a forester's chainsaw); diesel fuel (motorina) is more widely available than petrol in the mountains. The only stove that I am aware of that can burn diesel is the MSR XGK model. It only takes one occasion when you find that diesel is available but not petrol to make you wish you had a stove that runs on it. Methylated spirits (for Trangia stoves) is surprisingly widely available, even in small rural shops; let the shopkeeper smell your fuel bottle – no țuica jokes here, please.

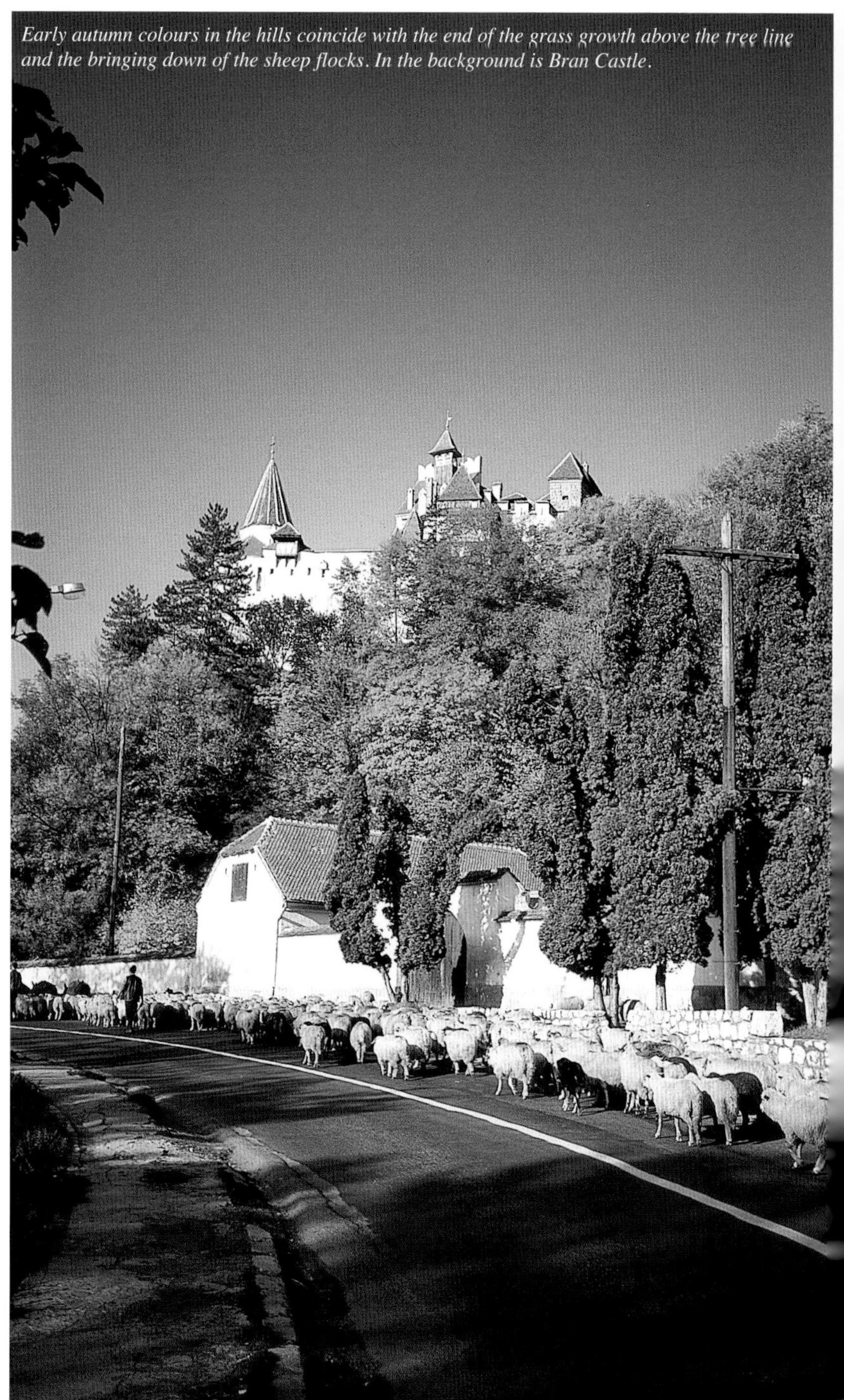

Early autumn colours in the hills coincide with the end of the grass growth above the tree line and the bringing down of the sheep flocks. In the background is Bran Castle.

Airlines do not accept bottles of fuel or gas cylinders on board, so fly with your fuel bottle empty; even in the remotest areas you can usually find at least a chain-saw or generator that runs on petrol, whose owner can be persuaded to part with a half-litre. One of the pleasures of backpacking in the Carpathians in Romania is the richness of the forests. In great contrast to the Himalaya, you do not cause environmental damage by having a small cooking fire. You do not of course need to take all the food you are going to eat. If you have decided to venture into the regions where you will need to be self-sufficient, calculate the number of days you will need food for. Add one or two days' supply of food as a reserve and pack the lightest possible food that you can and items that contrast with what you can find in the mountains – such as muesli. Dehydrated meals (mainly available in Bucharest, apart from powdered mashed potato which seems to be everywhere) are much more palatable if you take some herbs. You should aim to be eating the last food in your rucksack on the morning you return to habitation and cafes.

Drinks

Romania is an immensely boozy country. There is little in the way of licensing laws and all locally-made drinks are very cheap; even imported Scotch is not especially pricey.

Tea and coffee are as widely drunk as elsewhere in Europe. British visitors are pleased to discover that it is a country that shares a passion for tea. Much of the tea drunk is herb tea and it is very pleasant. Various local infusions are popular – examples are mint and lime flower. Coffee is often served rather as it is in Turkey, in very small cups, very strong and sweet, but western-style coffee is also widely available.

Beer is one of the country's delights – not least for the price of the stuff in the provinces. The beer with the highest reputation comes from Transylvania, from the town of Reghin; Aurora and Ciucaș from Brașov and Ursus from Cluj are also good; nearly ubiquitous now is the Bergenbier brand and Gambrinus is making a comeback. Avoid Fulbier and Malbier. Almost all beer in Romania is bere blondă – in other words lager. However dark beer is now reappearing (Bergenbier are brewing a quite drinkable version). Of whichever hue, beer is mostly drunk bottled, though very tasty draught can very occasinally be found.

Wine is a matter of pride to Romanians, though you should not expect anything very special from shops in small towns and villages in the hills. Various grape varieties are grown, such as Pinot Noir (the commonest), Chardonnay, Cabernet Sauvignon, Merlot, Riesling, Muscat and the indigenous Fetească. In fact, every region grows wine; Murfatlar, near Constanța makes some good red from Cabernet Sauvignon and other grapes, Cotnari, near Iași, is the source of a good sweet white. From the Târnave valley in central Transylvania comes good dry Riesling (the Riesling grape becomes a dry white wine in Romania) and good sparkling. For a recommendation for a good claretty red, I would suggest a Cabernet Sauvignon from the Dealul Mare region – in fact Valea Călugarească, just north of Ploiești. I have never tasted anything acceptable from the Arvinex label (near Arad). Whites (Riesling apart) tend to be sweet and should be reserved to drink with a dessert course; there are some excellent dessert wines such as Grasă de Cotnari. Sparkling wine, also on the sweet side, can be very good; the so-so Angelli brand pretends to be Italian but is actually local. I prefer Athenée Palace or Panciu. In fact the better restaurants in Sinaia can usually be relied upon to serve some good reds. Romanian Pinot Noir is widely exported; try some before you leave home to toast your forthcoming travels!

Spirits are drunk as heavily in Romania as elsewhere in eastern Europe; ţuica (pronounced 'tsweeka') is the national drink. It is a very potent clear spirit, normally translated as being plum brandy. In fact it can be made from cherries, apples, grapes, apricots or other fruit. The home-made 'pocheen' variety is of better quality than that bought off the shelf. An even stronger version is palinca; the Maramureş version being known as horinca. If you really want to amaze a Romanian you can explain that home distilling is illegal in Britain. Romanian brandy (coniac) is good; most comes from Focşani or Panciu in southern Moldavia.

FLORA AND FAUNA

This subject is dealt with in more detail at Appendix H. Suffice to say here that the mountains of Romania are the most wildlife-rich mountains in Europe, with more than half the continent's population (excluding Russia) of brown bear, wolf and lynx, not to mention a tremendous wealth of flowers, birds and reptiles. Full information on the mammals, other vertebrates and flora (not to mention more information on birds and the ecosystems) of the Carpathians are given in my book *Romania a Birdwatching and Wildlife Guide* (see bibliography). The amateur naturalist exploring Romania's mountains will be rewarded with many species not found, or unusual, in the British Isles. Thanks to the sheer extent of the Carpathians and the lack of chemicals used in hill farming in Romania, the country offers tremendous rewards for anyone interested in birds (see Appendix H).

A WORD OF WARNING

Many writers of guidebooks to specific regions or countries are so captivated by their subject that they fail to prepare their readers for some of the less pleasant aspects of being in the area they write about. In the case of Romania, however, the media has done a very effective job of painting an unfairly black picture of the whole region, so that the traveller who does venture there is a brave soul indeed. Romania is most certainly not the land of hardship, brutalism, pollution, crime and orphans that has been portrayed in the west since the revolution of 1989. It is bitterly ironic that the media of the democratic world has put across this image of Romania, bearing in mind that, unique among the revolutions of that year, Romanians braved the guns of their hated dictator and died in hundreds in a quest for just that democracy. This is a point of view you may well have put to you when in the country.

The feature which first-time visitors to the former communist bloc can find off-putting is the shabbiness of the towns, especially the large cities. Almost everything you come across in terms of buildings, transport, cars, roads and so on is more old-fashioned and less well maintained than we are used to in the west. In Bucharest you may meet taxi-touts who view a newcomer as a source of hard currency and a naive target for sharp practice. Once beyond them you find yourself in a country where people are fascinated and delighted to find you visiting their country.

Since the revolution there has been an increase in petty crime, but in my experience it is not as prevalent as some guidebooks would have you believe. As elsewhere in the world towns pose some risk, the mountains almost none. My recommendation is to use common sense

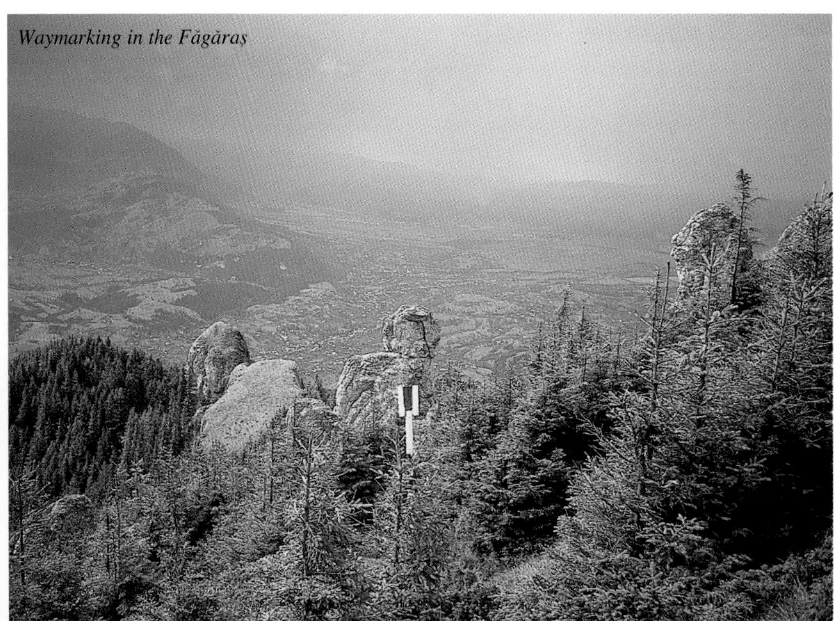

Waymarking in the Făgăraş

when confronted by the con-man type of thief in Bucharest or Braşov – and be vigilant in centre of cities. Many Romanian hikers will leave their rucksacks lying on the footpath whilst they climb a nearby peak. However, some western hikers may possess equipment unobtainable in Romania; do not tempt fate. If you are walking alone, you may want to approach a shepherds' hut, or other hikers camped around a Salvamont shelter in the evening to enjoy their company (though I much prefer being alone). If you insist on glorious isolation, camp out of sight where you are not seen on your approach and you are not likely to be disturbed. Urban pickpockets pose a constant minor threat – gypsies and non-gypsies alike.

Bears and wolves do not represent a threat to mountain hikers and campers. It is sad that wolves have a fearsome reputation for there has never, anywhere been an attack by a wolf on a human being; they are shy and timid animals. I regularly camp wild, have never taken American-style precautions agains bears – slinging food over a high branch on a rope some way from the bivouac – and have never found a bear to take an interest in me. The unfortunates who are killed by bears in Romania (it does happen) are shepherds who set about preventing bears taking their livestock with axes. The many bears I have encountered have beaten a retreat on my approach.

Romanian sheepdogs

The only specific warning that I want to issue about walking in Romania relates to the sheepdogs; I have well-developed 'dog sense' and have been attacked innumerable times, forcing me to defend myself desperately. I have been badly bitten several times. The breed is called Ciobănesc de Munte 'Mountain Shepherd Dog', and resembles a compact version of a Pyrenean, in a variety of coat colours. The dogs are there to protect their flocks from the predations of wolves and bears, and so try to 'see off' a lone walker by running at him,

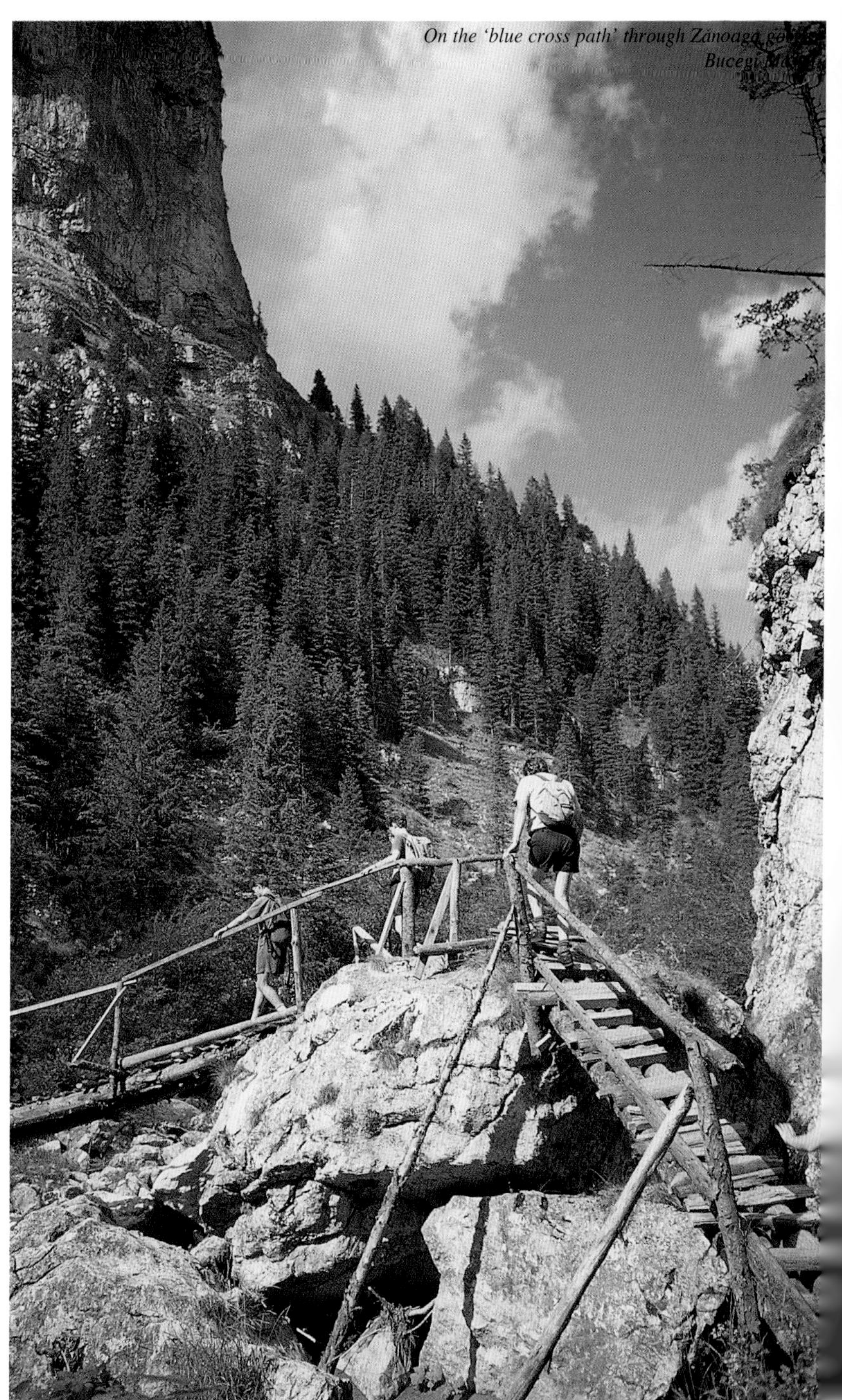

On the 'blue cross path' through Zănoaga go
Bucegi M

barking. They usually try and bite as well. Keep your distance from sheep as much as you can and to take a few precautions. Carry a few stones in your pocket; practise throwing them at stationary targets in quiet moments and above all do not hesitate to throw them as soon as the dogs come within range. The act of bending down to pick up a stone normally causes a single dog to retreat – but not if you are alone and the dogs are in their inevitable pack. The shepherds do not mind – their dogs are there to defend their charges against bears and wolves. Do not to turn your back on the dogs. If you see a flock of sheep in your path, shout to catch the shepherd's attention so he can call in his dogs. At night the dogs are at the herders' huts, down near the tree line, safely away from the ridge tops – but they are more vigilant and vicious at night. If you are unlucky enough to sustain a dog bite while in Romania, you will need a course of rabies injections – you may want to consider having these before leaving home. Above all, abandon all your soft western impressions – borne of first-hand experience of large dogs that are pleasant pets – in a little-walked-over stretch of mountains, a pack of uncontrolled Carpathian sheepdogs away from the shepherd will normally unhesitatingly try and kill you – they know how and are very good at it. Space here prevents me from explaining their method of attack – but I can tell you it is effective.

Please remember that there are inherent dangers in any expedition into mountains anywhere. Safety in the mountains is simply a matter of common sense allied to experience. This applies equally to the Carpathians in Romania as to anywhere else in the world.

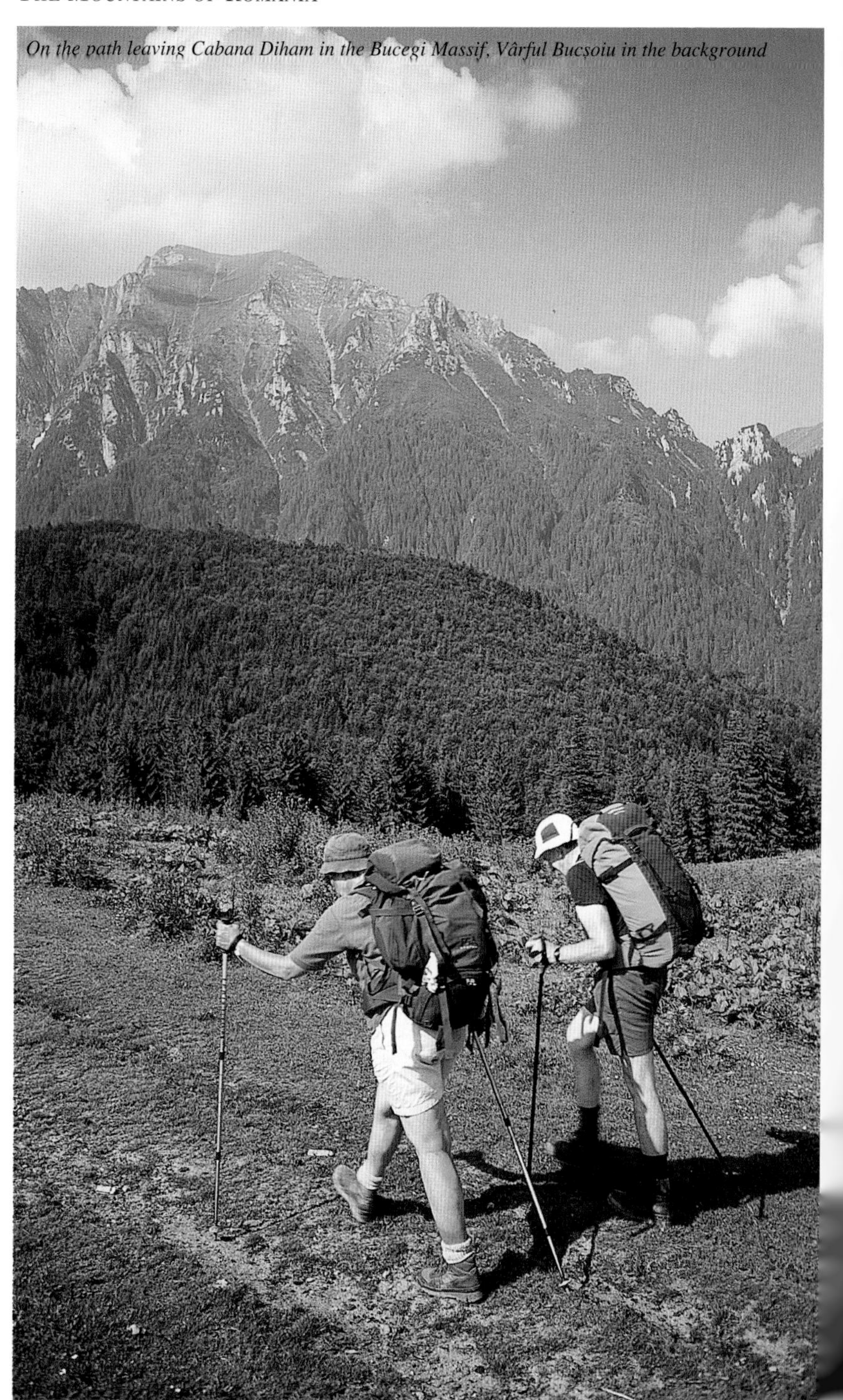

On the path leaving Cabana Diham in the Bucegi Massif, Vârful Bucşoiu in the background

CHAPTER TWO

The Bucegi Massif

The Bucegi is the most accessible massif in the country, which makes it ideally suited to a first visit. It also makes an appropriate range from which to venture further, into more remote and challenging areas, by getting you used to the waymarking and general conditions. Not only is it more accessible, it has a proportionately greater amount of cabana and hotel accommodation available than other areas of the Carpathians. From here there are waymarked trails taking you west, across the Leaota massif, off the northern side of Omu to the valleys around Bran, thence to the Piatra Craiului and so to the Făgărăș, which can then be connected to the western Carpathians.

Do not be put off by the popularity and accessibility of the eastern side of this range – if you use the cable cars as access and then walk well away from them you will find the solitude the mountain walker seeks. However, many of the cabanas do become quite busy during school holidays, especially during August; happily the great majority of those staying at the cabanas do not venture far along the mountain paths. The itinerary described below starts in the mountain resort of Sinaia – well worth a visit in its own right – and continues to finish in Bran, leading on to the following chapters on the Piatra Craiului and Făgăraș.

The geology of the Bucegi (pronounced 'boo-chedge') is largely of carboniferous limestone and conglomerate; at Peștera Ialomiței is a cave, open to the public, lit and liberally supplied with slippery wooden duckboards and rotten ladders inside; access is via the new monastery built inside the cave mouth. (Peștera means 'cave'.) The massif takes the form of a horseshoe, opening towards the south, in the centre of which is the artificial Bolboci lake. A dirt road snakes up the middle of the horseshoe, giving access to the various cabanas in the valley. It makes its way up over Păduchiosul (literally 'the lousy one') spur at Șaua Dichiului, described in more detail as a mountain-biking route in Chapter One.

The western side of the horseshoe is as deserted as the eastern side is busy; moreover it provides some of the finest views, not only of the high peaks of the Bucegi and Piatra Craiului, but also of the peaks and forested valleys of the Carpathians lying to the west. A few days of walking in the Bucegi will give immense variety – high cliffs and crags and precipitous paths, areas of flower-strewn meadows and deep natural forests of pine and beech. Being a horseshoe, rather than the more usual ridge feature found in Romania's Carpathians, the Bucegi is criss-crossed with a number of paths, instead of the one ridge path with a number of access routes that you tend to find elsewhere.

Around the highest point of the Bucegi horseshoe (part of the Carpathian watershed) runs the boundary between the counties of Brașov to the north and Dâmbovița to the south; this is also the boundary between the former Habsburg lands of Transylvania to the north and Wallachia to the south. Along the eastern side of the Bucegi runs the boundary of the two Wallachian counties of Prahova and Dâmbovița, both named after their respective rivers.

The towns of the Prahova valley

Below the eastern edge of the Bucegi massif is the Prahova valley, which gives its name to the county ('judeţul') stretching south from the Bucegi and its associated mountains, all the way to the oil town of Ploieşti. As well as being home to a substantial population in the towns of Predeal, Sinaia, Azuga and Buşteni, the valley is important as the corridor of communication by rail and road from Bucharest and the plains of Wallachia, through the Carpathians to Braşov and Transylvania. The most important towns in the valley are Sinaia and Predeal. From Sinaia and Buşteni cable cars ascend more than 1000m onto the eastern ridge, making this part of the Bucegi an immensely popular spot, winter and summer.

This accessibility is both a blessing and a curse – it has caused damage to the environment in various spots, thankfully localised to areas near to the road and cable cars. However it means that in Sinaia, Buşteni or Predeal you can step off a train direct from Bucharest and walk straight into the mountains, perhaps (in the case of Sinaia and Buşteni) via a cable car ride to gain the top of the ridge. Whilst the top of the eastern ridge is damaged by development, the walks ascending from the Prahova valley are superb, with many flowers and a very good chance of seeing chamois. The towns themselves have quite a distinct character; Sinaia is full of old villas, has the classiest hotels of the valley, is the biggest resort in the valley and the most expensive. Buşteni has the most spectacular situation, right beneath the craggiest and most dramatic part of the eastern wall of the Bucegi. Like Sinaia, it has a cable car, only much more dramatic, sailing high above the Jepii gully to the Bucegi plateau at Babele. Predeal is the highest and is the start point for walks to the Piatra Mare and Postăvaru as well as the northern Bucegi.

Access

Frequent trains daily depart Bucharest's Gara de Nord for Braşov, passing through Sinaia, Buşteni and Predeal. The

Cabana Poiana Izvoarelor in the Bucegi

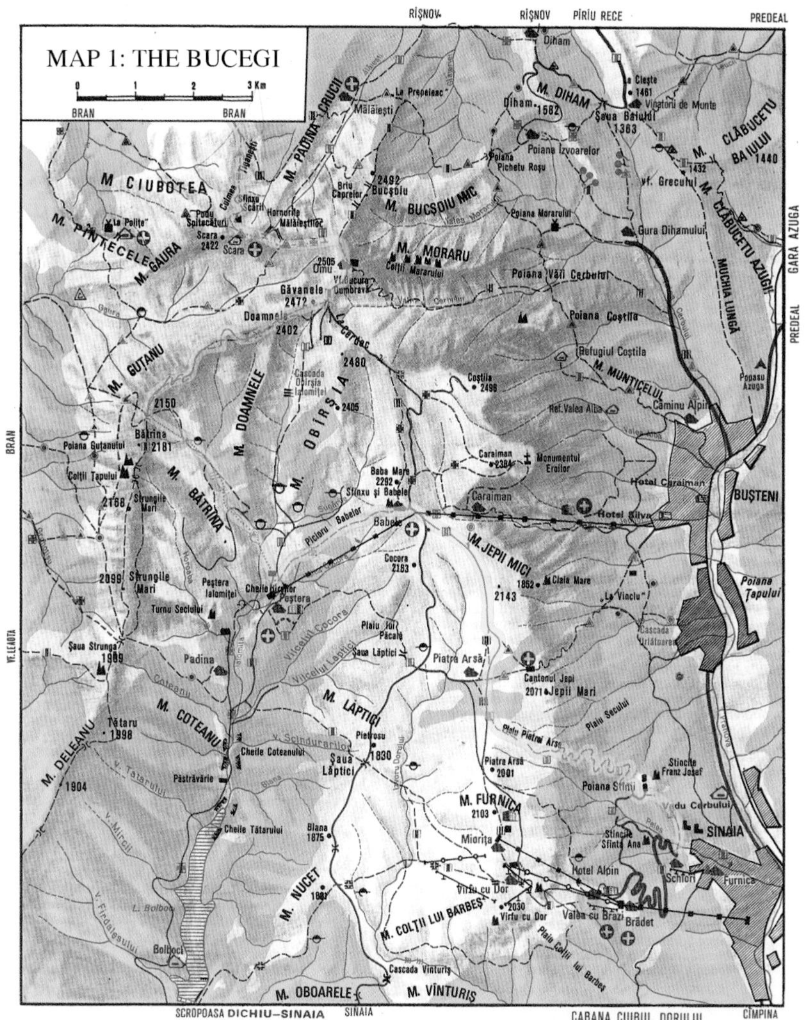

journey to Sinaia takes between 100 and 150mins, to Buşteni and Predeal correspondingly more. Almost all trains stop at Sinaia and Predeal, some at Buşteni. The walking itinerary starts from the station in Sinaia. The main street of these three towns is the Drum Naţional (henceforward abbreviated to 'DN') number one, from Bucharest to Braşov.

ITINERARY THROUGH THE BUCEGI MASSIF

There follows a suggested itinerary in the Bucegi, taking you from Sinaia through the best of the Bucegi to Bran village, with its castle. There is an addition, taking you through the forests and over Diham, Clăbucet and Postăvaru, finishing at Poiana Braşov, and an alternative finishing in Braşov itself. This itinerary is a

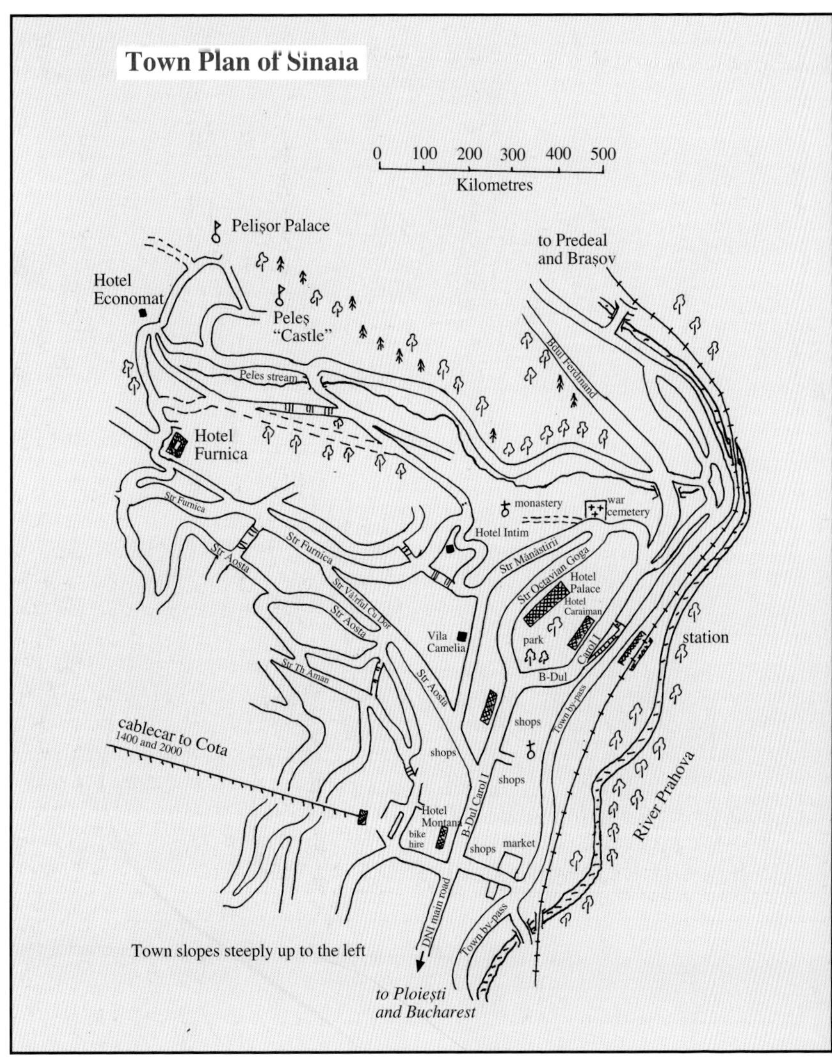

fine introduction to walking in Romania's mountains, starting as it does from Sinaia station. It also connects with the walk through the Piatra Craiului and Făgărăş and the mountains further west in the following chapters. Whilst the itinerary below is of a week, three or four days is in fact enough to see the Bucegi. The best approaches to the summit of Omu are from Poiana Izvoarelor via Mălăieşti or perhaps Bucşoiu, Gaura Gully or Şaua Bătrâna. Other fine walks to the summit of Omu are firstly from Buşteni either via the Jepii gully, starting near the Hotel Silva or (better) via Cerbului Valley, starting up the red triangle route from Cabana Caminul Alpin. There are also two routes from Bran, via Poarta Valley and Vf. Scara or the Şimon valley. It is also possible to start in Predeal, behind the market place on the east side of the main road, the blue stripe path towards

The Sphinx – natural sculpture in conglomerate rock at Babele

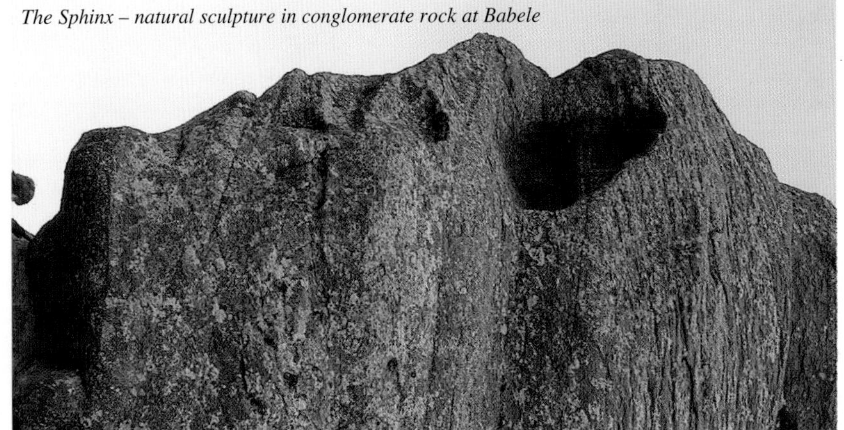

the Bucegi starting from the uphill end of Strada Plăieșilor. The last viable alternative start point is the little cluster of hotels at Pârâul Rece, the path taking you via Cabana Belvedere. The best exit from the Bucegi is from Omu cabana (highly recommended but inevitably busy over summer weekends), over Vf. Scara, then the red stripe route (not the yellow triangle path) via Țigănești and Clincea spurs to the centre of Bran via Poarta.

Day One

Sinaia to Caraiman cabana, 10km (7 miles). Altitude gained 1136m (3726ft)

Starting from Sinaia station (see map 'Town Plan'), head up the steps across the road from the main entrance and then bear left along a cobbled path to bring you up to the main road. Turn left on the main road, and walk southwards; turn first right up Strada Octavian Goga (though signs seem to be lacking). There is a taxi rank at the bottom of the street and a park on your right. Immediately after the Hotel Palace you come to a T-junction facing the war cemetery with the two cannon. Turn left here and cross the cobbled road to follow the cobbled footpath up to the monastery. From the monastery continue steeply uphill along Strada Furnica; do not go along the drive to the castle.

Opposite the Vila Dumbrava turn right up Strada Schiorilor, cobbled and steep. Follow this up to the half-timbered Furnica Hotel on your right and the sign to Peleș Castle to the right. Bear left here and follow the road uphill between villas (signs for 'Cota 1400'); the DN102A road becomes cobbled and makes a hairpin bend to the left (you can take a short cut). You see gates on the right with armed guards; these are the approaches to Foișor, used by Ceaușescu and still a Chequers-style presidential residence. You pass a milestone with a white figure 4 in its blue top.

At the first (left-hand) hairpin in the woods out of Sinaia turn right on a cobbled track (blue stripe waymarks) with an arrow painted on the wall. Contouring along the hillside, this is the access road to the private Cabana Vulturilor. Cross over the Peleș stream at a stone arched bridge and bear right. Briefly down the hill turn left along a cobbled path with the occasional bannister heading up in the forest.

Half an hour's walk brings you to a road at a large hay meadow in a clearing with houses and a drinks stall to your right; this is Poiana Stânei ('Shepherds' Hut Clearing'), often now referred to by its pre-communist name of Poiana

Reginei ('Queen's Clearing') or Poiana Regală. Take the path up the steps behind the cafe to a fine lookout across the Prahova valley (Stânciile Franz Josef); this detour of 150m is well worth the effort, if only to see the bronze plaque set on the crag commemorating a visit by Austrian emperor Franz Josef, a surprising survivor of the communist period.

From the private chalets head west on the road along the south side of the clearing and as you re-enter the forest turn right off it, steeply up through the pine and beech trees. The path is well waymarked (blue stripes all the way), steeply up through the forest and then along a spur giving views up the Prahova valley. After climbing out of the forest you enter a gully, the path being well worn. It is then waymarked with 'bus stop' type signs across the plateau towards the sports pitches and hotel at Cabana Piatra Arsă.

Continue along the plateau, north for 1.5km from Piatra Arsă, across the plateau through dwarf pine and then across the grass to a well signed junction, where the blue disc route turns right to head north-east, down to Caraiman cabana, with the admirable Mr Mazilu the cabanier. The yellow stripe route to Babele cabana (not an especially attractive path) also takes you to the top station of the cable car, should you wish to go back down into the valley at Bușteni.

Day Two

Caraiman cabana to Omu cabana, via Padina and Șaua Bătrâna 13km (8 miles). Altitude gained from Caraiman to Babele, 175m (574ft). Altitude lost from Babele to Padina, 675m (2214ft). Altitude gained from Padina to Omu, 980m (3215ft).

The rather mundane plateau-top walk to the summit of Omu via La Cerdac is one of the most popular in Romania; it will take you around three hours. My route, descending into the valley at the head of the Ialomița River and climbing up to the rim of the Gaura gully is an exciting mountain walk. From Caraiman the direct route is to head initially steeply up the gully, west (blue stripe waymarks), across the plateau to Babele, the large cabana being just north of the top station of the cable car. I suggest you start by going up the bank to the right as you leave the cabana, following the blue disc route (with some exposure) round to the fine viewpoint of Caraiman Cross. From the cross there is a very steep climb, west, up a bank (red cross waymarks) to Babele cabana. From Babele (the cable car can be unreliable) the blue cross route is well signed (and eroded), heading down to the bottom station of the cable car. To your left now is a rough track heading left, south to the very swish Hotel Peștera (very welcoming to hikers in quest of good hot food and drinks), also immediately south-west is the tiny hermitage ('Schit' in Romanian) and the modern monastery built in the entrance to Peștera Ialomiței cave. Walkers interested in wildlife should note that the valley-bottom crags around Peștera are a breeding site for several pairs of Wallcreepers. Eschewing these attractions, turn right at the bottom of the slope when you meet the track near the cable car and head north along it for 1.5km to a junction where you turn left (to the right is a direct short cut, straight north up the Ialomiței stream to Găvanele and Omu). Your track climbs north-west, marked with an occasional red triangle. Finally, a further 1.5km from the junction the track swings left, while your path continues north-west, up the broad grassy Doamnele Valley (still with red triangle waymarks). Your reach a path junction at the very top of the slope, at the lip of he west-facing escarpment of the Bucegi just north of Șaua Bătrâna. Turn right here, steeply up the grassy slope of Vf. Gutanu (2246m, 7369ft); on the far side of the summit you head along the top of an escarpment with fine views of the cliffs of Gaura to your left. A mile east along the well waymarked path east from Gutanu brings you to the top of Doamnele, from where there are fine views of Omu and the cabana on its summit. At Găvanele, a boulder the size of a large house, you find the path junction and a lot of erosion. Turn left here to follow the obvious path (in fact a track) angling up towards the summit of Omu.

Omu is (by my reckoning) the ninth highest peak in Romania, being 39m (128ft) lower than the country's highest, Moldoveanu (2544m, 8346ft) in the Făgărăș. On a clear day there are exceptional views north-west to the jagged outline of the Făgărăș, the arable plains of the Bârsa Depression and the great stretches of forest surrounding the high pale crags of the Piatra Craiului. As well as the excellent cabana there is a weather station at the summit; the latter is open all year, whilst the cabana is shut in the depths of winter between January and April. Try and avoid being at Omu on Friday and especially Saturday nights when it can be very full, as it can on weekday nights in August. Mălăiești cabana has been rebuilt, following its destruction by fire in spring 1998. There is usually someone at the mountain rescue building.

Day Three

Omu cabana to Bran, 18km (11 miles).
Altitude lost 1745m, 5725ft.

From the front door of Omu cabana turn left past the front of the weather station and pick up the combined red cross and yellow triangle route heading due west across a narrow plateau with superb views to the north. 100m of descent from Omu brings you to a high col and a path junction. (To the right the path plunges down into the Mălăiești Valley, to the right down into the Gaura Gully – a fine walk leading to the Șimon valley and so to Bran.) Keep straight on, the path angling gently up across a slope down to your left. On the summit plateau of Scara keep right at the path junction where the

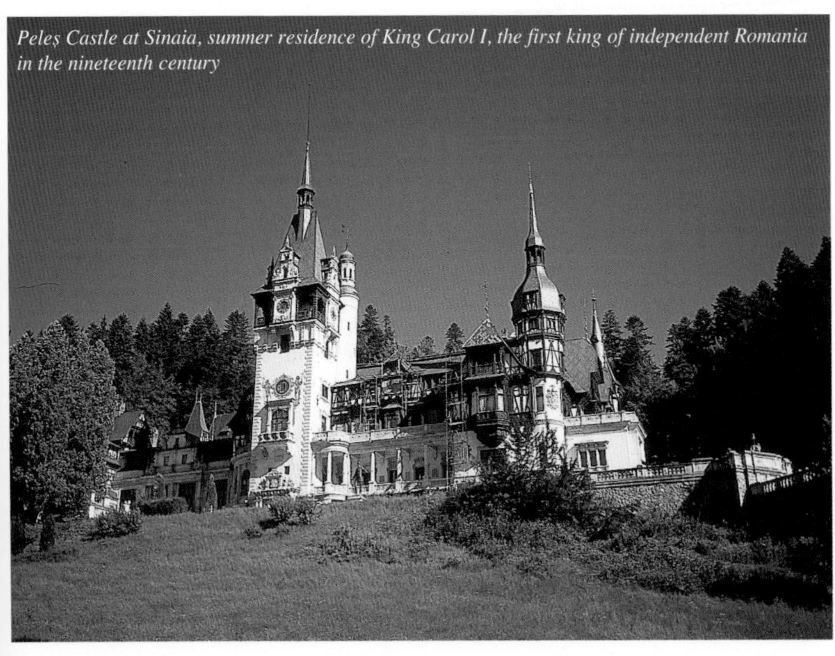

Peleș Castle at Sinaia, summer residence of King Carol I, the first king of independent Romania in the nineteenth century

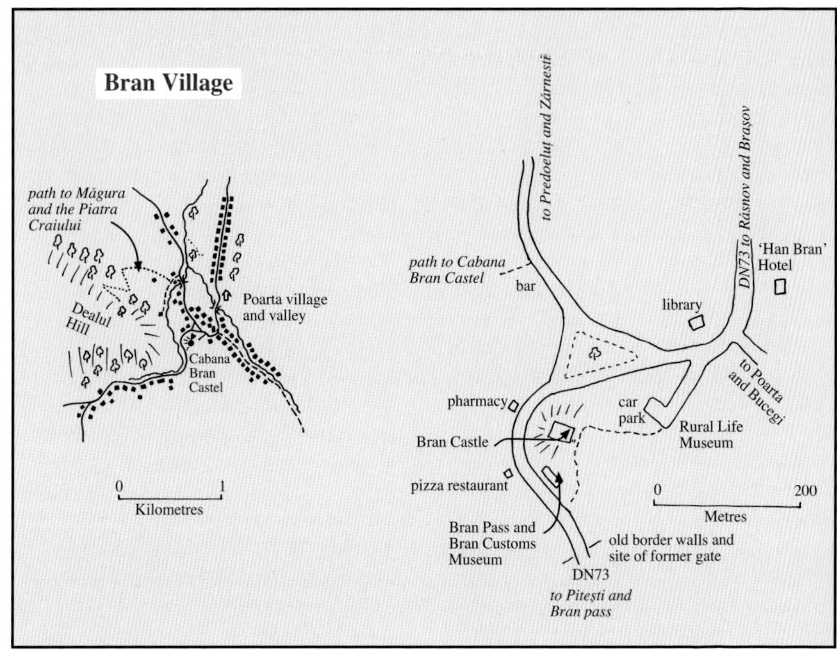

yellow triangle path heads left, north-west down into the Poarta Valley. Stay on the red stripe route north to a tricky descent with cables among crumbling conglomerate and along the Clincea spur. You reach a broad platform on the spur, whereupon the path angles away, down to the left and eventually into the forest, where it is easy to follow all the way to the first grazed clearing on a saddle — Poiana Pănicerului. There is a small spring in the trees well signed just off to the left here, the path heading into the trees near a rudimentary picnic table. Turn right at this clearing and take care to find the waymarked path heading initially north-east down from it. The red stripe route continues, well signed through the farms of Poarta into the centre of Bran village.

There is a delightful link route on to the Piatra Craiului from Bran; it is described after 'Day One' in Chapter Five – The Piatra Craiului and Iezer-Păpuşa Massifs.

Bran village and castle

To find Bran Cabana turn left at the T-junction at the bottom of the road down the Poarta valley: after 100m you come to the small park in the centre of the village around the bend. Turn right so that the park is on your left (Str. Sextil Puşcariu) and bear right at the road junction at the far side of the park. Walk for about 60m along the road and turn left down a footpath adjacent to a scruffy unnamed bar with a fence on your right; it leads you to a footbridge over the river and the cabana. As you meet the main road descending from Poarta turn right; Hanul Bran is a few yards along on the right. The village now has plenty of accommodation in small pensions and private houses as well as the hotel and cabana; it makes an excellent base for day walks (see Appendix A).

CHAPTER THREE
East of the Prahova

The mountains lying between the Prahova valley in the west and the Buzău valley to the east – the Piatra Mare, Gârbova, Baiului, Grohotiș and Ciucaș – are an area of largely grassy sheep-grazed ridges rising above forested valleys; the two massifs with areas of crags are the Ciucaș and the Piatra Mare. The strip in the west is well covered by maps – there are a number of cabanas and consequently numbers of local walkers. As you head east along the Carpathian watershed you very soon enter a much wilder area, briefly interrupted by the roads and buildings in the Ciucaș. The vast stretches of forest run uninterrupted all the way to the Eastern Carpathians, beyond the Buzău valley. None of the ranges to the east of the Prahova is as high as the Bucegi – they are comparatively rounded summits with little in the way of bare crags between Piatra Mare and the Ciucaș. However they do provide a wild and fascinating link route, along the Carpathian watershed.

The preceding chapter described walks relatively busy along high-level routes; the attraction of the region to the east of the Prahova is that, being less spectacular, it has no cabanas between Piatra Mare and Ciucaș and therefore remains much more of a wilderness. Paths are unsigned and there are almost no waymarks; more critically, between Predeluș pass and the Ciucaș there is effectively no map available. The area is therefore better suited to the walker who has spent some time on more well-trodden paths and has the feel of Romania's Carpathians.

The itinerary of this chapter describes a route heading from west to east, or 'anti-clockwise' around the Carpathian circle in Romania. It is therefore in the opposite direction to all the other itineraries, which run clockwise. It can be followed to connect with the itinerary across the Vrancea and Penteleu mountains. There is a choice of routes, along the Carpathian watershed, from the busy trails and cabanas of the Prahova valley into a relatively wild region. Mapping for this chapter is limited to the quite good 'Postăvaru – Piatra Mare' sheet; east of its coverage you are on your own.

THE PIATRA MARE MASSIF

The Piatra Mare lies to the east of the Bucegi, on the eastern side of the Prahova valley; like the Bucegi the access to them is from the valley. The massif offers an excellent day walk to the summit from Predeal. In comparison to the Bucegi the Piatra Mare is notably less walked by locals, especially since the destruction of Piatra Mare cabana in 1992; the nearest alternatives are the roadside Dâmbul Morii or Susai to the south. The waymarking is good. The geology mirrors that of the Bucegi itself – conglomerate and limestone. There is a small ice-filled cave, Peștera de Gheața, near the summit. A walk of about four hours, mainly through forest, leads from Predeal to the summit; it can also be reached by a fine walk south, up from Dâmbu Morii cabana and campsite complex which lies a short distance from Brașov on the DN1 main road.

Access
The Piatra Mare is very accessible, on its western side, where the main DN1 road and main railway line run along the Timiș valley and over the Predeal pass; the town

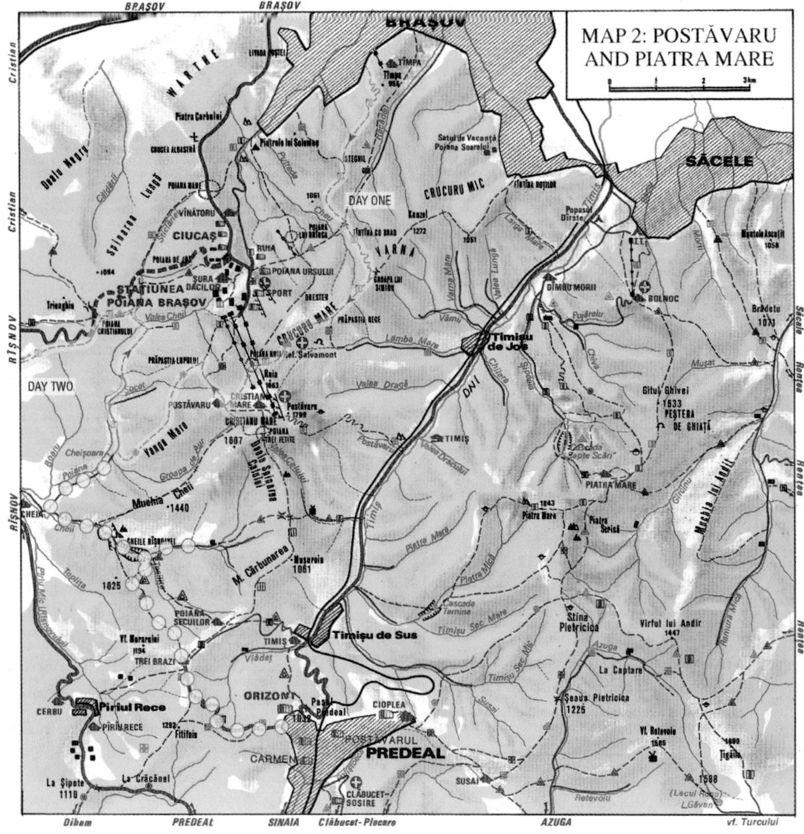

of Săcele is at its foot to the north. From Popasul Dârste campsite (a cheap place to stay when visiting Braşov – see Appendix A), a road leads east to the BTT campsite and ski lift up to Bonloc cabana (see Appendix A) and from there heads south (blue stripe waymarks), past a short diversion to Peştera de Gheaţa ('the Ice Cave') to the summit. In the east a forest road heads all the way up the Gârcin valley from the eastern end of Săcele, turning right off the DN1A as you head out of the town towards the lake. At the confluence of the Gârcin and Rămura Mică valleys (at some foresters' huts 6km after leaving the DN1A) the forest road keeps left, south up the Rămura Mică valley, whilst the yellow triangle path heads up the Gârcin valley, south-west to Piatra Mare cabana. From Săcele to Piatra Mare summit by this route is approximately 14km (8 miles). The routes from Dâmbu Morii cabana to Piatra Mare are described in more detail below. In fact, the easiest walk-in is from Predeal – follow the instructions into the Gârbova below.

Day One

Dâmbu Morii cabana to Lake Găvan bivouac site, 18km (11 miles). Altitude gained from Dâmbu Morii to Vârful Piatra Mare 1143m (3750ft)

This short day's walk gives time to reach Dâmbu Morii from Braşov or Predeal, or indeed Bucharest; there is a railway halt served by personal and cursa trains at Dârste, 3km north. Dâmbu Morii is also a useful place to stay whilst visiting the city of Braşov (there is also a good spot for wild camping near the old city – see Chapter Four). There are a number of possible routes from Dâmbu Morii to Piatra Mare summit; I have chosen this one because it offers the best views along the way.

From Dâmbu Morii cabana turn left, south up the tarred road, past the post office on the right and an alimentara on the left. At the end of the houses it forks by a fire warning sign. Turn right past a barrier along a rough track heading into a grassy area and then left off it, following the red disc 'bus stop' signs up the grassy slope to the forest edge ('Peştera de Gheaţa prin Şirul Stâncilor 2hrs'). To the right at the fork the road continues (yellow stripe waymarks) to Şapte Scării ('Seven Stairs') waterfall. Follow the red discs, twisting steeply up in the trees along the ridge; after about 2km you reach a signed junction with the 'Drumul Familiar' path to the right in a gully. Keep left, soon to bring you out to a broad gully where the path, steep and drily slippery, follows the Şirul Stâncilor crags at their foot; frequent overhangs give shelter in rain. There are views back to the left to Braşov and the landmark wooded Tâmpa hill with the mast and station on its summit; the views get even better with the ascent; towards the top of Şirul Stâncilor you can see back down to Dâmbul Morii.

At the top of the gully the path swings to the left among undergrowth, well marked with 'bus stop' signs. It then resumes its ascent among the tall spruce trees to the top of Piatra Mică spur (1614m), where you meet the blue stripe route from the left, coming up from Bunloc via the cave at Peştera de Gheaţa, 200m away. In fact it is something of a disappointment, being more a deep cleft than a cave. To get in requires some basic scrambling skills. Turn right on top of Piatra Mică ('Cabana Piatra Mare 45min'). As you continue steeply up the spur you have the first views to the right of the square tower and short mast on top of Postăvarul with, beyond, the rounded dome of Vârful Codlea. A clearing at the top gives views of the pale crags of the summit of Piatra Mare.

The approach to the former Piatra Mare cabana is along a level path, heading south-west to an old junction with the yellow triangle route from the left, from the Gârcin Valley and the eastern end of Săcele. Turn right here to bring you to the ruins of Cabana Piatra Mare. You pass two paths leading to the right; follow the red stripe waymarks through the trees, the path swinging right, west, over Vârful Piatra Mare (1843m, 6047ft), with views of Postăvaru and the Bucegi. Head back the way you came from here to head south (red stripe waymarks), descending across the plateau with plentiful 'bus stop' signs to an obvious junction with the blue stripe route down the Piatra Mică valley past the Tamina waterfall to Timiş de Sus – see 'Alternative access' below. Turn left at the path junction, south (blue triangle waymarks), descending across some crags to the east of Piatra Scrisă, crossing several streams before reaching the long, nettle-filled clearing of Pietricică (alt. 1405m, 4610ft) with some shepherds' huts (disused in 1996). At the uphill end of the clearing a signpost points the way to Predeal (blue disc waymarks); keep right here, down through the clearing to see a blue triangle on the left on a tree-trunk; the junction is not well marked although a post remains where once there was a signpost.

Here you turn left, the path ahead marked with red crosses heading in a short distance to Şaua Pietrica and thence along the forested ridge to Susai cabana (see

Appendix A) and down to Cioplea cabana and Predeal. Follow the blue triangle route east along the (not very distinct) main Carpathian watershed. The path descends to reach the good forest road 1km from the Pietricica junction at a broad col in the forest; continue across the road on the obvious wide path over the wooded summit of Vârful lui Andir (1447m, 4747ft) where it turns south, climbing as it does out of the trees to some shepherds' huts and a path junction 1.5km south-south-east of Vârful lui Andir; turn right here. The red and blue triangle route is clearly marked, down to the right, into the Azuga valley to Lake Găvan, also known as Lacu Roșu (alt. 1450m, 4757ft).

To continue this itinerary turn to the Lake Găvan to Muntele Roșu cabana walk on page 58.

Alternative access from Timiș de Sus

From Timiș de Sus railway halt turn right and walk 900m south alongside the main DN1 road, past a two-arched stone bridge over the Timiș stream; immediately beyond this you find a sign pointing over the river (blue stripe waymark) – 'Cascada Tamina dus-intors 2½hrs, Piatra Mare 5hrs'). Follow this along a forest track to turn immediately right off it, into the spruce and up to Cascadă Tamina. This well-used path takes you to the summit plateau of Piatra Mare.

THE GÂRBOVA AND BAIULUI

The Gârbova (sometimes and formerly always spelt Gîrbova) lies south of the Piatra Mare and is really the mountain hinterland to Predeal (see Map 3). In winter the Clăbucet cable car makes it a popular ski area. The Gârbova has three cabanas – Susai, Clăbucet Plecare (destroyed in a gas explosion in 1999) and Gârbova itself (details at Appendix A). The Baiului lies south of the Gârbova, a long north–south ridge sandwiched between the valleys of Prahova and Doftana: they reach up to 1847m (6060ft) and have not been developed with paths and accommodation as have the higher mountains to the west. East and south of the excellent and easily-available 'Postăvaru and Piatra Mare' sheet there is at present no mapping available.

Access

Predeal has more than a dozen trains a day; they take about half an hour from Brașov, about two hours from Bucharest. The town's main street is the DN1 main road. The Gârbova is also accessible on its eastern side by the road heading north up the Doftana valley from the village of Doftana, just east of Câmpina. This road becomes increasingly rough as it climbs to the north to reach Buzău pass (alt. 1295m, 4248ft).

A forest road reaches into the heart of the Gârbova, running up the Azuga valley (Valea Azugei) from Azuga. It starts in the centre of Azuga near the bridge; after 5km it reaches a fork at the foresters' huts and Păstrăvarie (fish farm for trout). To the left the route heads north up the Limbașelului valley. Keep right here, north-east and upstream up the Azuga valley, following it for approximately 14km (9 miles) to a junction in a wide open area on the valley floor. Turn left here, due north for 1.5km along a good forest road to Gârcin pass, marked by a Romsilva sign; the road continues down the Gârcin valley to the eastern end of Săcele) is on the main Carpathian watershed. Turn right here, south-east along the ridge in the spruce forest, the path marked with blue triangles and follow the directions in 'Day One' below. It is also possible to reach Lake Găvan in a fine and wild long (29km, 18 miles) day's walk north along the Baiului ridge, heading east from Sinaia, starting at Piscul Câinelui cabana. However space

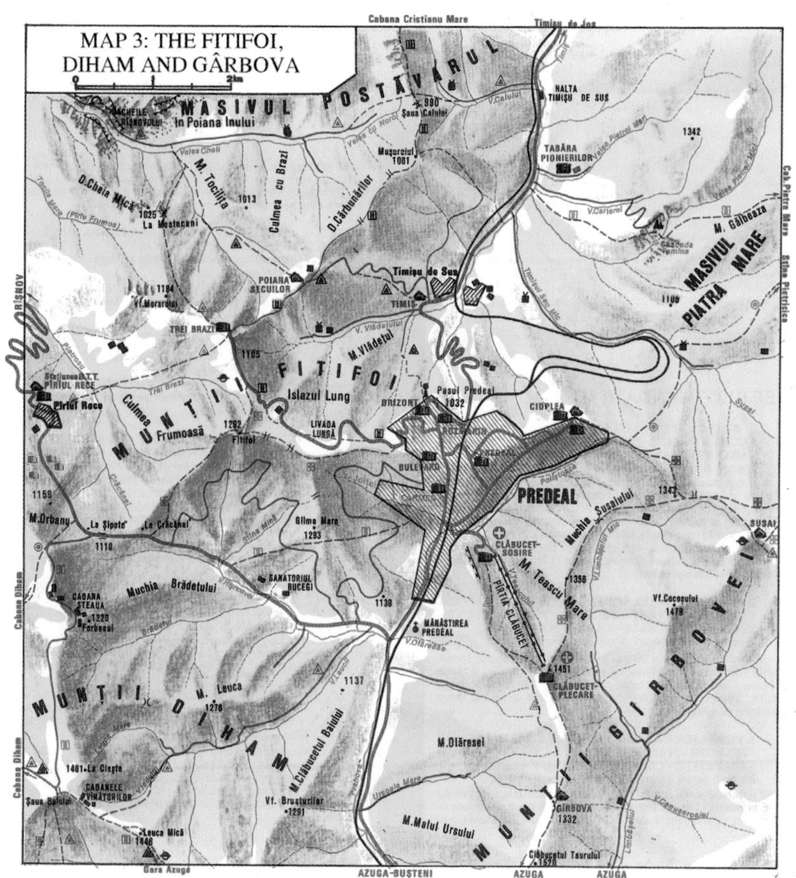

precludes me from describing it in detail here.

Day One

Predeal to Lake Găvan bivouac site, 12km (7miles). Altitude gained from Cioplea to Șaua Pietricica, 115m (377ft)

This short day's walk gives time to reach Predeal from Brașov or Bucharest. From Predeal station, turn right on the main street and first right after about 200m, signed 'Cioplea'. You go over the railway and follow Bulevardul Libertății, a cobbled road running uphill with villas set back on either side of the road. It swings right just after Hotel Cioplea, to head east-south-east and becomes a well made gravel road through the spruce trees, to a junction with a gravel from the right along the Polistoacă valley from Predeal; keep straight on, the path forking to the left into the trees. At this point the blue disc route to Piatra Mare via the Timiș Valley turns left. Keep right here, heading just south of due east on the very well waymarked path (wide and used as a logging track). You cross over a forest road, now ascending just east of due south to bring you to a T-junction of paths on the top of the Muchia Susaiului Ridge (alt. 1324m).

To the right the blue cross route takes

you along the ridge and up to Clăbucet Cabana. Turn left at the junction to head east along the ridge, the path wide and well marked all the way. After 1km and some ascent you come to a fork where the red and blue cross routes divide; the red cross bears left to join a goood forest road heading east to reach the Azuga valley. Keep right here (blue cross waymarks) up to Susai cabana. (An alternative route to Susai, involving less walking in the town is to head south on the main DN1 road. Turn left about 600m south of Predeal station along a road signed 'Teleferic', under a low railway bridge, thence up Clăbucet ski slope on the chair lift the blue triangle path to the right of the. From Clăbucet Plecare cabana at the top, head north-east (blue cross) north and then east along the ridge to Susai.)

The high standard of waymarking is sadly not maintained beyond Susai, with its wind generator.

Leave the cabana along the well trodden path, east across the clearing. There is no sign or waymarking; at the eastern end of the clearing, just as you are about the enter the woods, look to your left to see a red triangle on a fir tree. There is no path across the grassy clearing; turn left off the well used path and head north-east, into the woods (red triangle waymarks), along the ridge and steeply down into the Azuga valley where you meet a forest road at a T-junction. Turn left here, over the bridge and north along the road. Take care here; 50m after the bridge, turn right (red triangle waymarks) and go steeply up through the trees, heading east along a spur.

After about 30mins you reach a grassy clearing with a small hut on stilts on the left. At the far end of the clearing the path is more obvious as it dives back into the conifers to bring you to a second clearing and a small saddle with fine views. The path is now heading just east of north towards the top of the Retevoiu ridge. Just over the top of the ridge it swings right past the Retevoiu foresters' cabana and heads south-east along Plaiul Lacul Roșu to the ridge-top pool in the woods known as Lake Găvan (or Lacul Roșu). I suggest you walk a few minutes down into the head of the Azuga valley to obtain water, rather than using the pool.

Days Two and Three

Lake Găvan bivouac site to Muntele Roșu cabana, Ciucaș (about 40km of ridge walking)

This is a walk across an unvisited region, along the main Carpathian watershed and the old-style county boundary between Brașov to the north and Prahova to the south. From the western side of the lake (in fact, pool), head north (red triangle waymarks), down to cross the infant Azuga, briefly down along a forest track, then bear right and up along a path into the forest for 1km to a path junction on the ridge between Vârful Țigaile (1699m, 7409ft) and Vârful lui Andir (1447m, 4747ft). You are now on the north–south Gârbova ridge and the main Carpathian watershed. Ahead, a path (supposedly marked with blue and white stripes) heads north to the eastern end of Săcele along the Clăbucet ridge and the Cărbunarilor ridge. Ignore this to turn right and head south-south-east steeply up to the grassy summit of Vârful Țigaile. The next 2km are straightforward ridge walking along grassy moorland above the forest beside the old border trench; the path heads just south of due east from the summit; after 1km it swings right to head south and gradually swings left, all along the ridge, to meet an unnamed pass (1643m, 5390ft). You now head south, the forest climbing up the ridge to meet you; 2km from the pass you reach Vârful Turcu (1833m, 6014ft) among the trees. Continue south, the ridge swinging east; ahead you see the lump of Vârful Paltinu (1900m, 6234ft). The path climbs steeply to the right (west) of the summit, contouring along the western side. The path is obvious – almost a track.

Having crossed to the south side of the main watershed you see an obvious path turning left and heading downhill across the southern side of Paltinu. Follow this, offering easy walking south-east and then east. Much of the way you are following an ancient sunken track – probably a border marker rather than a route. The ridge narrows as you descend steadily towards the beech forest at Buzău pass (1298m, 4258ft). As you enter the forest you are on a clear route; there are a few old waymarks on tree-trunks. At the pass you find a good forest road and a triple electricity pylon (the base of one marked '1659 – R160') but no sign that you are on what should be a major walking route.

The route from Buzău pass is east, along a well used track in contrast to the route west from here. 1km east of the pass you leave the forest and turn left (the shepherds' track zigzags off to your right). You are now making your way around the head of the Tărlung valley, marked on some maps as the Doftana Ardealana – the Transylvanian Doftana (the 'real' Doftana valley is the one heading south from here).

Looking north-east, ahead as you leave the forest you see a rounded hilltop; reaching the top of the ridge follow the path along the south side, fairly well defined. 3km from crossing the road at Buzău Pass the path passes below the unremarkable summit of Vârful Sloeru Marcaşanu (1592m, 5223ft) and here swings to the right. The crags of the Ciucaş are now over your left shoulder; for the next 8km your heading is south-east, so that at times you seem to be heading away from your target. Between the Buzău pass and Bratocea there are a further three points where the path descends from the grassy moors to enter beech forest. At each of these it is quite well defined and a few trunks have red stripe waymarks.

Making your way south-east along the ridge, the path descends very briefly into beech forest about 4km south-east of Sloeru Marcaşanu; you go across a fine little clearing on the col and climb gently out of it onto a plateau with a small lone pine on the left. Passing a shepherds' hut on the tree line to your right you continue across the plateau until suddenly the path drops by some rock outcrops back briefly into the forest. It is well worth relating the map to the ground here, looking ahead. Follow the well defined path zigzagging into the forest to a rocky col; you start to climb on the south side of the ridge and leave the forest at a lone natural rock pillar. The path swings left; altogether out of the forest for less than 1km here, re-entering as a well defined route. Your general heading here is just south of due east.

There follows about 3km of easy forest walking; it is straightforward and there is even the occasional old waymark on a tree-trunk. Finally exiting from the forest among some hay meadow you regain the ridge to your left and cross over it, on a good track with springs. Just ahead of you is the mass of Vârful Bobu Mare (1757m, 5764ft). Your track swings left across the west slope of the mountain to a shepherds' hut. At the base of a broad spur you turn right to head up the obvious path with a narrow little v-shaped valley below you to your right. It is a steep pull to the summit, where you find a steel survey marker. The path now turns left to head due north across the Bobu plateau as a prominent old trench. You are now walking along the Grohotiş massif; behind you it runs as a ridge south- south-west above the forest, offering an exit route to the village of Valea Doftanei (Teşila).

At the north end of the plateau you are on an obvious track; it zigzags steeply down to a broad col between the Bobu plateau and Vârful Babeş (1556m, 5105ft). Notice the border trench continuing steeply up the face of Babeş. Bear left here, along the track contouring north along the base of Babeş, passing a spring before re-entering the forest at a vast spring just below to the left. The track takes you north-east along the Plaiul Sterp ridge on a rutted cart track through mature spruce forest to meet the DN1A road at the Bratocea Pass with its concrete sign marking the boundary between the counties of Braşov and Prahova. Here a sign points the way onward to Vf. Ciucaş (4–4½ hours), and back the way you came to Pasul Buzău (two days – I did it with a full pack in eight hours). Now turn to Route D below for directions onward into the Ciucaş.

THE CIUCAS MASSIF

The Ciucaş massif (pronounced 'chew-cash') lies to the east of the Bratocea pass on the DN1A road from Braşov to Vălenii de Munte and Ploieşti. It is a compact massif (200 sq. km), consisting of two ridges of conglomerate rising out of the forest, one reaching its highest point at Vârful Ciucaş (1954m, 6411ft) the other at Vârful Gropşoare (1883m, 6178ft). The latter is popular with climbers and makes an exciting walker's ascent, assisted by cables attached to the rock. The compact nature of this range means that it lends itself particularly to day hikes from the cabana at Muntele Roşu. The massif is distinctive, with a number of unusually-shaped rock outcrops. Rising so far above the surrounding forested hills the very tops offer some of the best all-round views in the Carpathians. Thanks to the Emil Cristea club in Ploieşti, the paths are very well signed and waymarked – I recommend the Ciucaş for fine, challenging walking with few other hikers. However be warned – with its limestone-based conglomerate geology, water is scarce in the Ciucaş; the high paths have no springs. Even Cabana Ciucaş has no water suppply; it is carried up from the delightful Fântâna Nicolae Ioan (alt. 1360m, 4462ft) spring, far below in the forest. The limited size of the Ciucaş means that the walking directions below are given as alternative approach routes, rather than Days One, Two, Three, and so on in the massif.

To the east and south-east of the Ciucaş lie the Tătaru and Siriu massifs, bounded on the north-east by the Buzău valley. This is a wild area which is crossed by a number of remote paths. If you walk into the Ciucaş as a continuation of the walk across the Vrancea and Penteleu (Chapter Twelve) you will cross this region from the Buzău valley in order to reach the Ciucaş.

Access

Access directly to the Ciucaş is probably easiest by bus (or lift) from outside the main railway station in Braşov, along the twisting DN1A road making its way southwards over the Bratocea pass (1263m, 4144ft), into the Telejean valley and eventually to the oil town of Ploieşti. This road runs past the resort of Staţiunea Cheia, from where an access road snakes up to Muntele Roşu cabana. You can also leave the road well before the pass, at Babarunca cabana, and walk into the Ciucaş from there. There is one bus per day from the bus station outside the railway station in Braşov to Cheia and Babarunca cabanas; it travels on to Vălenii de Munte.

It is also possible to approach the area from the north-east, having walked across the Vrancea massif and made your way to the village of Vama Buzăului (see Chapter Twelve and 'Alternative approaches', below). There are four trains per day from Braşov to

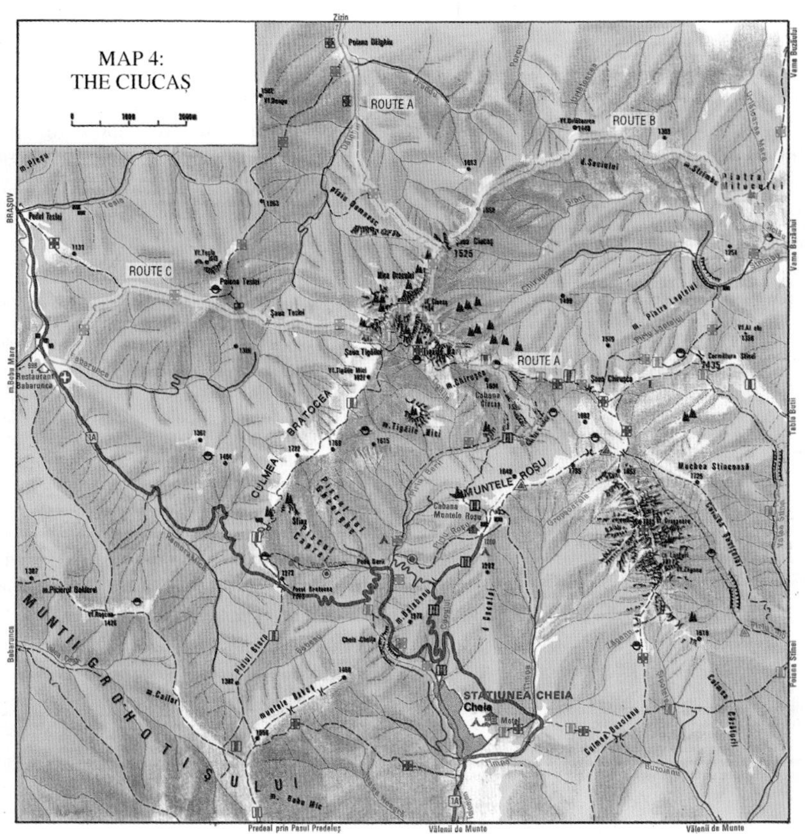

Intorsura Buzăului, taking an hour to cover the 36km. From the bus station by the train station you can catch a bus to Crasna and on to the Buzău pass (alt. 643m); arriving trains are met by departing buses. There are also buses from Brașov or Săcele to the village of Zizin, east of Tărlungheni (likewise, see 'Alternative approaches' below). Another possibility (offering much the shortest journey time from Bucharest) is to take the train from Bucharest to Ploiești Sud, and change there onto the personal train that takes two hours to cover the 50km to the village of Măneciu; from here take a bus or lift north along the DN1A to Cheia.

Alternative approaches to the Ciucaș

Route A: Zizin village to Ciucaș cabana, about 20km (13 miles). Altitude gained from Zizin to Vârful Ciucaș, 1274m (4180ft)

From Zizin head up the Zizin valley for 15km on the forest road over a minor pass to the village of Dălghiu. Turn right in the village to head south along the Dalghiu valley; after 2km the valley splits into the Prundu and the Dalghiu. Take the Dalghiu valley to the right, heading south: 1km after this fork you come to another fork, this time with a path (blue cross waymarks) heading up the spur between them; follow it southwards and then south-east to Şaua Ciucaş pass (1525m, 5003ft). Turn right here (red cross waymarks) up past the crags of Gemenii Ciucaş and Mâna Dracului ('Devil's Hand') on the right, to the summit of Vârful Ciucaş (1954m, 6411ft); it lies 1.5km south-east of Şaua Ciucaş. Keep left at the summit (red stripe waymarks) to head south-east for about 500m, down to a col, past the crags of Babele la Sfat on the right. Continue south-east, past Vârful Ţigaile Mare to the right and down to the Chirusca plateau and Ciucaş cabana (see Appendix A).

Route B: Vama Buzăului village to Vârful Ciucaş, about 16km (10 miles). Altitude gained from Vama Buzăului to Vârful Ciucaş, 1248m (4094ft)

This route may be walked as a continuation of the itinerary through the Vrancea massif, for which see the Vrancea section (Chapter Twelve). From Vama Buzăului head south, up the Buzău valley along the tarred road for 2km before turning left to head south-east along a rough road where the tarred road heads west, up the Dălghiu valley. 9km from the junction you reach the settlement of La Strâmbu. Turn right here to head west, then north-west up the Strâmbu valley for 2km and turn right (blue cross waymarks), heading north for less than 1km, up to the crags of Piatra Miticului. You meet the blue cross path at the crags, heading right, north, back to Vama Buzăului.

Your path lies due west for 500m, then turns right at a junction to head north along the top of a prominent ridge above the forest. 1500m west-north-west of Piatra Miticului you reach a col; the path continues due west along the south side of the ridge, continuing west across a broad saddle so that you are now on the north side of the ridge, heading along the banks of a stream in the forest. You reach the source of this and climb up to a col just south of Vârful Urlătoarea (1410m, 4626ft). The path drops off the ridge once more to the south; altogether 6km after Piatra Miticului it brings you to Şaua Ciucaş, where you turn left and follow the directions in Route A to reach Ciucaş cabana.

An easier alternative to this is to keep left at the junction 2km west of La Strâmbu, heading along the forest road into the Strâmbu valley. 3km west of La Strâmbu you reach the forest cabana (Cabana Piruşca). Turn left here, initially up the Pârâul Laptelui ('Milk Stream') valley, then almost immediately left out of it, to head steeply up through the forest, heading south to bring you up to a shepherd's hut near Curmatura Stânei. Head west from here towards the summit of Piatra Laptelui ('Milk Rock'). From here the path turns left and heads south to Şaua Chiruşca, where you turn right and head west along the ridge towards Cabana Ciucaş.

There is yet a third alternative from Vama Buzăului. Continue on the tarred road 9km to Dalghiu, where a rough road turns right to head north-west to Zizin. Keep left here, up the Dalghiu valley for 2km, past a right hand turning, south-east up Prundu valley. The forest road forks; head due south between the arms of the fork, up a spur in the forest to Şaua Ciucaş, from where you follow the directions above to Ciucaş cabana.

Route C: Babarunca cabana to Ciucaş cabana via Vârful Ciucaş. Altitude gained from Babarunca to Vârful Ciucaş, 956m (3136ft)

Babarunca cabana is on the DN1A road, 22km from Săcele on the way to Valenii de Munte and Ploieşti; it is also used as a truckers' halt. At the wooden two-bed huts you see a sign pointing east to 'Vf Ciucaş 4–5 ore' indicating the red stripe route across the grass field towards a new house (built in 1995). Drop down on the

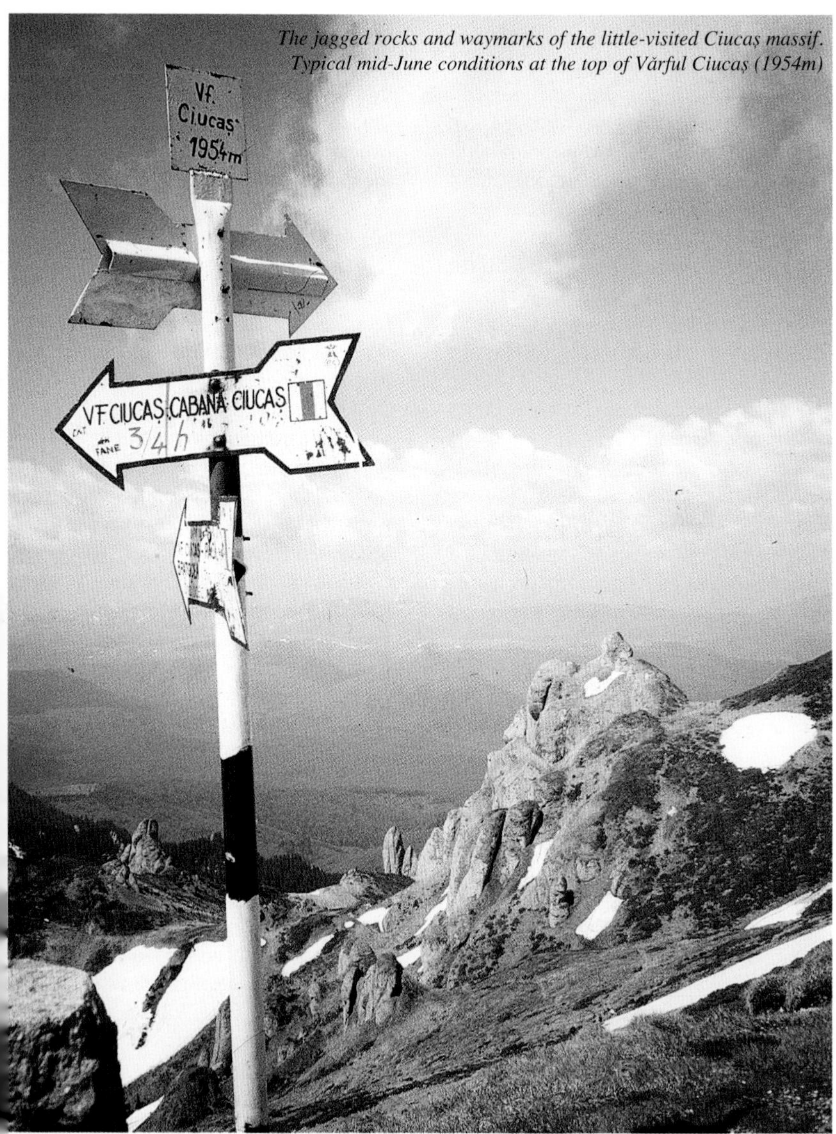

The jagged rocks and waymarks of the little-visited Ciucaș massif. Typical mid-June conditions at the top of Vărful Ciucaș (1954m)

far side of this through the beech trees and turn right along the forest road that runs up the Babarunca valley. Turn right on the rough road, with a new plantation on your left. After 150m you reach an obvious turning left, a well used but unmarked path heading north-west up the valley side through the trees.

1.5km of climbing brings you onto the Teslei ridge in the forest; you pass a junction with a path (red cross waymarks) turning left to head north-west down to Podu Teslei, back on the main road. Turn right to follow the ridge-top east to emerge from the forest by a shepherds' hut at Poiana Teslei, about 1.5km after the path junction. There are fine views west across the Baiului to the Bucegi beyond. Head east past the hut, ignoring a path to the left (blue cross waymarks), heading north-east to Poiana Dalghiului. The path returns to the forest and descends for less than a km to Şaua Teslei (1380m, 4528ft) and continues for about 2km climbing along a spur, latterly above the forest wlith the crags of Turnu Goliat ('Goliath's Tower') to your left. At the very head of the Babarunca valley you reach the path junction at Şaua Ţigailor, giving you the choice of keeping right, to the south of Vârful Ciucaş, down into the Ţigaile valley (red cross waymarks), or turning left (red stripe waymarks) for less than 1km to the summit of Ciucaş (1954m, 6411ft) and heading south-east from there. The two paths meet up just to the east of Ţigaile Mare, from where you head east to Ciucaş cabana.

Route D: Bratocea pass to Vârful Ciucaş, 8km (5 miles). Altitude gained, 682m (2237ft)

From the forest road at the pass, head north along the stony track into the trees, turning left immediately off it, briefly into the forest, heading steeply up. Reaching a grassy clearing you bear left with a telecommunications relay tower ahead of you. You rejoin the twisting track as it swings round the clearing and follow it zigzagging up to the tower. As you reach the fence round the tower, turn right, steeply up a bank and follow the well waymarked (red stripe) path up the spur with the spruce forest on your left. The route is easily followed to the signpost at Şaua Ţigailor at the crosspaths junction. Keep straight ahead here, perpendicularly up the slope and then swinging right to the summit.

Yet another alternative (recommended) is the walk from Cheia village to Cabana Ciucaş via Vf. Gropşoare (14km, 9 miles; altitude gained from Cheia to Vf. Gropşoare 970m, 3200ft). To start this, follow the main DN1A road east from the PECO petrol station. Pass the radio dish on the left hand side of the road; continuing along the road you pass two bridges with the usual yellow and black roadside railings. 500m beyond the second bridge turn right at the signpost (red cross and blue stripe waymarks, 'Cab. Ciucaş 5 hrs, Val. Stanei 2hrs'), heading east into the mixed pine and beech forest. The path takes you east, steeply up onto the Culmea Buzoianu ridge, from where you head north along the forested ridge and up to the crags of Vf. Zăganu and on over Gropşoare to Chiruşca pass and west to Cabana Ciucaş.

East from the Ciucaş

At Ciucaş cabana a sign points the way north 'Pasul Boncuţa 5 ore'. This is the path along the main Carpathian watershed route to the Siriu massif, leading eventually to the Penteleu and Podu Calului massifs. This is unknown country and, the Siriu itself apart, is almost entirely forest.

CHAPTER FOUR
The Mountains around Brașov

The mountainous hinterland to the city of Brașov – dominated by the Postăvarul massif – offers fine walking. The combination of this with the city of Brașov, Romania's second city and perhaps its finest city-centre, rivalling Prague or Cracow on a small scale (without the hordes of visitors), means that the area is very well worth exploring. There are a number of good cabanas, so that much of the walking can be enjoyed as day walks from a base. There can be very few cities in the world where, with the aid of a short cable-car ride, twenty minutes from the old town square, you can be stepping over the droppings of wild bear in the forest. The itinerary below involves a walk over the Postăvaru, starting in the old town centre of Brașov and taking you on to Râșnov, with its regular trains and buses on to Zărnești, start point for the Piatra Craiului. There are also buses from Râșnov on to Bran.

Access

Brașov is the easiest city to reach from Bucharest (I discount Ploiești), served by almost hourly trains, taking three hours, and trains from every other city in Transylvania, most of them direct. There are four trains and one bus per day from Budapest. It is well served by other international trains coming in from the north and west, so that, if travelling overland into Romania, you do not have to go via Bucharest. There is also one train a day to and from Vienna, Prague, Paris via Basel and Warsaw via Cracow.

To catch a bus to any of the start points of the walks described in this or preceding chapters, things are not quite so simple. There are three bus stations. The first is outside the main station, the second on the far (north) side of Cetatea, on the right hand side of Strada Avram Iancu as you head north. To catch a bus

The Bucegi massif, seen from the Postăvaru, near Cabana Cristianu Mare in early May

Day walks from Poiana Brașov

Anyone embarking on one of the popular centre-based holidays at Poiana Brașov should endeavour to obtain the excellent, green-covered Poiana Brașov and Piatra Mare walking map (try Stanfords in London, The Map Shop in Upton upon Severn – See Appendix C). Poiana Brașov is a good centre for walking, with a wide choice of walks of every grade, from easy strolls north of the resort across the Poiana Mare clearing and over the Spinarea Lungă ridge to the fields overlooking Cristian, to challenging ascents such as the one up the south side of Postăvaru to Poiana Trei Fetițe. The paths around Poiana Brașov are very well waymarked, with many self-explanatory walkers' signposts; they lead into superbly wild forest a very few minutes from the resort. The geology of the massif – largely conglomerate – has resulted in a number of paths that follow old fossilised scree slopes now overgrown. These can be very tricky walking, the ground hidden in foliage – frequently nettles – and very apt to trip up the unwary walker.

Staying in Brașov

Brașov itself is simply one of the most rewarding cities in central Europe in which to spend a few days. Description of its attractions, however, lies out of the scope of the present book. The only cheap central hotel is the Aro Sport (do not confuse it with the Aro Palace); also reasonable and well-sited is the Hotel Postăvaru. There is a campsite at Dârste near the main road to Predeal – catch a Predeal-bound bus and ask for the campsite. 2km further is the pleasant cabana at Dâmbul Morii, with the advantage that it is the start (or finish) point of walking routes up into the Piatra Mare. If you want to camp wild whilst visiting Brașov, there is an excellent spot no more than 30 minutes' walk from the town. A grassy clearing in the pine forest has a clear stream flowing across it. To reach it, follow the instructions below for the walk to Cristianu Mare cabana – it is highlighted in the walk description. At Pârâu Rece and Trei Brazi there are some pleasant rural hotels; by using these it is possible to enjoy a number of well signed walks from a centre base for a few days.

View of Brașov from the top of Tampa Hill: the city seen here is entirely German; the Romanian quarter, known as Schei, is hidden in the valley to the left

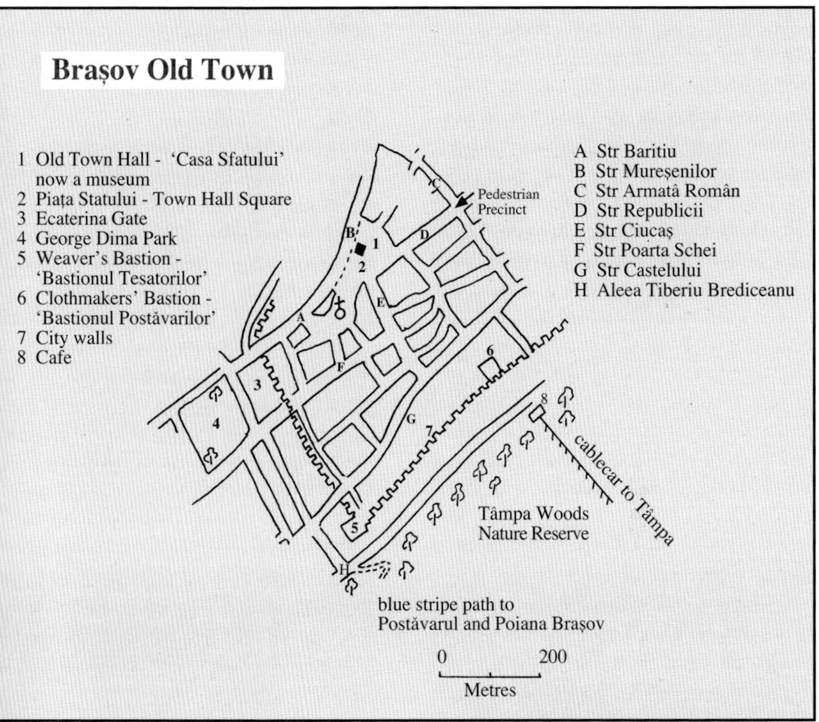

(number 20) to Poiana Brașov, head north along Strada Mureșenilor from Piața Sfatului, past St Peter and Paul's (Magyar) Roman Catholic church. The stop is on the corner of Bulevard Eroilor, on the south-east corner of Parc Central. Buses to Predeal and Săcele (for the Piatra Mare mountains) leave from the south-east of the city, on the corner of Calea București and Strada Poienilor, outside the Autocamion factory. However there is a special delight in walking straight out of a fine city into the mountains. In Brașov you have a choice of bidding farewell to the red-tiled Medieval cluster from the top of Tâmpa (reached by cable car or well signed path from the bottom station) or, perhaps better, walk from the city walls themselves.

ACROSS THE POSTĂVARU MASSIF

(See Map 4 in Chapter 3.)

Day One

Brașov to Cristianu Mare cabana or Poiana Brașov, 10km (6 miles). Altitude gained from the summit of Tâmpa to Cristianu Mare cabana, 750m (2460ft)

From the courtyard of the Black Church (Curtea Johannes Honterus) make your way south-south-east along Strada Brenkner and turn right along Strada Poarta Schei. At the end of the street you see the three arches of the Schei Gate. Turn left immediately after the gate, up Aleea Tiberiu Brediceanu, a quiet avenue with a the school sports ground and then the town tennis club beneath Bastionul Țesătorilor below you on your left. You reach the end of Str. Petofi, stretching away to the right; do not be diverted onto the blue stripe path but bear right on the well marked (and well trodden) blue cross route taking you south-west contouring along the steep hillside with the gardens of the Schei district to your right.

After about 300m you reach a clearing with a waymark on a tree on the far side, whereupon the path leads steeply down to reach a small shrine on a grassy slope. Turn round here for superb views back across Brașov. The path takes you into the pinewoods, up the first of two grassy clearings, either of which would make good camping spots; be discreet, however. The second clearing (Poiana Stechil), much higher and with a memorial cross, marks the junction with the blue stripe route from the left, coming from the top of the Tâmpa cable car.

Alternatively you can leave Brașov using the Tâmpa cable car (it usually operates seven days a week, 0930–1930). From the top station turn right on a gravel path heading south west along the Tâmpa ridge. After less than 100m it swings left, off the ridge, with a number of paths turning right. Keep along the spine of the ridge, with superb views into the old town of Brașov immediately below you. Confusingly there are a few yellow triangle waymarks on the trees here. Keep heading south-west to rejoin the vehicle track at a saddle (Șaua Tâmpa), on the far side of which the pine forest starts. A blue cross path (not the one described above) comes up onto this saddle from your right, from the Schei quarter of the old part of Brașov.

Look for a yellow signpost at the edge of the trees. Head south-west from here (blue stripe waymarks) along the ridge; a number of tracks cross the path – take care at the junctions. 2km after Șaua Tâmpa you reach Poiana Stechil and the blue stripe path from Schei Gate.

The paths, now united, continue south-west along the ridge and head down to the left, into the Răcădău valley where you meet the blue triangle path at Fântâna cu Brad ('Spring with a Fir Tree'). Head south (blue stripe waymarks) up the side of the valley, up to the clearing on the ridge at Groapa lui Simion (1340m, 4396ft), a steep 2km from Fântâna cu Brad. Turn right here to follow the Crucura Mare ridge along, with views ahead of Postăvarul summit and of the Piatra Mare over your left shoulder. 3km after Groapa lui Simion you meet a minor junction with a path down the the right (blue disc waymarks) to the Peștera de Lapte ('Milk Cave'), also taking you back down to Poiana Brașov. Keep straight on here, on a track (in fact a ski-run), taking you out onto the ski slope at a broad flat area. This is Poiana Ruia. Cross over this, under the cable car, and into the trees (red cross waymarks) taking you up through the woods to Postăvaru cabana (1602m, 5256ft) and on up to Cristianu Mare (1704m, 590ft). This is one of the best run of Romania's cabanas; there is also a superb view out across the Bârsa Land.

By heading west (blue triangle waymarks) from Fântâna cu Brad junction you can continue through the woods to the eastern end of Poiana Brașov, or turn right and head back into Brașov at Pietrele lui Solomon. The bottom station of the cable car up to Cristianu Mare is at the far western end of Poiana Brașov, just south of the Șura Dacilor restaurant. Poiana Brașov is well supplied with maps on boards, though they are not very useful.

In order to continue either to Trei Brazi or to the town of Râșnov from Poiana Brașov, follow the road downhill into the centre and turn left at the Șura Dacilor restaurant to head west (blue stripe and yellow cross waymarks) along the Poienii stream. 1.5km after leaving Poiana Brașov you arrive at a confluence of streams (the Sticlarei joining the

Good mountain huts and good waymarking – signpost outside Cabana Cristianu Mare

Poienii from the right – the north) in the forest and a path junction. Turn left here to follow the Cheii stream down through the forest, heading south. In dry weather in summer it disappears into watersinks and then reappears as you walk through the fine little gorge in the forest. You join the end of a forest track and walk down this; in places the track is the stream bed. You exit from the forest in some fine hay meadows and continue down the stony road to a wooden shed on your right; to your left a similar stony track heads up the Valea Lungă. Now continue from this point below.

Day Two

Cristianu Mare cabana to Râșnov, 16km (10 miles). Altitude lost to Râșnov, 1000m (3281ft)

This is a day of walking in varied forest, with occasional views of the Bucegi, Piatra Craiului and Postăvaru mountains. Turn left out of Cristianu Mare cabana, and make your way north-west down the blue cross path to the left hand side of the ski slope as you look down towards Poiana Brașov. In a few minutes you reach Postăvaru cabana; now take care. The red cross route heads south-west from the cabana and is well marked and used, bar the short stretch near the cabana itself. Five minutes from Postăvaru you reach an informative sign, pointing the way left to Poiana Ruia and Brașov. Turn right here (blue cross waymarks) through the trees, back out to the Lupului ski run.

You cross the piste, heading for a black shed. The blue cross path continues down, south from the shed, through the trees and then steeply down a gully with fossilised scree in a clearing; this is the Vanga Mică valley. The path, well signed, swings right out of the gully and north into the forest, still descending for rather less than 1km. Here you exit from the trees back on to the Lupului ski run to find yourself at the junction with the red disc path turning left, signed to Cheia cabana, taking you via the Groapa de Aur valley. Turn left here, back into the forest, descending (red and blue disc waymarks). After just over 1km you reach a signpost in the forest, pointing the way left to

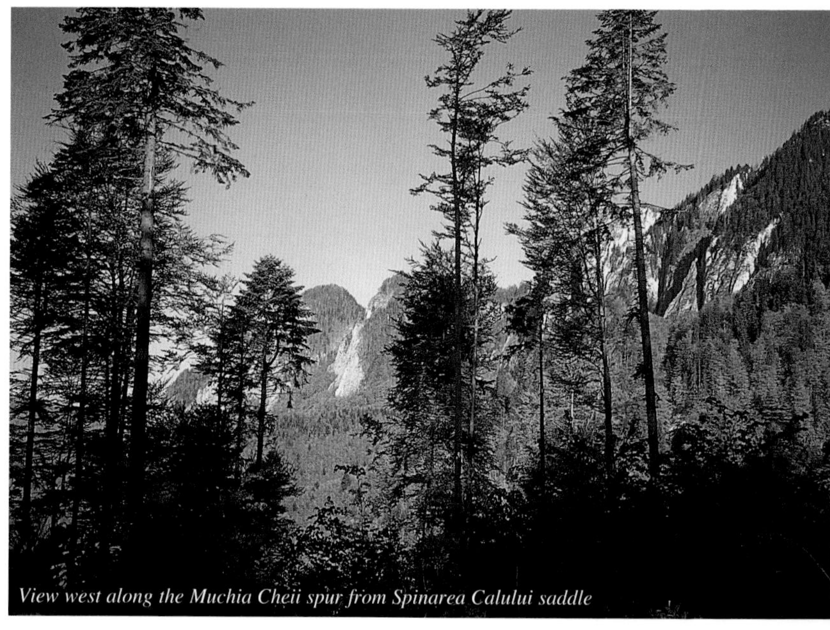

View west along the Muchia Cheii spur from Spinarea Calului saddle

Groapa de Aur; keep right here and continue to descend through the forest, into the Valea Lungă. The path steepens, takes you down a small v-shaped rocky gully and brings you to a grassy patch at the end of a track – a good camping spot. This is the Valea Lungă.

Follow the track down the valley to a junction by a wooden shed on the right beside a poplar avenue. 1km after this, at a right hand bend, the red disc path direct from Postăvaru comes in from the left. Keep on down the valley (very popular with Romanian families in the summer who come to camp and have barbecue lunches by the stream) to a memorial cross to one Leoca Dorin Alexandru; immediately after this turn right, off the track over the stream and north across a hay meadow in the bottom of the valley with the tree-lined river on your right. At the far end of the meadow turn left to head north-west, steeply up the right hand side of a tributary valley on a well-defined path with the occasional blue disc waymark on the trunks of the beech trees.

This takes you uphill, twisting for 1km through the forest, to the top of the Piscul Lung spur. 1.5km after leaving the Poienii stream you see a large blue triangle with 'Scouts 1994' on a trunk; fork left here, to reach a path junction with a signpost nailed to a tree on top of a ridge in the forest. Turn left here to head west (blue stripe waymarks) and then south-west along the ridge towards Râşnov. After about 1km you exit from the trees with fine views to your left, down the Valea Neagră and across to the Muchia Cheii ridge to the south-east.

At this point there are a number of rounded rock outcrops; you keep just to the left of the top of the ridge. The wooded spur of Dealul Bogdan stretches away to your left; you reach a grassy clearing with a signpost. A few minutes' walk south of here is the Bisericuţa Păgânilor – the pagans' holy shrine where sacrifices were made. Return to the clearing and head down, south-west (blue stripe waymarks), to the signed entrance to Peştera Râşnoavei cave. From here, little waymarked, the path heads west, steeply down with conifers on your right, then swings right, out of the Cărbunarilor valley to bring you after a few hundred metres of easy traversing descent with excellent views of the Piatra Craiului ahead to a grassy clearing, backed by beech forest.

Turn right out of the clearing (blue cross waymarks) north-east into mature beech forest. The path twists and turns around the head of the Popii valley, at one point climbing steeply for a short stretch and finally gaining the Dealul Cernit ridge at a narrow spine in the woods, where the path heads downhill in a sunken logging track down the left hand side of the ridge. Eventually, 4km after Râșnov cave you reach the road by a walkers' signpost opposite the Cetatea Râșnov Hotel (known to the locals as 'Acapulco'). There is a campsite here with small 'Wendy-houses', and it makes a good refreshment stop. Go up the tarred drive (past the walkers' map painted on a steel plate), with the football pitch on your left. As you reach the hotel the lane continues, bending to the left to head up through the trees to Cetatea Râșnov, 600m from the hotel. This is very much worth a visit and has superb views down onto the old centre of Râșnov. It never was a castle in the sense of being intended for permanent occupation, but was built as a refuge for the inhabitants fo Râșnov in time of Turkish (or Tartar) invasion. Its effectiveness depended, of course, on a reasonable water supply; the well took from 1623 to 1640 to dig out.

Râșnov has a station on the branch line from Brașov to its terminus at Zărnești, the journey Brașov–Râșnov taking around 20 minutes. Zărnești is the best start point for walking into the Piatra Craiului and the Făgărăș.

Link Route South towards the Bucegi

Cristianu Mare cabana to Trei Brazi cabana via Râșnov gorge, 18km (11 miles). Altitude lost to the Cheia valley, 1050m (3445ft); altitude gained to Trei Brazi cabana, 328m (1076ft)

Follow the directions above for Walk Two from Cristianu Mare to Trei Brazi via Valea Lungă as far as the wooden shed in the meadow by a poplar avenue (the confluence of the Lunga and Poienii valleys). From here simply follow the track down the Poienii Valley through Cheișoara gorge and out into the open fields towards Cheia cabana (serving good food). Turn left at the road junction before the cabana and walk up the track through the short but spectacular Râșnov gorge, hung with climbing ropes for the army's use. Despite this disturbance, the gorge is a nest site for a colony of Alpine Swifts. About 1km after the gorge, the road forks at a bridge with a walker's signpost. Turn right here (yellow and blue triangle waymarks) and immediately right again (blue triangle waymarks) very steeply up in the deciduous forest. You come to the top of a ridge, out of the woods and descend a grassy bank into what seems to be a chalky dry valley – a favourite haunt of numbers of butterflies in high summer. The path is well waymarked with striped poles through the scattered trees. You re-enter the beechwoods, heading south-east and ascend gently to leave the woods at a clearing grazed by cows. Ahead to the left is Poiana Secuilor cabana. Keep right once you reach the rough track to take you to Trei Brazi hotel, 700m south-west of Poiana Secuilor.

There is a more direct route from Cristianu Mare to Trei Brazi, but it involves a very steep descent and is not recommended unless you are experienced and fit. Whilst the path is well marked, for much of the descent down the south face of Postăvaru you will be clutching at

Râșnov citadel, near Brașov – one of the many old fortifications on the mountainous rim of Transylvana

tree trunks. From the steps of Cristianu Mare cabana look south, towards the top station of the cable car and pick up the path (yellow stripe waymarks) that swings right, heading south-east through the trees and contouring along the steep slope at the head of the Valea Seaca. Less than 1km of gentle ascent around the summit from the cabana, the path brings you to the tiny tussocky clearing of Poiana Trei Fetițe ('Three Little Girls' Clearing'). The path descends very steeply from here and negotiates two sharp spines, before taking you along the forested Spinarea Calului ridge (yellow stripe waymarks) before reaching the broad clearing at Poiana Secuilor from where you follow the track 1km to Trei Brazi.

Exit from Trei Brazi to Predeal or the Bucegi

There is an easy exit walk of an hour and a half from Trei Brazi down to Predeal; leave the hotel along the tarred road heading south. As you enter the woods a path (blue cross waymarks) turns off to the right; take care here for there are no waymarks visible from the road. Head perpendicularly up the very steep slope, picking up the waymarks as you approach the summit of Fitifoiu (1292m, 4239ft). Here you meet a T-junction of paths (all of them blue cross waymarks). At the summit is a signpost nailed to a tree; turn left to head west and then west-south-west through mature forest, downhill to rejoin the road just above the Orizont Hotel above Predeal. To head on into the Bucegi, avoiding Predeal, turn right at the t-junction on Fitifoiu and follow the blue cross waymarks down, south-west towards the DN73 main road. Turn left on this for about 600m, ascending steadily until you see a well-used track turning right into the trees, signed to Diham cabana. Follow this track, and the well-marked paths into the Bucegi.

CHAPTER FIVE

The Piatra Craiului and Iezer-Păpuşa Massifs

This chapter covers two quite contrasting ranges. The Piatra Craiului is a high crest of white limestone rising sheer from the forest; the Iezer-Păpuşa is a more massive crescent-shaped feature, of gentler contours, much of it grassed over. Both offer a worthwhile approach to the Făgărăş; only the Piatra Craiului, however, is worth travelling to for its own sake. Its sharp, narrow crest commands views of an enormous area of plains, mountains and forests. It is the most dramatic ridge-walk in Romania and one of the most enjoyable in Europe.

The hinterland to the south of these mountains is delightful. The DN73 is one of the most scenic roads in Romania, heading south-west from Braşov via Bran to Câmpulung, from where you head north to Voina cabana, start point for the walk north across the Iezer-Păpuşa into the Făgărăş. West of Bran and Moieciu the next village is Fundata, site of the Nedeia of the Mountains festival on the last Sunday in June – a trade fair in its original sense, where livestock and implements were traded and offering the chance to experience the opening scene of Hardy's Mayor of Casterbridge *come to life. There is a cabana nearby (not in Appendix A), Dealul Şasului ('the Saxons' Hill'). The German settlers in the region were, and still are, called 'Sas' – Saxon – by the Romanians, which is as inaccurate as continental Europeans calling all British people 'English'. This area was formerly one of those more densely settled by Germans.*

West of here is Bran pass (1240m, 4068ft), also marked as the Giuvala pass. Here you cross the boundary from Braşov county to Argeş, and the border between Transylvania and Wallachia. From the pass the road descends to the limestone gorges of 'Bridge of Dâmboviţa' and the turning right for Dâmbovicioara village and Brusturet cabana, at the southern end of the Craiului. Beyond the gorges you pass through the villages of Rucăr, Dragoslavele and Nămăeşti. The first two have a wealth of delightful wooden houses. Sacheverell Sitwell spent a few days in Rucăr in 1937 and was charmed by it as 'the perfect little mountain town' (see Bibliography, Appendix C). The church at Dragoslavele is worth a visit, as is the rock church at Nămăeşti with its hermits' cells.

THE PIATRA CRAIULUI

The Piatra Craiului is a dramatic limestone ridge rising sheer from the surrounding forested hills. In spite of its small size (22km, 14 miles long), it deserves a section all to itself because it stands apart from its neighbours, and within its small area it offers one of the most spectacular ridge walks in Europe. It is separated by a considerable area of forest from the nearest similar terrain (the Iezer-Păpuşa ridge to the west, the Bucegi to the south-east, the Făgărăş to the north-west) and has a rich flora, including the endemic Piatra Craiului Pink *Dianthus callizonus*, growing just above the treeline; there is also a small herd of chamois.

The best way to explore the Piatra Craiului (the name means 'royal stone') is to make a number of day walks from the fine cabana at Curmătura, situated at the top of a clearing sloping down to the south, between the arms of the Piatra Craiului and Piatra Mică. From here there

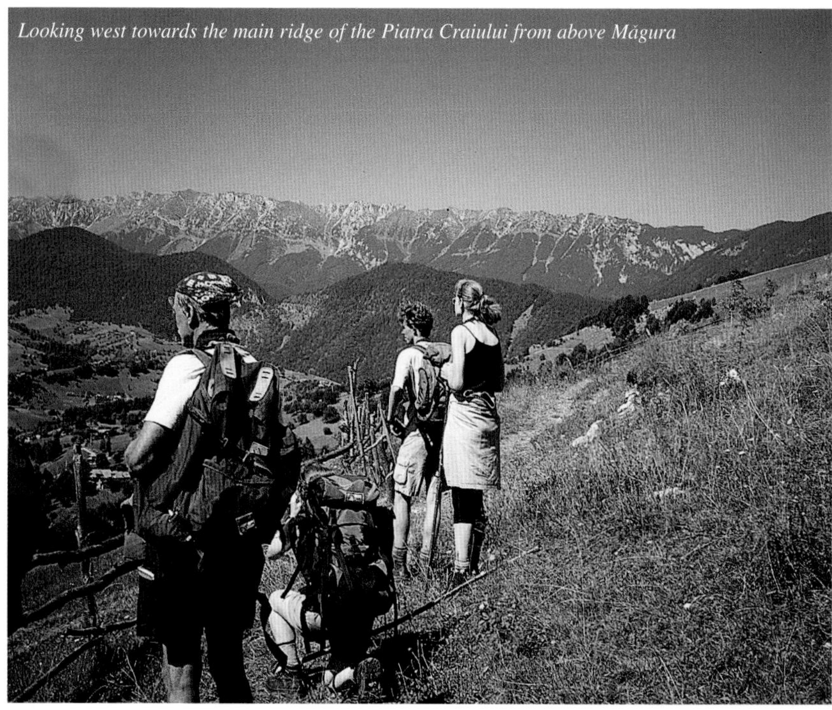
Looking west towards the main ridge of the Piatra Craiului from above Măgura

are enough spectacular day walks to fill most of a week. In the evening you will be given acetylene lamps with a naked flame. Do not take these up to your room and blow out the flame: the chemical reaction will continue to give out poisonous, inflammable gas. The dining room, with its purely decorative corner bar, is remininiscent of alpine refuges in Austria.

This is a cabana, where, due to its inaccessibility from the road, you may find little or no drinks. Unfortunately it can get very crowded in August. There are many more walks available in the Piatra Craiului, other than those I have outlined below; these, however, are around the south-western end of the Craiului ridge and are really only reachable if you are camping or staying in one of several refuges. Brusturet cabana is nowhere near as convenient for the high part of the range as Curmătura.

Access

If travelling specifically to the Piatra Craiului, the best way to reach it is to travel by train to Zărnești, 45 minutes' ride from Brașov. There are six trains a day from Brașov (departing at 0600, 0830, 1350, 1550, 2030 and 2335); hourly trains connect Brașov with Bucharest. Zărnești has a good supply of shops, a post office, two good daily markets, several cafes and a pizza parlour. There are two produce markets at Zărnești; the bigger of the two is at the extreme eastern end of town, adjacent to Zărnești halta railway halt (the stop prior to it is Tohanu Vechi). The other is in the centre of town; turn right out of the station and walk 1km to find the town hall on your right, opposite the complex commercial. Turn right here, down Str. 1 Mai, to see the market on your right. At the beginning of Str. 1 Mai is a good map on a board with hikers' information.

Day One
Zărnești station to Curmătura cabana, 8km (5 miles). Altitude gained from Zărnești to Șaua Curmătura, 940m (3084ft)

To reach Curmătura from Zărnești station, turn right out of the station building and walk up the main street into the old town. In summer, especially at weekends, trains are often met by drivers offering lifts to Plaiul Foii or Gura Râului cabanas, saving a lengthy walk along a dirt road. If you are walking head along the main street for 1km from the station, keeping left at the hikers' information board on the way. You reach a small square with a blue sign pointing the way to Gura Râului cabana. Turn right here, into Strada Barițiu and and pick up the signs to Plaiul Foii cabana: the road takes you out of the village and along an avenue of poplar trees, heading west up the beautiful Bârsa Mare valley. About 400m out of Zărnești turn left (blue and yellow stripe waymarks) south-west heading up towards the sheer wall of the Piatra Craiului. 2km after leaving the road you reach a stream. Turn left, upstream, south (yellow stripe waymarks) steeply up through the trees,

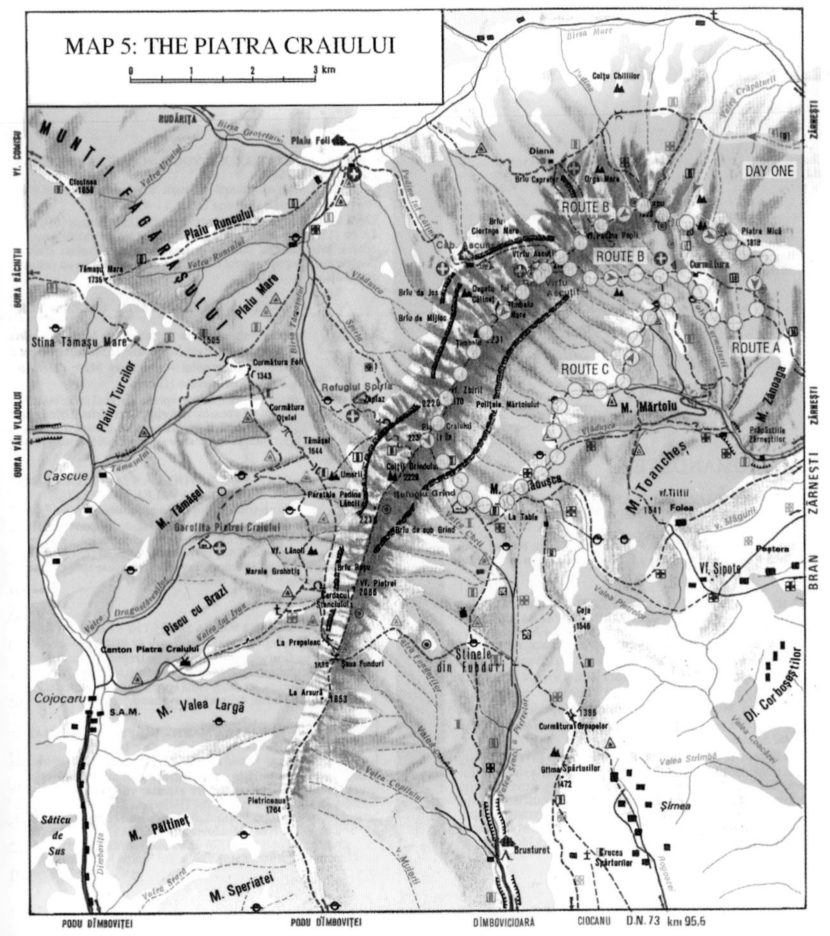

eventually bringing you through a rocky gully – Valea Crăpăturii. At the head of this is prominent pass – Şaua Curmătura, with a viewing platform. Keep straight ahead from the pass, dropping steeply through the pine trees to bring you after a few minutes to Curmătura cabana (see Appendix A).

There is an alternative, adding 3km to the direct Curmătura pass route; it involves a less challenging ascent, fewer fine views along the way, but the chance to eat at Gura Râului cabana. Follow the sign to Gura Râului cabana from Zărneşti and walk up the Râul Mare valley past the cabana and the quarry on the left until you find yourself in a steep wooded gorge. 2km after the cabana you find a signpost on your right near a spring with a shrine and a wired-off electricity sub-station adjacent to the left-hand turning to Măgura. This is Botorog's Fountain; turn right, steeply up through the trees (yellow stripe waymarks) to emerge in a large clearing beneath the crags of Piatra Mică – this is Poiana Zănoaga. A path turns right (blue disc waymarks) – the route up to the top of Piatra Mica. Keep left to continue more or less contouring (yellow stripe waymarks) to Curmătura.

If you want to walk through the gorge you can, adding a further 2km to the Poiana Zănoaga route, taking you through the delightful Prăpăştiile Zărneştilor gorge, whose sheer rock walls offer a number of climbing routes and nest sites for Alpine Swift. Continue south-west along the road through the gorge – you are now in Prăpăştiile Zărneştilor. You pass the climbing hut belonging to the Zărneşti-based Torpedo club and, where the gorge begins to open out, the road makes a hairpin bend to the left. Turn right here, steeply up into the forest (blue stripe waymarks), along the Muchia Curmăturii ridge to the clearing below Curmătura cabana.

Link Route from the Bucegi to the Piatra Craiului

Alternative One: Bran to Curmătura cabana, 16km (10 miles). Altitude gained from Bran to Măgura, 380m (1246ft); from Zărneşti gorge to Curmătura cabana, 678m (2220ft)

This route connects with the walk over the Bucegi; Bran is also a good base in its own right for exploring the northern and western side of the Bucegi and is reached by a number of buses a day from Braşov. It is also reached by a day's walk from a number of cabanas in the Bucegi see Chapter Two. It is a delightful approach walk to the Piatra, through the forest and across hayfields with wonderful views of the Şimon (pronounced 'she-mon') valley and Moieciu de Jos village.

Be warned that for a part of this day there is no map nor any waymarking; you are, however, making your way towards an easy landmark – a church. I have walked every possible variant a number of times and have found that the only route that would be easy to follow for the first time is along the dirt road through Predeluţ. However it is nowhere near as exciting as the meander over the ridge through the scattered farms of Măgura, with the superb view of the Piatra Craiului in front of you.

From Cabana Bran Castel head down the drive and turn left at the end of the trees on the left, along an attractive narrow slightly sunken lane. This takes you uphill and into an orchard, passing a house on the left. In the orchard the lane, now grassy, swings left and starts to zig-zag up the rudimentary ski-slope that has been cut out of the forest cloaking the hill slope. When you reach the top, there is a very fine viewpoint from the trees, west up the Moieciu Valley and south to the Bucegi. Turn right and head west, along the edge of the wood on your right. After 1km of walking outside the forest, you reach a saddle with an obvious path head-

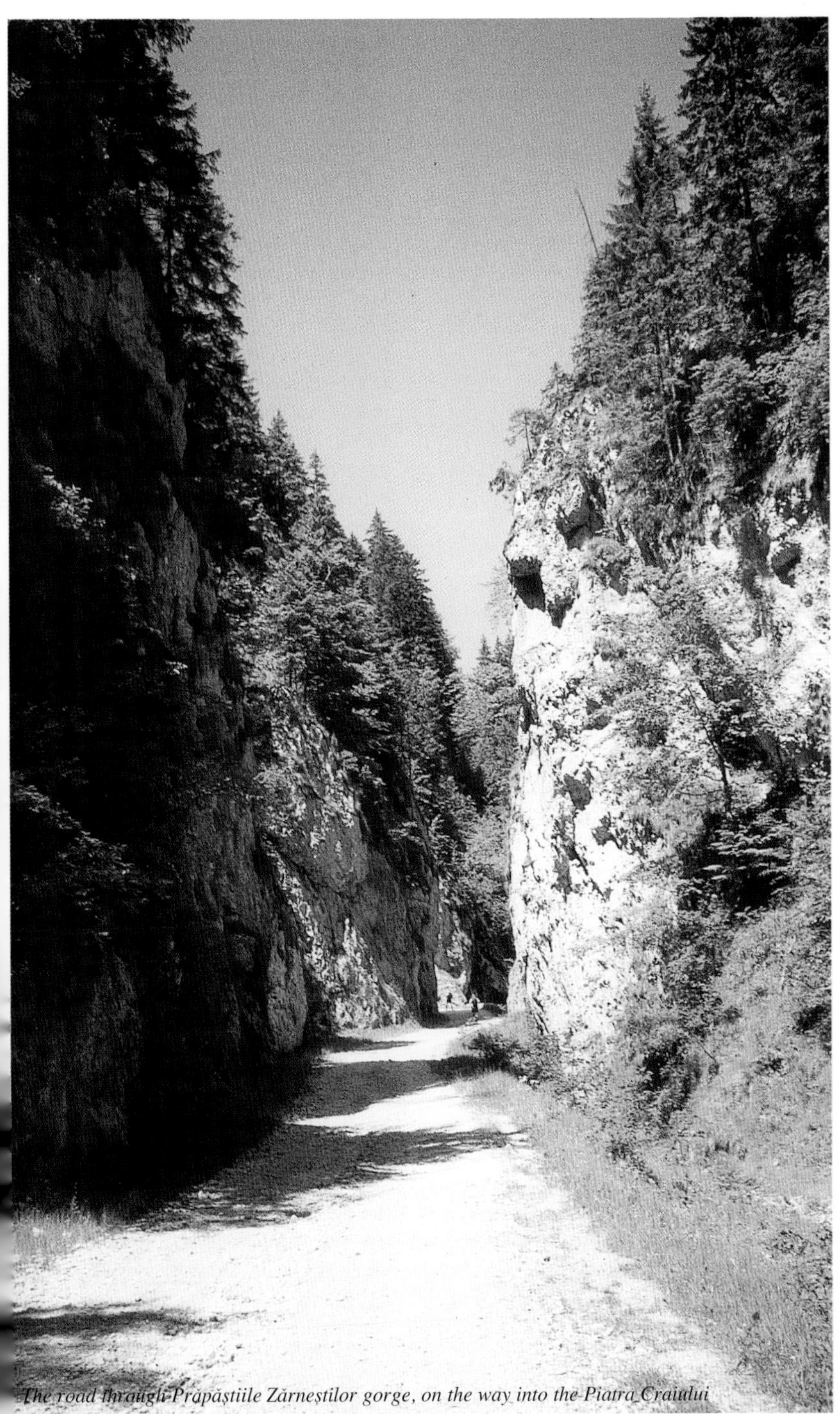

The road through Prăpăștiile Zărneștilor gorge, on the way into the Piatra Craiului

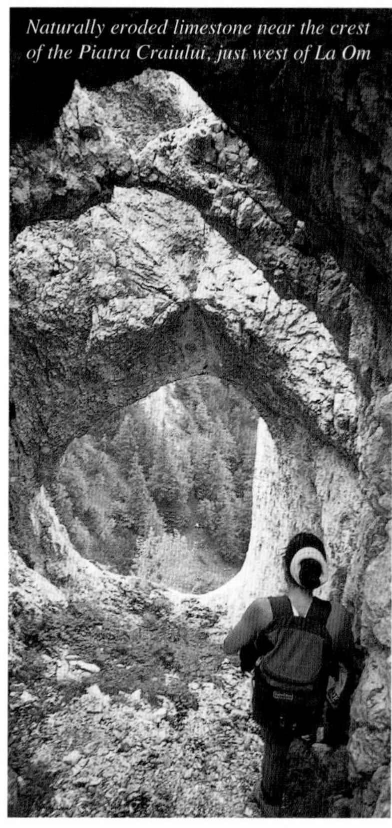
Naturally eroded limestone near the crest of the Piatra Craiului, just west of La Om

ing left across the grass from a tiny wooden barn; follow this, contouring across the hillside to some loney cottages, where you continue with your compass, heading west towards the dispersed village of Măgura. It is in this stretch that you are likely to miss the way. There is no centre to Măgura, simply a great number of scattered farmsteads. The church is prominent – visible from far and wide; make your way to it. Its west wall has frescoes of Saints Peter and Paul. Continue following the road west-north-west, past the church on your right onto to the left hand turning to the village itself and the village of Peștera (the fourth house on the right up this road has opened as a small shop and cafe). Continue straight ahead past the turning; the road drops into the valley bottom at Botorog's fountain. Now pick up the directions for the route from Botorog's Fountain to Curmătura (see Day One, above).

Alternative Two: Bran to the Piatra Craiuluin on the rural road, via Predeluț and Gura Râului cabana

Turn left at the bottom of the cabana steps and walk down the drive to the tarred road by the bridge. Turn left, through Predeluț, the road turning to a rough surface. Follow this road for 5km until the blocks of flats of Zărnești come into view. As you descend across the fields to Zărnești you can head to the left, north-west across the meadows to meet the road by the the tall brick-built cabana (Gura Râului) on the south side of the road. Turn left along the road and walk 1km to Botorog's fountain.

Day Two

Curmătura to Plaiul Foii, 6km (4 miles), 5 hours of very steep ascent and descent.

Altitude gained from Curmătura to Vârful Padina Popii, 520m (1706ft); lost to Plaiul Foii, 1141m (3743ft)

Head west from Curmătura along the obvious track (blue stripe waymarks), then turn right off the track in the trees, climbing steeply up to the ridge. You reach a narrow saddle near Vârful Padina Popii, halfway between Turnu and Vârful Ascuțit, and then descend on the other side down a narrow gully filled with scree. After a long slow descent you reach the woods and the shelter at Diana. You continue on down through the woods to emerge into grassy meadow (yellow triangle waymarks). You reach a road, turn left and arrive at Plaiul Foii, with fine views back up to the wall of the Piatra Craiului. Another pleasant cabana, this one with its own hydro-electricity plant which generates power. From Plaiul Foii it is an easy walk of 3hrs along the dirt road much frequented by horses and

Day walks in the Piatra Craiului, using Curmătura as a base

Route A: The Piatra Mică circuit, 4km (3 miles). Altitude gained, 346m (1135ft)
In common with all the walks in the Piatra this is slow going as you make your way up the crags. Allow 2½ hours for this walk. From the cabana make your way north up through the trees to Şaua Curmătura, then turn right to take the blue disc route up to Piatra Mică, with its tall wooden cross (1815m, 5957ft). Like the climb of Turnu, this involves a certain amount of hands on the rock. There are superb views to the Făgărăş, down into the Bârsa valley, straight down into Zărneşti town, and across to the Bucegi. Continue past the cross, down through the scrub of dwarf pine, steeply down into the forest proper, to join the main route to Curmătura from Botorog's fountain.

Route B: The ascent of Vârful Ascuţit, 8km (5 miles). Altitude gained, 680m (2230ft)
This is a challenging day walk of around seven hours. The ascent and descent are slow and tricky, with cables. Walks along the crest of the Craiului are best not attempted in rain or strong wind. Turn left out of the front door of the cabana and make your way up to Şaua Curmătura; turn left here (red disc waymarks), up and out of the trees and onto the rock. There are cables as you make your way up Turnu (1923m, 6300ft), from where a path (red cross waymarks) descends north to the Bârsa Mare valley. From the top of Turnu head south-west (red disc waymarks) along the sharp crest of the Piatra Craiului ridge to Vârful Padina Închisa, followed immediately by the pass of the same name. The path continues south-west, along the left of the crest itself, passing below Vârful Padinei Popii (2047m, 6716ft). 500m west of here is Vârful Ascuţit and its refuge, a plastic igloo on the grass; turn left here (blue triangle waymarks), down into the forest and back to Curmătura.

Route C: The ascent of La Om, 12km (8 miles). Altitude gained, 768m (2520ft)
La Om (2238m, 7342ft) is the highest peak along the Piatra Craiului ridge. This walk can be extended (given the energy and the gear with which to bivouac) to exit from the Piatra Craiului by descending from Şpirla refuge, from where you can walk on to the Făgărăş or the Iezer Păpuşa. Head west from Curmătura (blue triangle waymarks) up to the col just to the west of Vârful Ascuţit. This is a challenging day's walk of some eight hours. Take the blue stripe – blue triangle route westwards from the cabana and follow it up to Vârful Ascuţit, with its igloo-shaped shelter. Now follow the waterless ridge along to the south west, the rocks marked with a red disc. 1km south of Ascuţit shelter is Ţimbalul Mic summit (2231m, 7320ft). Should you wish, you can carrry on to the end of the Piatra Craiului ridge: a path takes you all the way, past Şaua Funduri and Pietriceaua to the village of Podu Dâmboviţei – there is a roadside cabana in Rucăr, 5km along the road.

To return to Curmătura take the path which drops down to the left just after La Om (red stripe waymarks), descending to Grind refuge. Turn left at the path junction below Grind, heading down, due east (red stripe waymarks) to the low col at La Table. Follow the Vlăduşca stream down, north-east, for half a kilometre (red cross and triangle waymarks) to a second junction near Stâna Vlăduşca shepherds' hut. Turn left here to head north, contouring and then going over the Mărtoiu ridge, on the far side of which you turn right on the track heading east, down from the shepherd's hut. After about 800m along this track you turn left off it, north (red triangle waymarks) to Curmătura. Take care; a number of paths tempt you to descend to your right, taking you well away from Curmătura.

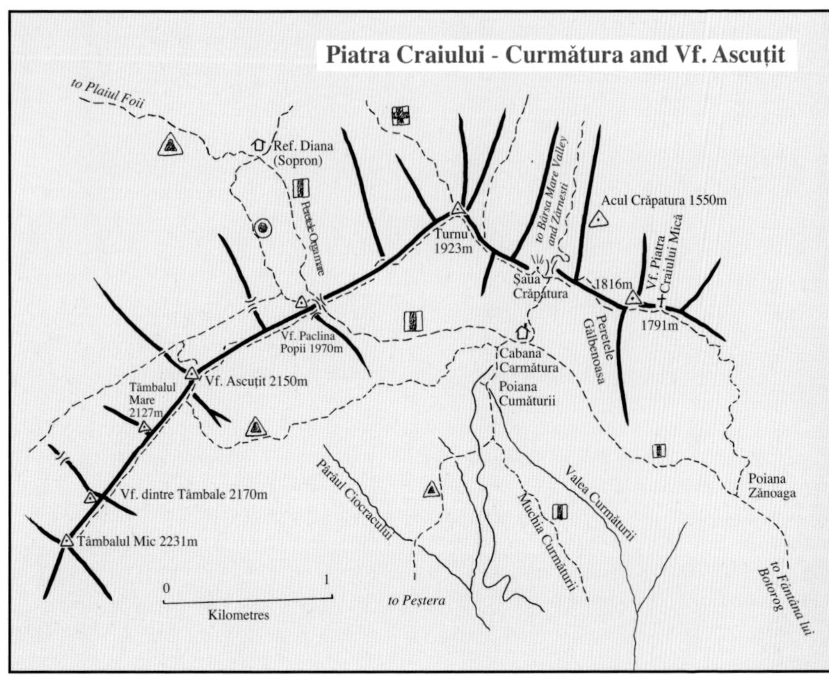

carts, into Zărneşti, from where you can take the train to Braşov. Equally it is a fine starting point for the walk into the Făgărăş, dealt with in Chapter Six.

Day Three

Connecting walk to the Iezer Păpuşa: Plaiul Foii cabana to Cuca cabana, 20km (13 miles). Altitude gained from Plaiul Foii to Curmătura Foii pass, 518m (1700ft); from the Dâmboviţa valley to Păpuşa summit, 1470m (4800ft)

From Plaiul Foii cabana cross the bridge and turn right on the road. Turn left at the fork and head south (red and blue triangles, blue stripe and red cross waymarks) up the Bârsa Tămaşului valley. Soon after some shepherds' huts a path turns left off the track that leads up to Şpirla refuge. Keep right, up the path (red and blue triangle and blue stripe waymarks) towards Curmătura Foii pass and past the right-hand turning on the path (blue stripe waymarks) and continue up to the Tămaşu at Curmătura Foii pass (1367m, 4485ft), on the watershed ridge between the head of the Bârsa and Dâmboviţa valleys. This is the easternmost end of the Făgărăş ridge and the connecting saddle between the Piatra Craiului and the Făgărăş. To the left are views of the western wall of the Piatra Craiului, as well as Padina Lăncii, Marele Grohotiş, Cardacul Stanciului, and Funduilor. A path to the left from the col goes to Garofiţa Pietrei Craiului refuge and a number of routes to the top of the Piatra Craiului. To the right is the red stripe route along the crest of the Făgărăş, heading initially through the woods, over Vârful Tămaşu.

From Curmătura Foii Pass head south-west (yellow triangle waymarks), down to join the forest road heading down the Tămaşului valley. You cross over the Dâmboviţa river at its confluence with the Tămaşului. Turn right up the valley along the road up to Pecineagu lake for 2km until a forest road turns left,

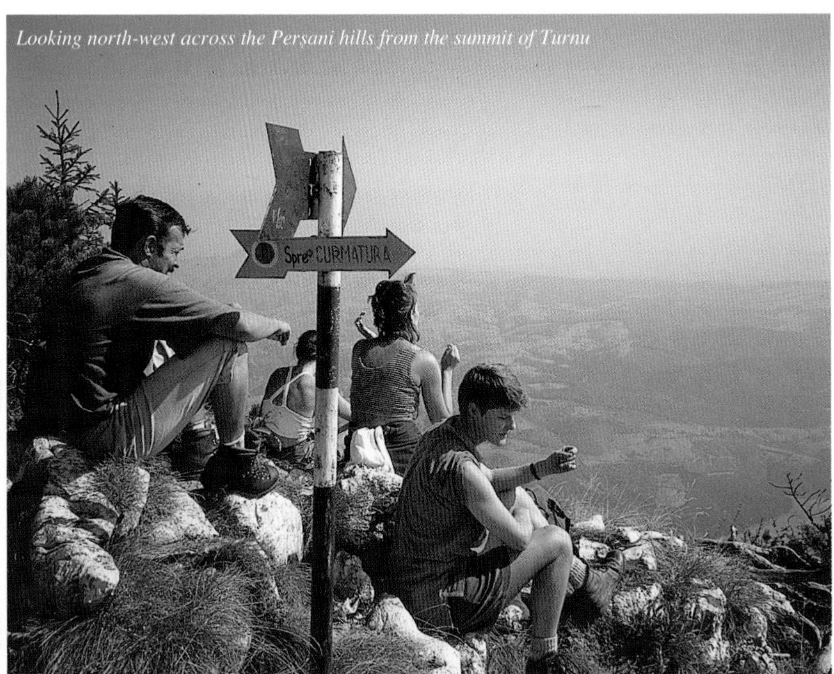

Looking north-west across the Perșani hills from the summit of Turnu

west up the Dracsinu valley. Turn left up the valley, then right after about 800m (blue stripe waymarks) up through the forest to the Dracșinu ridge. The path leaves the forest near a shepherd's hut and heads west and then south-west along the ridge to pass just to the west of the summit of Vf. Cascoe (2329m, 7641ft). Along this stretch there are fine views of the western wall of the Piatra Craiului and the Bucegi beyond. Ahead to the right are the high peaks of the Făgărăș; due north are the plains of Transylvania.

From Vârful Cascoe you descend south to a col to be joined by the yellow triangle route from your left (in fact a short cut, over Plaiul Cascoe and Plaiul Roșca, but its start in the Dâmbovița valley appears to be unsigned). Ahead to the south is the summit of Păpușa (2391m, 7844ft), the path lying along the east of the ridge. The path passes to the right of the summit of Păpușa and the red stripe ridge path heads away to the right. Keep left at the path junction near the summit to take the path heading due south along the ridge to Grădișteanu summit (2148m, 7047ft). Just after the summit you reach Poiana Sf. Ilie ('St Ilie's Clearing') and a lake marking the head of the Argeș valley. Turn right here, south-west (yellow triangle and blue stripe waymarks) across the Grădișteanu plateau, eventually zigzagging down to the new cabana at Cuca. If there is no room here it is an easy road walk of just over 4km down the Cuca valley to Cabana Voina.

Walking on from the Piatra Craiului

The walks above involve a descent on the north side of the Piatra to Cabana Plaiul Foii, where you return to 'the madding crowd's ignoble strife'. If you are backpacking you may well prefer to follow a ridge-top route all the way to the Făgărăș. To do this, you should make your way (either along the top or up from La Table) to Şaua Grind, 500m south-west of La Om summit on the main ridge. Descend past the rock arches from Şaua Grind on the north side and turn left at the path junction just inside the forest, contouring and then ascending along the base of the high cliffs to head south for 1km to Şaua Tămaşelului, where you turn right (red stripe waymarks), north-west to Curmătura Foii and on to the Făgărăş.

THE IEZER-PĂPUŞA MASSIF

The Iezer-Păpuşa (pronounced 'yayzer-puh-poosha') is a crescent-shaped range enclosing the head of the Târgului river; a number of tributary streams tumble through the pine forest, converge around Voina and head southwards towards Câmpulung. This town gives rise to the alternative title of the Iezer-Păpuşa – 'Câmpulung Muscel's Mountains'. You will find far fewer walkers in the Iezer-Păpuşa than in the Piatra Craiului – principally because it is a harder range to reach – reached only by a dead-end road heading up the Târgului valley and the forest road running up the Dâmboviţa valley to the dam holding back Pecineagu lake. The highest summit is Vârfu Roşu ('Pink Peak' – 2469m, 8100ft). The area around the top of the Iezer ridge is alpine in nature.

Access

If travelling direct to the Iezer-Păpuşa (although it is a fine, challenging walk over the Piatra Craiului) it can be reached from Câmpulung. Câmpulung has a station on the branch line from the junction at Goleşti ('Golesht'), outside Piteşti; no less than eleven trains leave Bucharest Gara de Nord for Goleşti, although all bar two are the agonisingly slow cursa or personal. Accelerat trains leave at 1350 and 1900 and take 90mins. There are six trains up the line from Goleşti to Câmpulung per day, taking 80mins. You may well want to take the bus or hitch-hike the delightful 50km journey from Bran or all the way from Braşov. From Câmpulung it is a 12km (8mile) walk up the tarred road, past Râuşor dam and lake to Cabana Voina (see Appendix A). The itinerary above details a route reaching Cuca cabana, taking in the Piatra Craiului.

The itinerary below is a point-to-point route which involves a walk along the top of the Iezer-Păpuşa, before taking you into the Făgărăş. It leads on to the Făgărăş range and makes a fine approach to the Făgărăş traverse. The cabanas in the region are not located so as to provide one every night, so unlike the Bucegi, you will have to bivouac out on some nights, such as whilst traversing along the Mezea–Călţunu ridge.

Day One

Cuca cabana to Izvorul Dâmboviţei bivouac site, 19km (12 miles). Altitude gained from Cuca to the summit of Iezer, 1472m (4830ft)

This walk is the continuation from Day Three of the suggested walk across the Piatra Craiului above. There are no cabanas within a day's walk if you are heading towards the Făgărăş; you will need to spend one night out. From Cuca cabana retrace your steps all the way to Păpuşa summit (2391m, 7844ft), where the yellow triangle and blue stripe route heads north, to the right, to the Dâmboviţa valley. Keep left here, heading north-west along the main ridge, going down to Spintecăturii Păpuşii pass, past the cross. From Vârful Păpuşa to the pass is rather less than 1km. From the pass the red stripe route goes just south of due west, keeping to the south side of the ridge, past Vf Tambura (2294m, 7526ft), Fracea (2242m, 735ft) and Bătrâna (2341m, 7680ft), following the red stripe route all the way.

To the north you look down into a number of glaciated valleys; to the south

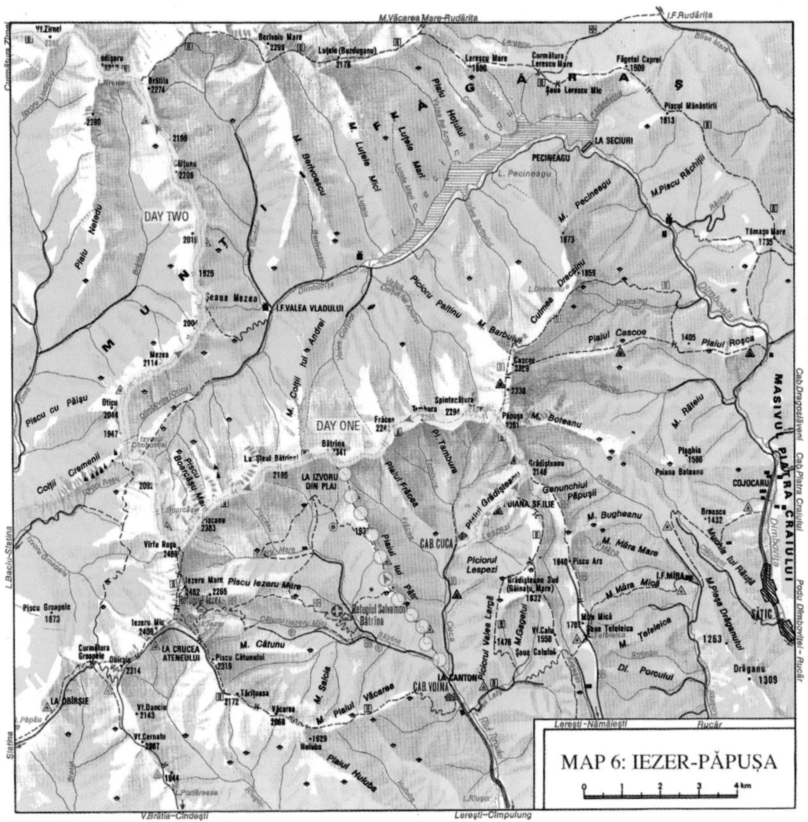

are grassy slopes. Just before Vârful Bătrâna you have the option of an escape route, turning left to head south-east, along the Plaiul lui Patru spur, following the red triangle waymarks to Voina. Keep west along the main red stripe route, north-west, past the spring at Izvorul din Plai to the path junction at Curmătura Bătrânei pass (2195m, 7202ft), some 6km west of Vf Păpuşa. From the pass your route is just south of due west, still keeping to the south side of the ridge, over Piscanu summit (2383m, 7818ft) to Vârful Roşu (2469m, 8100ft), the highest summit on the Iezer ridge. Immediately before the summit is a path junction where you turn right, the path zigzagging down due north and along a spur. Just in front of you are the crags of Colţii Cremenei ('the Flint Teeth'). You pass a junction with a path heading off to the right, initially along a ridge and then down into the Dâmboviţa valley to the gravel road to the lake, leading eventually to the village of Satic. Immediately after this is a pass (Curmătura Oticului) just at the eastern end of the Colţii Cremenii. Immediately below you on the right is the source of the Dâmboviţa; the area around offers good shelter where you can camp at a suitable distance from any shepherds' huts.

Exit from the Iezer to the Doamnei valley

1km south of Vârful Roşu (the option of climbing Iezer peak en route) is the old

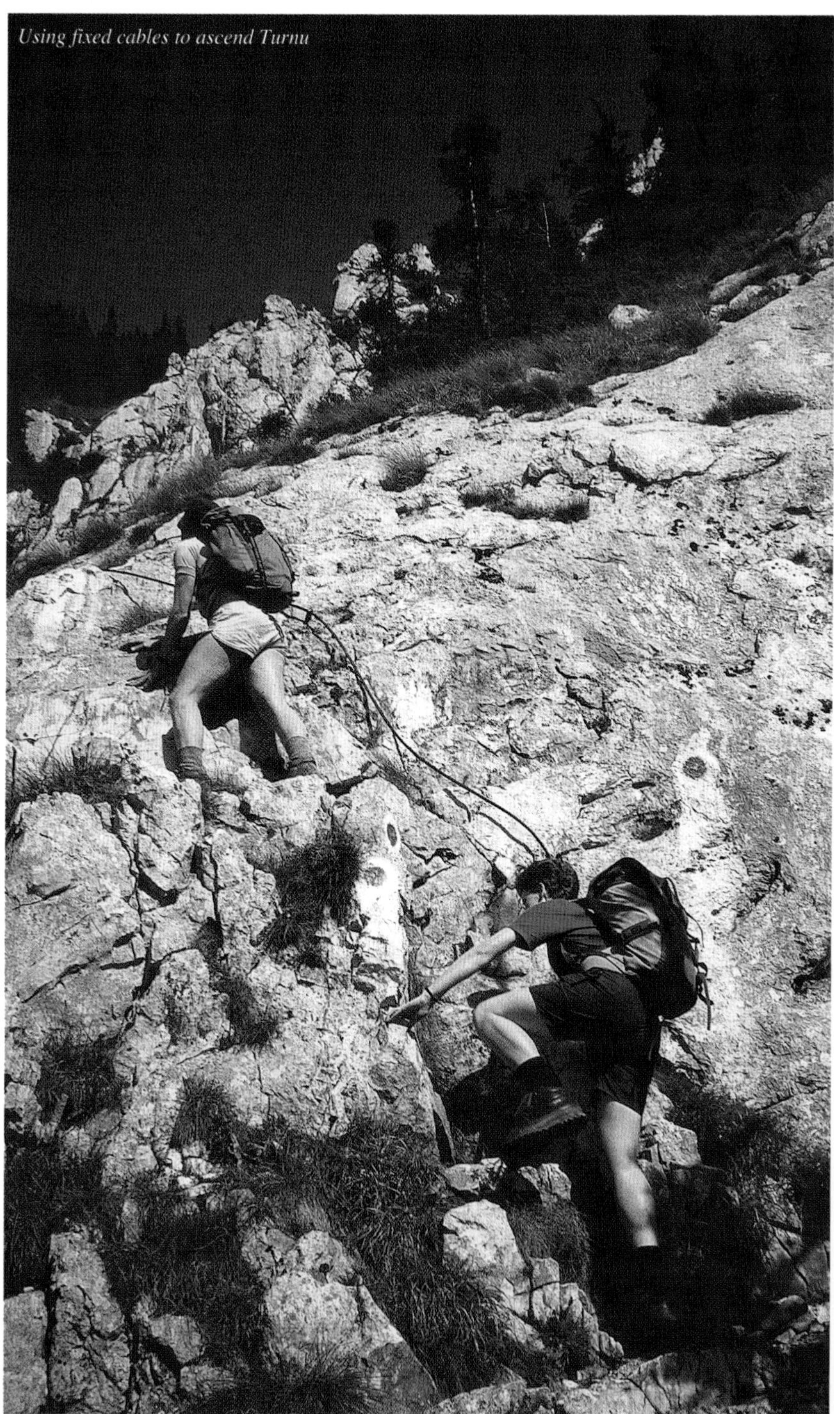

Using fixed cables to ascend Turnu

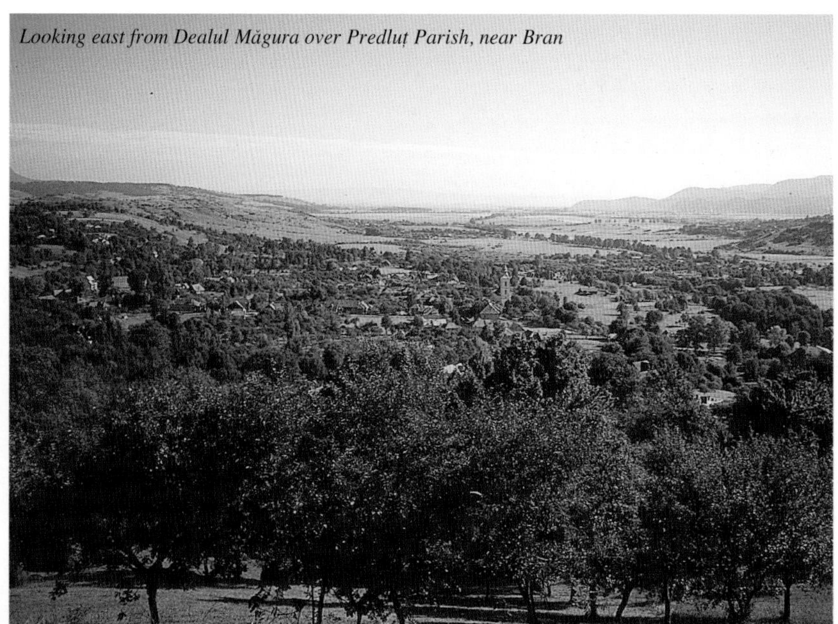

Looking east from Dealul Măgura over Predluț Parish, near Bran

Iezer refuge (alt. 2165m, 7100ft), now just another shepherd's hut, although rather more substantial than most. You are likely to find it occupied by a flock. Head south from the summit (red triangle waymarks), climbing for 1km to the summit of Iezerul Mare (2462m, 8077ft) then south for a further 1km to the path junction at the cross (Crucea Ateneului). Turn right here to follow the cart track south-west along the south side of the Iezer ridge, to the south of Vârful Obârsia (2314m, 7592ft); from this point on the contours of the Iezer are gentler. Just over 2km beyond the cross the track swings left to head south-east along the Cernatu spur; keep right to head west, zigzagging steeply down to Curmătura Groapelor pass (2030m, 6660ft).

From Curmătura Groapelor your route lies south-west around the head of the Bratila valley and along the south side of the main Iezer ridge, well above the tree line. 5km west of Curmătura Groapelor is Vârful Papau (2093m, 6867ft), the path keeping well below it on the south side. South of Vf. Papau runs the Jupineasa spur and a path along it runs to the village of Cândesti, in the Bratia valley. Turn right, less than 1km south-east of the summit of Papau to contour south-west (red triangle waymarks). As you descend, the path swings sharp right, west then north-west into the forest, then out of it to continue along a narrow strip above the trees on either side past a shepherd's hut by Vf. Setu (1720m, 5642ft), 3km south-west of Papau. The path descends into the forest, onto a forest road down to Slatina village in the Doamnei valley. A tarred road runs down the valley to Domnești village, on the DN73C road, halfway between Câmpulung and Curtea de Arges. Domnești has shops and accommodation.

Day Two

Izvoru Dâmboviței to Șaua Zirnei refuge in the Făgărăș, 23km (15 miles)

From Izvoru Dâmboviței head north (red triangle waymarks) with Boarcașu lake down to your right. You are now making

Wayside cross – troita – Peştera village, near Bran

your way around the headwaters of the Dâmboviţa river. The path continues due north, passing to the east of Oticu summit (2044m, 6700ft) to a pass on the ridge. At Oticu the ridge turns right to take you north-east; the path zigzags up and skirts Mezea summit (2144m, 7034ft) to the south and descends to Şaua Mezea (1870m) and continues due north along the grassy ridge above the forest, climbing steadily to Călţunu summit (2206m, 7237ft), 3km before the junction with the path along the main Făgărăş ridge. You reach the main Făgărăş path just north-west of Bratila summit (2274m, 7460ft). At intervals on either side of today's walk there are shepherds' huts which can offer shelter in bad weather. From the path junction by Bratila summit you can return to Zărneşti via Plaiul Foii by turning right (red stripe waymarks). To reach Zirna refuge, turn left and keep heading due west, the summit of Vârful Ludişoru (2310m, 7580ft) – 1km due west of Curmătura Bratilei – in front of you. You are now on day one of the Făgărăş itinerary, starting at Rudariţa, to the west of Plaiul Foii cabana.

CHAPTER SIX

The Făgăraş Chain

The Făgăraş are the highest of Romania's Carpathians; in the entire chain they are only surpassed in height by the High Tatra in Poland and Slovakia – this is a small isolated massif in contrast to the long crest of the Făgăraş. Described below is a superb ridge-top walking route running over all the main summits and giving access to the few prominent peaks that lie away from the main ridge. It is supplemented by a list of access routes to the main ridge top path from the north. This chapter also describes the Cozia massif under a separate heading.

The railway line from Sibiu to Braşov runs along the Olt valley, and access to the Făgăraş can be gained from stations in the towns and villages along it. Access was greatly improved to the stretch of the Făgăraş between Moldoveanu and Negoiu by the building of the TransFăgăraşan highway under Ceauşescu. This runs from the Olt valley near Cîrţa southwards to the town of Curtea de Argeş. Both towns are worth visiting for their monasteries, the one at Cîrţa being a Cistercian foundation, the oldest Gothic building in the country, and Transylvania's first monastery, dating from 1202. Curtea de Argeş is the burial site for Romania's royal family.

The TransFăgăraşan road tends only to be open for around four months of the year, June to September. Even in the height of summer its surface is generally running with meltwater and rocks the size of dustbins can be found lying in the road. The road is highly controversial – held by some to be a pointless piece of Ceauşescu propaganda, by others to be a noble achievement. One effect of the TransFăgăraşan highway is immediately noticeable as you approach the area around the road, walking from Podragu cabana: it has had – or rather the visitors that it has brought have had – a damaging effect on the environment, with increased litter and erosion.

The Făgăraş is the most dramatic part of the ancient border between Transylvania to the north and Wallachia to the south. The fact of the Făgăraş being the marches of the Hapsburg Empire is lent more drama by the Olt valley to the north, between Făgăraş town and Turnu Roşu, being densely inhabited, to a great extent in the past by Saxon settlers, whereas to the south lie many miles of high forested hills before the Olt valley finally makes its way onto the plains of Wallachia. For this reason most of the cabanas in the Făgăraş lie on the northern side of the watershed; their existence is owed to the Siebenbürgische Karpatenverein. During the communist period the range was popular with East German climbers and walkers.

If you are travelling by car in the area of the Făgăraş in early spring (too early to tackle the higher parts) the hillside covered in wild narcissi near Şercaia is remarkable. A special reserve, the Poiana Narciselor, has been created on the east-facing slope of the Şercaia valley to protect it. To reach it, head south from Şercaia (14km, 9 miles, east of Făgăraş town on the DN1) on the DN73A towards Zărneşti. After 4km you reach the village of Vad; turn right in the village to head into the Scurta valley.

A fine visit to the best of Transylvania's cities and the Transylvanian Alps would be to spend a day or two in Braşov at one end of the traverse and a similar amount of time in Sibiu at the other; short, direct train journeys connect access points for the mountain walk with the two cities.

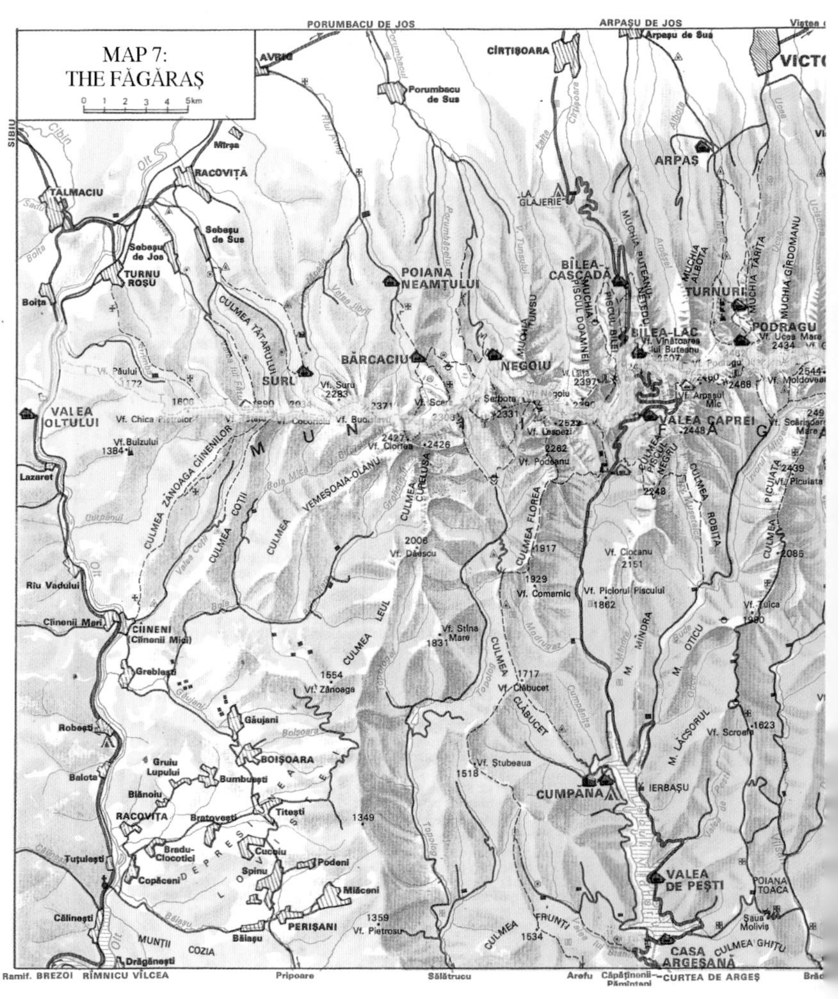

Topography

It was the Făgăraş that first earned the title 'the Alps of Transylvania' – a name bestowed by the eighteenth-century French cartographer Emmanuel de Martonne; it later extended itself to the whole Carpaţii Meridionali – the Southern Carpathians. In fact the name 'Transylvanian Alps' is much less known inside Romania than out of it. The Făgăraş comprises a ridge running east to west, some 75km long; it is best explored by taking a walk along all or part of the main spine. The Făgăraş escarpment is characterised by very steep slopes and short dramatic spurs to the north and long ridges with gentler slopes to the south. On their northern side the Făgăraş rise dramatically

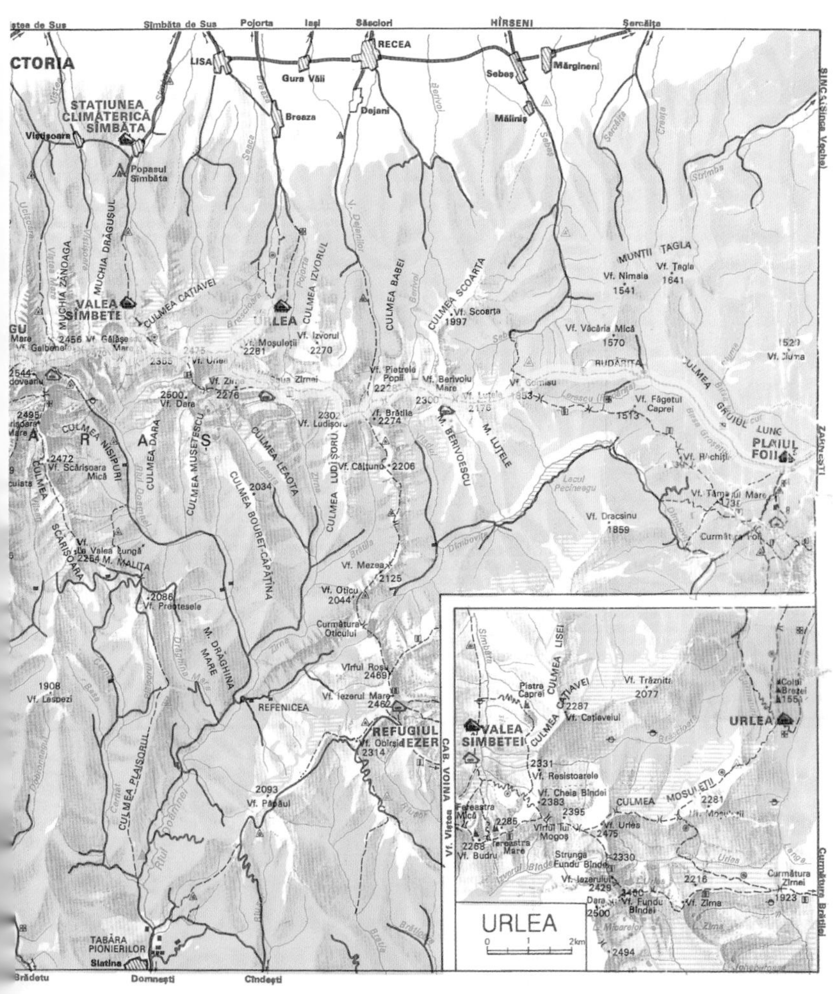

from the flat land of the Făgăraş Depression, a few minutes' walk taking you from the flat grassy fields into the steep Carpathian forests. On the southern side a series of long parallel forested ridges run into a large stretch of largely uninhabited country towards the plains of Wallachia. Along the valleys that divide these ridges, a number of gravel forest roads give access from the DN73C road from Curtea de Argeş to Câmpulung.

The chain contains a total of some seventy lakes. In the heart of the range these are glacial tarns, the largest being Bâlea and Urlea. They are known as the ochii marii ('the eyes of the sea'); a lake in the Slovak High Tatra is called Morskoe Ozero (meaning the same).

The River Olt flows east to west along the northern side of the Făgăraş and, at the pass and town of Turnu Roşu ('Red Tower') turns south, cutting the Făgăraş from the Lotrului to the west as it flows southwards into Wallachia through a fine 50km (30 mile) gorge. The fact that it breaks through what would otherwise be a watershed indicates that the Olt river predates the orogenic uplift of the Southern Carpathians.

Geology

Unlike the Piatra Craiului to the south-east, the geology of the Făgăraş is largely of igneous rocks, in this case crystalline schists rich in flakes of mica, together with gneiss and granite; at the very ends of the east–west ridge are areas of conglomerate and limestone. Whilst the Piatra Craiului is one long ridge, the central section of the Făgăraş is made up of a series of more or less pyramid-shaped peaks, linked by sharp arêtes. On the northern side of the main watershed ridge, steep escarpments drop away to the forests. The south-facing slope, appparently a dip slope, is generally grassed over. The summit path for much of its length follows the ridge top, a few metres to the south, with occasional views to the north.

Weather

The Făgăraş is often the first mountain area to receive snow and the last to see it thaw – patches lying in the corries right through the summer in some parts. Since the weather in Romania tends to come from the north-west, the Făgăraş does create a prominent rain shadow. A typical summer's day in the Făgăraş will start with quite clear skies, but after about nine o'clock you can often find cloud covering the northern slopes and the main peaks. This is actually an argument in favour of camping, allowing a first-light start, rather than staying in a dormitory room in a cabana, where breakfasts may be served later than you want. You can also avoid some very wearying ascents and descents to and from the main ridge route by camping near to it.

Access

The itinerary below starts at Plaiul Foii cabana, assuming a walk or a lift from Zărneşti station (trains from Braşov – see Piatra Craiului) or over the Piatra Craiului and perhaps the Iezer-Păpuşa as well. In summer, weekend trains are often met by drivers offering a lift to Plaiul Foii, saving a lengthy walk along a dusty road.

The Braşov–Sibiu railway line follows closely the foot of the Făgăraş range on its northern side, with a number of stations giving access to paths heading up to the south – Beclean, Ucea de Jos, Voila, Viştea, Cârţa, Porumbacu de Jos and Avrig. Most of these stations have paths waymarked from them, heading south to the Făgăraş. Details of the walking approaches from these are given after the details of the main east–west ridge route below, under the heading of 'Alternative approaches into the Făgăraş'. At the western end the best access point is the station at Podu-Olt junction, where the Sibiu–Braşov line meets the one from Craiova to Sibiu. In fact, the most popular route along the Făgăraş for Romanians is from Sâmbăta de Jos to Sebeş-Olt (Podu-Olt Station) or vice versa. The walking itinerary below ends at Halta Valea Mărului in the Olt valley. Ucea de Jos is the station for the town of Victoria, just north of the central and highest part of the Făgăraş; buses meet the trains. There are two daytime trains from Bucharest that stop at Ucea de Jos. See below for directions from Victoria under 'Alternative Approaches'.

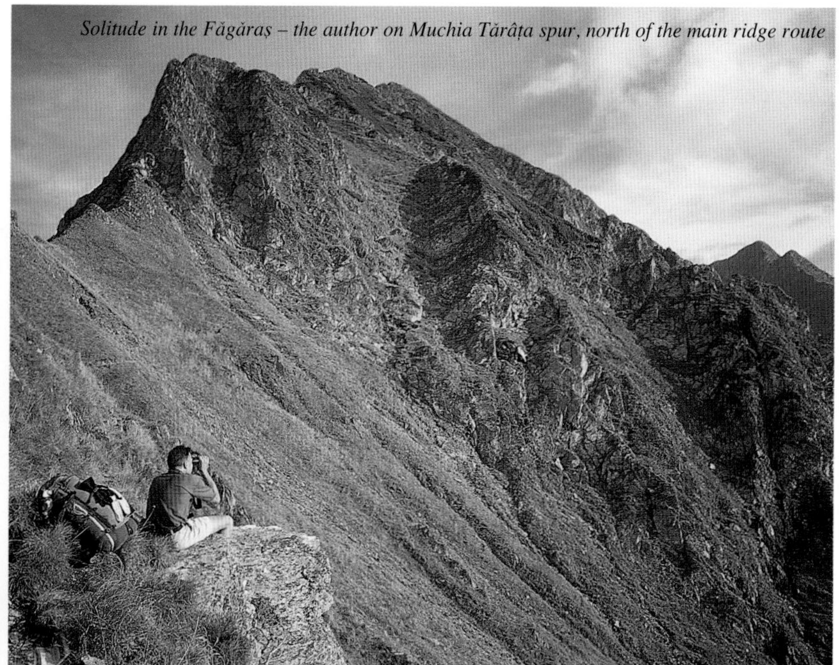

Solitude in the Făgăraș – the author on Muchia Tărâța spur, north of the main ridge route

ITINERARY ALONG THE FĂGĂRAȘ RIDGE

The itinerary below describes a challenging route from east to west, along the highest part of the range, taking in six peaks over 2500m (8000ft), and including the two highest mountains in Romania, Negoiu and Moldoveanu. It varies from easy walking along obvious footpaths over grassy moorland to tricky clambering over high crags in the central section around Negoiu and just west.

The start at Plaiul Foii cabana continues from the Piatra Craiului. If you approach the Făgăraș from Plaiul Foii you will find it a very long day's walk to Urlea cabana. The first shelter you reach is the refuge at Berivoiu Mare – a tiny Nissen hut on a small plateau just south of the ridge. In general the northern slopes of the massif tend to be more spectacular than the southern. However the ridges that head away to the south are less frequented by walkers. This east–west Făgăraș traverse is a major mountain expedition; if you are travelling to Romania especially to do this, be warned; it is not to be tackled lightly. Nothing in Britain comes close to this in scale. If you have tackled the Cuillins, the Aonach Eagach, Striding Edge and others in the past you will find these mere dwarfs in comparison. The real challenge to the walking lies in the central section, between the Șaua Zârna pass in the east and Șaua Cleopatrei pass in the west. The approach to the central Făgăraș, along the eastern and western extremities of its ridge, is relatively straightforward walking along grassy moorland. The striped iron 'bus stop' signs that are found so frequently in the Bucegi mountains are less common in the Făgăraș, with upended slabs of rock painted with the waymark taking their place. The paths can therefore be harder to follow under snow. I consider that in

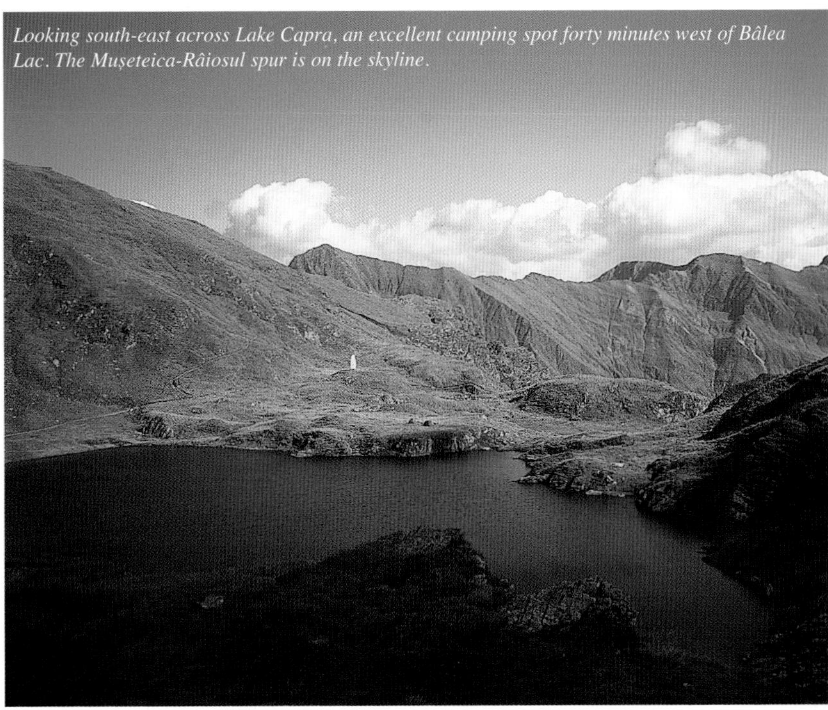
Looking south-east across Lake Capra, an excellent camping spot forty minutes west of Bâlea Lac. The Muşeteica-Râiosul spur is on the skyline.

fact there is much to be said in favour of a traverse starting in the west, with the prevailing wind behind you.

Access to the start

Zărneşti station to Plaiul Foii cabana, 12km (8 miles) on road

Follow the directions in 'Day One' in Chapter Five, The Piatra Craiului, and instead of turning left when you reach the stream, follow the road all the way up to Plaiul Foi. 5km from Zărneşti you reach a military-looking watchtower and a road junction at Crucea lui Gârniţa. A signpost points the way to Vârful Ciuma ('Plague Summit' – 1630m, 5347ft) to the right. Keep left here, up the Bârsa Mare valley, to reach Plaiul Foii cabana (see Appendix A).

Day One

Plaiul Foii cabana to Urlea cabana, 33km (21 miles). Altitude gained from Rudăriţa to Berivoiu Mare, 1451m (4760ft)

The walk starts with 9km (5½ miles) of forest road from Plaiul Foii to Rudăriţa. Your best chance of getting a left from Plaiul Foii to Rudăriţa is to wait on the road early in the morning, when trucks usually carry forest workers up from Zărneşti and horse-drawn carts bring peasants up the valley. From Rudăriţa turn left along the forest road up the Lerescu valley, turning left off it (red stripe waymarks, not red crosses, as marked on the map) up to the Lerescu saddle in the forest. Alternatively you can take a lower route, initially climbing steeply up the spur to the west of Rudăriţa to follow the ridge along (red disc waymarks), over Vârful Vacaria Mică (1570m, 5151ft), joining the red stripe route just east of Vârful Comisu. In spite of the signpost at Rudărița telling you the latter route is shorter, it is not, generally taking two hours longer. Soon after leaving the forest road along the Rudărița valley you cross the stream, after which there is a steep climb of half an hour to the ridge. From Lerescu saddle turn right (red stripe waymarks), westwards along the crest, through a patch of felling to emerge from the trees at Vârful Lerescu (1690m, 5544ft) with its wooden triangulation survey point. You descend back into the conifers, heading west to the path junction at Comisu. Here the red disc route over Vacaria Mică comes in from the right, also the blue triangle route taking you northwards to the Sebeș valley. Ignore this turning to head west (red stripe waymarks) as the path takes you onto the moorland, just to the south of Comisu peak (1883m, 6178ft), then over an unnamed hill, followed by Lutele (2176m, 7140ft), after which you come to a turning to the left to the refuge near Berivoiu Mare. Whilst walking the ridge itself there are fine views to the right, deep into Transylvania, and to the left across the Dâmbovița valley to the Iezer-Păpușa and the western wall of the Piatra Craiului. After the refuge the next peak, following the now less frequently marked red stripe waymarks, is Vârful Pietrele Popii (2228m, 7310ft). Soon after this you come to a signpost indicating the red triangle route northwards down the Dejanilor valley. Continue due west to the junction where the red triangle route turns away to the south, along the Cațunu Ridge, all the way to the Iezer-Păpușa range. For this stretch the path is generally on the southern side of the watershed, across grassy moorland. Keep heading due west, the summit of Vârful Ludișoru (2302m, 7552ft) in front of you. The path turns to the north here, following the dramatic watershed around to the saddle of Șaua Zârnei (1923m, 6309ft), where you find an igloo-shaped shelter. The path forks, the red stripe route keeping along the watershed to Vârful Zârna (2216m, 7270ft). Take the right hand path (red disc waymarks), steeply down into the Urlea valley and then up to a path junction at a pass on the Culmea Moșuleții ridge. Turn right to head north-east (red disc and blue triangle waymarks) along the ridge and then down a tricky descent through the spruce forest to Urlea cabana (see Appendix A). A hard and spectacular day's ridge walking has brought you deep into the heart of the Făgăraș. You may well want to rest on the following day, or have an easy day walk. (Note that there is a more challenging, higher ridge-top route from Plaiul Foii into the Făgăraș, along the ridge to the south of the Bârsa Groșetului Valley and over the Vârful Tămașu Mare.) From Urlea it is a five hour walk down to the station at Voila, following one of several paths (blue triangle, red cross or red disc), all of which meet the driveable track heading northwards down the Breaza valley to Breaza village, and so, 10km (6 miles) further, to Voila.

Day Two

Urlea cabana to Valea Sâmbătei cabana via Vârful Dara, 16km (10 miles). Altitude gained to Vârful Dara, 967m (3713ft)

Retrace your steps up to and then along the Culmea Moșuleții ridge (red disc waymarks) to Moșuleții saddle. Keep right here, due west as the path keeps north of the top of the ridge past Vârful Urlea (2475m, 8120ft). Just west of here, at Mogoșolui saddle (2344m, 7690ft) is the junction with the path going south (red stripe waymarks) to Vf. Fundu Bândei and Vf. Dara (2500m, 8202ft) – a recommended excursion. This done, continue west (red stripe waymarks), over Vf. lui Mogoș (2395m, 7856ft) and along a very narrow arête to the pass between Vf. Urlea and Vf. Mogoșului, where the blue triangle short-cut route from Urlea cabana meets the main ridge route. Keep left here to head west (red stripe waymarks), past Vârful Mogoşului (2395m, 7857ft) and then on to the junction with the red disc route.

You have a choice of routes to Valea Sâmbătei cabana. To the right, the shortest path (red disc waymarks) takes you over Vârful Cheia Bândei (2383m, 7818ft). Just after the summit the path splits again, the right hand route going along the Culmea Caţiavei ridge, to the crags at Piatra Caprei, then zigzagging down to meet the red triangle route in the Sâmbăta valley below and just to the north of the cabana. Slightly less challenging than this is the path zigzagging straight down into the Sâmbăta valley to reach the hut.

A more interesting route than either of these is to turn left, keeping to the ridge to take you past the crags of Colţul Balaceni (2285m, 7497ft) to bring you to Fereastra Mare ('Big Window') saddle (2180m, 7152ft) with views down the Sâmbătei valley to the flat plains of the Olt Depression. At the pass a path descends to the right, down to the cabana. Turn right here (red triangle waymarks) down across glacial rubble to the bowl at the head of the Sâmbăta valley. The path is well waymarked past a shepherd's hut to the Salvamont refuge point and, immediately after, Valea Sâmbătei cabana (alt. 1401m, 4596ft – see Appendix A). This cabana was built between 1931 and 1934 by the Sighişoara section of the SKV and was known therefore by the German population as the Schässburger Hütte.

If you are still feeling energetic, a good three-hour circuit walk takes you up to Piatra Caprei ('Goat Crags') and Vârful Resistoarele (2331m, 7647ft). Start by heading south down the valley to some shepherds' huts, where a path turns right and zigzags steeply up to Piatra Caprei rocks and on to Culmea Caţiavei ridge. There is an escape route out of the Făgăraş from Valea Sâmbătei, northwards down the Sâmbăta valley to the road to Staţiunea Climaterică Sâmbăta (see Appendix A) and the fine Constantin Brâncoveanu Monastery. If continuing on by train you should turn left to head for Victoria, not Voila.

Day Three

Valea Sâmbătei cabana to Podragu cabana via Moldoveanu, 16km (10 miles).
Altitude gained from Valea Sâmbătei to Moldoveanu, 1143m (3750ft), and up and down subsequently

From the cabana retrace your steps southwards to the cirque at the head of the Sâmbăta valley. As you cross the stream the path splits into three, like a bird's foot, with the red triangle route by which you descended taking you to the left. The right hand path takes you over the Drăgaşul ridge to Vistişoara lake. Take the middle path (yellow triangle waymarks), steeply up the glacial till onto the ridge at Fereastră Mică ('Little Window') pass. Turn right along the ridge towards Vârful Gălăşescu Mic (2410m, 7907ft), then down to Şaua Gălăşescu pass, also known as Fereastra Răcorelelor (2311m, 7582ft), from where the path climbs steeply up to a spur to the south of the summit of Gălăşescu Mare (2470m, 8103ft).

You have magnificent views of the waterfalls and the hollows of Piatra Roşie to the west, and from the top, towards Dara, Muşetescu and the Bândea valley. Continue west to a saddle, from where you traverse along the south-facing slopes of Vârful Galbenele ('Yellow Summit', 2456m, 8058ft). Down to your left are the mountain tarns feeding the tributaries of the Doamnei stream. The day's walk is now in a pattern of traversing the south side, near the crest of the main Făgăraş ridge, making

View of the main Făgăraș chain, looking across the Ucea Mare from the Tărâța spur

its way from saddle to saddle of the ridges that run away into the forests further south. There is a steep climb to the spur running southwards from Hârtopu Ursului ('Bear's Den') peak, followed by that running south from Portița Viștei peak (2310m, 7579ft), then the red-painted Salvamont refuge. Continuing west you reach the path junction at Șaua Viștea Mare, followed by a steep climb up to Viștea Mare peak (2527m, 8290ft). From here you can turn south for a few minutes' walk (red stripe waymarks) along the arête to reach Moldoveanu peak (2544m, 8346ft), the highest point in Romania.

From the summit head steeply down to the cliffs by Șaua Orzanelei (2305m, 7562ft), the head of the Orzaneaua Mare valley. From here the path heads along the left hand side of Vârful Ucișoara and Ucea Mare (2434m, 7985ft). An hour after Șaua Orzanelei brings you to the climb up the southern flanks of Vârful Tărâța (2414m, 7920ft, spelt 'Tărița' on the map – it means something like 'cornmeal'). From the summit of Tărâța the peaks of the Tărâța ridge stretch away to the north, the various individual summits diminishing in height in the distance. From the spur running from the summit of Tărâța (now on the detail Map 8) the path continues due west (red stripe waymarks) with a turning off to the left, leading to the blue triangle route heading down the Izvorul Podul Giurgiului valley. Keep to the right here to bring you to the path junction at Șaua Podragului, saddle (2307m, 7569ft). Here the east–west ridge route meets the route which crosses the Făgăraș from the town of Victoria in the north to the cabanas around Vidraru lake to the south.

If you want to turn left, the blue triangle route zigzags down into the valley of the Izvorul Podul Giurgiului where it

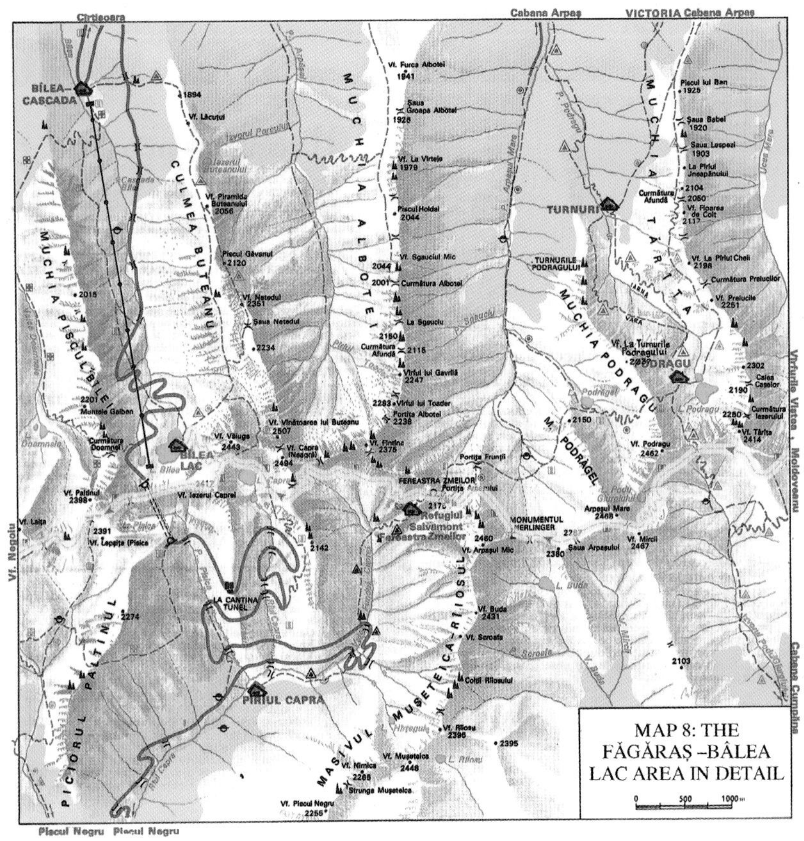

meets the red and yellow triangle route at a bivouac site near a shepherds' hut. From here it heads south-west down to the forest huts at Canton Buda and along tracks through the forests of the Buda valley to the TransFăgăraşan road at Lake Vidraru. From Şaua Podragului to the TransFăgăraşan is about 20km (13 miles). At Podragu saddle turn right instead (red and blue triangle waymarks) for 1km, down to Podragu cabana (see Appendix A). This area, with a number of cabanas quite close together, and just 5km from the TransFăgăraşan Highway, is often busier than the eastern stretch of the Făgăraş.

Podragu itself offers some fine day walks – it is ideally located in the highest part of the Făgăraş. Whilst these are not part of the itinerary of the Făgăraş traverse, the spurs running northwards from the main chain of the Făgăraş deserve exploring, not least because they see many fewer visitors than do the peaks along the central spine, combined with the fact that they offer excellent perspectives of the whole ridge – perspectives that are not given the walker who stays on the main ridge.

Day Four

Podragu cabana to Bâlea Lac cabana via Portiţa Arpaşului, 12km (8miles). Some scrambling with chains. Altitude gained from Podragu to Vârful Mircii ridge, 325m (1066ft), and more up and down subsequently

This is one of the most spectacular walks in all of the Carpathians. From Podragu cabana there is a choice of routes to Portiţa Arpaşului. The higher route with better views retraces the route of the evening before, following the red triangle route up to Şaua Podragului. From the pass you turn right to follow the red stripe route, descending on the southern side of the main watershed to cross the Izvorul Podul Giurgiului stream, draining the lake of the same name (2250m, 7382ft), in whose waters is reflected the peak of Vârful Arpaşului.

From here it zigzags up to the col between Arpaşul Mare (2468m, 8097ft) and Vârful Mircii (2467m, 8094ft) and heads due west, skirting the southern side of Arpaşul Mare peak to descend to the Şaua Arpaşului pass (2287m, 7503ft). This pass, unlike so many crossed on this route, is not a pass across one of the spurs heading south from the main Făgăraş chain, but takes the path across the main watershed so that you are now walking on the northern side of the Făgăraş ridge. You pass Vârful Pâru de Fier (2380m, 7808ft, marked on the map but not named) to the right. This marks the top of the former back wall of the glacier that occupied the Buda valley; Buda lake is all that remains. Soon afterwards you reach the Paul Nerlinger memorial, dating from 1934, then drop on the north side of the watershed with the summit of Arpaşul Mic (2460m, 8070ft) above you to the left. You now climb to the top of one of the biggest of the southern spurs of the Făgăraş, the Muşeteica–Râiosul ridge.

If you are a committed scrambler you would do well to head south along this ridge. The summit of Muşeteica itself (2448m, 8031ft) gives much the best views of the whole Făgăraş chain. It is well worth the tricky detour to see these, because none of the summits along the Făgăraş ridge give such a perspective as this one does, lying 3km south but a similar height to the tops of the Făgăraş. There is a path heading along the arête of Muşeteica–Râiosul, although it is not marked on the map and is tricky in places. If you do not want to return to the main Făgăraş watershed it is possible to follow the ridge southwards, down to Strunga Muşeteica pass and over the summit of Pescu Negru (2248m, 7375ft). Here you pick up the blue cross path heading west down to the DN7C trans-Făgăraşan road, just north of Canton Piscu Negru or east and south, down to the Buda valley.

From the point where the red stripe route crossed the very northernmost end of the Muşeteica–Râiosul ridge, a red disc route turns right to Portiţa Frunţii and the Arpaş Valley. Head south-west here to bring you to Portiţa Arpaşului (2175m, 7136ft), and then around the head of the cirque at the head of the Fundul Caprei valley, where there are chains attached to the rocks. You reach the path junction at Fereastra Zmeilor ('Dragon's Window').

A lower-level alternative route to Şaua Arpaşului takes the blue stripe route westwards from Podragu cabana, over the Muchia Podragu ridge and then zigzagging down to Podragel lake, before climbing southwards over the ridge of the same name and taking you into the dramatic cwm at the very head of the Arpaş valley. The path takes you round this to reach the Portiţa Frunţii pass and so to Portiţa Arpaşului pass. At Fereastra Zmeilor you meet the yellow triangle route taking you to the left, to the mountain refuge, a red-painted hut. It lies just south of the main ridge on the yellow triangle route which continues down the

Fundul Caprei valley to the trans-Făgăraşan road and the former Pârâul Capra cabana (see Appendix A).

To reach Bâlea Lac cabana follow the red stripe route around the rim of the cwm at the head of the Fundul Caprei ('Goat's Bottom') valley, over a ridge and traverse around the northern side of Capra ('Goat') lake, an excellent camping spot. As you approach the lake, you pass a junction with the blue stripe route taking you down to the former Capra cabana, then a sign to the private Cota 2000 cabana at the southern entrance to the road tunnel on the TransFăgăraşan. Keep right here to follow the red stripe route, taking you up to Şaua Caprei (2315m, 7595ft).

The path down to Bâlea Lac cabana (burnt down in autumn 1995 but being rebuilt in 1999 and 2000 – see Appendix A) turns right here, marked with blue triangles and eroded by the many poeple who make their way up here by road and cable car. The cabana itself is on a peninsula on the eastern side of the lake, but I always have preferred the delightful Vila Paltinu on a knoll at the roadside. If you want to avoid the roadside area, head due south from Şaua Caprei (2315m, 7595ft), following the less used path (red stripe waymarks) to Vârful Iezerului (2417m, 7430ft), from where you head west for 1.5km to Vârful Paltinu (2399m, 7870ft), on the far side of the TransFăgăraşan, which you cross over the top of the tunnel, scarcely being aware of the road at all - and blissfully ignorant of its presence below you in the tunnel if you are walking in mist. For the continuation from there, turn to the following day.

Day Walk from Bâlea Lac

Central spurs of the Făgăraş. Altitude gained from Bâlea Lac Cabana to Vf. Netedul, 325m (1066ft); descent to Bâlea Cascada cabana, 1117m (3665ft); ascent from Bâlea Cascada Cabana to Curmătura Doamnei, 968m (3167ft)

This walk takes in two of the northern buttresses of the Făgăraş range, with the attraction that it can be shortened by taking the cable car back to near the start point. Near the eastern shore of the lake you see a three-way walkers' signpost; take the blue disc route, signed 'Şaua Văiga 1¼–1½ hrs' and follow it north-east, steeply up on to the Culmea Buteanu ridge at Şaua Netedul Pass (2234m, 7329ft). From the pass you head south, over Vârful Netedul (2351m, 7713ft), less than 500m away, and then follow the spur down for 2.5km, over Găvanul (2120m, 6955ft) and Piramida Buteanului (2056m, 6745ft) before turning left and descending back into the forest after Vârful Lacului. You cross the TransFăgăraşan road and descend to the cabana at Bâlea cascada (see Appendix A), at the bottom station of the cable car.

The return route (red cross waymarks) heads north from the cabana along the Bâlea river, crossing it before you reach the waterfall. It then zigzags east, up through the woods and makes its way over the Muchia Piscul Bâlei ridge in the woods (there is no path along the top) and descends into the Doamnele valley, following the river upstream towards the cwm with Doamnele lake in its bottom. The path follows a tributary up the side of the old bergschrund, zigzagging as it makes its way up to Curmătura Doamnei pass (also known as Curmătura Bâlei, 2202m, 7224ft) and back to the TransFăgăraşan road.

MAP 9: THE FĂGĂRAȘ – THE NEGOIU AREA IN DETAIL

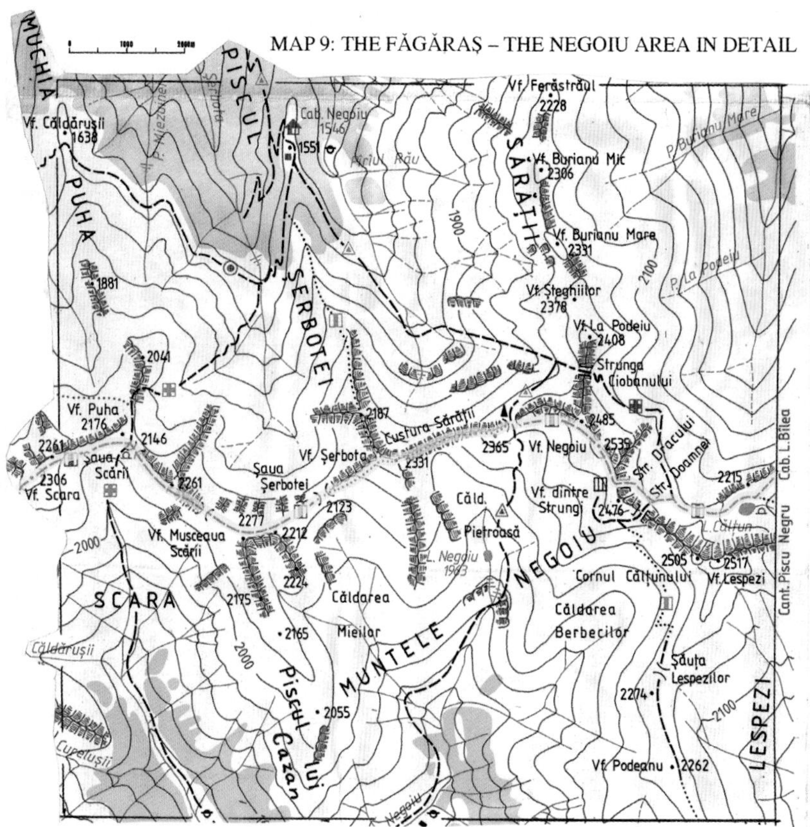

Day Five

Bâlea Lac cabana to Negoiu cabana via Negoiu summit, 14km (9 miles). Altitude gained from Bâlea Lac to Negoiu summit, 501m (1643ft), with more up and down

Note that part of this day – the climb of Strunga Dracului – involves a long, difficult stretch of scrambling with cables. Adjacent to the eastern shore of the lake is a three-way signpost. Take the blue stripe route, signed 'Șaua Paltinului ¾ hr' and follow it south, then west as it makes its way up around the Bâlea bowl to Șaua Paltinului (2330m, 7644ft). You find yourself, still on the northern side of the Făgăraș watershed, looking down into the head of the Doamnei valley. The path swings left, north of Vf. Paltinu (2398m, 7867ft), crosses to the south side of the main ridge and turns right to head southwest, to the junction with the blue disc route which leads down to the roadside cabana at Piscul Negru. You pass to the south of Vârful Laița summit (2397m, 7864ft), followed by Laițel (2390m, 7841ft), with some cables fixed to the rock on this stretch. You now leave the detail Map 9 and descend steeply along the south side of the ridge to the Sibiu Salvamont refuge at the alpine tarn of Călțun lake (2147m, 7043ft).

At the refuge the second blue stripe route descends on the southern flanks of the Făgăraș to Piscul Negru cabana. From the refuge head north (red stripe waymarks), with Lake Călțun on your left, up

Lake Călțun and the Sibiu Salvamont refuge, just south of the main Făgăraș watershed

across boulder-scree, over a col and down to a path junction 700m west of the lake. Here a path turns right (red cross waymarks) towards Negoiu cabana over Strunga Ciobanului ('Shepherd's Pass'), over the Piscul Sărații spur and avoiding Negoiu. Keep left here, to a second junction with a path to the left (yellow and blue stripe waymarks), going up to Strunga Doamnei ('Lady's Pass'). This offers a climb of Vârful dintre Strungi ('Between the Passes Peak', 2476m, 8123ft) and a walk south out of the Făgăraș, to Arefu village or Cumpana cabana, and may be followed all the way to the Cozia massif and also offers an approach to the Căpățân – a fine sequel to the Făgăraș.

From the junction with the yellow stripe route, continue up to Strunga Dracului. This is a very difficult stretch, with perpendicula chains and cables fixed to the rock. From the pass it is a short climb to the top of Negoiu and on, heading west on the south side of the ridge for about 500m to Șaua Negoiu; turn right here, down off the ridge to the north (blue triangle waymarks) via Popasul lui Mihai saddle and Piatra Prinzului to Negoiu cabana (see Appendix A).

If you are following a day stage plan different from this and want to head directly from Negoiu to Vârful Șerbota (2331m, 7648ft), be warned that this is the most difficult stretch of the Făgăraș traverse, marked on the accompanying map with just a dotted line. It is more a scramble than a footpath and is extremely hard going. West of Șaua Cleopatrei the path descends, then climbs on the northern side of the Făgăraș ridge before crossing over and descending into Caldarea Pietroasa above Negoiu lake on the southern side of the ridge. The climb to the summit of Șerbota is the trickiest part of the Făgăraș traverse and is probably best tackled as part of a day walk from Negoiu cabana without a full rucksack, leaving all but what you need for the day at the cabana. (However in September 1999 I left Negoiu Summit at 4pm in continuous wind and drizzle and pitched my tent at Lacul Avrig in the dark.) West of Vârful Şerbota the going is much easier.

Day Six

Negoiu cabana to Suru cabana via Scara and Budislavu summits, 16km (10 miles). Altitude gained from Negoiu to Budislavu summit, 825m (2707ft), and more detail up and down

(Note that I have had to use Suru as the end point owing to the day stages. However it is but a shelter, whereas Bârcaciu is a very fine cabana and highly recommended.) From Negoiu cabana head south (blue stripe waymarks); 600m from the cabana turn left, up, out of the trees and along the Şerbotei ridge to a point just to the west of the summit of Vârful Şerbota (2331m, 7648ft). There is an easier route, right (blue cross waymarks), south-west, up towards Şaua Scării ('Staircase Pass', 2146m, 7041ft) and a seemingly temporary Salvamont refuge on the main Făgăraş red stripe route.

From Şerbota summit head west (red stripe waymarks) down to Şaua Şerbotei (2123m, 6965ft) with a roofless shelter. You climb up to an unnamed summit (2122m, 6962ft) at the head of a short spur heading off to the south. The main Făgăraş ridge is a narrow crest here; it swings to the north-west and descends to Şaua Scării, where you meet the blue cross path described above. This continues to the south, down into the Topolog valley, where after 3km it meets a forest road at some huts. This road can be followed all the way to the village of Sălătrucu. 4km south of the huts the red triangle route turns left up to Clăbucet summit (see previous day for further description).

From Şaua Scării head west along the main ridge (red stripe waymarks) as it takes you just to the south of the summit of Vârful Puha (2176m, 7139ft), then west, just south of the main ridge. 800m west of Şaua Scării you reach the summit of Vârful Scara (2306m, 7566ft). Several well-used paths descend west to the grassy plateau around Şaua Gârbovei (2125m, 6972ft – the junction with the red cross route heading north along the Bârcaciu ridge and down to Bârcaciu cabana – see Appendix A). Continue along the ridge, over Vârful Gârbovei (2188m, 7178ft), and down to a pass where you cross over to the north side of the ridge. It is possible to head south-west along the main ridge from this pass to climb to the summit of Vârful Ciortea (2427m, 7962ft), at the head of the two spurs: the Culmea Vemeşoaia–Olanu ridge, leading away to thesouth-west and the Culmea Cureluşa ridge (not named on every map), with Vârful Dăescu (2006m, 6581ft) away to the south.

From the pass, take the path (red stripe waymarks) north-west for 1km, down to Lacul Avrig (2103m, 6900ft). In the past there was a refuge here; it is still popular as a bivouac site. The path takes you round the northern shore of the lake, past the junction with the blue disc path heading to the right, down the Avrig valley to Bârcaciu cabana. Keep left here, up to the top of the back wall of the cirque to reach Portiţa Avrigului (the 'Gates of Avrig') pass (2178m, 7146ft). The path contours and then climbs to Budislavu summit (2371m, 7779ft) with its very British cairn-like rock pile, then zigzags steeply down to Curmătura Roşiilor, a col on the main ridge. Keeping round the rim of a cirque on the southern side of the main ridge (red stripe waymarks), you pass to the south of Vârful Suru summit (2283m, 7490ft) to reach Curmătura

Surului saddle (2113m, 6998ft). Immediately after Suru saddle turn right, north, down (red triangle waymarks) to Suru shelter (see Appendix A).

If you want to walk to the the fine small town of Avrig (station on the Sibiu–Braşov line; this is one of the very few stations between Făgăraş and Sibiu where Accelerat trains stop – four each way per day and more slow trains), head north from the cabana (red triangle waymarks) along the Muchia Moaşei ridge: 1.5km north of the cabana you come to a path junction. Turn right here (blue triangle waymarks), down into the Moaşa valley by a forester's hut: a forest road takes you past Lunca Fiorilor to meet the Avrig river at Podu Jibrii. Here you join the Avrig valley and follow the road northwards (occasional red cross waymarks), down to the town. From Suru there is a quick exit from the Făgăraş, following the red triangle route through the woods along the Muchia Moaşa ridge to cross the Suru stream just before the village of Sebeş de Sus, from where there is a road to the railway halt at Sebeş Olt; this is altogether 14km (9 miles), altitude lost 1120m (3674ft). There is also a valley walk (red disc waymarks), taking the forest road from just below the cabana straight into the village of Sebeş de Sus.

Day Seven

Suru cabana to Valea Mărului railway halt, 19km (12 miles). Altitude gained from Suru cabana to Vârful Cocoriciu (Moaşa), 584m (1915ft); lost from there to Valea Mărului, about 1650m (about 5500ft)

I have written this day's route as ending at Valea Mărului ('Apple Valley') because this is the westernmost end of the Făgăraş ridge and followed by the red stripe marks. However I recommend you finish by taking the well signed red cross route to Turnu Roşu and the station at Podu Olt, where Accelerat trains stop and you return direct to Bucharest. The red stripe route to Valea Mărului is quite difficult to follow on the descent.

From the cabana make your way back along the red triangle route as it zigzags up the spur of Fruntea Moaşei to the path junction before the crags of Vârful Gorganul (1840m, 6037ft). Keep right here to head south (blue triangle waymarks) to the right (west) of Gorganul, reaching the main red stripe route at a signpost 300m to the west of the summit of Vârful Moasa (2034m, 6673ft) – also known as Vârful Cocoriciu. Turn right here to descend gently, heading due west, to a pass with a spring serving both sides of the watershed – Şaua la Apa Cumpănita, also used as a bivouac site. There is a junction here with a path turning left (blue triangles), heading down into the forest and then south-west along the Muchia Colţii ridge, to a junction with a road heading down the Colţii valley. You can keep left at this junction to continue over the summit of Vârful Măgura (1258m, 4160ft), to descend to the village of Câineni (station on the Podu Olt–Râmnicu Vâlcea line). (There are also trails heading west into the Lotrului massif.)

Head west along the main watershed (red stripe waymarks), up to the summit of Vârful Tătarului (1890m, 6200ft). Just west of the summit, you come to a junction with a path turning right (red disc waymarks), north-west, down into the trees and along the Fatu spur to the forest road to Sebeş de Sus. The red stripe route continues down the valley, having now become the Sebeşu, and on to Sebeşu de Jos and Sebeşu Olt station. It is 12km (7 ½ miles) from Vârful Tătarului to Sebeş Olt station. To continue along the now almost vestigial remains of the Făgăraş ridge, head west from Vârful Tătarului (1890m, 6201ft) across grassy moorland 500m after Vârful Tătarului you reach a path turning left (red cross waymarks)

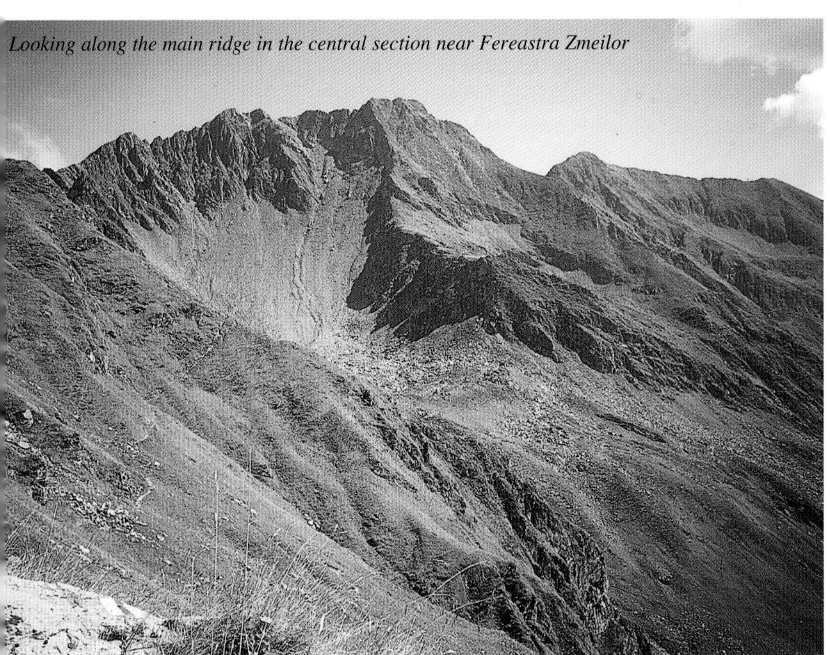

Looking along the main ridge in the central section near Fereastra Zmeilor

heading down into the trees and south-west along the Culmea Zanoaga Câinenilor ridge (highest point 1712m, 5617ft), bringing you to the village of Câineni. Just over 1km west of Vf. Tătatului you reach a col – Prislop pass; the red stripe and red cross route continues west for 500m to the summit of Chica Fedeșului (1820m, 5971ft).

The path now keeps to the northern side of the Făgăraș ridge, past Chică Lacului (1649m, 5410ft), 1km west of Fedeșului. Here you meet the junction with the red cross route, heading right, into the trees, keeping to the left of the wooded summit of Dealul Pleșii (1242m, 4075ft) and down through the geological reserve to the town of Turnu Roșu.

Continuing westwards along the very end of the Făgăraș ridge, the path skirts the summit of Vârful Chica Pietrelor (1606m, 5269ft) to the north and then descends to the tree line. This effectively is the end of the Făgăraș traverse. You are at a path junction; the red stripe route emerges from the trees for a short spell then continues initially north, towards the summit of Vârful Păului (1172m, 3845ft), a north–south ridge covered in beech and birch trees with a large clearing on its western flank. From Vârful Paului there is a descent of 4km over the end of the the Culmea Strimbanu ridge and into Valea Mărului to reach the railway halt of the same name (alt. about 320m, 1050ft), 2km north of the roadside restaurant and cabana of Valea Oltului (see instructions below in reverse for approach 6). This junction marks the end of our walk along the Făgăraș ridge. There is however no river crossing by Valea Mărului halt or the cabana. To cross the Olt, head south along the east bank to a steel bridge immediately south of the Valea Boului. The railway halt is on the east bank of the Olt.

If continuing on by public transport, the best exit is to follow the red cross route along the Dealul Pleșii ridge and then the forest Culmea Petriceaua ridge, all the way down to Turnu Roșu. Turnu Roșu ('Red Tower') recalls the fortress that formerly guarded the gateway to the Olt gorges and the route through to Wallachia. From here, or rather the nearby Podu Olt station, there are almost hourly trains to Sibiu. If you are continuing on the Căpățân – which I recommend – and do not want to make the lengthy walk south from Negoiu to the Cozia, I suggest you take a train from Podu Olt to Lotru. There are seven trains per day, taking 75 minutes.

Alternative approaches to the Făgăraș from the north

This section details the walking routes up onto the main Făgăraș ridge from various start points on the northern side, working from east to west. It follows that the latter access routes will be used by those interested in doing the Făgăraș ridge route from west to east, which has the advantage of the prevailing weather coming in behind you. Having walked them, I have reached the opinion that much the finest approach is 3a – the traverse of the Muchia Tărăței spur.

Route 1a: Făgăraș to Vârful Comisu via Sebeș, 18km (11 miles). Altitide gained, 1350m (4430ft)

Head south out of Făgăraș town on the road to Hârseni and on to Sebeș, 12km from the centre of Făgăraș. Keep heading south out of Sebeș on the rough road through Măliniș and up the Sebeșu valley (sporadic blue triangle waymarks). 8km (5 miles) south of the road junction in Sebeș village the road forks; keep left here and 4km later the valley starts to swing to the right to head south-west; the forest road dwindles to a cart track and turns left to head south, steeply up a tributary of the Sebeș to some shepherds' huts near the tree line. The path takes you up to just west of Comisu summit, where you join the main red stripe ridge route.

Route 1b: Făgăraș to Vârful Ludișoru via Recea, 16km (10 miles). Altitude gained, 1720m (5643ft)

The village of Recea lies 13km (8 miles) south of Făgăraș, reached by buses from the town via Hurez and Săscioara. Head south out of Recea, along the road to the village of Dejani, following the rough road south, up the Dejanilor valley. 10km south of Recea the track crosses the river, begins to climb more steeply, now as a path (red triangle waymarks). You reach the main ridge route near a bivouac site just east of Vârful Ludișoru.

Route 1c: Făgăraș to Mogoș pass via Breaza and Urlea cabana, 25km (16 miles). Altitude gained, 1710m (5600ft)

Head south-west out of Făgăraș along the road to Hurez, 4km from the centre of Făgăraș. Turn right in Hurez, on the dirt road, to head south-west to Iași and on to the villages of Gura Văii where you turn right for 2km along the road to turn left at a crossroads to Breaza (3km south-west of Recea village and also reached by bus from Făgăraș). From Breaza head south along the valley of the same name for 2km until the road forks at some cabins. Either route will bring you to Urlea cabana, the right (blue triangle waymarks) running along the Brezcioara valley, with the possibility of diverting to the left instead with red disc waymarks along the ridge. This latter is the recommended route. The left route runs south up the Pojorâța valley and then turns left to climb very steeply, direct to the cabana. The route to the main ridge route heads up to the south-west, to the summit of Vârful Moșuleții (2278m, 7474ft) where you can turn right to Vârful Urlea to join the main route, or steeply down into the Urlea valley and up to rejoin the main ridge route at Șaua Zârnei.

Route 2: Voila railway halt to Sâmbătei pass via Valea Sâmbătei cabana, 20km (13 miles). Altitude gained, 1580m (5200ft)

Voila halt is the access point for Sâmbăta de Jos village, 2km to the south. Head south along the road from Sâmbăta de Jos, keeping right in the village of Sâmbăta de Sus as the road heads south-east towards Lisa. After 9km (5 ½ miles) from Sâmbăta de Sus you reach the cabanas of Stațiunea Climaterică Sâmbăta and Popasul Sâmbăta, much used as a campsite by the locals. From here head south up the valley, the road soon becoming unsurfaced. You enter the forest, pass several cabins, at the last of which the road dwindles to a track. Keeping to the east of the Sâmbăta river, you pass a waterfall and then some shepherds' huts, followed by the cabana itself. The path beyond the cabana is described in detail in 'Day Three' above.

Route 3: Victoria town to Moldoveanu via the Viștea pass, 18km (11 miles). Altitude gained from Victoria to Moldoveanu, 1984m (6500ft)

This route makes it possible to step off a train from Brașov (or Bucharest) in the morning and be on the summit of Moldoveanu by dusk in summer. In this way you can enjoy a walking holiday in one of Romania's other ranges and still climb the country's highest summit as a one-off. I would recommend the return from walking elsewhere as being the best stage at which to tackle Moldoveanu, bearing in mind that a degree of fitness is needed. In fact the best way round to make this ascent would be to camp on the summit ridge near Portița Viștei pass and make the short ascent to the summit via Vârful Viștea at first light.

The unremarkable small town of Victoria (with a hotel in the main square) is on the Sibiu–Brașov railway line; alight at Ucea de Jos. Trains are met by buses running into the town. The bus station lies on the western extremity of the town. The municipal open-air swimming-pool is adjacent – useful if you have descended and have a long wait for the next bus on the heat of the plains. Turn right (east) out of the bus station to bring you to a junction with a road with an industrial railway line running along it. Turn left here past a walker's signpost and walk 500m north up the road. Just before the entrance to the Viromet chemical plant, turn left onto the concrete road beneath a gantry and head along this across flat fields of grass for 5km, the surface deteriorating to gravel. You come to a right hand turning with a walkers' signpost. Turn right here and after less than 1km you come to a barrier where the road enters the forest.

You are now heading south up the Viștea Mare valley, past a few orchards and cottages, then the forest closes in and the road climbs more steeply. This valley during August is red with wild raspberries; in parts the wild raspberry seems to be the commonest undergrowth plant. The forest road finishes and the path climbs more steeply, crossing the stream several times on tree trunk bridges. The deciduous forest turns to spruce and then opens out (red triangle waymarks painted on rocks). 1km after leaving the forest you come to a shepherd's hut. The final ascent up the head of the valley is steep, across boulder scree, haunt of marmot. About 8hrs after leaving Victoria you come to the Portița Viștei pass with a signpost. Turn right here to make the steep ascent up to Vârful Viștea, described in 'Day Three' above.

Route 3a: Victoria town to Șaua Podragului via Muchia Tărâței spur and Podragu cabana, 17km (10 miles). Altitude gained, 1730m (5700ft)

Follow the directions above to the Viromet plant and turn right at the

Plenty of waymarking but not much of a path! An easy stage of the tricky clambering section from Şaua Cleopatrei, east of Negoiu, west to Şaua Scării

entrance on a concrete, signed to Arpaş cabana. The road takes you across open grassland straight towards the mountains in front of you; ignore a right hand turning to Arpaş cabana and continue north (blue stripe waymarks). Shortly after entering the forest, the valley splits; take the track heading to the right, up the Ucişoara Seacă valley. 1km after the Arpaş turning you reach a path turning left off the track, heading south up a spur in the forests (blue stripe waymarks). Turn left here, briefly up to the crest of a spur in the forest. Now go right, south and keep right as the track splits; continue up and south, over the minor summit of La Şeuta (1203m, 3946ft). The path continues to ascend through the forest to the spring at La Şipot. The path now climbs steeply, zigzags up through the forest to the west of Vârful Boldanu (1679m, 5508ft) and then path splits, the right hand path contouring straight through the trees to Turnuri cabana. Keep left, for the excellent travers of the Tărăţei spur, keeping to its western side. There are superb views and chamois aplenty. Finally, among what appear to WWI trenchworks at Curmătura la Calea Calelor (2190m, 718ft) – the accompanying map inaccurate here – you turn right and descend to the lake and briefly up to the cabana.

Route 4: Arpaş station to Şaua Podragului via Arpaş and Turnuri cabanas, 21km (15 miles). Altitude gained, 1750m (5741ft)

Gara Arpaş is on the north side of Arpaşu de Jos village; head south through the village towards Arpaşu de Sus (5km away) and onwards, south-east up the Arpaşu valley towards Arpaş cabana. Just south of the cabana, heading south, a path turns off to the left (blue triangle waymarks), south to La Şipot. Continue along the

Arpașu Mare valley (red triangle waymarks). After a further 2km, shortly before the forest road ends, the path turns left off it and zigzags very steeply up the valley sides and then contours along through the trees, before swinging up to the left again to cross a tributary stream, the Pârâul lui Ban. From here it contours along, south, to a junction at the end of the Piscul Podragului ridge. To the right the red disc route heads around to the west of the ridge and on up, out of the trees to Podragel lake. Turn left here, south-east (red triangle waymarks), to cross the Podragu stream at a wooden footbridge, recrossing it again shortly afterwards to head up into the trees and then south to Turnuri cabana. There is a choice of routes on to Podragu cabana, from where the red and blue triangle route takes you up to Șaua Podragului.

Route 5: Avrig station to Portița Avrigului pass via Poiana Neamțului and Bârcaciu cabanas, 21km (15 miles). Altutude gained, 1600m (5250ft)

Head south-east out of the town along unsurfaced the road up the Avrig valley for 1km, to the road junction at Podu Jibrii (Gura Jibrii). Turn right here, south for 4km along the Râul Mare to Poiana Neamțului Cabana, all on a forest road. 200m south of the cabana turn left, steeply up a forest track (red cross waymarks) which takes you into a valley (the Comanesei); turn right after 15 minutes at the end of the track, zigzagging west, steeply up the valley sides to reach the crest of a ridge in the forest – the Piciorul Bârcaciului. The path turns left to head just east of south to reach Bârcaciu cabana after 2km. Immediately behind the cabana you reach a cross-paths; to the left the red disc path heads east to Negoiu cabana, over two of the spurs running north from the Făgăraș ridge; ahead the red cross route makes its way up onto the Muntele Bârcaciu ridge to join the main red stripe Făgăraș ridge route just west of Vârful Scara. Ignore these to turn right (blue disc waymarks) through the trees. Just over 1km after the cabana you finally exit from the forest near a shepherds' hut and start to ascend towards Avrig lake, lying in its dramatic cirque. From here follow the directions in 'Day Six' above to continue along the main Făgăraș route.

Route 6: Podu Olt station and Turnu Roșu to Chica Lacului or the former Suru cabana

Podu Olt station stands away from any settlement, immediately below the steep wooded hill of Chicera Veștera – a wonderful place to alight from the train. Turn right onto the road out of the station and immediately left, down the poplar avenue, signed 'Turnu Roșu 3km'. In fact it is only 2km; you reach a bridge over the River Olt and follow Strada Valea Caselor – the main street (the name means 'Valley of the Houses' and takes its name from the stream that flows down the middle beneath walnut trees) through the village of Turnu Roșu – not much in the way of shops but a fine village bar. Passing the bar you reach the war memorial on the left; immediately after this turn right, just before house number 221. 100m down this street turn left, just before the ochre-painted farmhouse number 237. The street ends at a gate, becoming a grassy track across a field. Look at the far side of the field to see a metal gate in the fence at the top of the slope; bear left off the track to follow the obvious path to this. A prominent path takes you up, through alder scrub to a flat grassy platform; tree trunks are few on which to fix the red cross waymarks but the path is well defined as it takes you into the forest, along the Culmea Petriceua ridge. There is no water available on this path once you have left Turnu Roșu until just before the main Făgăraș ridge.

Looking down the Bâlea valley from Şaua Caprei

A less attractive alternative is to turn right from Podu Olt station to make your way up to the site of Suru cabana; 2km along the road to Avrig, north-east from the station, you cross the Olt River and take the second of two turnings along unsurfaced roads, to Sebeşu de Sus road, just south of east from Sebeş Olt station – the second turning off the DN1 main road. At the far end of the village you come to a bridge over the Moasa Sebeşului river. Ahead, the track offers an alternative route all the way up the valley to Suru cabana. Instead, turn left here to make your way through the trees up to the end of the Culmea Moasa ridge, the path swinging round to the right so that it ends up heading almost south. 5km after the village your pass junction with a path to the left (blue triangle way-marks). Keep heading along the ridge here, a steady easy climb bringing you to Suru. Beyond the cabana (and now out of the forest) the path is steeper, zigzagging up to a junction where the blue triangle route heads to the right, south and then west to follow the dwindling ridge route towards the Olt valley, while the red triangle route to the right takes you up to Curmătura Surului pass.

Route 7: Valea Mărului halt to Chica Lacului and the former Suru cabana

Valea Mărului halt is served by six trains per day heading south from the junction at Podu Olt and a similar number heading north. There is no bridge over the river for access to the road nor is any habitation visible from the halt.

There is an old walker's signpost at the halt; follow the footpath north, parallel to the railway track, seeing the red stripe waymarks on a concrete electricity pole on the left. The path becomes a grassy track, contouring along the steep hillside. After 400m you come to a sharp left-hand bend in a gully with bushes. A path turns right, steeply up a bank through young False Acacia trees to bring you to a grassy slope. Head east, straight up this, past a shed on your right, following a fence steeply up the hill. At the top of a spur you come to a more prominent track heading into the wood, well waymarked with red stripes.

After nearly 3km of relentless ascent in the forest you come to a broad clearing at a shepherd's hut. Now take care: this clearing occupies the western slopes below the summit of Vârful Păului (1172m, 3845ft). This is shown on many maps as being out of the woods; in fact the summit, a north–south ridge, is densely wooded. From the shepherd's hut turn right to head just east of due south, contouring across the clearing, past a large spring fenced off in grove of birch. The path continues, not well defined, through the expanse of dock. Keep contouring, over a grassy spur, to the southernmost point of the clearing where you see a red stripe mark on a tree and the path continues, well defined, contouring along the side of the Strîmbanu ridge until you reach a small clearing on the saddle east of Vârful Păului. You exit from the trees at a grassy summit west of Chica Pietrelor and the path becomes ill-defined. Keep to the north side of the ridge and follow the well-defined path contouring back into the beechwoods, around a very steep gully, then crosses a stream below a stâna. The path contours along the tree line on the north side of Chica Pietrelor until you find a wide sheep-grazed bowl above you to your right. Bear right to head up this, past some springs to meet the junction of the red cross and red stripe routes on the tussocky expanse of the main Făgăraș ridge-top at Chica Lacului (alt. 1649m, 5410ft).

THE COZIA MASSIF

The Cozia massif (Map 10) is a small mountain block to the south of the western end of the Făgăraș. Thus protected from the north winds by the Făgăraș and the Lotru range, it stands guard over the valley of the much-dammed River Olt as it makes its way southwards, through the beautiful gorge of the Olt Defile, out of the Southern Carpathians onto the plains of Wallachia. There is little in the way of climbing to be enjoyed in the Cozia; there are a few scrambling routes on Bulzu crags and Forfecii. It offers an opportunity of combining mountain walking with a visit to the monasteries on the flanks of the mountain, in the Olt valley. The most important of these, Cozia, is on the western bank of the River Olt, between Turnu and Căciulata.

Access

Access to the Cozia massif is from the DN7 road and the main Sibiu–Wallachia railway line, running down the narrow corridor of the Olt Defile. If you are travelling specifically to the Cozia, you need to take the train from Bucharest to Caracal (five per day, taking around 2¾ hours), where you change for the Sibiu-bound train up the Olt valley, taking about 90 minutes to Turnu or Lotru stations. In fact you may find it easier to catch a train from Bucharest or Brașov to Podu Olt (an hour from Brașov) and change to a cursa heading south, down the valley. There is one direct fast train per day from Bucharest to Lotru and also a direct personal.

If approaching Cozia from the Făgăraș, there are two possible routes. One is to take the option on the final day of walking down from the main Făgăraș chain to the village of Câineni, along the Zănoaga Câinenilor ridge (red cross waymarks – wrongly shown on some maps as blue stripes). There is a campsite

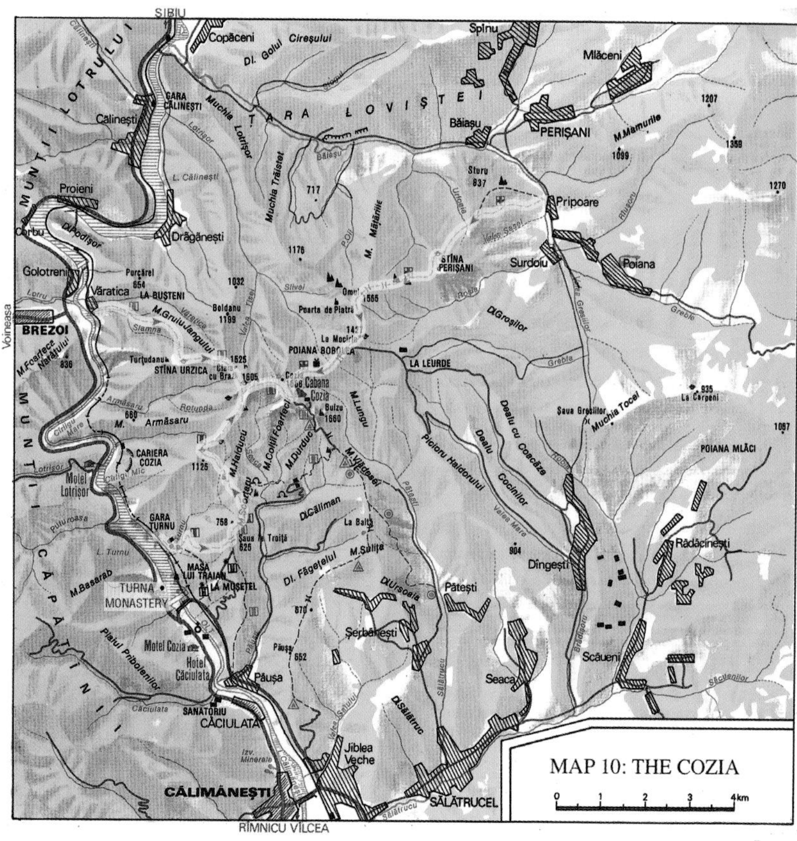

just to the north of the village, on the main road in the Olt valley. You may well prefer to camp in the woods short of the town. From Câineni it is a road journey of 26km, 16 miles south to Brezoi. There are also eight trains per day from Câineni to Lotru, the nearest station to Brezoi. You can also take the train down the Olt valley from Sibiu, alighting at Lotru station. You may well prefer to finish the Făgăraş traverse at Turnu Roşu (see above) and catch the train from nearby Podu Olt junction to Lotru. Podu Olt is the start point for trains heading south down the Olt valley. There are four trains a day along the Podu Olt–Piatra Olt line. It takes around an hour to make the very scenic journey from Podu Olt to Lotru. From Lotru station head south into Văratica village (blue stripe waymarks), heading due east up the Slamna valley. See 'Lotru station to Cozia cabana' below.

Crossing the Cozia massif

There is a very lonely link route to the Cozia from Strunga Doamnei pass, adjacent to Vârful Negoiu in the Făgăraş; it is about 78km (49 miles) and is supposedly waymarked with blue stripes through the forest as far as Arefu. It should only be undertaken by someone with experience of route-finding in mapless terrain, mostly in forest. You will need to have all supplies for at least three days and be prepared to camp wild. It takes you south along the Podeanu–Florea–Bolovanu–Frunții ridge, the watershed between the Topolog and Argeș valleys, and brings you 40km, 25 miles after Strunga Doamnei to Arefu village just west of the TransFăgărașan, south of the dam holding back Vidraru lake. From here it is a case of hiking or hitching along forest roads, west to Sălătrucu and further west, up to a pass down into the Greble valley to the village of Poiana, continuing through it to the hamlet of Pripoare.

Routes into the Cozia

Pripoare to Cozia Cabana, 12km (8 miles). Altitude gained to the summit of Omu, 1045m (3248ft)

From the northern end of the village of Pripoare (alt. 520m, 1700ft, served by buses from Curtea de Argeș), head west (red cross waymarks) up out of the valley towards the crags of Sturu (837m, 2746ft). In fact there are two routes, the right-hand one following the spur up to the summit of Sturu, whilst the left-hand, waymarked route takes you straight to a col (775m, 2543ft), immediately south-west of Sturu. From the col you head south-west into the woods and zigzag steeply up onto the Culmea Siriul de Pietre ridge by the shepherds' huts at Stâna Perișani, immediately north of Vârful Șoimului (1281m, 4203ft). You exit from the woods by some rocks and head south, at the edge of a clearing, before continuing to ascend in the woods, westwards along the ridge. 2km of steady ascent past a number of crags in the forest brings you over the rocks to Vârful Omu (1565m, 5134ft), where the path turns south, down to Poarta de Piatra, and the shepherd's hut at Mocirle. You reach a col on the main ridge, from where the red disc access route turns right to Poarta de Piatra. Head south-west, along the ridge for 1.5km from the col to join the access road, taking you across Poiana Bobolea clearing to Cozia cabana (alt. 1570m, 5150ft).

Lotru station to Cozia cabana, 10km (7 miles). Altitude gained, 1400m (4600ft)
From Lotru station walk south on the road for 1km to the hamlet of Văratica. In the village, turn left up the Slamna valley, following a track (blue stripe waymarks). Less than 1km east of the village, the path turns south, steeply up in a gully with the Gruiu Jangului spur above you to the left. The path becomes steeper and zigzags up to exit from the trees by the disused sheepfolds at Stâna Urzica. Here the path turns left to head due east with superb views west to the Lotru, before continuing back into the forest to reach a shepherds' hut by the crags immediately south-west of Vârful Rotunda. From the shepherd's hut the path turns left to head north-east, over Vârful Rotunda and down to a col before Vârful Cozia, less than 1km east of Rotunda. From Cozia it is a short walk south to the Cozia cabana (see Appendix A) and weather station.

Turnu station to Cozia cabana, 8km (5 miles). Altitude gained, 1060m (3478ft)
Walk down the road south from the station (alt. 510m, 1700ft) past Turnu monastery. Turnu, an outlier to the more important Cozia monastery to the south, grew up around hermits' cells lived in by monks from Cozia during the sixteenth century. There is an unattractive modern church and a facsimile of the sixteenth-century chapel destroyed during the First World War.

From the monastery the path leads up out of the Turnu valley to the east, into the woods and up to Șaua la Troița pass (625m, 2050ft), just over 2km from Turnu station. At the pass you meet the blue stripe route from the right, coming up from the village of Păuşa. Turn left immediately north of Şaua la Troiţa to head north, towards the right-hand end of the Muchia Traznița spur (758m, 2487ft). The path forks, the red stripe route heading away to the left, steeply up, northwards to Muchia Turneanu ridge, 2km to the north, where you exit from the trees and turn right to follow it to Cozia summit and cabana. It is also possible to reach Cozia from Şaua la Troiţa (673m, 2208ft) via Stânişoara monastery; turn right at the path junction 400m north of the pass to follow the blue stripe route north, with the crags of the Traznița ridge above you to your left. After about 1km, the path swings east, then meets a stream in the forest immediately below the summit of Vârful Salbaticu (803m, 2634ft). Follow the stream up to reach the clearing and Stânişoara monastery, founded as a hermitage in 1671.

Stânişoara is perhaps the finest of the monasteries in the Cozia massif, not just because it is off the beaten track. As with the monasteries of Bucovina, it is the setting which lends a powerful 'spirit of place'. From here is a superb view of Colţii Foarfecii. The path upwards from here becomes more strenuous, taking you past Damaschin's rock and up to Vârful Bulzu (1660m, 5446ft), where a cable has been fixed to a rock. Soon after Bulzu rocks you reach the access road to the transmission tower (not shown on the map). The final part of the walk is along the ridge to Cozia cabana.

Exit route: Cozia cabana to Călimanesti. Altitude lost, 1450m (4757ft)

From the cabana head south-east along the track to the television transmission tower and turn right off it where the track makes a left-hand hairpin. To your right is the rocky gully of the Valea Gardului. 1km from the cabana the path turns right, south, then south-east very steeply down the Muchia Vlădesei spur, assisted by cables as bannisters to a junction with the blue stripe route turning right to Colţul lui Damaschin rocks and Stânişoara monastery. You pass a shelter and cross with a wooden bench and table; keep left here, south-east down the spur (blue triangle and disc waymarks). After less than 1km you reach a pass on the ridge (976m, 3202ft), where a path turns left, down into the Pătești valley towards Sălătrucel. Keep right here, south along the Dealul Suliţa ridge; the path swings right to head south-west, along Dealul Fagetului ('Beech Tree Hill'), continuing in the trees to Balta pass. From the pass there is easy walking, south down the spur to meet the road on the east bank of the much-dammed River Olt, opposite Călimaneşti. To reach the town, turn right along the road across the top of the dam; keep straight on along the east bank for the station.

CHAPTER SEVEN

From the Olt to the Jiu

This chapter deals with mountain ranges lying between the valleys of the Olt and the Jiu, and describes the massifs of Cindrel, Șureanu, Lotru, Parâng, Latoriței and Căpățân, as well as the region of the valleys that drain south of the Căpățân, with their delightful monasteries. The eastern barrier is the mighty Olt Defile – see below – and the western is strictly the corridor of the Jiu and the Hațeg Depression as I include the Șureanu massif, north of the source of the Rivers Jiu, west and east. The mountains tend to be aligned from east to west; as a whole this region is a mountainous bridge connecting the higher and better-known Făgăraș and Retezat mountains. My recommendation for the best way to walk this is to finish the Făgăraș traverse by heading south to Cozia to start the Căpățân traverse from Brezoi and continue westwards across the Parâng, from where you can continue to the Vâlcan and on to the Retezat. The area described may be considered as a mis-shaped square with a city each corner – Sibiu at the north-east, Râmnicu Vâlcea at the south-east, Târgu Jiu at the south-west and Deva at the north-west. It is conveniently divided in the west by the Jiu Defile, where the river forces its way southwards between the massifs of Parâng and Vâlcan. The Jiu rises in the Carpathians, as the East and West Jiu. The Olt, however, whose valley was crossed from the Făgăraș to reach this region, flows from north to south right through the Carpathian chain, indicating that the river existed in approximately its present alignment before the uplift of the Carpathians in the same orogeny that threw up the Alps.

Mountain walkers familiar with the classic Himalayan walk, the Annapurna Circuit, will notice that the Olt is a replication in miniature of the Kali Gandaki river. This rises on the northern (Tibetan) side of the Himalaya which has carved the deepest valley in the world between the Annapurna massif to the east and the Dhaulagiri massif to the west, as it flows south, eventually to join the Ganges. In the case of the Olt, in the place of Annapurna read Făgăraș, Dhaulagiri read Lotru, Ganges read Danube. Even the holy sites in the valley are reproduced: for Muktinath Hindu and Buddhist shrine read Cozia Monastery. For all that contrasts in scale make the comparison seem initially ridiculous, it is valid, for the Himalaya were created in the same uplift that created the Carpathians, and the reason for the two rivers breaking the mountain chain is the same – that they continued to flow and erode their valleys downwards as fast as the mountains were pushed up.

Both the Olt and Jiu valleys carry important corridors of communication, both road and rail. Along the Olt valley run the connecting routes Râmnicu Vâlcea and the plains of Wallachia in the south to Sibiu and Transylvania. The Jiu carries the corridor of communication between the mining towns of Târgu Jiu and Petroșani, then up out of the Jiu valley, over the Merișor pass (755m, 2477ft) to Deva.

Unless walking straight through from the Făgăraș, the best entry point for this region is the city of Sibiu, effectively the finish point of the Făgăraș traverse. From here there are usually two buses per day from the railway station up to the tiny ski

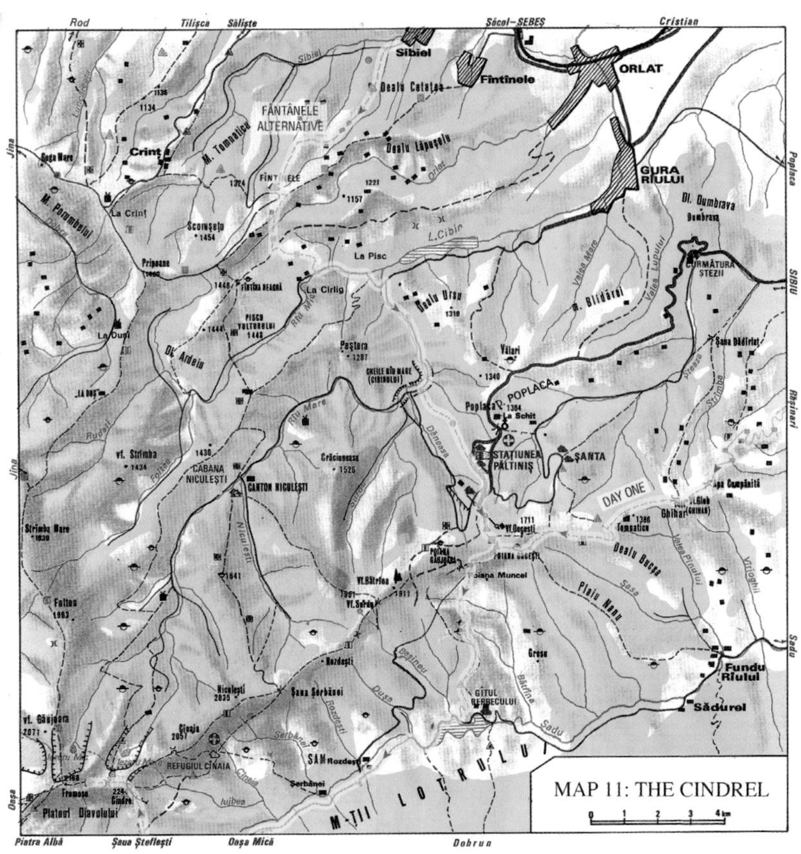

resort of Păltiniș. The city itself is well worth a day or two's exploration before departing for the mountains.

Access

If travelling to Sibiu by train from Bucharest, you will go via Brașov. You do not necessarily have to change; eight trains go direct, of which only one is a fast accelerat, leaving Bucharest at 1700, arriving in Sibiu at 2000. There are trains almost hourly from Bucharest to Brașov, taking three and a half hours or less. There are four trains a day from Brașov to Sibiu, taking between two and three and a half hours.

It is possible to continue straight from a westbound Făgăraș traverse – ended by descending into the Olt valley just to the south of the village of Boița. To the west of Boița is the (apparently mapless) Lotru range. The best bet would be to walk or hitch the 4km northwards to Tălmaciu, then head west up the Sadu valley along the DJ105G road 15km (9 miles) to Valea Sadului cabana, or a further 22km (13½ miles) to Gâtul Berbecului ('Ram's Neck'). If you finish the Făgăraș at Turnu Roșu, you will find buses and trains from Podu Olt, 2km north, to Tălmaciu. Pick up the itinerary below at day two – Gâtul Berbecului to Obârșia Lotrului ('Source of the Lotru'). Connecting the Cindrel direct to the Făgăraş in this way avoids Sibiu completely.

THE CINDREL MASSIF

The first part of our route takes us across the Cindrel ('Cheen-drell' – see Map 11). This is an east–west ridge rising out of the forests, some 35km (20 miles) long, with some fine glacial tarns. It is almost entirely of igneous rocks, with mica schist and gneiss predominating. On its northern side is our start point, the ski resort of Păltiniş, its chalets and hotels scattered pleasantly among the spruce trees, reached by buses from Sibiu. If visiting Sibiu, the Cindrel is an ideal area for day walks based in Răşinari or Păltiniş, as well as being the start point of our traverse of the western part of the southern Carpathians.

Day One

Sibiu to Gâtul Berbecului chalet complex, 14km (9 miles). Altitude gained from Răşinari to Ghinan, 881m (2890ft)

This day can be shortened by about four hours by taking a bus or taxi all the way to Păltiniş.) In order to make a full east–west traverse of the Cindrel, you should get out of the bus from Sibiu – buses depart from outside the railway station – at the village of Răşinari, site of an annual gypsy music festival on the third Sunday in April. From Răşinari follow the well waymarked track which turns left off the main road from Sibiu, up the Sibişel valley. 600m south of the road you turn right. The path, marked with red stripes, takes you up through woods west to the summit of Vârful Coastei (935m, 3068ft). From here it is a straightforward ridge-top route south-west to Apa Cumpanită, then, continuing south-west, over the summit of Vârful Glub (Ghinan) (1411m, 4692ft) and Tomnaticu to Vârful Onceşti (1713m, 5620ft). From the summit a track winds down to Păltiniş but by heading south-west from the summit, following the blue disc path across the ridge top clearing (Grădina Onceşti), you can avoid Staţiunea Păltiniş altogether. 1km beyond Vârful Onceşti you reach the clearing at Poiana Muncel; just after the clearing you turn left on a track, then left off it again to head south. You are now off the main red stripe route and following the red triangles due south to descend past the shepherds' hut in a clearing at Bătrânei in the forest, to the Bătrâna Mică sheepfold (marked on the map but not named). From here the path descends steeply to Gâtul Berbecului, on the shores of Negoveanu reservoir. This day can be shortened to a walk of just two and a half hours by taking a bus all the way from Sibiu to Păltiniş.

Alternative approach to the Cindrel

Sibiel Station to Fântânele cabana, 12km (8 miles). Altitude gained from Sibiel to Fântânele, 837m (2746ft)

This short day walk allows plenty of time to catch the train out of Sibiu; five per day call at Sibiel halt; the journey takes half an hour. Check before you leave that the train for Sebeş does stop in Sibiel; if not, alight in Orlat and walk up, or catch the bus from Sibiu instead. Whilst in Sibiel you should not miss the fine little gallery of locally-worked icons painted onto glass – a tradition in southern Transylvania. From Sibiel station head west along the road from the halt through the village. 200m after the last house cross a bridge and turn left to head south-west through beech woods up to the summit of Dealul (Vârful) Cetatea (1098m, 3602ft). The ruins of the fourteenth-century fortified citadel can still be seen on top of the hill. From here you continue south-west past the barns scattered about Poiana Godia along the Lăpuşel ridge (blue disc waymarks) to bring you to Fântânele cabana (see Appendix A).

There is an alternative route, turning left through the village of Fântânele, 1km west of the station; this takes you on a track the whole way.

Alternative Day One

Fântânele cabana to Gâtul Berbecului via Cibin gorge, 24km (15 miles). Altitude gained from La Pisc to Poiana Muncel, 995m (3264ft)

Leave the cabana to the south-west (red disc waymarks) across Piciorul Fântânelor ridge and down to cross the Orlat stream. Keep heading south-west to climb Runcuri hill in the forest to cross a path at Runcuri saddle (1267m, 4157ft) and descend steeply from there to meet the forest road running along the bottom of the Râu Mic valley at La Cârlig. Now omit the next paragraph and continue at the following one.

There is also a longer route, heading west from the cabana along the track, which runs over Pripoare summit (1400m, 4593ft) eventually to Jina village. 3km after the cabana you turn left off the track (red cross waymarks), southwards, up to Fântâna Neagra – 'the Black Spring' (alt. 1146m, 3560ft). You cross a path heading along the ridge at the spring. Head south-east (red cross waymarks) towards Vârful Curmătura, where you turn right to head south-west, along the ridge to Piscul Vulturului (1443m, 4734ft) and then descend, the path swinging to the right to head south, down to cross the forest track at the bottom of the Râul Mic valley at Strîmba. Heath south along a track from the junction, heading up the Foltea valley and then turn left to climb steeply up, heading south-east through the forest (red cross waymarks) over the ridge, heading east. You reach a track, giving access to Cabana Soarelui; turn right along it to head south, returning to the forest and then descending to cross the Râu Mare valley at Canton Niculeşti. Turn left and then immediately right here, so that you are heading south, up the Beşineu valley through the forest (red cross waymarks) which turns right after 4km to head south-west up to Şaua Şerbănei. There is also a slightly tricky path heading up from Canton Niculeşti, taking you south-east to Vârful Surdu (1951m, 6400ft) and on to join the main Cindrel ridge at Şaua Bătrâna. From Şaua Şerbanei turn left, now on the main ridge route (red stripe waymarks), taking you north-east over Vârful Rozdeşti, down to a col and then off the south side of the ridge. 2km east of Vârful Rozdeşti the path forks; bear right to head east (red stripe waymarks) to Poiana Muncel from where you follow the directions in 'Day One' above to head south to Gâtul Berbecului cabana. From the main Cindrel ridge you descend either from Poiana Muncel or Cânaia refuge to the Sadu valley and Gâtul Berbecului cabana. There is also a more direct route, taking you through Cibin gorge.

From La Cârlig, turn left, down the Râu Mic valley towards Cibin lake. After 2km on the forest road you turn right (red disc waymarks) near the confluence of the Râu Mic and Râu Mara at La Pisc (662m, 2172ft) up the forest road into the gorge. As the gorge swings round to the right, turn left, sharply back on yourself, initially on a grassy trakc (red disc waymarks) steeply up the path known as Calea Studenţilor through the forest to Păltiniş. Turn right on the road, south along the lower part of the loop road through Păltiniş. At the top end of the resort the road makes a hairpin bend to the left; keep straight ahead, under the ski-slope bridge, past Cabana Păltiniş on a good forest road to reach Poiana Muncel, where you turn left to descend south to Gâtul Berbecului cabana. At the shed at Poiana Muncel the red triangle route takes you steeply down past Bătrâna springs and the Bătrâna Mic sheepfold to Gâtul Berbecului ('Ram's Neck') cabana (see Appendix A).

If you have food you may prefer to stay at Cânaia refuge. From Păltiniș head up towards Vârful Oncești and then south-west (red stripe waymarks), to bring you along the ridge to the rocks at Bătrâna, past the path junction at Surdu and over Vârful Rozdești (1925m, 6315ft) to bring you to the pass at Șaua Șerbănei. Immediately after the pass the path forks; bear left (blue disc waymarks) to the refuge at Cânaia just south of the main ridge. This is a comfortable stage, although you should take your own food.

From Gâtul Berbecului cabana it is also possible to head south (red triangle waymarks) from the foresters' cabana at Rozdești, at the head of Lake Negoveanu south for 8km to the summit of Vârful Balindru (2207m, 7241ft), the highest point in the Lotru range. From here the path continues south to the settlement at Dobrun and Balindru lake in the Lotru valley. From here you can turn right to head up the valley to Vidru lake and the hotels at Vidruța – in all a walk of about 26km (16 miles).

Day Two

Gâtul Berbecului to Obârșia Lotrului via Cindrel summit. Altitude gained from Gâtul Berbecului to Cindrel summit, 1069m (3507ft)

From the cabana head west along the rough road up the Sadu valley to Șaua Șteflești, whence it continues south-south-west, down the Frumoasă valley to Tărtaru forest cabana on the DN67C road from Novaci to Sebeș.

If you are feeling very energetic you can retrace your steps all the way up to the main Cindrel ridge, at Vârful Bătrâna (1911m, 6270ft), and turn left to head south-west along the main Cindrel ridge (red stripe waymarks) to the south of Vârful Surdu (1961m, 6434ft) and over Rozdești, down to the path junction at Șaua Șerbanei. Here the red cross route turns right and leads off to the north, to Canton Niculești; 300m west a path to the left (red disc waymarks) leads to the refuge at Cânaia just to the south of the main ridge. From Șaua Șerbanei head almost due west (red stripe waymarks) – it is about 6km to the summit from Șaua Șerbanei pass. The path takes you just south of Vârful Niculești (2035m, 6676ft) and over Vârful Cânaia (2057m, 6749ft). As you approach the summit the ridge narrows dramatically between the Cindrel cirque on the right and the Lujbea Răsinarului cirque on the left.

However a more relaxed route to the summit is to follow the barely-used road up the Sadu valley for approximately 8km (5 miles) past the junction with the track descending from Păltiniș to the right, to the forest cabana at Șerbaniei where the blue disc route turns right, signed to Cânaia refuge. Turn right here, climbing steeply up through the trees, then out of them to reach the refuge. This is a delightful place to stay, overlooking the wide cirque of the Caldarea Iujbea, whose stream runs down to the Sadu river.

Keep heading west from the refuge, following the blue discs to bring you to a col on the main Cindrel ridge – Șaua Cindrel (2025m, 6643ft) – immediately west of Vârful Cânaia. (There is also a path from the refuge, red triangle waymarks, taking you round the cirque and down to the road pass at Șaua Șteflești.) Turn left at the col on the main Cindrel ridge (red stripe waymarks) south-west up to the summit of Cindrel (2244m, 7362ft), with fine views of the Retezat to the west. As well as our path from the summit of Cindrel there is also a path to the west (red cross waymarks) for 18km, all the way to Oasa cabana on the DN67C road south from Sebeș to Novaci. Head down to a col, and a glacial tarn, where the blue triangle route heads steeply down to the north, leading to Niculești and the Cibin gorge. Ignore this and keep heading west to Frumosu summit (2168m, 7113ft). Just west of the summit there is a path junction; take the right hand route (red cross waymarks) to Oasa.

From the summit of Cindrel, head south (red stripe waymarks) all the way down to the road pass of Șaua Șteflești. On the way you pass a junction with the blue triangle route turning left, back to Cânaia refuge. Keep right here, on down to the unnamed pass carrying the unsurfaced forest road, a westward extension of the DJ105 up from Tălmaciu and Gâtul Berbecului in the east (not marked on road maps; it connects with the DN67C to the west, north of Tărtărăul road pass – 1678m, 5505ft).

At the (unnamed) road pass cross over the road and head south, steeply up (red cross waymarks) to the east of Vârful Șteflești (2242m, 7356ft – a path goes to the summit). You are now off the southern edge of Map 11 and not yet on Map 12 – the Parâng. From Vârful Șteflești head west-south-west (red cross waymarks), over the summit of Vârful Crestești, and then south-west to bring you north of the summit of Piatra Albă (2178m, 7146ft). The path runs to the west of the summit and descends southwards to a col. The route further is marked with red stripes and marker poles, heading due west. You are now on the main red stripe route along the Lotru ridge, marked with paint on stones. The general alignment of the path is south-west towards the summit of Parângu Mare ahead. You pass a junction (now on Map 12, but not marked) with a track heading off to the left from a col above the trees, down to Vidra lake in the Lotru valley. The path continues steadily downwards across sheep-grazed grassland and past patches of dwarf pine, heading south-west along the Tâmpele ridge, leaving the summit of Vârful Tâmpa (1800m, 5905ft) to your left. The path passes well to the north of the rounded grassy summit of Tâmpa din Pârâu (1809m, 5935ft), then descends to a minor col. South from this col the Tâmpei valley drains to the western end of Lake Vidra. The col is the (unmarked) junction between the red stripe route heading west to descend to the DN67C road by the Tăraru pass (1678m, 5505ft). Your route is to the left here, heading south-west, following what should be red stripe waymarks over a number of tributary valleys and spurs feeding into the Tâmpei valley. The third of these after the col is a larger valley, the Muierilor ('Women's Valley' – peasant slang). The path – a well-used track – swings to the left to head south, then west as you meet the conifers in the Pârâul lui Mihai valley. The end of the route is marked by descent on a track through conifers to bring you onto the DN7C just east of the rather basic Obârșia Lotrului cabana (alt. 1320m, 4330ft) at the lonely crossing of two rough roads in the mountains; you can head west from here over the Șureanu Mountains for a day's walk en route to the Retezat – see below.

THE LATORIȚEI RIDGE

The Latoriței ridge is an east–west limestone ridge sandwiched between the Lotru to the north and the Căpățân to the south. At its eastern end is the village of Voineasa; its western end is marked by the Latoriței Șaua Ștefanu pass, on the DN67C road from Sebeș to Novaci. Along its northern side the DN67A road makes its way west up the Mânăileasa valley, from Voineasa, around Vidra lake to Obârșia Lotrului cabana. There is also vehicle access on the south side, the rough DJ175 road heading west from Hanul Latoriței, up the Latorița valley to Lake Petrimanu and from there south over the Curmătura Oltețului pass

(1620m, 5315ft) across the Căpățân ridge and down the Olteț valley to Polovragi. There are a number of climbs of varying grades in the Olteț gorge, between Polovragi and Curmătura Olteț.

If you are making your way west along the southern Carpathians, the Latoriței offers a ridge walk, leading to the Parâng, especially useful if you can get road transport from Văratica (see Cozia Massif) to Voineasa. The walking is fast and easy, all along a jeep track. It is probably best tackled as a two-day walk; Voineasa village or Hanul Latorița to Cabana Petrimanu and the next day from there to Obârșia Lotrului or Șaua Piatra Taiata in the Parâng.

THE PARÂNG MASSIF

The Parâng is Romania's forgotten high mountain range, dominating the mining town of Petroș to the west. The highest point in the massif is Parâng Mare ('Great Parâng' – 2519m, 8264ft), Romania's fifth highest summit. To the north, the Jiet valley, for part of its length a dramatic gorge, separates the Parâng from the Șureanu massif. To the east the Igoiu ridge connects the Parâng to the Căpățânii massif. Together, the Căpățânii and Parâng make a long east–west ridge running from the Olt valley in the east to the Jiu valley in the west. On its southern flank a number of parallel rivers drain southward towards the plains of Wallachia, many of them through attractive gorges. Unusually, this is one area where the forest cover seem to omit the usual spruce forests, the upper edge of the beech forests giving way to dwarf shrubs and grassland. The western end of the Parâng is accessible from Rusu cabana and is popular for skiing. The central part of the Parâng consists of two glacial hollows (Câlcescu and Roșiile), enclosing several tarns. There is some small-scale climbing available in the Cheile Galben gorge, immediately west of the Olteț gorge (see 'The Latorița Ridge' above); both gorges are located in the south-east of the massif, east of Novaci.

Access

If travelling specifically to the Parâng, the easiest way to get there is to walk from the town of Petroșani, on the railway from the junction at Simeria (on the main line from Sibiu to Arad). The line from Simeria heads south to Craiova; from Bucharest, Petroșani is best reached in a day's journey, changing at Craiova and Târgu Jiu; there is one direct train per day – a sleeper. It must be possible to walk from the Olt valley, in the region of Lotrișor, along the main Căpățân ridge, coming onto Map 12 in the vicinity of Vârful Beleoaia (2039m, 6690ft). Certainly the path heading along the ridge in the vicinity of Curmătura Oltului (1615m, 5298ft) is well marked. Curmătura Oltului is just to the south of Petrimanu cabana (reached by a track – blue stripe waymarks), by Petrimanu lake in the Latorița valley.

The Parâng can also be reached via the Căpățânii range from the area of the monasteries in the valleys that drain southwards from the Căpățân I range. A path (blue triangle waymarks) heads north from Polovragi to the summit of Beleoaia, whilst a gravel road runs up the Olteț valley, over the Curmătura Oltului pass to Petrimanu. Access to the southern flank of the Căpățân I and the Parâng is by bus; two buses a day run east from Târgu Jiu. The town is also reached by two buses a day from the town of Râmnicu Vâlcea, in the Olt valley. You may well want to try and catch a lift or walk along the DN67C rough forest road (19km, 12 miles) from Novaci to Rânca cabana.

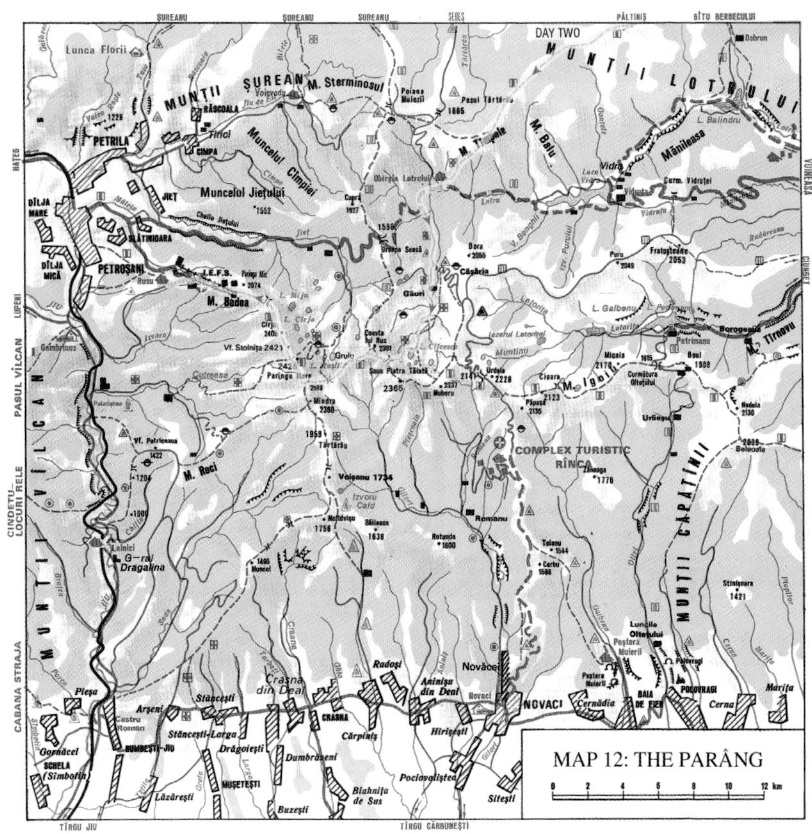

MAP 12: THE PARÂNG

Day One

Obârşia Lotrului cabana to Cabana Rusu, 30km (19 miles). Altitude gained from Obârşia Lotrului to Parâng summit, 1497m (4811ft)

From Obârşia Lotrului head south initially on the unsurfaced DN67C road towards Novaci. (This road leads to Rânca cabana, en route to Novaci; 4km down the rough road south of Rânca you come to a path leading off to the left (blue triangle waymarks) – it leads to Peştera Muierii cabana, near the 'Women's Cave' in Galbenul gorges.) After 2km you come to a road junction with the DN7A road heading west to Petroşani. Keep heading due south along the unsurfaced road south towards Rânca for a further 4km to a track leading to the right, signed with red crosses. Turn right here, south (red cross waymarks) up the Lotru valley, past the foresters' huts at Gauri (also known as Huluzu), on towards Câlcescu lakes, the track giving way to a footpath 5km after the junction.

You are now walking upstream along the infant river Olt towards Câlcescu lake (1935m, 6348ft). As you reach the lake shore you come to a path junction with the red triangle route taking you south-east up to the main Parâng ridge. Keep right here, around the western side of Câlcescu lake (red cross waymarks) through the scrub. The path leads you up the back of the old bergschrund of Câlcescu cirque and up to the pass at Șaua Piatra Taiata (2225m, 7300ft). Here you turn right, to skirt round to the south of (or over) Coasta lui Rus summit (2301m, 7550ft). You are now on the main east-west route (red stripe waymarks), along the top of the Parâng ridge and eastwards to the Căpățânii. To your right now is the glacial hollow of Lacu Roșii, dotted with tarns draining towards the Jieț valley. Turn right onto the red stripe route; very soon you come to a junction with a path (blue stripe waymarks), turning right, along a ridge to the north to Groapa Seacă pass (1598m, 5243ft) on the DN7A road. Keep left here to head due west (red stripe waymarks), to the left of the summit of Coasta lui Rus (2301m, 7550ft). You are now walking above the cirque of Roșiile to your right; you climb Vârful Picleșa (not marked on the map, 2335m, 7660ft), descend for a while the climb to the left of the summit of Vârful Gruiu (2345m, 7693ft). Another 2km of ridge walking brings you to the summit of Parâng Mare (2519m, 8264ft). This is the highest point in the Parâng and in front of you to the west are the jagged summits of the Retezat.

An attractive and lengthy route to the Vâlcan and the Retezat would be to head south (red cross waymarks) from Parângu Mare to Mândra summit (2360m, 7743ft), then right (red disc waymarks), south-west over the Reci ridge and Vârful Petriceaua (1422m, 4665ft) and down to the popas turistic at the monastery at Lainici in the Jiu valley. From just north of here a track turns west off the main DN66 Petroșani–Târgu Jiu road, to Schitul Locuri Rele ('Bad Places Hermitage'), and then up on to the eastern end of the Vâlcan ridge at Șaua Stâna and on into the Vâlcan.

To continue on to Rusu head north-west from the summit of Vârful Mândra (red stripe waymarks) to the lesser summit of Gemănarea (2424m, 7953ft), then Stoinița (2421m, 7943ft). Still within 2km of Parâng, you reach Cârja summit (2405m,7890ft). From here you descend with views across the Jiu valley and the Șureanu massif ahead; the path brings you to Șaua Caprelor (2195m, 7201ft) where you find a small roofless stone refuge. From Cârja westwards the going is much easier – its straightforward walking over the minor summit of Vârful Scurtu (2202m, 7224ft). The path down to Rusu turns to the left off the main Badea ridge at Șaua Izvorul (2050m, 6726ft) to keep to the south of Parâng Mic ('Little Parâng', 2074m, 6804ft). Cabana Rusu (alt. 1168m, 3832ft) is in a clutter of huts lying below Vârfu Badea on its western side and a few minutes' walk from the top station of the cable car (see Appendix A).

From Rusu cabana there is a track (assuming you wish to walk, rather than take the cable car) down to Petroșani town (red stripe waymarks). If you do not need the shops or hotels of Petroșani then I suggest you take advantage of the pedestrian by-pass offered by a rough road heading down the Sasul valley from just east of Cabanu Rusu, bringing you to Gambrinus hotel.

Alternative: The Parâng traverse – Peștera Muierilor cabana to Cabana Rusu, 40km (25 miles). Altitude gained from Peștera Muierilor to Parâng summit, 1934m (6345ft)

This walk across the Parâng is for those who have approached the massif by visiting the monasteries of Vâlcea. From Peștera Muierii cabana head north-west (blue triangle waymarks) along a ridge to the pass just to the south of the summit of Tolanu (1544m, 5066ft). You join the unsurfaced DN67C road and turn right toward the Rânca cabana complex (see Appendix A). From Rânca head north on the road to the Urdele pass (2141m,

Schitul Cioclovina hermitage, near the suggested start point across the Vâlcan to the Retezat

7024ft). Shortly after the pass turn left off the road (red stripe waymarks) along the main Parâng ridge. It takes you to the north of Vârful Mohoru (2337m, 7667ft), and around the impressive Câlcescu cirque to your right past Vârful Piatra Taiata (2365m, 7759ft) to the pass of the same name. From here follow the directions given in 'Day One' above.

THE ŞUREANU MASSIF

The Şureanu is an extensive block of almost completely forested mountains; it can be considered as a broad westward extension to the Cindrel, or a northward extension of the Parâng. It faces south-west across the glacial outwash plain of the Haţeg Depression to the much higher and much more visited Retezat. This massif is of metamorphic geology with some limestone areas around the margins. Its highest summit is Vârful lui Pătru (or Petru, 2130m, 6988ft); Vârful Şureanu itself is 2059m (6755ft). To the north-west the Şureanu slopes down to the fertile Mureş valley, on the far side of which rises the Apuseni – the mountainous hidden heart of Transylvania. There are a number of caves around the Şureanu; there is just one area of craggy relief, near the summit of Şureanu itself, the only area that raises itself above the forests of spruce with some beech. It is well supplied with cabanas – see Appendix A. A walk across the Şureanu (for which no map seems to exist) is a fine link from the Retezat to the Cindrel, though navigation is harder than across the higher and more satisfying Parâng, to the south.

THE CĂPĂŢÂN MASSIF

The Căpăţân ridge, running west from the Olt defile opposite Cozia for some 50km (31 miles) to the Olteţ valley, is something of a Făgăraş in miniature. Of igneous geology, the main ridge has a steep north-facing side, easily reached from the Lotru valley. To the south a number of parallel north–south valleys drain towards the pastoral landscape of Vâlcea. The ridge is higher in the west, its highest point being Vârful Ursului (2124m, 6968ft). This rocky, relatively unvisited crest offers a fine connecting walk west from the Cozia to the Curmătura Olteţului pass where you cross over into the Parâng. There are a number of climbs to be enjoyed in the Căpăţân: on Stagşoare, Pereţele Sântinela Cheii, Pereţel Livada cu Mesteacani, the north side of Sălcet and the north side of Claia Strîmba.

Access

Reaching the eastern end of the ridge is the same as for the Cozia, the best start point for walking being the halt at Lotru. From here make your way through Brezoi on the main DN7A road past the police station to the western side of the town and turn right, opposite Strada Lotrului, to head south up a cobbled street with a stream on your right – the Râu Satului. This becomes a track, taking you up onto the Căpăţân ridge.

THE LOTRU MASSIF

If doing the great traverse of the Transylvanian Alps from end to end, the Lotru ridge is the natural western sequel or precursor of the Făgăraş, a parallel east–west ridge to the Căpăţân, lying across the Lotru valley. The Cindrel is effectively a northern salient of the western end of the rather gently-contoured Lotru. The highest peak is Vf. Ştefleşti (2242m, 7356ft). There are no cabanas away from the nearby valleys and no climbing to speak of. The range offers a very pleasant connecting walk between the Retezat to the west and the Făgăraş to the east.

View of the main Retezat ridge, in the vicinity of Peleaga

CHAPTER EIGHT
The Retezat Mountains

After the Făgăraş, the Retezat is the range that has the most extensive truly alpine area above the tree line. I include in this chapter the Retezat's southerly neighbour, the Vâlcan (described first as it offers a natural approach to the Retezat from the Căpăţâni and mountains further east, covered in preceding chapters), and, briefly the Mic-Ţarcu mountains, to the north-west of the Retezat; the Mic-Ţarcu offers a pleasant exit route across comparatively unwalked terrain. The Retezat itself is quite different from other ranges in the Romanian Carpathians – a block-shaped massif with a landscape of sharp peaks, narrow, boulder-covered crests and tarns filled with natural glacial lakes. British walkers will find a scene that, in its highest parts above the tree line, contains outlines reminiscent of the Cuillins or the Mamores, much increased in scale. Certainly the mountain walker who enjoys peak-bagging, combined with exciting, ridge-top routes and challenging summits (a very few with a small amount of clambering) will find much to delight them in the Retezat – possibly more so than the Făgăraş. The itinerary consists firstly of a one-off north-south approach to the Retezat across the western Vâlcan; the principal itinerary is of an east-to-west traverse along the top of the Vâlcan and over the Jiu-Cerna pass into the Retezat, followed by a traverse across the central Retezat from Buta in the south-east to Gura Zlata in the west. Whilst walking in the Retezat valleys, with their lakes, pinewoods and expanses of crag and rubble, I have often been reminded of the scenery to be found in the Jasper–Banff–Lake Louise area of the Canadian Rockies. The high ridges themselves above the tree-line are a delight, with well-waymarked paths, mainly over areas of shattered, lichen-covered boulders.

Topography and geology

The geology of the central Retezat is entirely igneous, much of the rock rich in glistening mica. South of the Lăpuşnic valley the ridge over which the itinerary below approaches the Retezat is of limestone. This is the eastern end of the Godeanu ridge, stretching away to the south-west (and offering a superb waymarked route of about two days to the delightful old spa of Băile Herculane). The highest peak in the Retezat, Peleaga (2509m, 8232ft) is only just exceeded by Negoiu and Moldoveanu in the Făgăraş. The Retezat has the greatest concentration of post-glacial lakes in Romania, around a hundred, the number fluctuating because some of them appear and disappear mysteriously. The largest post-glacial lake in the country is here, Bucura, with an area of 8.86 hectares. Below the tree line are great forests, mainly of Norway spruce, also beech, birch and others. A unique feature of the Retezat is the wealth of boulder-fields, both high on ridges above the tree line and on the forest floor in some valleys on the north (eg. around Pietrele); these can make the going unexpectedly slow. In contrast to many other areas of the Carpathians, the Retezat is not just one simple ridge route but a block-shaped massif, offering a wide choice of routes; most of these are best tackled as day walks from a base. If you are using cabanas, the best way to do this is to spend a few days at both Buta and Pietrele (or Genţiana, which effectively operates as a cabana rather than merely a refuge). If you are carrying a tent you have a fantastic choice of glorious sites to pitch your tent (but illicitly – see in the following paragraph). Apart from the main Pietrele–Buta axis the Retezat is relatively little visited. The itinerary below describes a route connecting with the finish of the Parâng traverse, starting by heading up across the Vâlcan from east to west, then heading north into the Retezat, crossing the head of the Jiu de Vest valley. The logical conclusion to a traverse of the Retezat from the south or east would be to head away along the marked route south-west along the crest of the Godeanu ridge towards Băile Herculane (broadly described below) and so to the Almăj.

The Retezat National Park

The Retezat National Park covers most of the range and was the first created in Romania in the 1930s. The western part of the National Park, to the south-east of Gura Zlata cabana is a strictly protected core area known as the Gemene reserve – a stretch of alpine mountain habitat and lower forests that is of international importance. It protects an area of high alpine terrain as well as the forests of the valleys of Dobrunu, Cârligu and Cioaca Radeşului. Walkers are not allowed in this area, clearly shown on maps and with 'no entry' symbols painted on rocks and trees and its uphill boundary, running south along the ridge from Vf. Retezat, over Vf. Bucuraa and south-west along the ridge to Vf. Zănoaga; the area west and north of this ridge is a forbidden area. The prime factor in the creation of this reserve was the endemic flora to be found there. It is also an important habitat for the fauna of the Carpathians, including brown bear, wolf, boar, stone marten, chamois, lynx and more. The regulations of the Retezat National Park (not just the Gemenele reserve) forbid camping, largely because local hikers tend to set up base camps and stay for several days, all too often leaving quantities of litter when they depart. When not leading parties in the area, my walks have been lightweight backpacking expeditions, erecting my leaf-green tent in the dusk in an out-of-the-way spot and walking on early in the morning. Camping is permitted at specific locations; these are Pietrele cabana, Genţiana refuge, Poiana Pelegii, above Buta cabana, Gura Zlata, Râuşor cabana, Lunca Berhina, Câmpuşel and Stâna din Râu. Naturally these tend to be busy and in August may be crowded.

THE VÂLCAN MASSIF

The east–west ridge of the Vâlcan is 55km (34 miles) long and forms the southern side of the Jiu valley. To the south a number of rivers drain through the forests toward the basin of Târgu Jiu and the lake at Rovinari. The most notable of these is the Sohodol, with its limestone gorge and a number of caves, Gârla Vacii ('Cows' Pond'), Pârleazul ('Streamlet'), Peştera cu Lilieci ('Bats' Cave'), Tunelu, Nările ('Nostrils'). The DN672C road heads up the Sohodol gorge, past the cabana (see Appendix A) at its northern end and on through more limestone gorges, the Pătrunşa and Bulzul, up to the Dâlma Căzuţa pass (1152m, 3780ft), before descending to Valea de Peşti (small hotel – see Appendix A). In the east the Jiu gorge divides the Vâlcan from the Parâng. There are three spectacular sections of the Vâlcan ridge, these being, from east to west, the area of the summits of Straja, Sigleu and Oslea. The last, the highest at 1946m (6384ft), is reminiscent of a miniature Piatra Craiului without the trees. From either of the eastern summits there are wonderful views of the Retezat

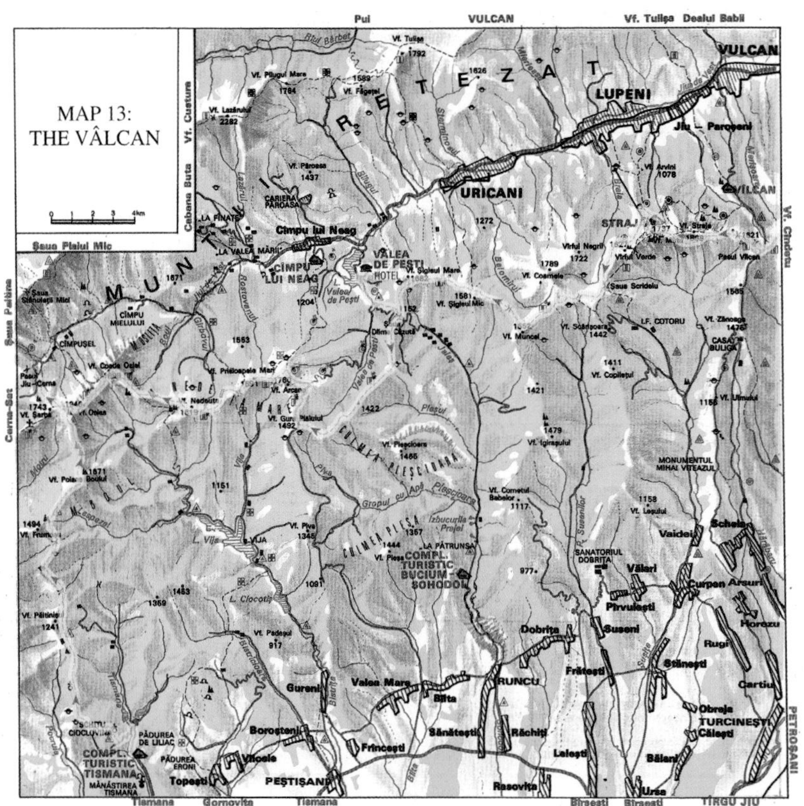

and Parâng mountains and across Ţara Gorjului ('the Gorj Land') to the south.

Access

The easiest access to the Vâlcan is from the north and west, arriving at Petroşani station and taking one the very frequent maxi-taxi minibuses from the road above the east side of the station to Uricani in the heavily-mined Jiu de Vest valley and head south from the town. However it makes more sense, whether walking from Cabana Rusu at the end of the Parâng traverse or arriving specifically in Petroşani to start walking in the Vâlcan and Retezat to begin a traverse of the Vâlcan from the eastern end. You can walk the 5km to the start point of the Vâlcan traverse, at Motel Gambrinus from Petroşani station. However there is a halt nearby, at Livezeni, served by a number of personal trains running between Târgu Jiu and Petroşani. From Motel Gambrinus, at the confluence of the Jiu and Jiu de Vest valleys, the well marked red stripe main ridge route climbs steadily southwards to the western end of the ridge.

The Vâlcan is not easy to reach from the south, where a number of long valleys drain towards Rovinari, or the west, where the Vâlcan ridge becomes the remote, scenic and very rewarding Mehedinţi hills. There is a route all the way to the south-western end of the Mehedinţi, above Băile Herculane. However one of the most rewarding walks is to head north across the western end of the Vâlcan from the monastery at Tismana; this is only for self-contained backpackers as there is no cabana. The walk makes an excellent approach to the Retezat. It is described in detail below.

The itinerary below connects with the finish of the last chapter, descending from Cabana Rusu to Petroşani. From the southern end of Petroşani the path heads due west up the Vâlcan ridge, dominating the valley of the Jiu de Vest and Vulcan, Lupeni and Uricani – coalmining towns all. There are fine views back to the Parâng and to the Retezat massif itself, lying to the north of the Vâlcan across the Jiu de Vest valley. The route described descends for a night halt at Câmpuşel, for this was the way I had to research it. However I strongly recommend this as a camping route and that you keep high, west along the Vâlcan, over Oslea and so to Jiu-Cerna Pass and into the Retezat. I start with a description of a fine north-south traverse of the western Vâlcan as a separate route.

The Western Vâlcan

Tismana to Jiu-Cerna pass, Câmpuşel, approx. 20km (13 miles)

This is an excellent long day's north–south traverse from Tismana Monastery across the western end of the Vâlcan, with views across scenery I found strongly reminiscent of the Cévennes. I describe it separately from the main route because it is an excellent walk in its own right and the best possible approach to the Retezat from the fine monastery at Tismana. In mid-summer this walk (along a path more for communication than recreation) is wonderfully well supplied with wild fruit – raspberries, strawberries and more. There are a few shepherds' huts and shelters along the way. About the only water point is the stream that rises immediately east of Vf. Frumosu (1494m, 4902ft), just after the path leaves the conifers.

Head north, up the road from the village and monastery at Tismana, past the hotel on the left. The road forks; keep left, past a tunnel into the rock on your left. The road twists up through the trees; after 2km you find yourself at a right hand hairpin around a spur with a wide gravel patch on the left of the road. A well made stepped footpath turns right off the road and heads up through the beech trees across weathered granite. You climb into the beechwoods along the spur, past a wayside shrine and bench; half an hour's uphill pull brings you to Schitul Cioclovina de Jos (450m, 1476ft), a white-painted wooden church in a steep clearing in the woods. There is a spirit of place here missing from the more famous and visited Tismana. If the chapel is closed a nun usually appears to let you in; there is a collection box inside the chapel.

The 1km of walking from the chapel itself is the only stretch where you will encounter any navigation problems. From your approach to the monastery you leave by turning left, past a dog kennel, at the time of my visit home to a vicious little cur. You re-enter the trees and immediately come to a second clearing on the left. The path forks; keep left (the right-hand version goes up to Cioclovina de Sus, a square stone, chapel on a knoll, about 75mins return walk); your path contours through the trees along the steep hillside up to your right. After less than 1km you exit from under the trees onto an old forest track with views to the west. Turn right to head north; after almost 1km you find yourself in a grassy clearing; the path leaves at the far end, into the woods.

From Cioclovina saddle (820m, 2690ft) you continue north along a ridge between the Pocruia and Tismana rivers.

Whilst the path is not as well waymarked with red triangles as it should be (look for blue borderless triangles or faded pink triangles with blue borders), it is easy to follow, past the rocks at Piatra Taiata and skirting the grassy summit of Vf. Păltinișului (1241m, 4071ft) to the east. You descend in the trees to Pojorița pass (1100m, 3609ft) and then the path skirts the grassy summit of Vârful Frumos (1494m, 4902ft with a wooden survey marker on top) rising above the spruce trees to the east; there is a diversion over the summit following the well-marked wheel-tracks across the grass. From here your route lies across open upland grazing and over the western end of the crags on Vârful Poiana Boului ridge (1671m, 5482ft). Vf. Boului is a prominent rounded summit with some exposed rock; the path goes back into mature beech forest before finally emerging again as you approach the western end of the craggy Oslea ridge (1945m, 6381ft). The final piece of ascent for the day, to the path junction at La Suliți pass (1703m, 5587ft) is hard (though well marked), but the reward of the views of the Retezat in front of you and the descent to the Jiu-Cerna pass are great. There is an excellent walk on into the Retezat proper, up to Cabana Buta – 16km (10 miles), altitude gained from Câmpusel to Piatra Iorgovanului, 834m (2736ft). The path (red disc waymarks) on up to Buta via Piatra Iorgovanului heads north up the Soarbete valley, from the road 1.5km west of Câmpușel.

The Vâlcan Traverse

Day One

Petroșani: Motel Gambrinus or Cabana Rusu to Straja cabana, 20km (13 miles). Altitude gained from Gambrinus to Straja summit, 1423m (4668ft)

This route (from east to west) is a continuation of the Parâng traverse, finishing at Cabana Rusu. The path you need from Rusu is the one heading south-west and then west, down the Sălătruc valley to Livezeni. Motel Gambrinus overlooks the main DN66 road just south of the junction with the DN66A to Vulcan. The red stripe route is marked from the motel car park, heading up through young birch trees and taking you up the Cândețu valley, finally emerging out of the forests just before the summit of Cândețu (1548m, 5078ft).

Head south–east from the summit for about 500m to a col, and turn right to follow the path for 1km along the south side of the main Vâlcan ridge, keeping above the forest until the path regains the main ridge by some exposed rock. The summit of Vâlcan, or Dragoiu (1690m, 5544ft), is skirted to the north and you descend for 1km to meet a cart track which you follow south-west along the ridge for 1.5km, joining the rough road from Schela to Vulcan just before Vâlcan pass (1621m, 5318ft). You can if you wish finish the day at Vâlcan cabana – turn right and walk 3km north along the road. To reach Straja cabana turn right off the Schela-Vulcan road at the pass to head north-west. After 1.5km following the red stripe route along the main Vâlcan ridge you reach Diul saddle (1540m, 5052ft). Here you turn right (an alternative route keeps to the northern side of the ridge passing to the left of this, the highest summit of the Vâlcan), following the blue triangle route to the summit of Straja (also known as Străjii, 1868m, 6128ft), with fine views north to the Retezat and east to the Parâng. The path descends west from the summit and then zigags down to Straja cabana (1445m, 4740ft), 2km from the summit. The cabana is north of the main spine, at the head of the ski-lift from Lupeni.

Day Two

Straja cabana to Valea de Pești over Sigleul summit, 22km (14 miles). Altitude gained from Straja cabana to Sigleul Mare, 237m (776ft)

From the cabana head north-west (blue triangle waymarks) through the trees for 1km to the Braia shepherds' huts near the viewpoint of Vf. Constantinescu, on a spur on the northern side of the main Vâlcan ridge. Turn sharp left here to head south towards Vf. Mutu ('Dumb Peak', 1737m, 5700ft); the path keeps well to the north of the summit and rejoins the main ridge route at Șaua Prislop (1550m, 5085ft). From the pass the red stripe route heads south-west, past a spring on the north side of the ridge (Izvoru Rece) and continues south-west well below the main ridge and the summit of Vf Verde (1627m, 5338ft) for 2km to Șaua Scrideiu, where the blue triangle route heads left, down to the forest huts at Cotoru and descending from the Vâlcan along the Șușița valley (there is also a route along the top of the Scărișoara ridge to the village of Curpen).

As you make your way south-west along the ridge from Șaua Scrideiu, the ridge and its path swings right, to head west, towards the summit of Coarnele (1789m, 5869ft). Once again, the path keeps well to the southern side and even crosses two streams just above the tree line as you make your way around the head of the Susenilor valley. Keep along the main Vâlcan ridge to Vârful Muncel (1553m, 5095ft). On the northern side of the summit the path swings right, north into the trees, descending along the ridge among the trees to Șaua Girloabele, 1km north-west of Muncel. Continue north-west, ascending, leaving the forest behind as you approach Sigleul Mic (1581m, 5187ft), the path skirting the summit to the north and following the main ridge north-west, keeping to the south side of Sigleul Mare (1682m, 5518ft). The path now turns left and descends due south past some shepherds' huts for 1km to reach the road from Runcu to Câmpu lui Neag at the Șaua Dâlma Câzuță pass (1152m, 3779ft). Turn right to reach the lake and hotel at Valea de Pești (alt. 910m, 2986ft), approx. 5km along the road. Alternatively, if you have camping equipment, the ridge-top continuation east on to Oslea is highly recommended.

Day Three

The Western Vâlcan and Oslea: Valea de Pești to Cabana Buta. Altitude gained from Valea de Pești to Vârful Oslea, 1036m (3400ft)

From Șaua Dâlma Câzută ('Fallen Hillock') pass head south-west (red stripe waymarks) through the forest, heading up to the minor summit of Vf. Custurea (1310m, 4298ft) in a small clearing. The path keeps to the left of the summit and heads south, along the ridge to Măcrișu (1422m), a wooded summit, and descends for 500m to a shepherds' hut (Poiana Stevioara), 2km from Șaua Dâlma Câzuță. Turn right here, to head south-west, along the ridge mostly in the forest to meet the rough road just south of Gura Plaiului summit (1492m, 4895ft).

At Gura Plaiului you turn right along the forest road towards Arcanu summit (1760m, 5774ft), the forest road skirting the summit to the east. The path contours along the north side of the ridge so that the summit of Arcanu – a good viewpoint with the Retezat to the north and the sharp Oslea ridge to the west – is above you to your left. A few minutes after Arcanu you come to a route heading off to the right, north-east down to Câmpu lui Neag. Keep left here to follow the twisting Nedeuța ridge, due west, to the summit of Prisloapele Mari (1591m, 5220ft). From the summit the path descends south-west to a col where you cross the red cross route running from north to south and connecting the Gârbovul and Vila valleys

Keeping above the trees, the path heads along the ridge to keep to the south of the summit of Nedeuţa (1619m, 5321ft), with its attendant crags to the west. 2km west of Nedeuţa summit you meet the red triangle path coming up from the left, from Vija lake and the Bistriţa valley. You begin the steep climb up towards the summit of Coada Oslei (1899m, 6230ft). 3km below you, north-west, is the logging settlement of Câmpuşel (1180m, 3871ft), reached by the path following the red triangles. Continue along the Vâlcan ridge (red stripe waymarks) south-west to Oslea summit (1946m, 6384ft). 1km west of the summit brings you to a path junction at a col – La Suliţi ('Spears') pass (1703m, 5587ft). Ahead, the path (red stripe waymarks) continues along the ridge of the Mehedenţi. Turn right here (red cross and blue triangle waymarks) north, down towards the unsurfaced road in the Jiu de Vest valley, this section being called the Scocol Jiului. There is no cabana but a good spot to camp near a kind of roadside picnic shelter. Rough though it is, this road connects the Jiu valley with the west. It can be followed all the way to Cerna-Sat village (and cabana) and 50km more to Băile Herculane.

From La Suliţi pass between the summits of Şarba and Oslea there is an exit route to the south (well established and easy to follow) to Cioclovina hermitage and Tismana monastery (described in reverse above).

THE RETEZAT

Access

If travelling specifically to Retezat, the best access is from the corridor of communication from Târgu Jiu to Deva, in the section between Petroşani and Haţeg. If travelling to the area by rail from Bucharest, trains to Petroşani go via Craiova and Caracal. There are five a day and the journey takes about three and a half hours. You will have to change either in Craiova or Târgu Jiu. There is also the branch line up the Jiu de Vest valley, terminating at Lupeni. This applies if you wish to approach the Retezat from the south, aiming for Cabana Buta. (In fact it is an easier journey from Bucharest to Pui station on the east of the massif, three hours' walk from Cabana Baleia, but you will have a long walk to the central Retezat along the waterless Culmea Lansitiu ridge – see below.)

If you arrive in Petroşani by train, head east over the footbridge and turn right on the road to catch a minibus to Uricani, from where you will probably have to thumb or walk 14km further up the valley to Câmpu lui Neag (the cabana now defunct). From here walk on to Buta along the well signed track up from the new cabanas at Cheile Buta (Buta Gorge). An alternative, if approaching the region from Wallachia, would be to take the train from Craiova to Motru and catch a lift or a bus up the Motru valley in the direction of Baia de Arama to Tismana, and walk north from there, described in detail below.

Two railway lines give access to the Retezat from the north; the main Petroşani–Simeria line via Subcetate Junction (6km, 4 miles, east of Haţeg) and the branch line east from Caransebeş to the terminus at Boutari (Băuţar), the latter with three (slow) trains per day. This latter route (east from Caransebeş) really only makes sense if you are approaching the Retezat from the west and are happy to spend a day walking east over the Ţarcu. The best access straight into the Retezat is by alighting at Pui (five trains each way per day on the Petroşani–Simeria line), some 22km (14 miles) from Baleia cabana – you may get a bus or a lift 8km (5 miles) to Hobiţa. It is possible to catch a through train from Simeria, on the busy Braşov–Arad line, with good connections from Budapest. If travelling direct to the Retezat it is effectively impossible in one day via the line south of the Carpathians; probably the best bet is to catch the evening sleeper to Arad (normally departing at about 2200hrs) and change in Simeria onto a stopper to Pui (about 80 mins).

An equally good start point is Ohaba de Sub Piatra, between Pui and Subcetate junction. From the railway halt make your way down the dirt road south to the main DN66, cross over and head south-west along the tarred road 2km to Salașu de Jos and on to Salașu de Sus (2km), Mălăiești (3km), and finally Nucșoara (4km). Continue south-west through the village; the road turns to a gravel surface and heads up the Nucșorul valley to cross the river on a high concrete bridge and heading south, up to Cabana Cascada and on to Pietrele cabana (see Appendix A).

From Pui, head south-east on the DN66 for 1km and turn right (DJ667 to Baleia) on to the unsurfaced road. You pass through Râu Barbat, 3km from the road junction and continue 5km to Hobița. Turn right in the middle of the village (a rusty walkers' sign behind a lamppost pointing the way) and walk 15km (9 miles) up the rough track to Baleia. It is also possible to head into the Retezat from Băile Herculane, spending two or three days walking the Cerna ridge and then the Godeanu.

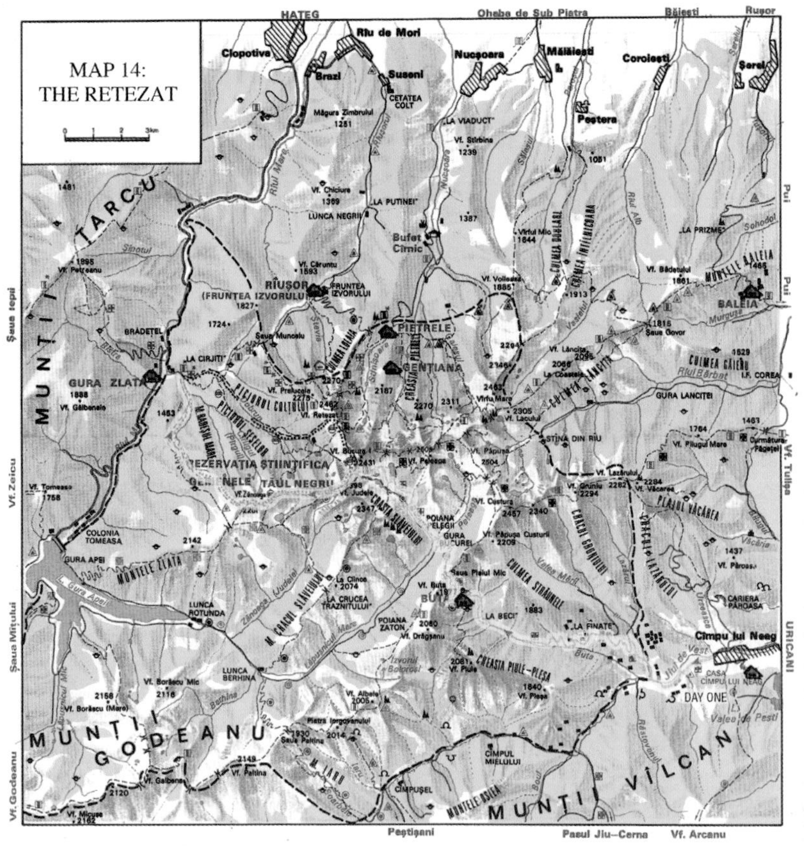

The main Retezat ridge

Day One

Câmpu lui Neag to Cabana Buta, 13km (7 miles). Altitude gained from Câmpul lui Neag to Buta cabana, 755m (2500ft)

This is an approach into the Retezat massif for those arriving in the area by bus from the railway station in Petroșani. The journey takes you past a number of coal mines, the last being an opencast pit at Câmpu lui Neag. From the bus stop in the town head west along the road up the Jiul de Vest valley. 3km after the town you meet the track coming down from the Marii valley on the right, signed 'drum forestier', leading up to Buta cabana. Ignore this and keep heading up the valley, past a sawmill on the left and an alimentara forestieră shop to a small dam on the left. Here the road forks, the left-hand fork going immediately over a bridge; there is a rusty walkers' signpost almost hidden in the foliage. Turn right here (Gura Butei) along a track to two new private cabanas (built summer 1994). Continue up the track for a few more yards to a small dam by the entrance to Cheile Butei gorge. Turn right (red cross waymarks) up into the woods with some very steep climbing to bring you to the large grassy clearing and La Fânețe huts. You reach the drum forestieră heading up to Buta cabana and turn left along it, largely in trees, along the Buta valley. After more than an hour walking along the forest track in the trees you reach the noticeboard about the National Park and picnic site at Lupeni (now red cross and blue stripe waymarks), bringing you through the Douglas fir reserve. There are views above the trees of the limestone 'cathedrals' of Piule (2081m, 6827ft) and Pleșa (1840m, 6037ft) summits high up to the left. The forest track dwindles and becomes steeper, heading straight up the slope. Buta looks across to the Străunele spur and is well run by its helpful cabanier, Bela. It was immediately rebuilt follwing destruction by fire in the late nineties. It is a good spot for birdlife, with tame crossbills feeding around the tables. The highest cabana in the range, Buta is the best base to explore the Retezat, with the highest peaks in the heart of the massif all climbable in a

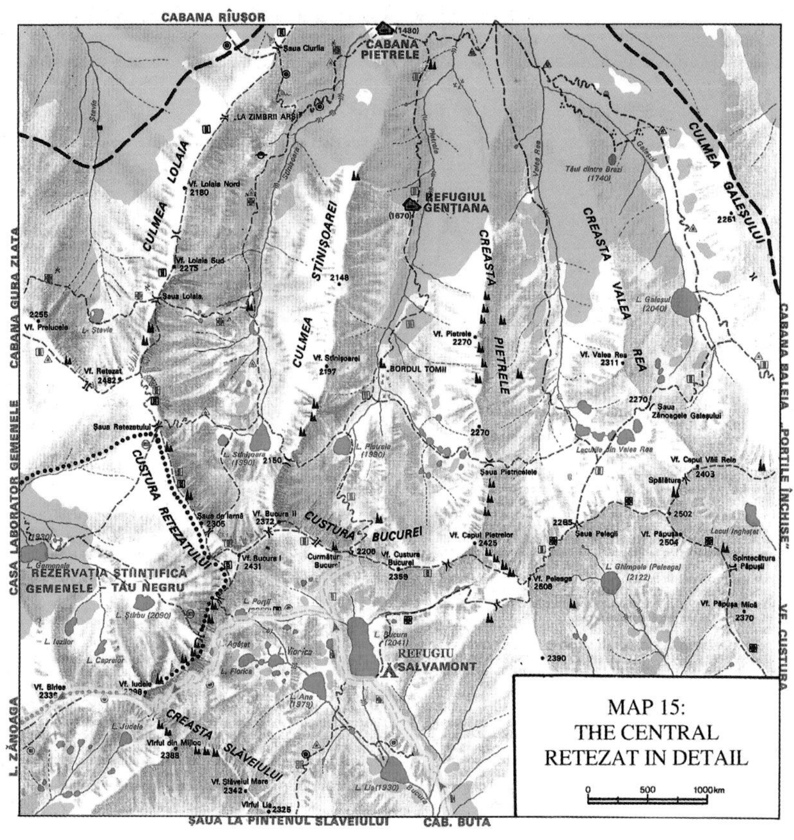

MAP 15: THE CENTRAL RETEZAT IN DETAIL

day's excursion – though to do all in the same day would be a considerable feat!

Day Two

Buta to Gura Zlata cabana, 22km (13½ miles). Altitude gained to Şaua Plaiul Mic 300m (984ft); from Poiana Pelegii to Vârfu Judele, 848m (2782ft); lost from Judele to Gura Zlata, 1623m (5325ft)

This is an itinerary that connects the two cabanas without going over the major peaks of Bucura and Retezat. The paths over these are well waymarked and well walked; you simply divert from the route described by continuing from Bucura lake up to Curmătura Bucurei and turning left to head west, steeply the north side of the ridge to Bucura, then continuing north-west along the Custura Retezatului ridge, over Şaua de Iarna pass, then Şaua Retezatului (2251m, 7385ft), up to the survey marker in the boulder-field on Vârful Retezat, thence along the Prelucele ridge, then left, down Muncelu to Gura Zlata.

In fact Gura Zlata marks something of a diversion away from the Retezat. If you have a tent, you will certainly want to vary this itinerary by camping closer in to the heart of the Retezat. You are not supposed to enter the Gemenele nature reserve, still less camp in it. There are a number of attractrive sites for camping outside its boundaries. Alternatively you can stay higher by heading north from the Bucura area in the heart of the massif to spend the night at Pietrele; see below for a suggested exit route from Pietrele to Baleia. Pietrele makes the perfect base for a fine day walk and scramble up the Stânişoara valley and over the Culmea Lolaia ridge from Şaua Ciulea to Şaua Lolaia, returning either along the ridge or back down the Stânişoara valley.

From the cabana head up the rough track at the back and turn right before crossing the stream to follow the variously waymarked path up out of the trees, latterly steeply up through a rocky gully to Şaua Plaiu Mic pass (1879m, 6165ft). Descend to the north from here, down into the Peleaga valley at a camping area and hut at Gura Bucurei, the confluence of the Bucura and Peleaga streams and the end of the rough forest road going down the glacial Lăpuşnic valley to Lunca Berhina and the lake at Gura Apei. Head upstream, north-west along the Bucura stream (red cross waymarks) through the Spruce trees towards the glacial tarns at the head of the valley. Near Lia lake you are joined by a path from the left, dropping down off the high crags of the Creasta Slăveielui ridge. Keep heading north towards the head of the valley (see Map 15); when you reach the moraine damming Bucura lake, bear left and follow the path round to the west of the lake, heading north. To the right of the lake the yellow cross route climbs up to Vârful Peleaga (2508m, 8228ft), passing the Tabără Mobilă Salvamont shelter on the eastern shore. This is a much-used campsite – a fine spot, or it least it would be without the ubiquitous tin cans (in usual Romanian style, there are signs around forbidding camping).

Near the northern end of the lake you see the very well walked blue stripe path continuing north to Curmătura Bucura pass (2206m, 7237ft). Turn left here to take instead the yellow stripe and red disc path heading west across the grass and crossing a number of springs. You pass several small pools and climb steeply before reaching Porţii lake (2260m, 7715ft). The screes plunging to the north shore of the lake give a fine echo; this a beautiful lake, one of my favourites in the Retezat. Ahead and above you is the craggy summit of Judele with a rocky pinnacle immediately south. On the western shore of the take lake a path (yellow stripes) going very steeply up towards a col just west of Vf. Bucura I (2433m, 7982ft). Keep left, leaving the blue stripe waymarks and head south-west (red disc waymarks) to the tiny Agăţat lake (2208m, 7244ft), beneath Poarta Bucura passes. The path continues twisting south-west, up to Judele pass (2370m, 7775ft) on the craggy Creasta Slăveiului ridge, just north of Mijloc summit (2388m, 7834ft). Although the detail map does not mark it, there is a route, heading left, south-east along the Creasta Slăveiului ridge, taking you over the crags of Slăveiul (2342m, 7684ft), Vârful Lie (2325ft, 7628ft) and down to Pintenul Slăveiului saddle (2235m, 7333ft), just to the south of the detail map. You can turn left here to descend back to Bucura lake.

Turn left at Judele pass, away from Vârful Judele (2398m, 7867ft), a diversion leading to the right, to the summit. You now join the main Retezat ridge (here the Muchia Ascuţită – the 'Sharp Ridge') heading west, the path spending most of the time on the left hand side of the ridge, past Bârlea summit (2338m, 7671ft) to a col before Vf. Şesele (2278m, 7474ft). The path now tends more firmly to the south side of this west-pointing spur, away from the heart of the Retezat. Towards Zănoaga lake, in a grassy bowl (an attractive but illicit camping spot) below Zănoaga summit (2261m, 7418ft) the main waymarked route drops right off the ridge and then

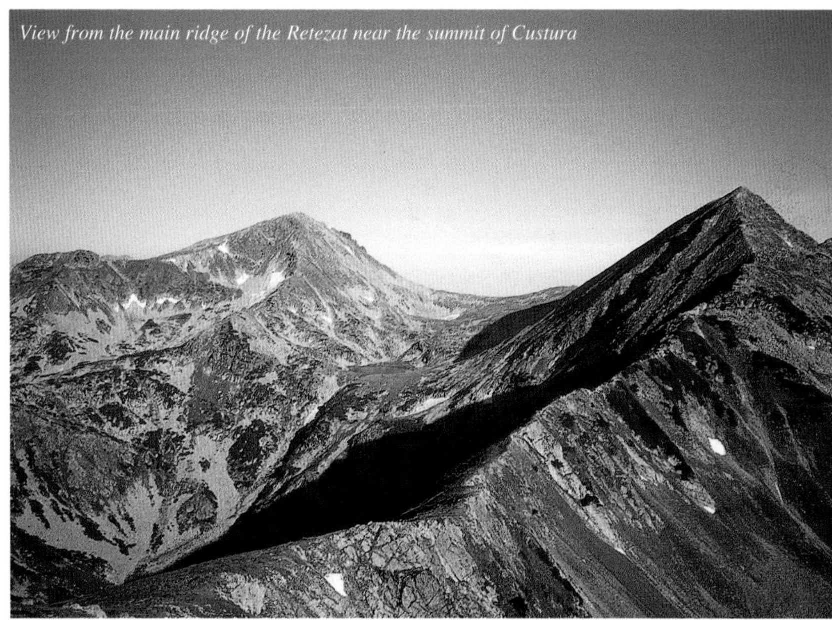
View from the main ridge of the Retezat near the summit of Custura

regains it on its western side. There is an alternative route along the crest of the ridge, over Şesele Mic, rejoining the main route 1km west of the lake. Once the ascent is complete west of the lake you find yourself heading due west across a grassy plateau with many springs – the Radeş-Zlata plateau; 2km west of the lake you reach a path junction at a broad grassy saddle. To the west the blue cross route, well marked with bus-stop signs, goes just south of the summit of Zlata (2142m, 7027ft, reminiscent of Dartmoor) and ends up at the track on the shore of Gura Apei lake.

Turn right here (red stripe waymarks) north-west to the shepherds' hut on the spur at Radeş (marked but not named on the map). The path then zigzags steeply down into the forest with the Radeşul Mare ridge on the right. From the Radeş hut you have 2hrs of very steep descent in the forest; the path twists and turns but tends generally northwards and is well trodden (red stripes and the occasional red triangle waymarks). You cross the Mareş stream in the woods and eventually you come to the confluence of the Dobrun stream and the Radeş, along whose valley runs a rough forest road. The spot 'La Cîrjiţe' on the map is a collection of foresters' huts. Walk down the road to the main road in the Râul Mare valley adjacent to Gura Zlata cabana (see Appendix A).

At the head of the road is Colonia Tomeasa, near the dam holding back Gura Apei lake – an environmental disaster on a horrific scale. It is possible to exit from the range by making a long day walk, heading up the road past the lake, then turning right on a path taking you due west to the summit of Ţarcu (2190m, 7185ft), from where the path turns to the north, descending to the mountain resort of Muntele Mic, reached by road from Caransebeş (station on the main Timişoara to Turnu–Severin line).

Exit from the Retezat: Şaua Paltina to Băile Herculane – the Godeanu Traverse (about 65km, 40 miles)

Şaua Paltina marks the junction of the Godeanu massif with the Retezat; it lies 10km (6 miles) south-west along the Drăgşanu ridge from Şaua Plaiu Mic. From Şaua Paltina (1930m, 6332ft) head west along the ridge, passing just north of Vf. Paltina (2149m, 7050ft). Still keeping to the north side of the ridge the path heads west and then south-west to a col, then just north of the summit of Scurtu (2090m, 6857ft), then descends south-west for 1km to a col; just after this col a path heads south, down to the Cernei valley. The main red stripe route heads north-west and then drops into the head of the Galbenu de Sud valley, on the north side of the Godeanu ridge, before making its way back onto the main ridge just over 1km east of Vârful Galbena (2194m, 7198ft). This summit, too, is skirted to the north, as is Borăscu Mic, 1.5km west. On the west side of this the path swings south-west to a col where you have the choice of keeping left on the main ridge, over Micuşa (2162m, 7093ft) or heading due west, down into the Micuşa Valley to rejoin the main ridge immediately east of Scărişoara (2210m, 7250ft).

The red stripe route now tends to the south side of the ridge, taking you past Vârful Bulzului (2245m); 1km west of here is a path junction on a broad col, where you need to head north-west past Vârfu Moraru (2284m, 7493ft) and west along the ridge for 7km (4 miles) to Vârful Godeanu (2229m, 7313ft), thence south-west to Vârful Olanelor (1990m, 6529ft) and Vârful Dobrii (1928m, 6325ft), altogether some 30km (19 miles) south-west of Vârful Paltina. The ridge now swings to the south as it becomes the Cerna, over the summit of Baldoveni (1800m, 5905ft), then Vlascul Mic (1733m, 5686ft), Arjana (1512m, 4961ft) and eventually south-west to the charming spa town of Băile Herculane. A tempting alternative is to head west from Baldoveni, down to Camena village then across country via Cozia and Obiţa in to the Pârâul Rece valley to Rusca and west to the village of Teregova where you pick up the blue disc waymarks into the Semenic, onto the eastern edge of Map 16.

THE TARCU MASSIF

The Ţarcu (often combined with the associated Muntele Mic to be called the Mic-Ţarcu) is a block of mountains shaped like a right-angle triangle; on the northern side runs the Bistra valley, on the western side the Timiş and to the south-east the Rece valley and the Râul Mare valley separate the Ţarcu from the Godeanu and the Retezat respectively. The Ţarcu is reminiscent in shape of the Brecon Beacons in Wales, without any major crags. It offers a worthwhile approach or exit route for a very long day to or from the Retezat. An interesting variation of this is to start or finish at the Dacian-Roman archaeological site of Ulpia Traian at Sarmizegetusa on the north of the massif.

The easiest point of access is the town of Caransebeş, on the main Timişoara–Bucharest railway line; at least three through trains from Bucharest stop per day; they take around 7hrs to cover the 435km (270 miles). Buses go up to Muntele Mic resort (see Appendix A).

The Ţarcu Traverse from Gura Zlata cabana to Muntele Mic is approximately 42km (26 miles); accommodation is available part-way at Cabana Prietenii Munţilor. There is a hefty climb from Gura Zlata to Vf. Petreanu of 1140m, 3740ft. Start by heading north along the road down the Râul Mare valley from Gura Zlata and turn left after less than 1km along a forest track taking you up the Valea Mare in the forest to the shepherds' huts at Părăginosu and finally out

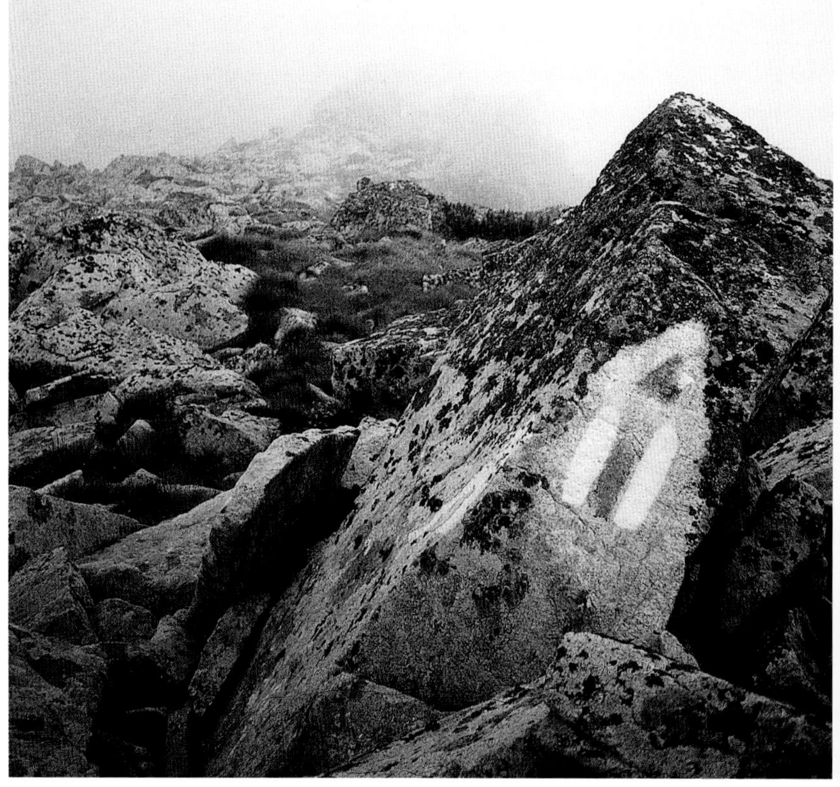

In fog the efficient waymarking is appreciated, especially where the path becomes ill-defined across scree of lichen-covered boulders as here in the Retezat

of the forest at Poiana Idovanu, then north-west along a spur to the summit of Petreanu (1895m, 6217ft). From here it is a relatively straightforward walk south-west along the grassy ridge just above the forest, over the summits of Bistra (2153m, 7064ft), then Vf. Pietrii and Bloja – both summits having excellent views of the Retezat. 3km south of Vf. Bloju you reach Șaua Iepii (1727m, 5666ft); continue south-west along the Baicu ridge over the summit of Nedeia and on, south-west to Vf. Țarcu, from where the red stripe route heads east-north-east down to Prietenii Munților cabana and then along a ridge in the forest north to Muntele Mic ski resort.

CHAPTER NINE

The Mountains of Banat

This chapter deals with the extreme western part of the Southern Carpathians, west of the Timiş Corridor, carrying the international railway line and DN6/E70 road from Orşova to Caransebeş. It consists of the Semenic, Anina, Locva and Almăj ranges. The Southern Carpathians reach their westernmost extremity in the latter range, where the Danube forces its way through a natural barrier before making its way to the Black Sea. I have also included brief coverage of walks available from the delightful eighteenth-century small spa of Băile Herculane, clustering in the bottom of the Cerna gorge.

The flavour of the area is almost more Balkan than Carpathian, facing across the Danube to Vojvodina, the province of the former Yugoslavia, and with a markedly milder climate than the Carpathians further east. The whole area – the highlands of the Banat – is a remote corner of Romania, cut off by the looping Danube, forcing its way through the Balkan S-bend. These are low but craggy mountains, offering challenging walking when the higher main ranges are closed by snow.

It is an area characterised by rolling deciduous forests, largely of oak and beech. It is notable for its caves and gorges; notably the Cheile Nerei (Nera gorge) in the south, also Caraş gorge and the Minişului gorge in the south-west which carries the DN57B road from Iablaniţa and Bozovici to Anina. At the eastern end of Caraş gorge, hidden in the forest, is Peştera Comarnic, where you can take a guided tour through its 400m of calcite crystals, 'cave pearls' and various creations of soluble lime; there are numbers of other caves that are not laid out for organised visits. The town of Reşiţa in the north of the range is Romania's own Swindon, being the home of the country's locomotive building industry. The area traditionally provides a recreation area for the notoriously militant steel workers from the town.

Access

This can best be described as 'difficult'. Reşiţa Sud is on a branch line from the junction at Caransebeş and is altogether usually 8hrs by train from Bucharest, depending on connections. It is quicker to reach the area by train from Belgrade than Bucharest. The old state bus depot, east of the station by the Universal main store, now seems defunct. To find a bus or communal taxi to Caraşova, head south from Reşiţa Sud station, under the town flyover and the overhead coal-conveyor, to the bus shelter on the right. It is possible to travel by bus from Caransebeş, both to Reşiţa and to Caraşova village. If travelling to the area by train, the branch line to the mining town of Anina is spectacular.

ITINERARY

The itinerary below explores the Anina range, rather than the Semenic; what little of the Semenic that lies above the tree line has been developed for skiing and is not especially attractive.

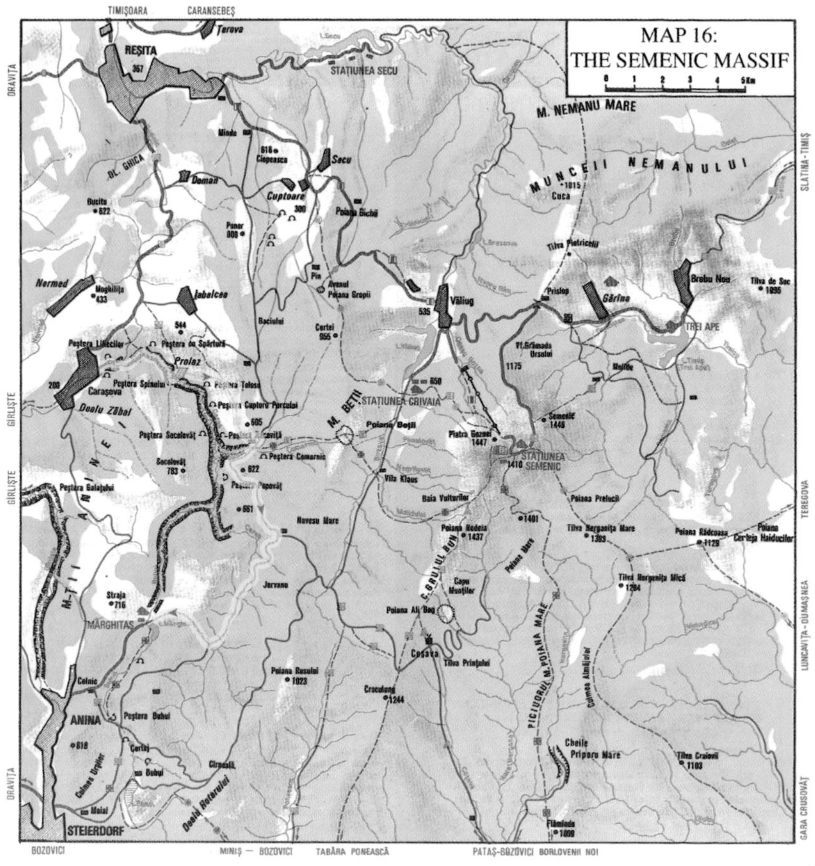

Carașova to Stațiunea Marghitaș, 25km (16 miles)

The approach to Carașova from Reșița is along the winding DN58 road, which skirts the village to the east, crossing over the Caraș river on a viaduct. As you descend towards the village the 'Râu Caraș' is announced. Leave the road here, heading along the south bank of the river (ie. with it below you to your left). There is also a marked path on the north bank but it merely leads to an over-deep ford – I have had numerous such wettings in the course of researching this book. There are a number of flat streamside campsites in the bottom of the gorge; at one point the path takes you through a tiny cutting. After 5km the valley opens out and you turn sharp left, down off the path through the trees to cross the river on two cables. Around you is a scattering of farmsteads known as Prolaz. There is a rudimentary path into the gorge beyond here but it is not recommended; this is the access for a number of caves in the gorge – Peștera de sub Cetate II, Liliecilor, Cuptoru Porcului, Tossu, Socolovat, Spinului, Spartura, Racovita, Popovat and others before reaching the manned cave complex at Comarnic.

To continue onwards to Comarnic, leave the river-bank here and head straight up the slope, past a little green and white farm building towards some fruit trees. You find a sign pointing left, also with blue stripes, to the DN58 road by the Iabalcea turning. Keep right here, perpendicularly up the slope among hazel coppice. This is extremely steep; at the top you exit from trees and keep straight ahead, south-east. The path is well marked with blue stripes on stones and tree trunks.

As you approach a low wall enclosing some cultivated ground bear right, the path descending now between hedges to turn right on a stony farm track, leading to an extensive plum orchard. This is straightforward walking; the path takes you back into the forest, always well waymarked, and descends to the clearing in the valley-bottom at Comarnic; turn right on the forest road. Somewhere an unmarked path turns right off the forest road to head south along the bottom of the Caraş valley but I could find no sign. The walk along the forest track with milestones is pleasant and easy, through clearings. 4km from Comarnic, you reach a tiny col with the Canton Silvic buildings of Navesu on the left. Just ahead you look into a bowl and a clearing; turn right off the track here to take a short cut, down a tussocky slope to rejoin the forest track and follow it to the collection of buildings either side of the track at Jervani.

The path onward from here to Marghitaş is not marked but is easy to follow. Continue south along the track from Jervani, through young trees. Now take care. 400m from the cottage at Jervani you reach a stand of tall spruce on the left as you re-enter the mature forest. Turn right here (a triangle cut into the bark of a tree) and follow the obvious old path angling south-west up the valley side. This swings round to the right so that you are walking almost due north as you exit from the forest to a heathy area. There now follows an easy stretch with no path. Look across to your left to a low ridge above you; bear left to make your way to the top of it, keeping the edge of the forest on your left. Descending due west on the far side of the ridge, go perpendicularly down the slope to find a track with concrete electricity cables exiting from the forest. Turn right and follow this for 1.5km to Staţiunea Marghitaş.

Continuing from Marghitaş, it is possible to avoid Anina (something to be desired) by turning left off the tarred road after 3km on a rough forest road to Peştera Buhui and continuing by turning right after the cave to head south for a further 3km to Motel Diana. Head east from here 1km on the road to the col between Anina and Şteierdorf and follow the road down through Şteierdorf to the road junction 1.5km south-east of the village. From here I have found no problem in obtaining a lift for the further 30km (19 miles) to Bozovici. From here the road heads south along the Nera valley to Şopotu Nou, the entry-point for Nera gorge.

Nera gorge

Nera gorge (Cheile Nerei), longer, deeper and wilder than Caraş, offers a wonderful day walk; accommodation is available at Canton Silvic Valea Bei, reached by rough track north-east from the confluence of the Bei valley with the Nera at the western end of the gorge. Situated amidst a vast area of forested hills, it is an enchanting valley protected as an extensive nature reserve. At various points along the gorge are meadows overlooked by crags. Here isolated farmsteads cultivate plots with horse- and ox-drawn ploughs. The path through the gorge, some 30km (19 miles) long through the intricate winding valley, is occasionally steep and tricky in parts, especially the section north-west of Lacul Dracului. At the western end by Cotul la Cîrlige you have to wade; this is not possible in spring when the water level is high – a further reason to approach the gorge from Șopotu Nou in the east.

Access

If travelling direct to Nera gorge (it is well worth the journey), the nearest rail access is via Oravița, then bus or hitch 30km (19 miles) south to Sasca Romana, the entry point for the western end of the gorge. However, train travel to here, whilst undeniably scenic, takes an interminably long time. Better to take the train to Băile Herculane, then bus or hitch from there along the main road 20km (12 miles) to Iablanița (or personal train) and bus or hitch from there 40km (25 miles) to Bozovici, thence to Șopotu Nou. It is also possible to do a day walk south from Anina (in fact the dwindling satellite village of Șteierdorf), along the Beuș valley to the western end of the gorge.

Walking directions

At the northern end of the village of Șopotu Nou the tarred road through the village crosses the tributary of the Nera on a concrete bridge. A wide rough track heads north from here, with the river on your right; by the bridge is a corroded information board about the gorge. This track takes you straight into the gorge, on the south bank. Past the scattering of farms at Driștie it dwindles drastically, until you begin to think you are on the wrong side of the river; there are no waymarks. Finally, climbing above the river the track finishes in a steep clearing; contour across this and climb slightly to find a good path contouring through the beech forest along the valley. After ten minutes of walking you come to a small clearing with two sheds below on your right. Here small suspension bridge, rather reminiscent of rivers in Nepal, takes you across to a farmstead on the north side, where you continue downstream (the yellow stripe route north through the woods to Izvoru Tisiei departs from behind the farmstead but is hard to find – ask the helpful farmer, Mr Nicolae Crăciun.

Heading west, the gorge now opens out to Poiana Meliugului, an enchanting expanse of meadow with a fine farm below the cliffs. Bear left off the main track here to follow the river-bank to a second bridge over the river. On the far side you turn right in the trees to reach a clearing with fruit trees and a tiny watermill where the Haimeliug stream tumbles out of the forest; this is probably the best site to camp – the last level grassy patch with a water supply. Now take care; cross the stream and bear left, the well worn path zigzagging up into the forest to a junction on a col where you go left to Lacul Dracului ('Devil's Lake'). This out-and-back path goes past a dramatic viewpoint; the lake itself is down by the riverside.

Băile Herculane

Situated in the Cerna gorge, where the river of the same name forces its way south-west, between the Carpathian ridges of the Munții Cernei and the Munții Mehedinti, Băile Herculane has a strong claim to be the most charming spot to stay in the country. The whole area is unrelieved natural forest, all of it deciduous, broken only by high limestone crags. Golden eagles nest nearby and I have seen them soaring over the town. The town is the perfect base for some low-level walking – but nevertheless very steep and challenging. Situated at a low altitude, it particularly rewards an early winter or early spring visit when more elevated areas of the Carpathians are under snow. Walking maps of the area seem to be unavailable; I will describe in detail just one: the out-and-back route to the top of Varful Domogled, together with instructions as to how to leave the town on the many waymarked trails. It is one of the finest areas of Romania for

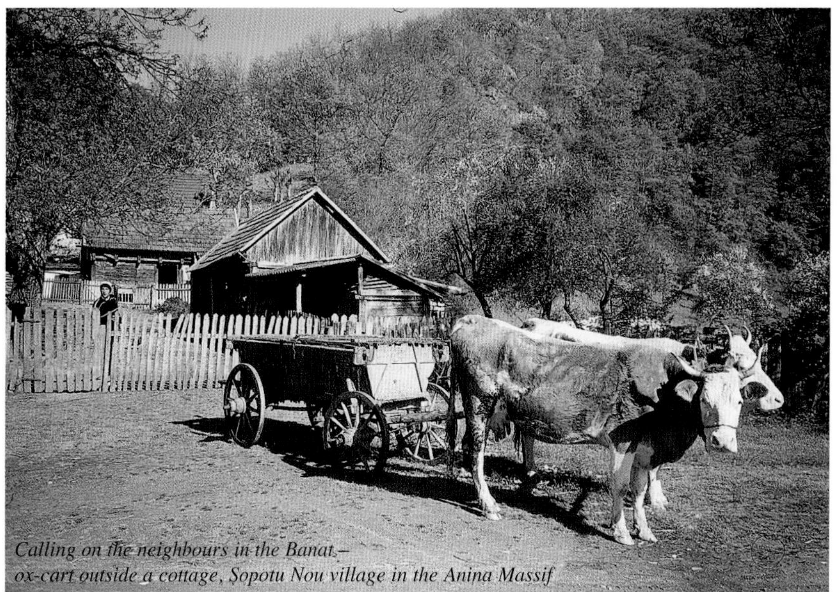

Calling on the neighbours in the Banat – ox-cart outside a cottage, Şopotu Nou village in the Anina Massif

walking, with wonderful scenery and good waymarked trails.

Access

Băile Herculane is 390km (244 miles) by road from Bucharest. By train the journey takes around five hours; there are ten trains per day from Bucharest, the stretch along the Danube being very scenic. The little spa lies 5km east of the main Craiova–Timişoara DN6/E70 road and the station; there are two roads heading up the Cerna valley, a fact apparently not acknowledged by any map. The southerly one is the through-route DN67D road up the Cerna valley; the one that turns exactly opposite the station serves the little town itself, via the modern satellite of Pecinişca.

Băile Herculane to Varful Domogled and back, 1105m (3625ft). 8km round trip. Altitude gained, 945m (3100ft)

From the Hotel Cerna in the centre of the spa head uphill, east, the road bending left past the Complex Comercial. Narrow and cobbled, it brings you up to the main road along the Cerna valley; turn right here, sharply back on yourself and head along the DN67D road, contouring above the town. You pass a fork with a minor road going right, back down into the town at a red-topped milestone; keep left here on the main road and ignore a flight of steps just after, on the left by a deep drain gully. 100m further you find a gap in the wall on the left with a variety of signs about the footpath and the nature reserve. The path (blue cross waymarks) is very steep but well graded, except where fallen trees have blocked the zig-zags, forcing almost perpendicular short-cuts up through the lower reaches of the forest of beech, hornbeam and sycamore. Ignore a right-hand turning as you start to walk clear of the forest. At a ruined hut turn right where the blue cross route heads left, down into the Tesnei valley, to a spring (this does not offer a route back into town). The path now (yellow stripe waymarks) takes you steeply up through open woods of Austrian pine scattered with snakeshead lilies in May, past a small diversion left to a cave. The summit of Domogled is a short east–west ridge with a truly magnificent view of all the surrounding hills and the Danube to the west, snaking across the plains east of Belgrade. The path continues east of the summit of Domogled to the main ridge of the Mehedinți, where you can turn right (yellow cross waymarks) and make your way back down to Pecinișca via Vf. Predelu, or left, taking you in theory on a ridge-top route all the way to a point above Cerna-Sat.

Paths onward from Băile Herculane

In order to leave Herculane to head north up onto the Cerna ridge, find the small Roman Catholic church immediately above the east end of Piața Hercules. A flight of concrete steps 20m west of the church door is the beginning of the trail (blue triangles) up through the forest to meet the red stripe route along the top of the Cerna ridge at Poiana Perii – the aptly-named 'Clearing with Pear Trees'. There are several hiking trails out of town to the Mehedinți ridge to the south, apart from the Domogled route. One is the yellow stripe route up the Prolaz gorge to the south of the town; follow the DN67D road south to the obvious wide trail coming out of the Prolaz gap, reaching the road at a left-hand bend by some gypsy squatters' shacks. Having climbed up through the gorge you find yourself walking along a flat-floored valley in the beech forest. You reach an obvious path junction, where the well marked yellow stripe route goes left up a tributary valley and the red dot route continues over the Mehedinți ridge to Podeni village. Alternatively, you can climb up via Șaua Padina; follow either of the roads north through Herculane to the point where they meet at the bridge over the Cerna. From here follow Strada Uzinei, a rough lane on the east bank and find a track bearing right (yellow stripe waymarks), eastwards through the woods at the end of the lane. A third is to head out of town, north along the road from the bridge above, for 3km, past Șapte Izvoare to the next left hand bend; two paths head right from here, one (red disc waymarks) Cascada Roșetu, the other (blue triangle waymarks) goes to the main Mehedinți ridge in the area of the karstic depression of Balta Cerbului. There are also two gorges well worth exploring, further up the Cerna Valley. These are Cheile Corcoaia, in the Cerna Valley itself, and Cheile Țăsnei, hidden up to the right, just above the head of Lake Șapte Izvoare, the dammed Cerna.

CHAPTER TEN

The Mountains of Maramureş

If Romania is a country for connoisseur travellers – which it is – then Maramureş is connoisseur's Romania. The highest mountains of the region, the Rodna, are the eastern end of an outlying arm of the Carpathians that stretches west towards Hungary from the main north–south chain of the Eastern Carpathians. This mountain extension encloses the two delightful valleys of the Izer and Vişeu (pronounced 'Ee-zer' and 'Vee-shay-oo'). These two valleys are the heart of the county of Maramureş ('Mahra-moor-esh'); in addition the Coşeu and Mara valleys run south from Sighetu Marmaţiei towards the Gutâi pass. This arm of the Carpathians has had the effect of isolating Maramureş from the rest of Romania, and indeed the world. The modern county, whose capital is now Baia Mare, stretches over the southern side of this ridge, but Maramureş proper lies to the north (its capital being Sighetu Marmaţiei). Maramureş was never part of the Roman imperial province of Dacia. Most subsequent invasions have passed it by, leaving its population little changed in millennia. Consequently this is a region which has a greater tendency to maintain traditional ways than other regions of Romania. Apart from this, from the point of view of attractive countryside, the lowland landscapes of the Iza and Vişeu valleys are hard to beat anywhere. No single name attaches itself to these outlying arms of the Carpathian range; west of the Rodna, across the Salăuţa valley (carrying the railway line northwards from Târgu Mureş and Bucharest) is the Ţibleş ('Tsee-blesh'). Further west lie the Lapuş, the Gutâi, the Igniş and finally the Munşţii Oaş – one long complex mountain ridge.

Access

If you want to make the traverse of the Rodna and its outliers starting from the extreme western end, then you should start at the village of Vama and walk east into the Igniş massif. If, however, you want to combine some walking up high with exploring the magical villages and valleys of Maramureş, I suggest you start at Vişeu ('Vee-shey-oo'). Considering that this is the farthest-flung province of Romania, hemmed in against the closed border with Ukraine, it is surprisingly simple to reach. There is one through train per day from Bucharest to Vişeu, continuing on to Sighetu Marmaţiei – a sleeper. Getting there by day involves changing trains – I do not recommend it. You can also catch a train to Baia Mare from Bucharest and find a bus or a lift taking you northwards along the DN18 road over the Gutâi pass. The start point at the western end of the Maramureş mountains is the village of Vama, 4km south of the town of Negresti-Oaş. It has a railway halt (six slow trains per day, taking an hour and a half from the start of the branch line from Satu Mare). Two days' walk south-east is the Hanul Pintea Viteazul cabana on the Gutâi pass, 26km (16 miles) by road from Baia Mare.

THE GUTÂI MOUNTAINS

The mountains of the west of Maramureş (from west to east, the Igniş, the Gutâi, Lăpuş and the Ţibleş) offer a wild and fascinating walk south-east from Negreşti Oaş to the Şetref pass, on the

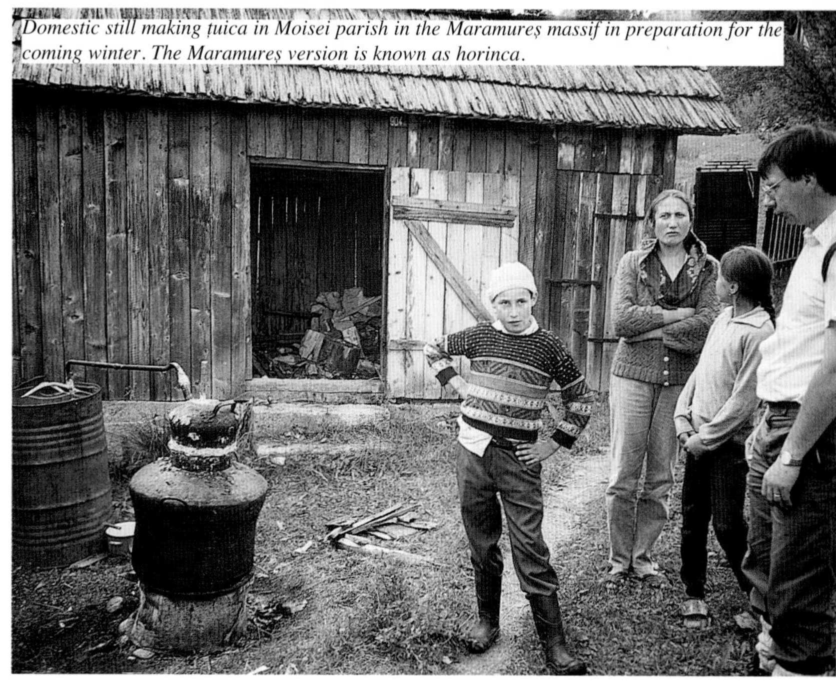
Domestic still making țuica in Moisei parish in the Maramureș massif in preparation for the coming winter. The Maramureș version is known as horinca.

DN17C road from Năsăud to the Iza valley. East of the pass the route continues into the Rodna mountains. Of extremely complex geology, the range offers some climbing, on Vf. Igniș and the Lespezi cliffs and especially the Creasta Cocoșului ('the Cock's Comb'), east of the Gutâi pass. This last is a very worthwhile target for a walk, with superb views northwards down the beautiful Mara valley with its string of villages; the mountain is a geological reserve.

Tucked into the southern flank of the Guțâi is the county's capital, Baia Mare. Whilst not a town to make a point of visiting (though Piața Libertății is attractive) it is not as polluted as some guides would have you think. From here you can walk straight from the town into the mountains. Make your way to the Usturoi restaurant by heading north from the Podul Viitor bridge (immediately north of Piata Libertății) over the Sasar river; turn left and then first right, to head north along Strada Petofi, along the west side of the park.

Access

Negrești-Oaș is the furthest point from Bucharest mentioned as a start point in this book. It is reached by branch line from Satu Mare (51km, 32 miles), on the main line continuing onwards from Baia Mare (nine trains per day). An alternative to this is to start from the village of Vama, with a halt on the same line (Vama Turului). There is one through train per day from Bucharest to Baia Mare – a sleeper. There are no daytime trains direct from Bucharest to Baia Mare, though there are from Brașov and the connections are reasonable.

My suggestion is that you cut out the long approach walk to the crags of Creasta Cocoșului and arrive by train in Baia Mare and take a bus from there to Valea Neagra – you may be lucky and find one going all the way (tarred road) to the cabana complex at Izvoarele. There is 12km (7½ miles) of zigzag road up from Valea Neagra to Izvoarele through the forest.

Day One

Negrești-Oaș to Izvaorele via Vf. Rotunda, 28km (17 miles). Altitude gained to Vf. Buiana, 810m (2650ft)

Head east out of Negrești-Oaș, on Strada Vrăticel, starting to the left of the Casa de Cultura. Turn right as you leave the town to head just south of due east along the rough road heading up the Tur valley. You go past the old Văraticel cabana, now a tabăra childrens' camp, walking on a former narrow-gauge forest railway. After 5km you reach a forest cabana on the left by a fork with an old quarry in the arms of the fork; keep left here (occasional red disc and older cross waymarks), due east, past a left hand turning 500m east of the fork. A further 1.5km brings you to a right hand turning, up the Balotei valley. Keep left, now heading north-east, up the Goroha valley. Turn left off the forest road along the bottom of the valley 1km after the Balotei junction to head due east, steeply up the south side of an east–west spur. 4km of ascent from the road brings you to a grassy col and a clearing – Poiana Buiana – and the junction with the red cross route to the south.

Head east from the col, down into the woods. 500m after the col a path turns left (red disc and blue cross waymarks). Keep right here, just north of due east, down through the trees and turn right almost immediately to head south-east, down to the bottom of the valley and then south across the river and upstream along it with the river on your right. The path ascends to a clearing and two paths turn right, offering routes back to Negrești-Oaș. At the second clearing turn left, off your south-bound route, and head north-east towards the dominant twin summits of Vf. Rotunda, 4km away; there are no waymarks but the path is well trodden along the Dealul Roasa ridge. After 2.5km you exit from the woods and descend to a col, from which a path turns right to head down the valley to the end of a forest road leading to Baia Mare via Valea Neagra and Firiza reservoir. This also offers an alternative route to Izvoarele. Head east from the col, the path taking you just north of Vf. Rotunda to a path junction immediately north-east of the summit, with the main ridge route all the way from Huta pass.

The Culmea Rotunda ridge runs in an arc south-east and your path keeps on its north-east side, largely through forest, swinging gradually to head east, reaching a col in the forest, then less that 1km later, passing Vf. Stânelor (1162m, 3182ft) on your right. Altogether 4km after Vf. Rotunda you meet a path junction at a col. Ascend east from the col; the path swings right to head south to bring you after 1km to a track on a pass – this is Poiana Lungă (1093m, 3586ft).

Cross over the road here to head south, on the right hand side of the forested ridge, passing a tiny lake on your right and then a second after almost 1km. 1km after the second lake, the path now heading east and ascending, you reach a junction at the top of a forested ridge running away due south; turn right here to head along the top of it, then out of the trees to the summit of Vf Pleșca Mare (1292m, 4239ft). From the summit head south-west, steeply down and back into the forest 1.5km to reach the forest road. Turn right along it, descending south along the Stedea Valley for about 500m to reach a track junction by a foresters' hut. Turn right here and head south-west uphill for about 300m to a col where you turn left to head south in the forest, towards the crags of Pietrele Lucii, the path swinging right to keep to the west of them, contouring along the west side of a north–south ridge, past Vf. Breze (1253m, 4111ft) and then descending down a valley to a foresters' road, continuing south-east to Izvoare by turning left after 1.5km of forest road. The complex of Izvoare stands in a large area of cleared forest in the mountains. There is what must be the highest tennis court in Romania and a series of wooden sculptures from the 1980s.

Vf. Gutâi and Creasta Cocoșului crags, 1444m (4737ft)

From Izvoarele cabana, head east up the access road, away from the main DN18 road. The road dwindles to a track and brings you to a cross-tracks. Turn left to head north, towards the summit of Măgura above the trees. Follow the track as it swings right out of the trees, a path turning off to the left to the summit of Măgura. After 500m turn right to head north-east back into the forest, the track contouring around the flanks of Secătura. The track becomes a footpath and turns right to climb steeply up onto the craggy ridge.

On top of the ridge you come to a path junction; turn left along the ridge to the summit. The path south from the junction offers a route steeply down to the village of Cavnic. Looking down to the north from Vf. Gutâi you see the delightful villages of the western Maramureș Depression. Head south-east from the summit of Vf. Gutâi, back down through the forest to the road from Cavnic north over the mountains to Budești, just south of the Neteda pass (1040m, 3412ft). It would be pleasant to recommend a path continuing east across the Lăpuș and Țibleș mountains; sadly there is none.

Ieud to Șetref pass via Vf. Țibleș, 42km (26 miles). Altitude gained, 1290m (4232ft)

This can be used as an approach to the Rodna traverse outlined below. It is too much for a day's walk; perhaps the best way to tackle it is to visit the famous church in Ieud in the morning and then camp wild in the woods around Țibleș. Ieud has the country's oldest wooden church, dating from 1364; the village is the source of much of the craftsmanship seen in the Hanul lui Manuc courtyard hotel and restaurant in Bucharest.

From the church head south on the main street through this typically long straggling village. It runs into its satellite of de Ieud and 2km beyond this brings you to a track junction. Turn left to follow the track south-east up a tributary valley to the Ieud. The track becomes a path and takes you up out of the trees, over a watershed and into the Călimanul valley, where the path swings to the right, west and up through the forest to the summit of Vf. Măguriței (1242m, 4075ft). Here it turns left to head south, along a ridge through the forest to the summit of Vf. Stregior and then (occasional red stripe waymarks on tree-trunks), down to a col in the forest. The path ascends to Vf. Tomnatecul and out of the trees past a shepherds' hut to the summit of Vf. Țibleș (1839m, 6034ft) the highest summit on the ridge west of the Rodna massif. This is a fine viewpoint, the Maramureș depression spread out below you to the north and the valleys draining towards the Someș to the south. Head south-east from the summit (red stripe waymarks), turning left after 1km to head north-east down a valley. The path becomes a track and continues down the Fiadul valley.

After about 4km of track walking you come to a junction; turn left at a cluster of buildings. The track immediately deteriorates to a path and climbs north-east towards the summit of Vf. Comarnicele (1065m, 3494ft) which you pass to the east. Continuing north-east from the summit, it descends back into the forest along a broad ridge and then takes you back out of the trees by some shepherds' huts and up to the summit of Vf. Ştefaniţei (1181m, 3875ft). Beyond here the path is well trodden, north-west down through the trees to for 2km to Vf. Fântânele (978m, 3209ft), where you swing right, following a broad ridge – the Culmea Şetref – to an unnamed grassy conical summit with scattered small pine trees. The path continues south-east here to a bank of trees, where it swings to the right, now a cart track along the top of a grassy ridge with scattered trees. You have your first sight of the DN17C road, snaking up from Săcel. As you start to descend you see the new Cabana lui Patru built in the summer of 1996. The track becomes sunken and eroded and brings you to the cabana at the pass. Now pick up directions for 'Day One' of the Rodna massif, below.

THE RODNA MOUNTAINS

The Rodna is a compact massif, bounded on the northern side by the DN18 road as it makes its way eastwards out of Maramureş over the Prislop pass from the Vişeu valley into Bucovina. To the south and east the Rodna is bounded by the Someşul Mare (Bârgău) valley, in which is the old-fashioned town of Rodna itself. 7km to the east of Rodna, the last settlement but one as you make your way up out of the Someş valley to the Rotunda pass (see itinerary below), is the village of Şanţ, scene of a midwinter festival at the end of December.

The highest point in the Rodna massif is Pietrosul (2303m, 7555ft), dominating the little mining town of Borşa – the ugliest possible settlement amidst the finest possible landscape (though you rapidly walk out of it, heading up towards Pietrosul). The higher reaches of the Rodna are not well supplied with cabanas; in order to explore this area you will have to be self-contained. In the east of the area it is possible to make excursions from a base in Borşa town, Statiunea Borşa ski village (rather pleasant), Moisei or the Han on Prislop pass (the former Puzdra cabana, still marked on some maps, has been burnt down). The area around Pietrosul is a nature reserve, covering some 3000 hectares, clearly marked on walking maps. It was set up to protect the flora and fauna of the region, including chamois; there are a number of endemic plant species. There are moves afoot to declare the area a National Park – since 1980 it has been a UNESCO biosphere reserve. The area north of the summit of Ineu is also a nature reserve – the Bila-Lala reserve, covering the sources of these two valleys.

Given the lack of high-level cabanas, I have written this itinerary as being from bivouac site to bivouac site; low-level accommodation is however available all round the Rodna (see Appendix A). A complete Rodna traverse is recommended, from Şetref pass to Rotunda pass, from where you can contine into Moldova, across the Suhard to the town of Vatra Dornei and from there south-west to the Caliman or north-east to the Rarau-Giumalau. However, if you want to restrict yourself to the highlights, I recommend Şetref pass to Borşa via Pietrosul (possible in a day given an early start) or a two-day walk east along the ridge to Vf. Ineu – surely the loneliest of Romania's 2000m (6500ft) summits and to Rodna town, with its station (six trains per day from the junction at Ilva Mică, one of them direct to and from Bucharest – a sleeper).

Access

The itinerary below describes an eastbound traverse along the crest of the Rodna, continuing from the Ţibleş mountains. Alternatively you can arrive by train and start at Romuli or Dealul

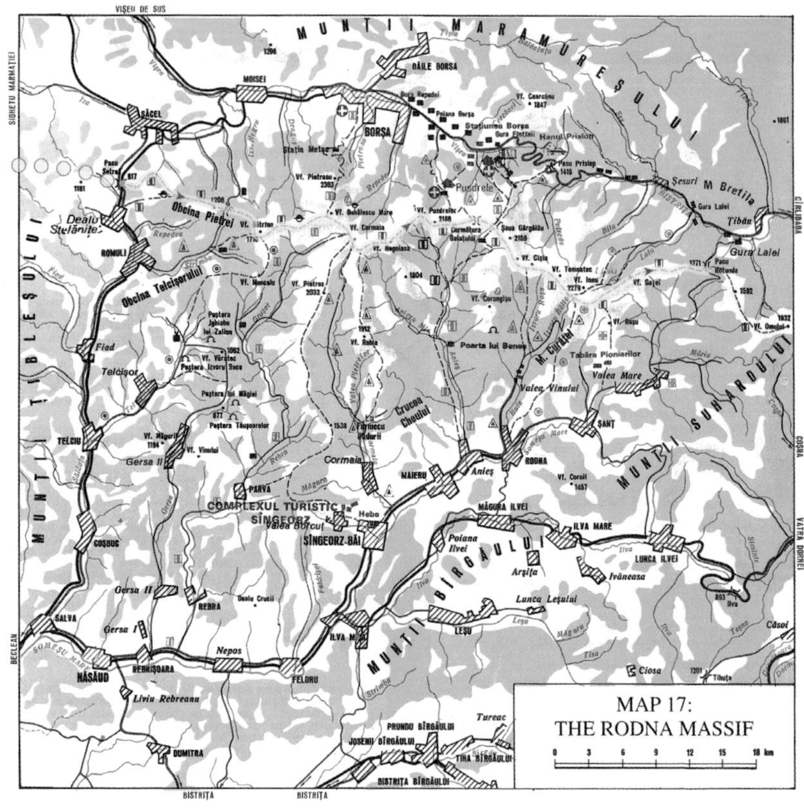

MAP 17: THE RODNA MASSIF

Ştefaniţei (walking 3km north along the road to Şetref Pass). You can also start walking from Moisei or Borşa. If the choice is between the routes from Dealul Ştefaniţei or Romuli I would recommend the former, via the pass and the open ridge with its fine views rather than valley route through the forest from Romuli. Şetref pass (817m, 2680ft) lies 8km (5 miles) south of the road junction in Săcel on the DN17C towards Romuli and Bistriţa. Four trains per day travel each way along the scenic single-track line north from the junction at Salva, stopping at the villages of Romuli, Dealul Ştefaniţei and Săcel. It continues to Vişeu de Jos, from where four slow trains connect with it up via Moisei to Borşa station, 2km west of the town centre. To walk up into the Rodna from Borşa, take one of the maxi-taxi minibuses that meet the trains and alight in the centre of town. Walk east from the main crossing in the town (the sign north to Baia Borşa) and turn right, south, immediately after the Perla Maramureşului Hotel on the north side of the road. You find yourself walking along a wide street with the hospital on your left; just before it ends (200m from the main road), turn left over a concrete bridge over a stream near the 'Rodna' bar in a small wooden shack. Head south up a steep stony track between fences and gardens; continue on this as it becomes the path up Pietrosul.

Day One

Șetref pass to Buhaescu Mare Hollow, 21km (13 miles). Altitude gained from Șetref Pass to Buhaescu Mare summit, 1305m (4281ft)

From the Hanul lui Patru (Peter's Inn) at Șetref pass two tracks head east. Take the right hand, rougher of the two which immediately forks – it does not matter which you take. Gullied and steep, they take you up a grassy slope and rejoin. Ahead you see the obvious path, climbing south-east up the broad grassy slope through belts of spruce, bringing you to the top of Vf. Posiosu (1103m, 3619ft) among the trees, 2km from Hanul lui Patru. You now descend steeply to a col and continue east to some shepherds' huts by a second col at Capul Muntelui. Climbing south-east through the pines and then across fields, you meet a track (blue triangle waymarks) coming in from the right (Dealul Ștefaniței) at the shepherds' huts at La Jgheaburi, 1.5km from Capul Muntelui. Head east from here through the clearing along the top of the Preluca cu Bulboci ridge, taking you over the summit of Muncelul Râios (1703m, 5587ft), with fine views of the higher peaks of the Rodna mountains ahead. Head east (red stripe waymarks), descending steeply through the forest to reach a clearing at Pietrii pass (1190m, 3904ft) where you cross the track from Moisei to Romuli. The area around the pass has been felled and is dominated by an unnamed conical craggy summit immediately west. At the pass two tracks turn right, both to Romuli; a better track descends left to Moisei. Continue east along the ridge and back into the spruce forest.

From the pass the path ascends gently to the east as a track; bear immediately left off it onto the ridge-top route, climbing steeply to a clearing and then swinging right, heading south-east along the side of a wood, bringing you to a path junction; bear right here, heading south for 700m to a second junction by a trig point survey marker (a wooden post and tripod). Here you are joined by the red triangle route from the right, coming up from Romuli. Turn left here to climb up out of the trees to the summit of Vf. Bătrâna (1710m, 5610ft). Head east from the summit, down to Șaua Bătrânei (red disc route heads off to the right, south to Vf. Nedeia, from there west to Tomnatic summit and thence back to Romuli or down into the Telcișor valley to the village of the same name, 4km from Telciu railway station).

Keep left at Șaua Bătrânei Pass, north-east along the northern side of the Rodna ridge watershed (red stripe waymarks) – fairly easy walking above the tree line with fine views behind you of the Țibleș and ahead to Pietrosul. Reaching the tree line again the path swings right, following the ridge-top, climbs past an unnamed summit to the left (north) (1764m, 5787ft) and then descends to Podul Bătrânei pass. Heading east along the ridge, 1km after the col you reach a path junction, offering you the choice of the ridge-top route over Vf. Gropilor (2063m) and Vf. Buhaescu Mare (2122m, 6962ft); the alternative lower-level route keeps to the south side of the main ridge and the two rejoin at Tarnița La Cruce pass (1984m, 6509ft), 1km south-east of Buhaescu Mare summit. There is a useful bivouac site north-east of Buhaescu Mare; to reach it take the blue stripe path to the left, along the ridge to the north of the summit, passing over Vf. Rebra (2221m, 7867ft) and on to Curmătura Pietrosului pass, where you turn right to walk down to the bivouac site near two small tarns.

Day Two

Buhaescu Mare to Șaua Gargalău, 16km (10 miles)

No figure for ascent has been given for this day as it is a walk of several small-scale ascents as you head east along the ridge. From tarns below Buhaescu Mare head south-east and down, following the stream past a shepherds' hut to a path junction just beyond where you turn right, to head south-west up past a small tarn to Tarnița La Cruce pass (1984m, 6509ft), where the winter route to the south of Buhaescu Mare summit joins you from the right. Turn left at the col to follow the red stripe ridge route as it keeps to the left of the crags of Vf. Obârsia Rebrii (2052m, 6732ft). Just south-east of the summit you come to the junction with the blue stripe path to the right; it heads south-west, down the Gușeț valley, becoming a forest road and running all the way to Parva village – it also offers a route to Telcișor and Telciu. Keep left here along the red stripe route below Șaua Obârsia Rebrii pass (1985m, 6735ft).

The main ridge route now avoids two major summits on the top of the ridge, Cormaia (2033m, 6670ft) and the more impressive Vf. Repede (2074m, 6804ft). These are left to your right as the path contours around the impressive cirque at the head of the Repede stream. I suggest that, conditions permitting, you follow the high path over the summits. The paths reunite at Șaua Intr' Izvoare pass from where you head east, the path splitting at Tarnița Negoieșilor col to pass either side of Vf. Negoiasa (2041m, 6696ft). Again, conditions permitting, I recommend the higher, right hand path; the two reunite 1.5km north-east of Negoiasa at the second col, Tarnița Bârsanului pass, from where a cart track leads down to the right, eventually reaching Anieș village.

The route now runs north-east along the ridge-top to a path junction just before Șaua Puzdrele pass, between the summits of Puzdrele (2189m, 7182ft) and Laptelui (2172m. 7126ft). Cross through this col, now on the northern side of the watershed; rather less than 1km a path (blue disc waymarks) turns off to the left, taking you down to Puzdra cabana (see Appendix A), offering an alternative night stop. You rejoin the ridge 1km east of Vf. Laptelui and find a second turning left to Puzdrele cabana; keep heading due east along the ridge route, south of Vf. Galatului, bringing you to Șaua Galatului pass and on east, keeping south of Vf. Cailor (1931m, 6335ft) to Șaua Gargalău (1925m, 6316ft), where level ground and a spring offers a useful bivouac site.

Day Three

Șaua Gargalău to Rotunda pass, 24km (15 miles). Altitude gained from Șaua Gargalău to Vf. Ineu, 354m (1161ft)

Șaua Gargalău marks the junction of the main Rodna red stripe route to Rotunda pass and the exit route via Știol to Prislop pass and the DN18 road. Alternatively you can walk north from here to Stațiunea Borșa (a good alimentara shop and accommodation – see Appendix A).

From Șaua Gargalău pass head south-east, climbing steadily east-south-east for 1.5km to Vf. Gargalău summit (2159m, 7083ft), descending to a a col before climbing Vf. Claii (2117m, 6945ft), less than 1km south-east of Vf. Gargalău, the path now something of a switchback as it drops and then ascends again in a similar distance, still heading south-east to La Cepi (2101m, 6896ft), then swinging right, down to a third col and up to the east of Vf. Omului (2135m, 7005ft). It now swings left, down to Șaua Cisa and up the summit of the same name (2039m, 6690ft) and down, due east, to the path junction at Tarnita lui Putredu. Here the blue triangle route turns off to the right, south down the Cisa spur and into the Izvoru Rosu valley and along a rough road to the resort of Valea Vinului (see Appendix A).

Keep heading east along the Rodna

ridge route, to the right (south) of the summit of Coasta Neteda (2060m, 6758ft), 1km from the path junction. From the summit the path heads south-east, along the craggy Ripa Coasta Neteda ridge via Şaua Putreda col (2051m, 6729ft) to Şaua cu Lac col (2140m, 7021ft), 1km south of the summit of Vf. Ineu (2279m, 7477ft); turn left at the col to head north to Şaua Ineutului (2228m, 7310ft), from where a path continues north to Ineu summit and continues north-east along the Creasta Picioru Plescutei spur. From Şaua cu Lac the blue disc path descends past Lala lake (1815m, 5595ft) along the Lala valley and a forest road to the lonely hamlet of Gura Lalei (1015m, 3330ft) on the DN18 road.

Once you have made your out-and-back climb of Vf. Ineu return to Şaua cu Lac. Head east from here (red stripe waymarks) bringing you after 1km to Şaua Ineului (do not confuse with Şaua Ineuţului) immediately below the summit of the same name (2222m, 7290ft). Here the path forks; to the right the blue cross route heads south-east, along the Piciorul Ineuţ ridge to the crags of Vf. Roşu and then south, offering an exit to the village of Şanţ.

Bear left at Şaua Ineului, leaving the summit to your right and head north-east along the Dosu Gajei (Muntele Gaja) ridge to Şaua Gajei (1789m, 5870ft) after 2km, now with the forest on your left. Continuing north-east along the south side of the ridge, you pass Vf. Gajei above you to the left, 5km from Ineut. The next landmark is a shepherd's hut at Prelucile, after which the path zigzags down, south-east to the forest edge to a junction. Turn left to head north-east, still above the tree line, past Nichitaş summit to a col from where you head east, down into the forest to Pasul Rotunda (1271m, 4170ft), where a clearing and a spring offer the chance of camping. The pass carries the rough DN17D road north-east out of the beautiful Someşul Mare valley over to the Bistriţa Aurie valley and the main DN18 road east to Bucovina. To continue further, south-east along the watershed, see the Suhard Massif below.

The Vaser valley narrow-gauge forest railway

From the top of the Borşa ridge the view to the north is of the forested mountains of Maramureş, stretching away to the border with Ukraine. The stretch of hills that give their name to the county of Maramureş are separated by the Vişeu valley from the Borşa massif and rise to their highest point at the wooded summit of Toroiaga (1930m, 6332ft). The delightful Vaser valley, taking you far from any road, gives access to the Maramureş mountains. Something that is well worth travelling to the region to discover (Explore Worldwide run a tour that involves a day here – see Appendix F) is the delightful miniature railway that runs up this valley, north and east from the town of Vişeu. The line was built in 1933 and is not marked on road maps, although the Vaser valley is. The line still mostly uses steam. Apart from footpaths, the railway is the only way to reach the logging settlements along the valley.

There is one train per day, up the line, leaving Vişeu SIL station (as opposed to the main CFR, at the western end of town by the bridge over the river) supposedly at six in the morning – though often later. It takes between four and five hours to reach Coman at the end of the line. The train descends on the same day, so it is possible to make a day excursion up the line and back. Two hikes suggest themselves, neither of them waymarked with any symbol, although the paths can be followed. Bearing in mind that you will have to

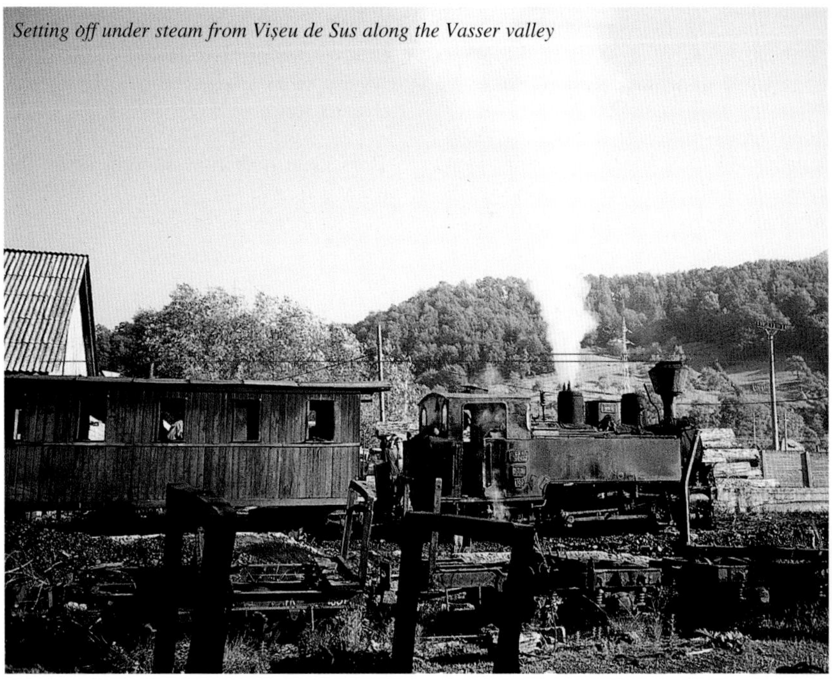
Setting off under steam from Vişeu de Sus along the Vasser valley

travel up the Vaser valley by train first, both will take two days to complete. You will need full camping gear; there is no accommodation to be found in the Vaser valley.

Do not head north out of the valley. Romania's border guard is a specific part of the army. They take a dim view of any foreigners wandering the remote border with Ukraine. They may stop you whilst travelling on the railway to ascertain that you are not going near the border. The walks in the Maramureş mountains are on paths little used by recreational walkers; they are for the experienced walker only, who has enough experience of map and compass in poor conditions to be able to navigate with only the most rudimentary map.

One suggested walk is from **Catarama Vaserului to Prislop Pass** (the DN18 road) via Tarniţa Bălăsinii (23km, 15 miles, altitude gained to Tarniţa Bălăsinii 800m, 2600ft). Catarama Vaserului is the last halt before the end of the line at Coman. A forest track heads south up a tributary of the Vaser from here (an alternative takes you up to Şaua Gilu and back to Băile Borşa – about 8 hours). Turn left off the forest track to head south-east, straight up the Piciorul Cataramei spur, reaching some isolated shepherds' huts near the top. The path takes you over Prislopul Cataramei pass (1644m, 5394ft), passes some more shepherds' huts and goes south-east to the next summit on the ridge, Vf. Jupania (1853m, 6080ft). Here the path turns to the right, down off the ridge and reaches the pass of Tarniţa Bălăsinii (1471m, 4830ft). From here the route lies all along the forest track which for most of its length keeps to the top of a high ridge.

An alternative is the walk from **Macârlău to Băile Borşa** (altitude gained to the Maramureş ridge 830m, 2723ft), largely on forest tracks; from

Macârlău (a railway halt and a couple of huts) head due south up the valley of the same name, passing a track junction just before a forester's hut. Keep heading south-south-west as the track dwindles to a path and brings you to the top of a gentle col in the woods between the summits of Vf. Piciorul Caprei (1804m, 5918ft) and Vf. Toroiaga (1930m, 6332ft). Bear left along the ridge and pick up a path bringing you along a spur with the Sacu valley to your right. You find yourself on a forest track: as it swings round the end of the spur above the farms at Băile Borșa; the path runs straight down the extremity of the spur, bringing you back to the road as it runs into the village.

Typical architecture of the Moti people in the Apuseni – a cottage in the parish of Cheia, near Râmet, Trascău massif

The old church and the new, Râmet Monastery, Trascău massif

CHAPTER ELEVEN
The Apuseni Mountains

'Transylvania had been a familiar name as long as I could remember. It was the very essence and symbol of remote, leafy, half-mythical strangeness; and, on the spot, it seemed remoter still, and more fraught with charms.'

Patrick Leigh Fermor, *Between the Woods and the Water*

The Apuseni are the mountainous heart of Transylvania. Just as the Eastern Carpathians ('Carpaţi Orientali') are alternatively known as Carpaţi Răsaritean ('Răsarit' meaning 'dawn'), the name Apuseni is derived from 'apus de soare'; these western mountains are indeed 'the mountains of the sunset'. The region is uniquely important in Romania's history, for the gold and silver deposits of the Metaliferi range were the primary reason for Emperor Trajan's invasion, giving rise to the country's Latin language and national identity. The Apuseni (pronounced 'Apoo-sen'), unlike the Carpathians proper, is a labyrinthine tangle of mountains contained within the angle of the Eastern and Southern Carpathians. It is bounded to the south by the Zarandului range and the corridor of communication running along the Mureş valley from Deva to Arad, to the north by the Crişul Repede valley, draining west from near Cluj to Oradea and the border with Hungary, to the west the Bihor and Codrul ranges slope down to the plains of Crişana. It is a region where superb scenery, much of it of limestone gorges and great forests, combines with delightful villages and valleys in which a traditional way of life persists, unchanged in centuries. This area is rich in interest for travellers in quest of folk music, art and traditional costume, as well as the mountains themselves. This is probably the best area to explore on a mountain-bike, with long, empty (and rough) roads in the forests.

Topography and geology

These are not the highest of mountains – the highest peak, Cucurbata Mare or Bihor, reaches a modest 1849m (6066ft). An attraction of the Apuseni, however, is that some superb walking can be combined with a visit to the nearby city of Cluj, one of eastern Europe's finest city-centres. The preceding three chapters have dealt with mountains that rear above the populated inhabited valleys below. The Apuseni is quite different. The name attaches itself to a region of mountains, intersected with a number of valleys. In some Romanian guides you will scarcely see the name feature at all, but each massif separately dealt with – Trascău, Vlădeasa, Bihor, Codrul and the Munţii Metaliferi. The last is a range of ancient crystalline rocks rich in mica and, as their name indicates, the ores of a number of metals, including gold. However, for the most part, the Apuseni is a limestone area, with the country's greatest wealth of karst features and lime-loving alpine plants. In the Turda gorge is a pocket of sun-loving plants more usually found in Mediterranean regions. Most of the Apuseni is made up of rounded peaks with the usual endless in spruce forests broken up by grassy meadows. Beneath these lie labyrinths of swallow-holes, underground rivers, gorges and caverns. The gorges can fill to overflow their paths with alarming speed – indeed some of the paths involve quite deep wading when the river flow is at normal. As well as limestone there are areas of igneous geology – the basalt pillars of Detunata near Bucium and the volcanic Vlădeasa in the north-east of the region.

The Moți people

The inhabitants of the Apuseni are referred to as being a distinct mini-nation, known as the 'Moți'. One of the first things you notice is their distinct architecture, with tall steeple-shaped thatched roofs on cottages and barns alike. Visitors are told of valleys whose population has changed little since the time of Trajan's invasion; certainly the region produced more than its fair share of Romanian patriots and rebels during the time of Austro-Hungarian rule. Here can be found villages without any recognisable streets or layout, just scattered in the valley, with peasants' way of life little changed in centuries. The region has a tradition of folk music stronger perhaps than anywhere else in Romania; Bartok found inspiration for much of his music in the folk music performed in the valleys of the Bihor massif. The Apuseni region is also rich in local festivals, mentioned in the text below. In addition to these, the village of Săvârșin in the west of the Apuseni, in the Mureș valley (67km, 42 miles, west of Deva), holds two notable festivals, on 30th January and 27th November.

Itinerary across the Apuseni

Precisely because the Apuseni are not a remote mountain range or a simple ridge feature, a walk through them is not a straightforward matter of following a marked path from one mountain-hut to another. The paths and cabanas in the Apuseni do not lend themselves to this. Rather you will be walking for some of the time along gravel roads, much of whose traffic is horse-drawn carts. As an independent traveller, you may well find your planned itinerary changed by the offer of accommodation or a lift to a village you had never intended visiting. The first itinerary is a route taking you southwards, across the eastern side of the Apuseni plateau, where tributaries of the Mureș river have carved spectacular gorges and wooded valleys through the east-facing escarpment. It runs from Cluj, across the Gilău massif (or Muntele Mare), then across the Trascău massif and finishes in Alba Iulia on the main railway line. The itinerary itself can be incorporated with a journey on the delightful rural Arieș valley narrow-gauge railway line.

The walk across the Muntele Mare connects with a traverse of the Bihor and Vlădeasa massifs, starting at the village of Gârda de Sus, 43km (27 miles) from the end of Trascău traverse at Bucium, and finishing at the station in Poieni, on the main line from Cluj to Oradea, connecting with trains further north from Oradea to the Maramureș region, dealt with in the preceding chapter. Just west of the Bihor and Vlădeasa massifs is the Codru-Moma; it lies west of the Crișul Negru valley, flowing through Beiuș. There are no cabanas; access is along the slow branch railway from Oradea via Horod junction. The best way to explore the massif is as a two-day traverse with a bivouac half-way.

The itinerary below has largely been written as being from cabana to cabana. However, to be self-sufficient when walking in the area would be an advantage. It is the perfect area in which to camp wild in the forest.

Access

Cluj can be reached by overnight train from Bucharest, thus saving the cost of a hotel. By day there is one through train from Bucharest; it takes seven hours (five trains a day from Brașov; journey time 5hrs). There are three buses a week and more frequent trains from Budapest. Neither the town's railway station nor the main bus station are close to the centre; the bus station is reached by heading east along Strada Budai Nagy Antal. I recommend you start by taking a taxi to Cabana Făget to start the walk into the Gilău and on into the Trascău.

THE GILĂU MASSIF

The Gilău massif (also known as the Muntele Mare) is a limestone, dome-shaped feature, reaching its highest point at Vârful Muntele Mare (1826m, 5991ft). From this summit the valleys of a number of rivers run in a radiating pattern, all of them eventually draining into the Mureș, flowing west from the Apuseni acrosss the Banat plain. To the west the Gilău merges into the Bihor massif (see below); in the south it is separated from the Trascău (see below) by the Arieș valley, with its narrow-gauge railway line from Turda 93km (58 miles) up to Abrud. In the north the massif is bounded by the valley of the Someșu Cald, dammed for much of its length. In the east the Ierii valley provides the main communication, with roads bringing skiers up to the popular cabana at Băișoara in the winter. The itinerary below takes you across the Gilău, starting from Cluj, walking across the Făget ridge and through Turda gorge. An alternative is to walk across the Trascău massif to Salciua and then head down the Arieș valley for 35km (22 miles) to the turning to Cheile Turzii cabana. There are two trains per day; alight at Plaiești.

Day One

Cluj (Făget cabana) to Cheile Turzii cabana, 28km (18 miles)

Făget Pădurea cabana lies on the outskirts of Cluj, a 20-minute taxi ride from the railway station, or can be reached by walking from the centre, heading south along the Calea Turzii from the old city gate of Bastionul Croitorilor ('Tailor's Bastion'). If there is no room inside the cabana, you can ask for one of the little huts set outside beneath the pine trees. Alternative accommodation can be found at Făget cabana (see Appendix A).

From Făget Pădure cabana head south-west (red stripe waymarks) up into the woods towards Vârful Peana (832m, 2730ft), the highest point of the Făget hills. The path takes you south-east, descending out of the woods into the Micuș valley, towards the hamlet of Micești, where you cross the river on the road. The path follows the river, turning right off the road, taking you through the village of Deleni and then along the river, south-east to the village of Petreștii de Jos. Turn left to head south-east through the village, leaving it on the DJ107 road to Turda. The road swings round to the north and east after leaving Petreștii; when you reach the end of Petreștii turn right down the last village side street turning off the main one, the street dwindling to a muddy track, then a footpath, then a tricky path taking you through the superb Turda gorge.

Cheile Turzii gorge is a spectacular cleft through a 600m (2000ft) high ridge – the Culmea Petreștilor; the path crosses the river several times in the bottom of the gorge, each time on a bridge, unlike Râmeț gorge. You pass the entrances to Cetateaua Mare cave on the right bank and Mic on the left – really one cave now split by the river. Beware; the limestone in the gorge wears to a very slippery surface, even when dry. At the far end of the gorge the path, now a wide gravel track, takes you up through the groves of birch and alder to Cheile Turzii cabana (see Appendix A). There is a path around the cliffs at the top of the gorge (red disc waymarks), shown on a map at the cabana.

An alternative to this is to catch a lift or a bus to Turda, from where a narrow-gauge line heads west, up the Arieș valley to Abrud (three trains a day). To reach Cheile Turzii cabana from the town you leave on the main DN75 road heading west up the Arieș valley to Abrud and turn right off the road at the end of the town at a roundabout (red blue cross waymarks), heading west along the north bank of the Arieș river; it is 6km (3½ miles) from leaving the road to the cabana. If you are in a hurry you can catch a bus, or perhaps a lift along the DN75 road, through the village of Mihai Viteazu to a right hand turning. Alight here and walk up the road into the village of Cheia; keep right at the fork in the village and follow the rough road uphill past the quarry, over the hill to the cabana (see Appendix A).

Day Two

Cheile Turzii cabana to Buru cabana, 12km (8 miles)

This is a short day's walk, giving plenty of time to explore the gorge from the cabana. You have the choice of walking into the bottom of the gorge or going up around its rim (red disc waymarks). I recommend you make a sketch from the map on the wall of the kiosk shop by the cabana as this is better than any printed map available. From the cabana head south-west (red triangle waymarks) to the Hășdate river downstream of the gorge. Cross over the concrete suspension bridge and turn left (red triangle waymarks) to take you, initially through the pines on the north side of the Arieș valley. You exit from them as you approach the summit of Dealul Bisericii (794m, 2605ft). The path continues for just over 2km to a second summit, Dumbrava (785m, 2575ft) and beyond it for 2km more to Dealul Borzești, where you re-enter the forest and descend steeply to the Borzești stream; turn left to head south-east down the valley through the Cheile Borzești gorge to the Arieș valley. Turn right on the main road for just over 1km to Buru Cabana. This is a short day's walk for the simple reason that the next cabana is a full day's walk away. The train from Buru to Ocoliș departs about 0720 in the morning. 8km (5 miles) south of Buru is the village of Râmețea, with a largely Hungarian-speaking population.

It is possible to head west from Râmețea onto the Trascău ridge and head south-west along it to the grassy col above Huda lui Papară cave – see the Trascău section below. A second possibility for continuing to the Trascău is to make your way 9km up the Arieș valley, initially on a track then a path (blue cross waymarks) taking you along the eastern side of the Bedeleu ridge for a spectacular full day's walk to Huda lui Papară cave. Yet a third possibility is to take a train or lift 27km (17 miles) up the Arieș valley from Buru to Salciua de Jos halt (the first stop after Poșaga) and walk up to Huda lui Papară cave and on to Râmeț; see the 'Access' section for the Trascău.

Day Three

Buru cabana to Băișoara cabana through Runcului gorge, 38km (24 miles) (16km, 10 miles, by train). Altitude gained from Buru to Vârful Scărișoara, 972m (3190ft)

You may well want to start the day by taking the train as far as the fourth stop, at Ocoliș. The DN75 road is not too busy – the walk along it is pleasant, and you may well get a lift. Turn right off the main road, heading up through Ocoliș. As you leave the village you are heading up the Ocoliș valley on a rough chalky track. Before you enter the gorge you pass a junction with a path up to Cheile Pociovaliștei (blue triangle waymarks); we later rejoin this path on the summit of Scărișoara. Keep heading north-west up the track (red cross waymarks), up the Runcului gorge, carved by the Ocoliș river through blue basalt. At the end of the gorge the path swings to the left and heads south-west, ascending some 600m through the trees to take you just to the north of the summit of Vârful Scărișoara (1382m, 4534ft), a rounded hilltop in the forests. 1.5km after passing the summit, now heading south-west across the plateau, you come to a junction with the blue triangle route. Turn right, west and then north (blue triangle and red stripe waymarks) to cross the forest road at the unattractive ski hotel of Băișoara cabana (see Appendix A).

There are several choices of how to proceed from Băișoara. You can head west and then south into Câmpeni, to follow the Trascău traverse in reverse order, or walk all the way to Padiș, missing out the Trascău, which would be a pity, or walk into Câmpeni and take the train to Salciua, there to start the Trascău traverse as detailed below.

If you want to head east out of the Apuseni, then the route takes you down to Muntele Filii cabana; cross over the road at Băișoara and take the blue stripe route past the bottom of the winter-only ski lift. It heads to the north and then round to the north-east, through the pine trees and down to Muntele Filii cabana in the Băișoara valley. There is a tarred road leading to the south-east to Turda, and a path (blue stripes and red triangles) east to Lita and eventually to Cluj.

Days Four and Five – Băișoara cabana to Câmpeni (hotel), 48km (30 miles)

This is written as a two-day section, assuming bivouacking in the woods en route. There is no accommodation heading west or south from Băișoara. From Băișoara make your way along the rough road through the forests as it runs past the ski lift, and up towards the summit of Muntele Mare (1826m, 5991ft), which you skirt to the south. Just before the end of the road a path (red cross waymarks), turns left, following a ridge south-west through the pines, over the minor summits of Neteda (1784m, 6853ft) and Sesu Lupului (1636m, 5367ft), eventually bringing you down to the village of Lupșa. If you turn right and walk into the village you will find the campsite and a small bar, where you may be able to find private accommodation.

To keep heading along the ridge of Muntele Mare ignore the red cross path to keep heading west along the road as it deteriorates into a path, marked by the occasional red stripe. It keeps to the southern side of the main ridge, passing through the trees as it dips into the shallow col between the valleys of the Iara to the right and the Valea Mare to the left. Swinging to the north away from this, you come to a fork with the red triangle route turning right to continue northwards to pass to the east of Vârful Dumitreasa (1638m, 5374ft), eventually heading out of the mountains at Gilău lake and so down to Cluj. Keep left here, following the main ridge (red stripe waymarks) west to Vârful Smidele (1644m, 5394ft). The path now descends on the northern side of the ridge, with the summit of Vârful Balomireasa (1632m, 4698ft) above you to the right. The path now swinging round to the right, you cross a path from the Someșu Rece valley to the north to the Bistrișoara valley to the south. 4km after this path crossing you meet the forest road heading north from Câmpeni. Turn right on this, then left after 500m to head north-west (red stripe waymarks) on the southern side of the watershed towards Vârful Sihla, further directions being given under 'Day Two' of the Trascău itinerary below.

THE TRASCĂU

The Trascău (pronounced 'Tras-ca'oo' – do not confuse with the Tarcau in the Eastern Carpathians or the Țarcu, north-west of the Retezat) is a dramatic limestone ridge running from north-east to south-west, marking the eastern flank of the Apuseni. It overlooks the city of Alba Iulia and the valley of the River Mureș. The highest point in the Trascău is Dimbău (1369m, 4491ft); this modest elevation belies the rugged outline of the range, with a good deal of exposed rock above the hill pasture and beech forest. A number of parallel valleys drain south-east into the Mureș valley – most of them have a string of farming villages along them, making this is the most densely populated area described in this book. It is characterised by tiny scattered hidden Moți villages with cottages of thatched roofs as steep as hayricks, hidden valleys with narrow muddy lanes along which ox-carts make their leisurely way. There is no one central ridge to the Trascău; rather the waymarked route threads its way through valleys, villages and gorges. The peaks of the Trascău are best tackled as day walks. Maps of the area are poor.

This is a region of typical karst scenery; the valleys cut deep into the limestone, resulting in a number of gorges. There are caves at Huda lui Papară, Poarta Smeilor and Bisericuta. The western side of the Trascău is marked by the Arieș valley, with its source in the heart of the Apuseni; it flows north-east to join the Mureș at the eastern end of the Trascău. The Trascău is, in my opinion, perhaps the most rewarding area of the Apuseni to explore, with its gorges, monasteries and dramatic high ridge. Râmeț monastery is the site of two major religious festivals, one celebrating the Holy Apostles Peter and Paul on 29th June and another the birth of the Virgin Mary on 8th September.

Access

The easiest access is from the DN1 (E81) along the Mureș valley; this also carries the main Bucharest–Cluj railway. Beiuș has several direct trains per day from the capital. From Beiuș buses make their way up to Râmeț monastery (18km, 11 miles). If heading south across the Apuseni you may prefer to do the first day walk in reverse, starting at Salciua de Jos halt and heading south, over the Arieș river on a footbridge and following the gravel road to Huda lui Papară cave, turning right as the road turns left out of the valley to follow an older track to the cave. There are two trains per day on the narrow-gauge line from Turda to Câmpeni. There is no rail link from the main line station at Câmpia Turzii to Turda; it has been replaced by a bus. To reach the gara mică for the narrow-gauge line head east along the DN15 towards Câmpia Turzii and turn right at the 'Zona industrială' sign to walk through the industrial plant to the station.

Day One

Salciua railway station to Râmeț cabana, 20km (13 miles)

You will probably find it quicker to reach Salciua by hitching a lift; the narrow-gauge train, like driving a sports car with the roof down on a cold sunny day, is a form of transport that looks better from the outside than experienced from within. Salciua is a delightful village with two festivals per year. From the station head east through the village on the DN75 towards Turda. Slightly less than 1km from the station you reach the end-of-the village road sign; turn right here, across the Arieș river on a wire pedestrian suspension bridge. You leave the village heading south-east along a farm track waymarked by blue crosses; turn right where the red cross route to Aiud gorge and cave keeps straight on. Follow the gravel track along the valley past ha

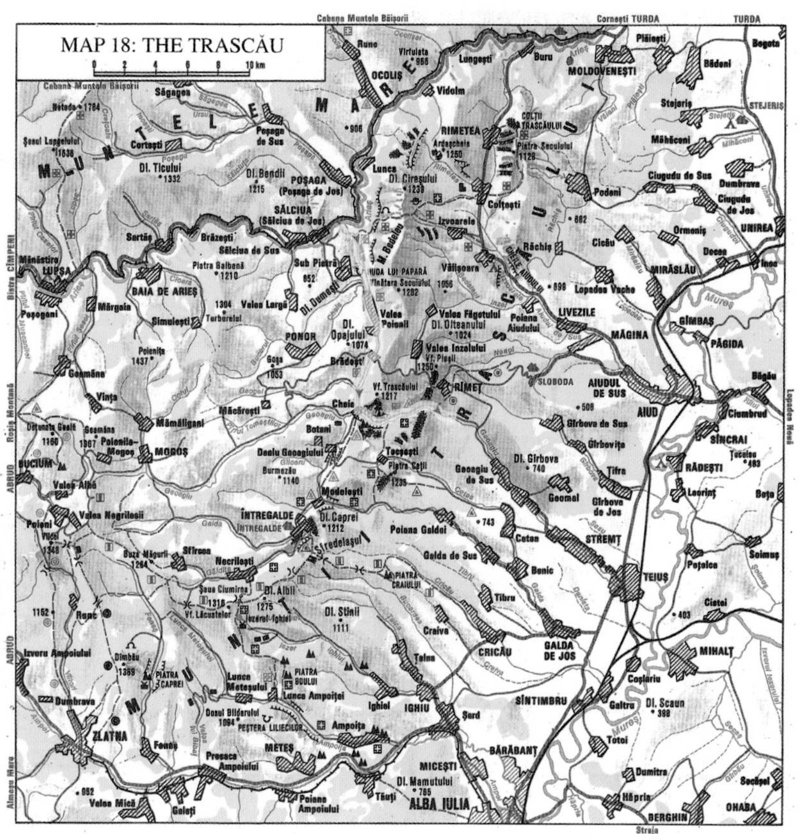

meadows and to the entrance to a small gorge and the entrance to Huda lui Papară cave (567m, 1860ft), 4km after leaving Sălciua.

Keep right by the apparently defunct ticket office for the entrance to the cave (itself well worth exploring) and follow the blue crosses along a stony zigzagging track, steeply up through the deciduous forest and out of the Galdiţa valley to a clearing on a ridge. The track swings to the left and descends back to the valley, where it is joined by a blue stripe route from the left, from the Bedeleu ridge. Head just east of due south to head up the valley with the river on your right to reach the dispersed village of Valea Poienii. This stretch is not well waymarked but is easy to follow; you join a well-used rough road coming in from the left.

At the hamlet of Brădeşti, on the main Trascău ridge you climb steeply up a meadow to reach a settled saddle on the main Trascău ridge. Turn right at the shop on the road from Râmeţ to Mogoş and head steeply down a rough track beneath trees among houses, into the Brădeştilor valley; it dwindles to a footpath along the valley bottom in the forest and brings you to a cross-paths among the trees at the delightful village of Cheia, 5km from the track-junction at Brădeşti. Turn left here, east, downstream along

On the trail near Brădești – Trascău massif

the valley to the beginning of Râmeț gorge. Here you have the choice of the cable-equipped and awkward (but dry) route along the side of the gorge or the scarcely believable gorge route, involving wading up to mid-chest height (I am 6ft tall) along the relatively slow-flowing stream with a firm bottom. In warm dry weather it is a delight. The two routes rejoin after 2km. A further 2km along a track brings you to the modern but unappealing cabana (see Appendix A). Along the Mânăstirii valley and in the gorges cables have been fitted.

There is a pleasant, easy walk down to the town of Aiud from Râmeț, taking you past the monastery, then turn left to Râmeț village (red disc waymarks). The path takes you from the eastern end of the village, up to a saddle and Pleasa Râmeților summit. Follow the ridge of Sultanului Hill (714m, 2342ft) and then descend into the Secături Valley. The final approach to Sloboda cabana (see Appendix A) is a steep descent of Oltenuli hill. From here there are 12km (7½ miles) of road into the centre of Aiud a pleasant town, with an old-world atmosphere and a wealth of old architecture.

There is an alternative approach t Râmeț cabana via Râmețea village fro Buru, adding about 3hrs to the abov walk. It is a superb walk, well wort doing, even if you end up camping for night in the forest. Head south from Bur along the road to Râmețea village an Aiud, heading up the Râmețea valley (g a lift if you can). As you enter the villag of Râmețea a path (red cross waymarks leads off to the left, up to Colț Trascăului summit, heading southwar along the narrow ridge and returning the road at Coltești village. This is diversion that will add an hour and a hal Heading south through Coltești villag turn right, west (yellow cross waymarks over the ridge running between Deal Cireșului (1239m, 4066ft) and Bedele You descend over some crags into th

Arieş valley and join the track heading south past Huda lui Papară cave. From here you follow the directions given above.

Exit route

Râmeţ cabana to Bucium, 37km (20 miles)

From Râmeţ cabana head south from just before the gorge (yellow cross and red stripe waymarks) over into the Cetea valley and south, to the right of Piatra Cetii crags (1233m, 4095ft), down into the Galda valley. Turn right along the track in the bottom of the valley (yellow cross waymarks), through a small gorge to the hamlet of Modoleşti. In Modoleşti turn left, still on a track, where now blue triangle waymarks have joined the yellow crosses. After 2km you reach the village of Întregalde with its cabana. The village lies at the confluence of the Galda and Galdiţa streams. Turn left, south (red triangle waymarks), up the southern side of the valley, onto Sfredelaşul hill. From the top of the hill a path takes you past the crags of the Piatra Craiului ('King's Rocks') down into the village of Cricău (red stripe waymarks). Ignore this to head south-west (red stripe waymarks), over Dealul Albii (1275m, 4183ft) to Şaua Ciumârna pass, on a karst plateau.

There is an exit route here if you want to leave the area via the town of Alba Iulia. Turn left at the pass (yellow cross waymarks) down to the small lake at Iezerul Ighiel (alt. 920m, 3018ft). From the forester's hut a rough road leads to the left, down to Ighiel village. Ignore this and keep on the yellow cross path, taking you down to the hamlet of Lunca Ampoiţei, past the crags of Piatra Bulzului (1029m, 3376ft) and Piatra Boului (1091m, 3579ft) on the left. At Lunca Ampoiţei you turn left onto the road, taking you through Ampoiţa gorges to Ampoiţa village. Continue through the village to the main road, where you can hitch to Alba Iulia, or instead turn right on the road for 2km, before turning off to the left in the village of Tăuţi, to take the path over Mamut hill (765m, 2510ft), and so into Alba Iulia. To return from Alba Iulia to Bucharest you need to take the train from nearby Vânţu de Jos junction to Sibiu (five trains a day, taking an hour and a half).

To reach Bucium from Şaua Ciumârna pass head west along the ridge to Vârful Lăcuştelor (1316m, 4465ft), across another pass, bringing you to the summit of Buza Măgurii (1264m, 4147ft). You approach Bucium, in fact a commune of more than twenty smaller settlements, past the campsite just to the north of Vârful Vâlcoi (1348m, 4422ft). North of Bucium ('Buchium') are the basalt crags of Detunata (1160m), a nature reserve. Bucium is actually the name of a local instrument, rather like an alpenhorn. To hear one being played you should visit the Maidens' Fair on the third Sunday in July, near Avram Iancu (see the Bihor massif below).

To connect with the itinerary through the Bihor-Vlădeasa, you need to walk the 14km (9 miles) down the road to Abrud. This is the terminus of the Arieş valley narrow-gauge line; there are three trains a day down the line. You need to travel 12km (7½ miles), three stops to Câmpeni, from where you catch a bus or a lift 31km (19 miles) to the road junction at Gârda de Sus.

It is also possible to walk all the way to the Bihor from Câmpeni. Head east out of the town on the DN75 towards Bistra village and Turda. The road follows the north bank of the Arieş river as you head downstream. The first tributary you cross, coming in from the north, is the Bistra river. An unsurfaced road turns left off the DN75 up the Bistra valley. Follow this due north, up out of the valley in the forests. 22km (14 miles) after leaving the main road you reach a junction with the

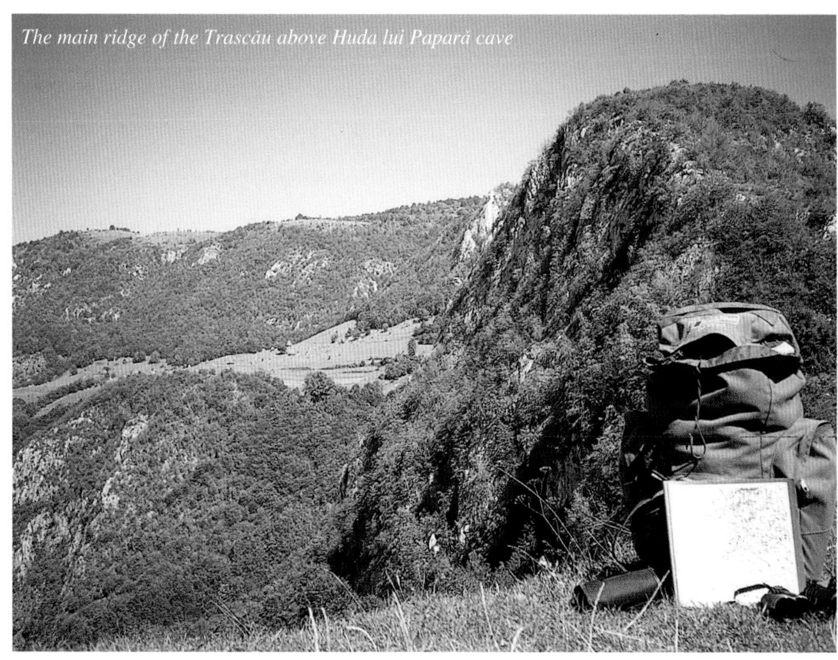
The main ridge of the Trascău above Huda lui Papară cave

main Muntele Mare ridge path (red stripe waymarks) heading due west from the cabana at Băişoara. Turn left now to follow this north-west up out of the forests to the southern flanks of Vârful Sihla (1670m, 5480ft). 2km south-west of the summit you reach a path junction, a right hand turning taking you to the summit itself. Keep left here to head west, after a further 8km (5 miles) reaching another forest road. Turn left along this to reach the crosstracks at the pass of Şaua Ursoaia and a private cabana (see map). Head west from Şaua Ursoaia (red stripe waymarks), along a watershed in the forest to Vârful Clujului (1399m, 4590ft). The track swings to the left after the summit, bringing you to Poiana Ursoaia pass. From here you have the choice of heading straight ahead, south towards Gheţaia and Gârda de Sus (red stripe waymarks) or turning left (blue stripe waymarks) to Padiş, as per the second alternative of 'Day Two' of the Bihor-Vlădeasa itinerary below.

THE BIHOR-VLĂDEASA REGION

This is the heart of the Apuseni, reaching a maximum altitude of 1849m (6066ft) at Cucurbata Mare summit. It is above all a karst region, where the rolling forested hills are honeycombed with caves and swallow-holes. There are some spectacular small gorges, described in the itineraries below. The settlements in this region, especially Arieşeni and Gârda de Sus, are delightful traditional villages whose inhabitants can still be seen wearing local costume on Sundays. The accompanying map must inevitably lose some accuracy in this area of bizarre geography – but it has plenty of inexcusable errors as well. There is an excellent 1:30,000 sheet of the Padiş area, of Hungarian origin (see Appendix C, maps).

Avram Iancu and the Târgul de Fete Festival on Vârful Găina

Just off the accompanying map, at the southern end of the Bihor ridge, is the village of Avram Iancu. Here, or rather on the summit of Găina (1484m, 4869ft), is where on the third Sunday in July the Târgul de fete (or 'Maidens' Fair') takes place. This was, and to an extent still is the event where the inhabitants of the region met annually to arrange spouses for their sons and daughters. The festival is still a spectacle of local costume and music, and is well worth getting to if you can. As events tend to start at dawn on the Sunday you need to arrive on the Saturday to see the best part of the fair.

It is quite easy to walk south from this map to Vf. Găina. Near the southern edge of the map the DN75 road is shown; 1km east of Şaua Vârtop pass, where it crosses the main north-south Bihor ridge is a ski slope; a path heads south from the foot of this on the roadside, up to Piatra Grăitoare (1658m, 5440ft) and continues south along the ridge, past a col and over Cucurbăta Mare (1849m, 6066ft), takes you across the forest road from Cristianu de Jos to Avram Iancu, south to Vârful Rotunda. You turn left here to walk over Găina and down into Avram Iancu (22km, 14 miles, from Cucurbăta Mare). The total walk from Arieşeni village will take about 9hrs. By road Avram Iancu is 22km (14 miles) west of Câmpeni (slow branch line from Turda and Câmpia Turzii) and 35km (22 miles) north of Baia de Criş, on the main DN76 road in the Crişul Alb valley. There is also a path signed with blue stripes, up from Halmagiu village, initially on the track up the Lungşoara valley, taking you up to Vârful Rotunda. It takes about 8hrs to reach Avram Iancu.

Itinerary across the Bihor

The itinerary below details a walk across the centre of the Apuseni, initially walking up to the resort complex at Padiş. It can be continued from the walk across the Gilău and Trascău, detailed above. Alternatively you can walk in from the west; this is suitable if you are arriving by train. Ştei (shown on older maps as Dr Petru Groza) is on the line from Oradea in the Banat region; there are three trains a day, taking nearly three hours.

Day One

Walk-in to the Bihor-Vlădeasa from Ştei (railway station) to Padiş cabana, 32km (20 miles). Altitude gained, 1080m (3500ft)

From Ştei take the DN75 road south-east towards Nucet (signed to Câmpeni), turning left after 8km up to the village of Sighiştel. From the eastern, uphill end of Sighiştel a path leads you (blue triangle waymarks) along the Sighiştel stream past the cave entrances of Peştera Măgura and Peştera Coliboaia. An hour and a half after leaving Sighiştel village you a clearing (Poiana Muncelului); continue east across it to reach a forest road climbing up from the main road. Turn right, east along the forest track and then left after 400m at a junction, north for 350m on a track. Turn right off the track, out of the trees, east (blue triangle waymarks), the path skirting the wooded summit of Vf. Ţapului hill (1475m, 4839ft) to the north and then heading north, down in the forest (red stripe waymarks), to meet a forest track. Follow this, downhill and contouring, downhill to a junction at a bridge (over thePăuleasa stream). Keep right here, past the forestry buildings of Canton Păuleasa to the principal Valea Galbenei, crossing the Râul Galbenei so that you are heading south-east on a better forest track, upstream with the river on your right. 1km after the second bridge turn left (Gheie Galbenei Gorge lies ahead – map 19 is inaccurate here) off the track onto a path taking you up, north-north-east, across the clearing of Poiana Florilor. You have 2km of ascent after leaving the road (after leaving the clearing, all in forest) before reaching Focu

MAP 19: THE BIHOR AND VLĂDEASA MOUNTAINS

Viu cave on your left. The path now swings to the east and becomes a rough forest track; Map 19 only marks the red stripe route turning north to the road here, but you can turn right (yellow disc waymarks), to head east, down through the forest to the gravel road running along Valea Cetății – the stream that flows south to disappear underground into Cetățile Ponorului cave; this is a worthwhile detour to your right – the road also taking you to the karst plateau of Lumea Pierduta – 'the Lost World'. To continue to Padiș, turn left on the road, then right off it at Canton Glăvoi buildings to head north-east (blue and yellow disc waymarks). for altogether 3.5km after leaving the road, through scattered trees and clearings to Padiș cabana (see Appendix A).

Information is available at the cabana for a number of day walks exploring the surrounding karst plateau; not all routes are well waymarked.

Alternative Day One

Gârda de Sus road junction to Padiș cabana, 23km (15 miles). Altitude gained, 705m (2300ft)

If you want to spend some time visiting the ice cave during this walk you should set off early. Head north on the rough road out of Gârda heading up the Gârda Seaca valley, plenty of waymarks indicating your route. The road itself gets to Gârda by turning right up the Ordencusa valley, through Ordincusii gorges and the entrance to Peştera Poarta lui Ionel to the village of Sfortea, skirting Vârful Stânişoara (1377m, 4518ft) and meeting the Poiana Horea road at Poiana Ursoaia, from where it turns left to head south to Gheţari. The total distance for this is 17km and will no doubt be your choice if you are on a bike. 5km up this road you can turn left (blue stripe waymarks) up to Gheţari. The better walking route is to keep left at the road fork just out of Gârda de Sus. After almost 1km you turn right over a bridge, crossing the Gârda Seaca river (red stripe waymarks). From the river the path goes up though the forest, climbs to the left, reaches a clearing and a farm and runs across the Scărişoara karst area near the site of the former cabana, burnt down in 1991. (The map is not accurate in showing a red stripe route following the stream to the left while a supposed red cross route heads straight due north.) You are walking through mixed woods, stands of young beech and fields of hay. At Gheţar you are in the wilds of the Apuseni; there is no main street, just houses at random. If you are lucky you may be offered accommodation in the village itself; if not press on to Padiş cabana. Whichever route you take from Gârda, the walk takes about 4hrs.

Near the village of Gheţari is the famous ice cave, Peştera de Gheţaru, or just Scărişoara; a number of other caverns contain the usual stalactite and stalagmite features. However ordinary caves can be visited anywhere in the world. Ones with subterranean glaciers are something special, so the one to visit is the ice cave. Analysis of the ice within the cave is helping to indicate climate change over the centuries. At the back of the cave is a chamber known as 'the church' for its ice pillars; there is also a natural ice sculpture resembling a bear.

Onwards from the cave the route lies mainly on rough forest tracks. Initially, you need to pick up the blue triangle waymarks from the cave exit along a footpath through the trees which heads down the hill, north-west from Gheţari, to join the rough road running up the Gârda Seaca valley. You turn right along this to follow it through various little settlements to the foresters' huts at Casa de Piatra ('House of Stone'). Along the way you can find examples of the village 'Troiţa'. In lieu of a church or even a priest several settlements shared one itinerant cleric (an arrangement lately adopted, with the addition of a car, in the English shires), the villagers holding services beneath these crucifixes, the proceedings conducted by the oldest and most respected male. Beyond Casa de Piatra the track takes you past the entrance to Peştera Coiba Mare cave on the left. At the end of the road you find a sign pointing the way up the Gârdişoara valley (blue stripe waymarks) north to Padiş cabana.

There is an alternative from Gheţari to Padiş, which takes you along the top of a broad water-less ridge, such is the porous nature of the limestone. Head north from Gheţari on the rough road (red stripe waymarks) which connects Gheţari with the rest of the world, running along the ridge between the Gârda Seaca and Ordencuşa valleys. 8km (5 miles) after the village you reach the junction at Poiana Ursoaia. Turn left along here, heading north, initially on a forest road. From here the path runs north-west (blue stripe waymarks) approximately following the limestone ridge of Calineasa, initially dropping to the east side of it through conifers and meadows. As the map shows, it then swings round to the left to regain the ridge at the hilltop of Calineasa, site of the famous Târgu de Dat festival of trading goods and disputes. The path drops again to the east side of the ridge, to the east of the unnamed summit of 1579m (5180ft). You climb back up towards the crags of Apă din Piatra ('Water of the Rocks') to Vârful Peşterii and the source of the Bătrâna river. From here the path continues north-west (blue stripe waymarks) across the hill and down to the road running up the Bătrâna valley to Padiş. Turn left on the road and head west for 1km to the cabana, on the way passing the blue triangle waymarks turning left down to the Gârdişoara valley and Gheţari, outlined above.

Day Two

Padiş cabana to Stâna de Vale via Cetatea Rădesei, 18km (11 miles). Altitude gained to Şaua Cumpănaţelu, 360m (1180ft)

From Padiş head west on the road (red and blue stripe waymarks) to reach a five-way junction of rough roads after 2km, in the grassy clearing of Şesul Padiş (or Platoul Padiş). Turn right here, north, still on the road (still with red and blue stripe waymarks), past a glacial pool on the left (Tăul Vărăşoaia) and then over the gentle Vărăşoaia Pass (1327m, 4354ft). You are walking along the forest road for this stretch; it passes to the right of Vărăşoaia summit and then runs along the watershed between the Crişul Pietros river to the left and the Someşu Cald on the right. 600m north of the pass turn right off the road at a left-hand bend, down some steps with a railing fixed to the rock (red disc waymarks), and into the Cetatea Rădesii gorge and cave complex; this path leads you to the much larger Cheile Someşului Cald gorge, at the downhill, eastern end of which a road leads east, down to Ic Ponor and eventually to the town of Huedin. A path explores the top of the Cheile Someşului gorge on its southern side and runs along the bottom of the gorge; when you have finished exploring, take the signed path (red disc waymarks) heading up, west-north-west up for 2km, out of the forest to reach the red stripe path and continue climbing up the southern side of the east-west Apuseni ridge to Cumpanatelu pass (1630m, 5348ft), where the track swings to the left to head west along the ridge top. There are views down to the Crişul Pietros river on the left. The rough road swings to the north as it passes through a hollow by Cârligatele summit (1694m, 5558ft), past Vf Fântâna Rece (1652m, 5420ft). You continue north-west along the ridge with wide views across the forests, down to Drăganu saddle, keeping east of Bohodei summit (1654m, 5558ft). 1km north-west of the summit is Şaua Bohodei, where you meet the blue triangle path coming up from Pietroasa and Canton Aleu in the Aleu valley to the left. Head west-north-west from here on the track, for 1.5km to a junction where the wider forest track heads left, east down to Budureasa. This junction is on the forest edge, 1km west of Vf. Poienii. Head north from here on a lesser forest track (red stripe waymarks), north initially descending, to the resort of Stâna de Vale. Alternatively you can stay on the forest road all the way. Stâna de Vale is 25km (15½ miles) east of the village of Beiuş, reached by road twisting up through the forest. A number of forest roads radiate from it, heading north and east to the Iad and Drăganului valleys, making the area ideal for cycle touring.

Onwards from Stâna de Vale

From Stâna de Vale there is the possibility of three alternative exits.

The first goes north-west (blue triangle waymarks) along the watershed between the Nimăeşti and the Iadului valleys as far as Piatra Tisei summit. Beyond the summit the watershed (still blue triangle waymarks) is between the Beiuş and Meziad valley. The path swings to the west and drops to the cabana and village of Meziad (see Appendix A), from where you can head down to Beiuș on the DN76 road and the railway from Oradea to Deva. There is also a walking route of seven hours north-east, off the map to the cabana at Leșu (see Appendix A). The path heads past Meziad cave, over Dealul Stogu summit and Hodrincușa summit (1027m, 3370ft), overlooking Leșu lake. You descend on a forest track to the north end of the lake and the motel-cabana.

The second exit route from Stâna de Vale heads north on a forest road to descend into the Valea Iadului ('the Valley of Hell'). You follow the valley northwards on the forest road past the Cascada Iadului waterfall and reaching the head of Leșu lake after 14km (9 miles). The forest road continues north to Motel Leșu and Bulz.

The third takes you east, back across the the Apuseni to Vlădeasa; from Stâna de Vale; an approximation of it is shown on the accompanying map; head east from Stâna de Vale (blue cross and red triangle waymarks) up the valley past the trout farm (păstrăvarie) up to a minor pass and down to the foresters' huts at Cantonul Ciripa, where you meet the road heading northwards down the valley to the lake. It is possible to turn left and take the low-level route to the lake and on down to Valea Drăganului cabana (see Appendix A). Alternatively you can turn right 3km along the lake shore, heading up the Zirna valley (blue triangle waymarks) to Vlădeasa cabana (see Appendix A).

The most attractive route to Vlădeasa crosses the Drăganului valley at Ciripa and follows the blue triangle route up to the right of the Moara Dracului valley, past the waterfall in the forest and the foresters' hut. You reach the ridge connecting Vârful Buteasa (1792m, 5880ft) to Vârful Britei (1759m, 5771ft). A path leads to the summit of Buteasa 2km to the north. Turn right, south (red triangle waymarks) along the ridge, skirting the summit of Vârful Briței to the east. You reach a path junction on the col between Vârful Briței and the crags of Piatra Tilharului; turn left. Adjacent to Piatra Tilharului is a simple refuge. Take care to follow the blue stripes here, east towards Vârful Miclău. The path follows the ridge around to the north, then west, over Vârful Nimăiasaor or Garda de Piatra (1589m, 5214ft). The path swings to the west, then drops down on the east side of the ridge, below a shallow col, Intre Munți. Here you meet the forest track heading away to the right to cabana Vlădeasa, also offering a route east down the Stanciului valley past the Rachitele waterfall to Rachitele village. Bear left instead (blue stripe waymarks) due north to Vârful Vlădeasa and the cabana meteorologica. The highest point reached on the walk is Vlădeasa summit itself, 1836m (6024ft), where you will find the met. station.

Onwards from Vlădeasa

My suggested exit route from Vlădeasa is the descent to Bologa station (20km, 12 miles). Head north-east (blue stripe waymarks) descending into the Visag valley, in the bottom of which the path meets a gravel road through, down to the Hent valley, where you turn left along the road into Bologa (railway station on the Oradea–Cluj line). Alternatively (look at the road map now, as this route is off the Bihor-Vlădeasa map to the north) you can walk across to the larger town of Huedin, the start point for heading into the Meseș hills and their remarkable wooden churches. Turn right at the Visag–Hent confluence, to reach the village of Săcuieu after 1.5 km. Turn left in the village to head up the rough road going east for 10km (6 miles) to Sâncraiu, where you turn left into the town of Huedin.

If you are heading in the direction of Cluj you may well want to extend your walk by heading down to the Henț valley, turning right to go upstream to the hamlet of Scrind Frasinet, and turning left to head up the Margăuța valley on a rough road taking you into the Măgura Călățele hills, to the village of Călățele with some fine wood carving on the houses, descending to Huedin through the Hungarian-speaking villages of Călata and Sâncraiu. If you turn left to head along the road up to Beliș and Stațiunea Fântânele you will come to Ardeleana cabana.

Trains to Cluj from Huedin or Bologa take around an hour; there are nine trains a day. There are a similar number of trains west to Oradea.

CHAPTER TWELVE
The Eastern Carpathians

Just as the Pennines in England were never considered to be a single entity until they were collectively named in honour of Italy's mountainous spine, so the Eastern Carpathians – the Carpați Orientali – are really a collection of smaller massifs divided by valleys and depressions. Viewed as a whole, they divide Moldavia in the east from Transylvania in the west. The region is well supplied with populated valleys – this is not a mountain barrier in the way that parts of the Southern Carpathians are; nevertheless the area offers plenty of remote mountain walking. The highest summit is Pietrosul Bistriței (2100m, 6890ft) in the Căliman; with Iezerul Căliman (2031m, 6663ft) the only summit in the Eastern Carpathians over 2000m (6500ft). Outlined below is a north–south Carpathian grand traverse.

The Eastern Carpathians consist of three parallel strips running north–south. In the west is an area of volcanic mountains, well supplied with spa towns (such as Borsec, Covasna and Băile Tușnad) taking advantage of the hot springs. Off to the east of the southern end of the region, in the Slanic valley, 26km (16 miles) north-west of Buzău, is Vulcanii Noroioși, a sort of Rotorua-in-miniature of bubbling mud pools. The central zone of the Eastern Carpathians is made up principally of limestone and crystalline formations; to the east is a region of sandstone ridges. Vast areas of forest cover the whole area. In general it can be summed up as a region of forested rolling hills with isolated areas of high crags.

International footpaths through the Eastern Carpathians

At the time of writing it is planned that the international E8 footpath will be connected with a route running southwards through the Eastern Carpathians. The result will take the E8 from the Dutch coast (an extension across England and Ireland is proposed), south-east across Germany, following a Rhine–Danube route into Austria, crossing into Slovakia and heading north from Bratislava across Slovakia into the Beskid mountains and so into Poland, heading east along the Carpathians into Ukraine.

It diverts from the main Carpathian chain to cross the border into Romania near Sighetu Marmației, then south across the Rodna, the Căliman and the Giurgeului and then along the 'east of the Olt' route outlined below, eventually running southwards across the Baraolt range to Brașov. From here it is proposed that it will follow a route west along the Făgăraș, Retezat, Godean and the north side of the Danube across the plains, crossing at Calafat into Bulgaria, then south-east to the Aegean coast in Greece, just west of the Turkish border (see Long Distance Paths Advisory Service, Appendix F).

The itinerary below outlines a walking route starting in the north and heading south, eventually to connect with the Ciucaș (Chapter Three). It is possible to connect the monasteries west of Suceava with walking in the Rarău and Giumalău and, similarly, a visit to the Neamț monasteries can be connected with walks using Lacu Roșu as a base. The southern part of the Eastern Carpathians can be considered to be followed by two parallel walking routes, following the mountain ridges either side of the youthful River Olt as it flows south towards Brașov. On the east of the Olt is the route running across the Căliman, the Giurgeului, Hășmas, Ciucului and Bodoc. The route effectively forks in the unmapped Ciucului, from where it is possible to take a yet more easterly route, across the Nemirei massif and into the Vrancea and Penteleu mountains. On the western side of the Olt valley you can walk south across the Gurghiului and Harghita ranges.

THE SUHARD MASSIF

The Suhard is a largely forested small massif running south-east from the eastern end of the Rodna towards Vatra Dornei. I would not recommend a journey especially to explore it, but it offers a useful connecting walk from the Rodna to the Giumalău and the Rarău. Its highest point is Vf. Omului (1932m, 6339ft). To the south-west of the Suhard is the Ilva valley, with a string of villages (see Rodna map). At the head of the valley at its eastern end, the road and railway cross the Ilva pass (893m, 2930ft) in the forests and descend into the Tesna valley. To the north-east of the Suhard is the less populated Bistrița valley, carrying the main DN18 Borsa–Vatra Dornei road from Transylvania into Moldova. At Cabana Runc at Vatra Dornei there is a sign indicating the walking time back to Rotunda pass as being 22hrs. The itinerary below assumes the end of an eastbound traverse of the Rodna, finishing at Rotunda pass. This is a remote spot, reached by unsigned rough road, snaking up 4km from the DN18 along the Bistrița Mare valley, west of Tibău village.

Rotunda pass to Vatra Dornei (Cabana Runc), about 38km (24 miles). Altitude gained from Rotunda Pass to Vf. Omului, 661m (2169ft)

From Rotunda pass head east up out of the forest (red stripe waymarks) to a shepherd's hut by the head of the Șes stream, flowing north; the path swings right, south-east to a second shepherd's hut on the south side of the ridge, from where you follow the path along the tree line and right, around the head of a valley draining down to your right; you are heading just west of due south for a short stretch until you reach a point just below an unnamed col and return to heading south-east on the right hand side of the ridge, passing below Vf. Cociorba (1592m, 5223ft); at a broad saddle betwen Cociorba and Vf. Caturii (1625m, 7103ft) you regain the top of the ridge by some springs draining to the north.

You now return to walking on the western side of the ridge, heading just east of due south above the trees, on the western side of the watershed, bringing you, 6km after the Rotunda pass, to an unnamed rocky outcrop with some shepherds' huts below to the south-west. At the pass here a path turns right, south-west down to a shepherd's hut and into the Marin valley. Keep left at the pass to head just south of due east from the pass to a second unnamed craggy summit (1723m, 5653ft); 1km beyond this you reach Vf. Omului (1932m, 6338ft).

From Omului it is some 30km (18½ miles) south-east to Vatra Dornei. The path keeps to the south side of the top of the ridge, past the foresters' hut at Cabana Pastorală Omu and contours around the head of the Runcu valley in the trees. Continuing south, you pass Pietrele Roșii summit (1773m, 5817ft) to the east, still in the forest and continue south to Vf. Diecilor (1631m, 5351ft) above the surrounding forest. Immediately south of the summit is a col on the ridge by a shepherd's hut – Șaua Diecilor ('Curates' Pass'). The main ridge-top route turns left to head east and descends back into the forest; you pass a lake below you to your right, nestling below Vf. Rotunda (1461m, 4795ft). 3km east of Vf. Rotunda you exit from the forest and pass a second lake on your right (Lake Iceana), the path swinging left to head north-west over the crags of Vf. Sveiţaria (1562m, 5125ft), followed by Vf. Bitca Târsalui (1548m, 5079ft). 3km east of here the path heads south-east, off the eastern side of the ridge after 2km, crossing a stream and then contouring around the eastern side of of Vf. Făraone (1715m, 5627ft).

Directly east of the summit the path turns right to head south, back into the forest for 1km before reaching a shepherd's hut and clearing at Tarniţa (1542m, 5059ft), where it swings left, south-east of Vf. Jacob summit and down to a col north-east of Vf. Livada ('Orchard Summit' – 1463m, 4800ft). Head south-east from the col, contouring along the east side of the ridge to bring you, 2.5km from Vf. Livada, to a clearing with shepherds' huts. The final approach to Vatra Dornei takes you along the Ouşoru spur, at Runcu cabana and wooden cabins (Appendix A).

THE BÂRGĂU MASSIF

The Bârgău (formerly spelt Bîrgău) is a lesser range south-west of the higher Rarău and Giumalău. Of volcanic origin, its highest point is Heniul Mare (1611m, 5285ft). It offers a short cut from the eastern end of the Rodna, south, direct to the Căliman over the Tihuţa pass (1200m, 3937ft), avoiding the Rarău-Giumalău. Accommodation is available at the high village of Piatra Fântânele, with a number of villas and the bizarre Hotel Dracula. Tihuţa pass – also known as the Bârgău Pass – is the 'Borgo Pass' of Bram Stoker's Dracula. The village of Leşu, in the Leşu valley at the western end of the Bârgău, holds the 'Rhapsody of the Triscasi' festival on the first Sunday in September.

Access

The Bârgău is remote and inaccessible; only the most dedicated hunters of the Dracula location will make their way specifically to it. It is bounded on its southern side by the DN17, running a lonely 83km (51½ miles) south-west from Vatra Dornei to Bistriţa. On the northern side of the massif runs the railway line from Floreni junction (west of Vatra Dornei) to Ilva Mica (eight trains each way per day).

Walking in the Bârgău

There is a wild walk from **Rotunda pass to Tihuţa pass** (about 47km, 30 miles); there are no cabanas and few waymarks. From the summit of Vf. Omului (see Suhard traverse, above) head south-south-west and descend back into the forest; after just over 1km of walking in the forest you exit from the trees, continuing to descend along the spur to the crags of Suhard (1415m, 4642ft). There are fine views of the wooded Creasta Munţii Inisiraţi ridge ahead.

From the summit of Suhard head south-west, down for 1km to Suhard pass (1200m, 3937ft). To your left a track descends into the Coşniţa valley, eventually meeting the main DN17 road at the Podu Coşnei village (station) 12km (7½ miles) west of Vatra Dornei. Head west-south-west from the pass, back into the forest; 1km of ascent brings you to Suhardul Mare summit (1326m, 4350ft), altogether 7km (3½ miles) from Omului. From the summit, now out of the trees head south-east along the ridge, which, 2km south of Suhard Mare, swings left to head south and then south-south-west in the woods. Approximately 4km beyond Suhard Mare you exit from the woods onto a plateau; a number of paths head south-east along the Păiuţa spur. There follow 6km (4 miles) of heading west along the ridge, in and out of the trees, to bring you to the rounded summit of

Cucureasa (1392m, 4567ft), 9km (6 miles) south-west of Suhard Mare.

North-west of Cucureasa a grassy spur descends towards the Someş valley. Turn sharp left at the summit, to head south, around the head of the Cucureasa valley to your left. The ridge swings left to head south-east, all in the forest along the ridge for 8km (5 miles) to Poiana Casteilor summit (1216m, 3989ft). Head south-west from here, crossing the rough road from the Ilva valley (west) to the Teşna valley (east). You continue descending gently for about 6km (4 miles) through the trees, crossing the snaking railway line. The path swings confusingly in detail here but takes you due south. Having crossed the railway you follow a stream up, south-west, past its source eventually to exit fom the trees on top of a ride. You are just east of a grassy sumit, Vf. Friu (1121m, 3678ft). Turn south from here along the forest edge for 5km to Tihuţa pass in the trees. To continue from here see 'The Căliman Massif' below.

THE RARĂU-GIUMALĂU MASSIF

The Rarău-Giumalău (pronounced 'Rahro-Je-oomahlo') massif is a compact block of mountains whose white crags just poke above the mighty forests of spruce. To the north-east of the Rarău are the painted monasteries of Bucovina. Starting with Vf. Bârnărelu (1321m, 4334ft), to the north-east of the mountain resort town of Vatra Dornei, the Rarău-Giumalău sweeps in an arc around the Bistriţa valley, finishing at Curmătura Prislop (1310m, 4298ft) pass, carrying the road up from Chiril in the Bistriţa valley to the village of Ostra. This pass marks the beginning of the Stânişoarei mountains, a largely forested ridge which extends for some 70km (43½ miles) south-east towards the town of Piatra Neamţ. In fact the Giumalău in the west and Rarău, at the eastern end of the massif, are quite different. Giumalău (1857m, 6092ft) is the highest summit of a number of undulating and open ridges. Rarău (1650m, 5413ft) is a tangle of white crags among the spruce, its eponymous cabana-hotel perched among the rocks. Its architecture is described by Dervla Murphy as 'by Swiss chalet out of Stalin'. The author broke her foot slipping downstairs on a drunkard's frozen vomit. As she comments, only in Romania would the culprit later identify himself and offer apologies.

Despite the fact that the Rarău-Giumalău has a sizeable town at either end (Câmpulung Moldovenesc – 'Moldovans' Long Field' – to the north and Vatra Dornei to the south-west), its paths are little walked. Both towns make pleasant bases.

Access

If you are travelling expressly to the Rarău-Giumalău, rather than continuing your walk from Rodna and Maramureş (Chapter Ten), you have a choice of several start points. The railway from Suceava to Vatra Dornei runs along the northern side of the massif, over Mestecaniş pass (1096m, 4000ft); there is a railway halt just south of the road (eight trains each way per day). The stations in Câmpulung Moldovenesc, Pojorâta and Mestecaniş all make good start points. Eight trains daily travel the line from Suceava; it takes about 2hrs to Câmpulung. There are six trains a day from Bucharest to Suceava, the journey taking about 6hrs. There is one train a day direct from Bucharest to Vatra Dornei, the start point for the itinerary below, a sleeper.

Walking the Rarău-Giumalău massif

The itinerary below connects with an extension from the Rodna mountains. If you are travelling specifically to walk in

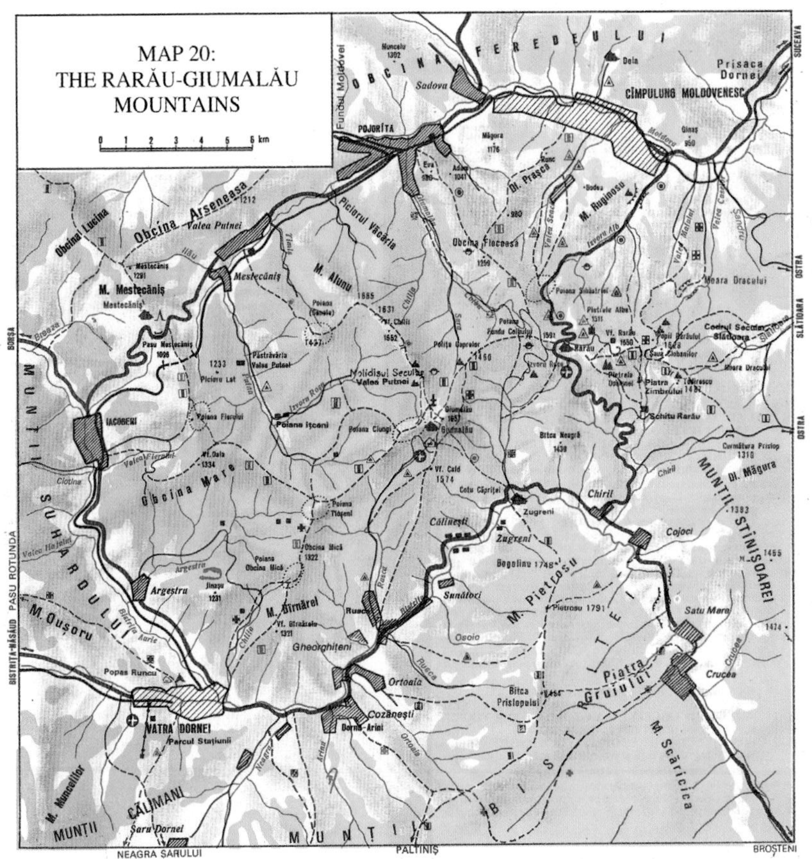

the Rarău-Giumalău, followed by the Căliman, the best start point is Câmpulung, finishing at Vatra Dornei (or continuing thence into the Căliman). You have a choice of no less than three paths out of **Câmpulung up into the Rarău-Giumalău**, in addition to the tarred road up to Hotel-Cabana Rarău. Much the best route is from the western end of town (blue stripe waymarks). Head west along Calea Bucovinei, the DN17/E571, towards Vatra Dornei and turn left along Str. Sirenei, then right at the sports stadium. You are now walking parallel to the main road, along Str. Sirenei, past the hospital on the left. The street dwindles to a rough road between houses and swings left to head south up a steep valley. Well marked with bus-stop signs the path takes you across the hay-meadows of the Runcu and to the main ridge. You can also head east along the main Calea Transylvaniei, the DN17/E571 to Gura Humorului from the main square in the centre with the statue of Dragoş Voda and the bison. Turn right along Str. Grigorescu, then first right along Str. Trandafirilor; continue to the junction with Str. Valea Seacă. Turn right here to head south up the valley (yellow triangle waymarks). The third possibility is to head out of town east along the main

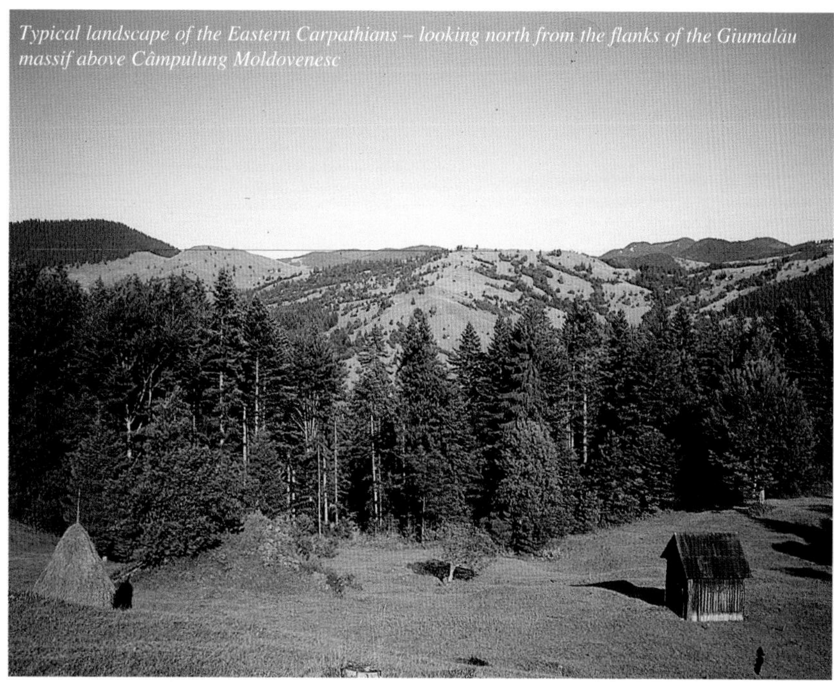
Typical landscape of the Eastern Carpathians – looking north from the flanks of the Giumalău massif above Câmpulung Moldovenesc

road, past the road up to Cabana Rarău, continuing for a further 1.5km to a left-hand bend, where you turn right, south along a track (red cross waymarks), taking you south up the valley into the Codrul Secular reserve and a small gorge, planked over with logs. This route is marked but not much used and is almost impossible to find on the descent.

An alternative is from **Vatra Dornei to Cabana Giumalău** (18km, 11 miles, alt. gained to Vf. Giumalău 1002m, 3287ft). Walk east out of Vatra Dornei on the main DN17B road; 1.5km east of the junction at the eastern end of town with the DN17 north to Iacobeni and Câmpulung turn left on a rough road down to cross the Bistrița river; 300m after the bridge turn right on a cart track (blue stripe waymarks) taking you up through the trees, and then out of them to walk over Vf. Bârnărel (1321m, 4334ft), continuing north to Poiana Obcina Mică clearing (1322m, 4338ft) and just east of north for 2km to the path junction at Poiana Ticșeni. Turn right here (red triangle/stripe waymarks), north-east along a ridge through the woods to Poiana Ciungi clearing. The crags surrounding Giumalău summit start in this clearing, as you climb above the tree line.

Giumalău summit (1857m, 6092ft) lies 257m (843ft) above the cabana. There are views west to the Suhard massif and the rocks at Pietrele Doamnei, 8km (5 miles) east. An alternative to Giumalău cabana is the cabana in the bottom of the gorge (a nature reserve) at Zugreni (Appendix A). Head south-east from the cabana (blue disc waymarks), through uninterrupted forest along the ridge of Colbu for just over 2hrs (881m, 2890ft) down to Zugreni cabana.

It is also possible to walk east up into the **Giumalău from Cabana Mestecaniș** (alt. 1096m, 3507ft), on the DN17 road. This is 16km (10 miles); altitude gained from Mestecaniș to Guimalău summit

761m (2500ft). (There is a tempting path from Mestecaniș north-west, following the red stripe waymarks along the Obcina Mestecanișului ('Birch-tree') ridge over Mestecaniș summit 1291m (4236ft) to Izvoarele Sucevei village, on the Ukraine border – about 12hrs total). To walk to Giumalău, cross over to the south side of the road from the cabana and head south-east along a track between fences (a sign to Giumalău 5–6 hrs, red stripes, Vatra Dornei 5–6hrs, blue stripes); you are heading towards the small opencast mine. After about 500m turn right (red/blue stripe waymarks), south, over the railway and to the path junction at Poiana Fierelui clearing. Keep left here (the right hand track running west down the Fierului valley to the village and station of Iacobeni); after 1.5km you reach the path running along the main east–west ridge of the Guimalău north-east of Oala summit (1334m, 4377ft). The junction is near a crossing of one of the tributary streams of the Putna. Turn left on the path which heads south-east in the woods along the Valea Putnei, then follows the Obcina Mare ridge on its northern side, continuing to head south-east, (red/blue stripe waymarks) to the junction at Poiana Ticșeni clearing. Here you meet the blue stripe route coming up from the right from Vatra Dornei. Keep left to head north-east along the ridge, following the red stripes and triangles to bring you to Poiana Ciungi and Guimalău cabana.

There is a day walk **east from Rarău to Slătioara** (18km, 12 miles, there and back; alt. lost to Slătioara, 790m, 2560ft), which also offers an exit route. Just to the east of Rarău are the limestone pillars of Pietrele Doamnei and the ancient forest of Slătioara – a worthwhile down-and-up day walk. The very intrepid may be tempted by a traverse of the Munții Bistriței – a mapless three-day route of approximately 85km (53 miles) from the Bistrița Valley to the Ceahlău massif.

THE CĂLIMAN MASSIF

The Căliman is a volcanic ridge running east–west for about 50km (31 miles), the highest volcanic part of the Carpathians; in the centre of the massif is a 10km (6 miles) wide volcanic crater. On its northern side this is now split by the valley of the Valea Neagra, a tributary of the Dorna. Inside the main crater are several secondary craters – Pietricelul, Haiței Peak and Negoiul Românesc. The Căliman is well known in Romania for its strange rock formations at Tihu, Rusca, Retitiș, and Tămalău, and the Twelve Apostles, so called because they resemble figures with their heads bowed in prayer. The Căliman has plenty of accommodation: Șoimilor, Salard and Galoia cabanas in the Mureș valley to the south of the range, hotels and Cabana Runc at Vatra Dornei and cabanas and a hotel at the slightly strange and very elevated village of Piatra Fântânele, just south of Tihuța pass, on the northern side of the massif. In the heart of the Căliman are three mountain shelters to which you will have to carry your own food – Lomașița, Bradu-Ciont/Puturosul and Luana, replacing the former refuge of Negoiul.

Access

The Căliman is easily accessible from the south via the Mureș valley, carrying the DN15 road and the Brașov–Baia Mare railway (two direct trains to and from Bucharest per day and a number of others, stopping at Toplița and Deda). From the north you can start at the terminus of the branch line at Dornișoara (two trains per day), and then follow the forest road south and then east along the Dorna valley (yellow disc waymarks) up to Luana shelter. The more likely approach from the north is by walking across the Bârgău, heading south from Maramureș to the Tihuța pass. From the north-east you can walk from Vatra Dornei. The shortest

route into the Căliman is to catch a bus from either Vatra Dornei or Bistrița to Piatra Fântânele. In order to continue further south you should follow the route suggested as an alternative exit to the spa town of Borsec and from there take the bus eastwards on the DN15 to Grințieș for the Ceahlău.

The walk south from Tihuța pass to Luana shelter is 28km (18 miles) and takes you over Pietrosul (2100m, 6890ft) the highest point in the Eastern Carpathians. Onwards from the Căliman, the most direct exit is to Toplița (railway station); alternatively it is a 35km (22 mile) walk to the spa town of Borsec.

THE CEAHLĂU MASSIF

The Ceahlău (pronounced 'Chakh-low') massif is a compact, craggy massif rising to 1900m (6233ft) just west of the town of Bicaz. It has a curious geology of marls, sandstone and conglomerate rock (the word is the same in Romanian). Legend has it that the daughter of King Decebal, the Dacian king who defended his country against the might of the Roman Empire, was transformed into Dochia peak, in the heart of the massif. This is supposed to have been the home of the Dacian gods, hence its soubriquet 'the Moldovan Olympus'; the massif is particularly rich in anthropomorphic names. The spurs leading from the central summit provided inspiration for Mihai Eminescu's poem The Ghosts. Postwar leisure development has meant that the Ceahlău is popular with the local population. There are hotels at Bistriţa, Durău (festival, second Sunday in August) itself and Brânduşa ('Crocus') – you are better off walking for less than an hour up to Cabana Fântânele or all the way up to Dochia, in the rocky heart of the massif. Bicaz lake (also known as Lacul Izvoru Muntelui – 'Lake of the Mountains Springs') was created by the building of the dam (serving a hydro-electric plant) in 1960; the resulting reservoir curls its way around the Ceahlău massif to the north and west. At Durău is the hermitage, adorned with paintings by the folk artist Nicolae Toniţa, incorporating local backgrounds into his depictions of the Bible.

The itinerary below describes a two-day traverse of the Ceahlău, pausing at Dochia cabana, probably the best of the three cabanas in the massif itself (Dochia, Fântânele and Izvoru Muntelui). In fact it is possible to walk across the Ceahlău in a long day, although an overnight stop is preferable.

Access

From the south, the Ceahlău is reached from Bicaz, the terminus of the branch railway line from Bacău via Piatra Neamţ (six trains per day of which one direct to and from Bucharest). Bicaz is on the DN12C road from Piatra Neamţ west via the Bicaz gorge to Gheorgheni; the itinerary assumes an approach from the north. There are buses from Piatra Neamţ and Târgu Neamţ to Durău. It is also possible to walk to the village of Hangu on the eastern shore of Bicaz lake from the monasteries of Văratec and Agapia (Chapter Thirteen). It should be possible to reach Grinţieş by walking south-east from Guimalău over the Bistriţa massif – see 'Day One' of the Căliman section above. Do not rely on the supposed ferry across the lake from the landing stage at Chiriteni, below Hangu.

Walking in the Ceahlău

The itinerary below describes several routes into and across the highest part of the Ceahlău, including an ascent of the highest summit, Vf. Toaca. If you finish the Stinişoarei traverse at Grinţieş village there is a walk of 5km (alt. gained to Obcina Boistie 230m, 754ft) to Durău. From Durău on to Dochia cabana, via the Duritoarei path, it is 6km (4 miles) (alt. gained 1025m, 3362ft).

Staţiunea Durău to Cabana Dochia, 5km, 3 miles. Altitude gained 970m, 3182ft

Head south along the road up through Durău as it swings round to the right. The second path turning off the road is at a car park. Turn left off the road at a signpost (red cross waymarks) through Poiana Cailor ('Horses' Clearing') and past a spring. (If you miss this turning, stay on the road for 500m and turn left off it (blue cross waymarks) south-west to the Rupturi river, the path following it upstream to join up with the red cross route at the waterfall.) Follow this south-east, steeply up Piciorul lui Bucur, muddy with its clay soil. You cross the forest road from Durău to Izvoru Muntelui and reach a path junction in the clearing at Poiana Vesuri. To the left the yellow triangle path heads north-east to Cabana Fântânele, 1.5km away. Turn right to head (red cross waymarks) south-west, across a few streams and past 'Bombişul Vesuri' – blocks of conglomerate rock. The path goes up some grit-stone steps and down to the Rupturi stream at the foot of the Duritoară waterfall (1250m, 4101ft), where the river pours 25m over a face of 'Ceahlău con-

glomerate' rock. Continue steeply upwards, on the left of the waterfall.

At the head of the waterfall the path leaves the stream and zigzags steeply up to Poiana Scaişului clearing. Half an hour later you reach the narrow terrace – Poliţa cu Ariniş, a fine vantage point with views of Rarău and Toaca summit and Piatra Ciobanului. The path heads west here and becomes more tricky around the confluence of two valleys at Jgheabul Arinişului. It continues to ascend through twisted pines to another clearing, Curmătura Piciorul Schiop (1705m, 5594ft) and a junction with a path to the right (blue stripe waymarks) down the Bistra valley to Bicazu Ardelean. The path (now also blue stripe waymarks) swings left, north-east across the Ocolaşu Mare plateau, past Piatra Lacrămata rock and across the northern side of Vf. Ghedeon (1845m, 6053ft), then east, dropping down to Dochia cabana (1750m, 5741ft), with its cable car for bringing supplies up from Izvoru Muntelui cabana below.

There is an alternative: the 'Drumul lui Baciu' route, via Fântânele cabana and the main summit, Vf. Toaca (1900m, 6233ft). It is a high, ridge-top route in contrast to the valley route above. Leave Staţiunea Durău past Durău hermitage (alt. 780m, 2559ft) and turn left up the Nicăn valley (red stripe waymarks). The path swings to the left out of the valley, crosses the forest road and continues to ascend south-east to reach Fântânele cabana (1220m, 4002ft). (A blue triangle path heads north, down 6km to Pârâul Mare village on the lake shore.) From Fântânele continue south (red stripe waymarks) now on a difficult climb up past Piatra Lata, Căciula Dorobanțului and onto the main Ceahlău ridge past Panaghia crags. From Panaghia the path goes south-east round Toaca summit (aka Ceahlău, 1900m, 6334ft), reached by a short diversion up some steps. You come to what the map marks as a Salvamont point, in fact used as a met. station, shortly afterwards reaching Dochia cabana.

Exit routes from Dochia cabana

To reach **Bicaz town** from Dochia, head south (red stripe waymarks) above the tree line to the east of Ocolașu Mic summit, then descending to the path junction at Poiana Maicilor ('Nuns' Clearing'). Ahead, the blue cross route takes you south over Văraticu (1365m, 4478ft) and Neagra summits (1141m, 3473ft), down a spur to join the road in the Neagra valley to Neagra village. Turn left here to head east (red stripe waymarks) either to Izvoru Muntelui cabana, or along the Bitca Popii spur to join the road at Furcituri, just west of Izvoru Muntelui village. There are regular buses from here into Bicaz.

An alternative to this is the walk to the lakeside village of Izvoru Alb (you may find yourself marooned at the lakeside); head east (blue stripe waymarks) from Dochia to the stand of larch at Polita cu Crini (1600m, 5249ft – protected as a nature reserve), near Piatra cu Apa crags. Descend into the forest, cross through La Arsuri clearing (1020m, 3346ft) and then over the forest road near Curmătura Lutu Roșu. From here head east (blue stripe waymarks) along the Chica Baicului spur down to Izvoru Alb (550m, 1804ft). Alternatively from the path junction near Curmătura Lutu Roșu you can turn right to descend to the cabana of Izvoru Muntelui and from there follow the road all the way down through the village of the same name to the dam.

It is also possible to walk from **Dochia to Bicaz Gorge cabana** via Bicazu Ardelean (31km, 19 miles; alt. lost from Stâninelor Saddle to Bicazul Ardelean 809m, 2654ft; gained from the Bicaz valley to Piatra Luciului 380m, 1246ft). From Dochia retrace your steps south-west (blue stripe waymarks) past Vf. Ghedeon (1845m, 6053ft) to the path junction (red cross route). Head south-west from here (blue stripe waymarks) to Curmătura Stăninele pass (1420m, 4700ft). A left hand turn here would take you south-east (red disc waymarks) to Neagra village past Poiana Stănile huts to Vf. Văratec (1365m, 4478ft); from here an exit path (blue cross waymarks) goes south in the forest past Vf. Negri (1141m, 3743ft) and down into the Neagra valley. To continue from Stăninelor saddle to Bicazu Ardelean head north-west, around the head of the Bistra valley to Curmătura la Scaune pass, just west of Jghiabul lui Voda crags. North of here a path (red disc waymarks) heads down the Pârâul lui Martin valley to Ceahlău village; another path (blue cross waymarks) heads north-west down the Slatina valley. Ignore these, heading south-west (blue stripe waymarks) down through the forest into the Bistra Mare valley and 8km along forest road to Bicazu Ardelean ('Transylvanian Bicaz', 580m, 1903ft) with its fine wooden church (spring festival, first Sunday in April).

From Bicazu Ardelean you have to walk west along the DN12C 4km to Bicaz Chei village. You pass the turning left to Damuc, then the track left up the Lipenieș valley to take the third left turning off the main road, up the twisting mountain road towards Piatra Arșița (yellow stripe waymarks). This path keeps parallel to the road above the gorge, north of Piatra Luciului to the path junction at Poiana Caprăresei. Here you can turn right to descend straight into the gorge, or continue south-west on a forest track down into the Bicaj valley. Shortly after crossing the river you have the choice of turning left down to Lacu Roşu resort, or right to Bicaz Gorge cabana (Appendix A).

Onwards from the Ceahlău, you can head west from Curmătura La Scăune (blue cross waymarks) over Vf. Lacurilor (1319m, 4327ft) to Curmătura Lacurilor and along the Obcina Tablei ridge (blue stripe waymarks), part of the Ceahlău, to the path junction near Curmătura Tablei with the path crossing the ridge (red triangle waymarks). Head west from here towards Vf. Chicere (1343m, 4406ft), the path keeping to the south of the summit. It brings you to Blaj pass (1070m, 3510ft), on the rough road crossing the ridge, from Bicazu Ardelean to Tulgheş village, on the DN15 road.

THE HĂŞMAŞ MASSIF AND LACU ROŞU

The Hăşmaş ('Hush-mash' – shown on some maps as the Curmăturii) is a limestone ridge running south from the Bistricioara valley, west of the Ceahlău. Its most notable feature is the 300m deep Bicaz gorge, a nature reserve. At its western, upstream end is Lacu Roşu – 'Red Lake', formed when a landslide dammed the valley in 1838 – the tips of some of the spruce trees can still be seen protruding through the surface. The lake gets its name from the reflection of the red clay on the flanks of Mount Suhard (1505m, 4938ft, reached by a path up from Suhard cabana), the same clay which precipitated the landslip that produced the lake. This north–south traverse of the Hăşmaş (or Hăghimaş) takes the walker across some of the best karst scenery in Romania. There is some fine cliff-top walking with superb views west into Transylvania. Bicaz gorge offers the best climbing in the Eastern Carpathians.

Access

The Hăşmaş is reached by the twisting DN12C road covering the slow 55km (34 miles) over the Pângărăţi (Bicaz) pass (1256m, 4120ft) south-west from Bicaz to Gheorgheni. The nearest rail access is Gheorgheni, on the main line from Braşov to Baia Mare (two direct trains from Bucharest per day).

Walking in the Hăşmaş

Bicaz Gorge Cabana to Piatra singuratică Cabana – 19km, 12 miles. Altitude gained from start to Hăşmăş ridge, 846m, 2356ft

This walk continues from the route described above, in the Ceahlău, which finished at Bicaz Gore cabana ('Exit routes from Dochia cabana'). From Bicaz Gorge cabana (note that it is used as a start point only; at the time of going to press it seemed permanently closed to the public), cross the river and turn right on the road. Turn left off the road after 500m to follow a path steeply up (red triangle and red stripe waymarks) up out of the gorge towards Şaua lui Ţifrea pass. At the pass follow the path south-west towards Şaua Varaşcău (1011m, 3317ft), now on a good unsurfaced road coming up from the resort of Lacu Roşu, in the valley above Bicaz Gorge. Turn left off the road at the pass, heading south-west and then south (red triangle and blue disc waymarks), into the forest and south-south-east, broadly contouring along the Hăşmaş ridge, past Vf. Ucigaşului (1407m, 4616ft) on your right. The path now descends into the head of the Ucigaşului valley as it flows south-east towards the Duritoarei gorge. After the shepherds' hut at Stâna Ucigaşului it

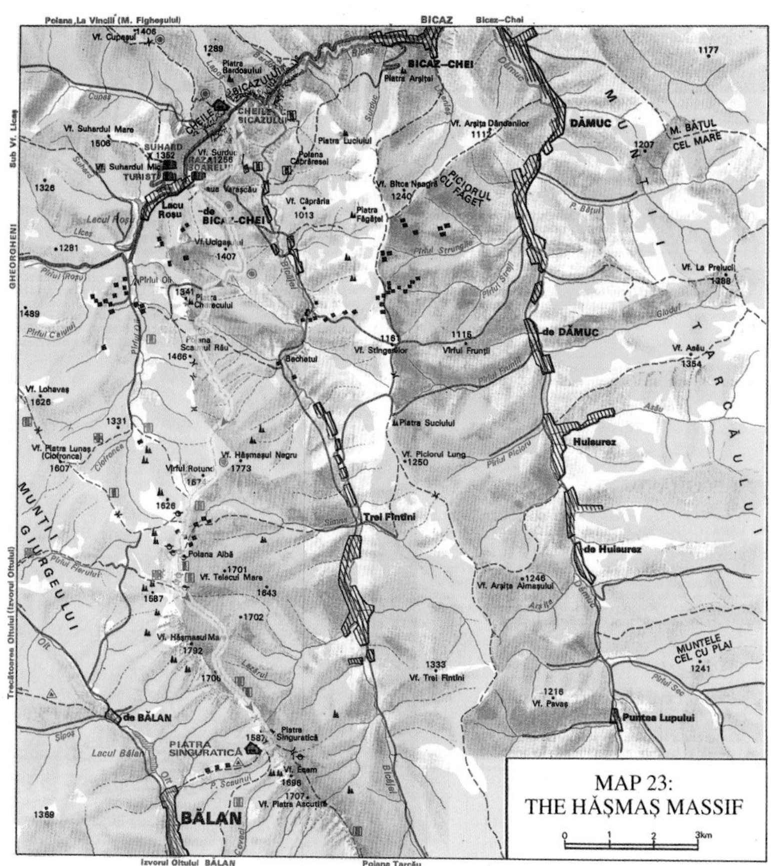

turns west to make its way towards Piatra Chereculu (1341m, 4400ft). Here it turns south and, keeping to the east side of the Hăşmaă ridge, heads south through Poiana Scăunul Rău ('Bad Seat') clearing (1466m, 4809ft). From the clearing a path turns left, straight down off the eastern side of the Hăşmaş ridge into the Bicajel valley. 1.5km after Poiana Scăunul Rău the path swings to the right, heading up to a pass just north of Vf. Hăşmaşul Negru (1773m, 5817ft)

The path now drops on the western side of the ridge, south to an unnamed pass between the summits Hăşmaş and Vf. Rotund (1647m, 5403ft) and then swings right, south of Vf. Rotund, heading south-west to a path junction just after the summit near a collection of shepherds' huts at Poiana Albă clearing (1515m, 4970ft). From here a path (blue stripe waymarks descends to the right, north, down to the forest road in the Pârâul Olt valley, back to Lacu Roşu. Ignore this to keep heading south for 1km to a second junction (path from the right – red stripe waymarks – heading north-west along the Munţii Giurgeului to Bicaz Pass on the DN12C, 10km to the north-west; note the possible route all the way south-east along the Giurgeului fron Stânceni and the Căliman Massif). From

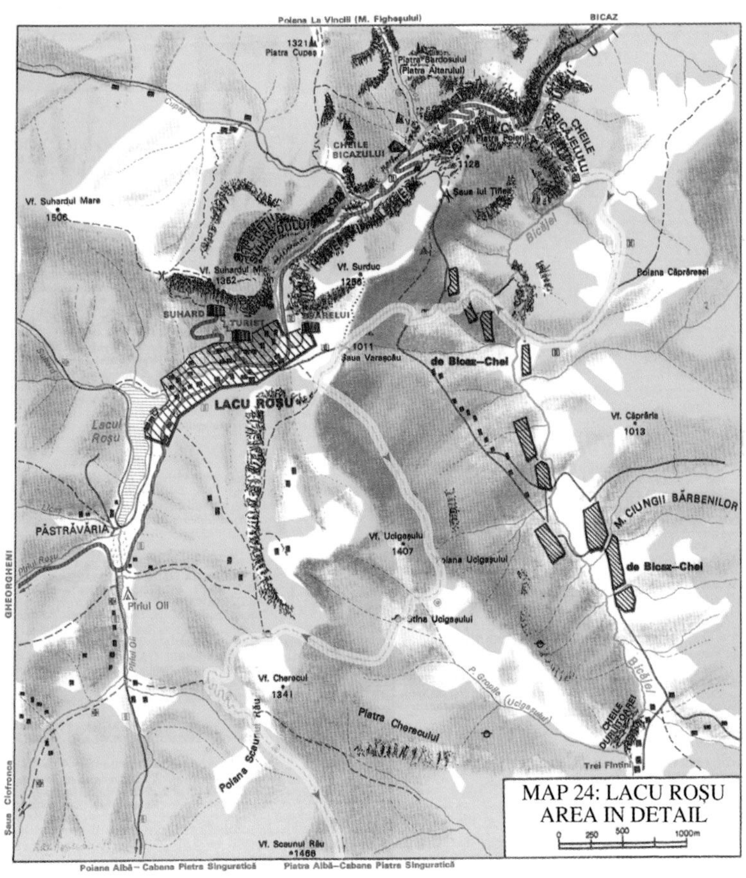

MAP 24: LACU ROŞU AREA IN DETAIL

this junction, keep heading south for 600m (blue/red stripe waymarks), past the junction with the route heading down the Pârâul Fierelui valley to the right (blue cross waymarks). Head back into the forest, skirting Vf. Hăşmaşul Mare (1792m, 5879ft) to the east (access route to the summit). The path now swings right, south-west up to Vf. Hăşmaşul Mic (1706m, 5597ft) on the ridge and then south-east along it to Curmătura pass (1470m, 4823ft) near Piatra Singuratică ('Lonely Stone') crags (1587m, 5207ft); the cabana lies a short distance down to the right from the pass (Appendix A). From here it is just 4km down to the village of Bălan, the highest settlement in the valley of the River Olt.

From Piatra Singuratică you need to decide whether you want to head south-west to Mădăraş cabana in the Harghita or continue south along the Hăşmaş to the Ciucului and Bodoc massifs. If the latter, turn to the Ciucului and Bodoc section below, after the Harghita.

THE HARGHITA MASSIF

The Harghita is a largely forested minor range of volcanic geology, with muddy forest roads and areas of wet peat reminiscent of parts of England's Pennine

Way. On the western flank of the Eastern Carpathians, it runs south from the Sicaz pass (1000m, 3281ft) on the road south-west from Gheorgheni to Odorheiu Secuiesc and reaches its highest point at Harghita-Mădăraş summit (1800m, 5904ft). The accompanying map (Map 25) is hampered by the creation of a large number of forest tracks often overlying existing paths. There are natural hot springs, for example at Racu, just north of Miercurea-Ciuc.

On its eastern side the range is bounded by the valley of the River Olt and the Ciuc depression, site of the county's capital, Miercurea Ciuc and source of the very pleasant Ciuc beer. The Harghita continue southwards as the Muntele Baraoltului, reaching their highest point at Vf. Cucu (1588m, 5210ft), just north-west of the spa town of Băile Tuşnad, 28 km (17 miles) south of Miercurea Ciuc on the way to Braşov. From here they dwindle away to the south to the area of the Saxon villages east of Braşov. To the west a number of valleys run down from the forests to the Szekler villages of Transylvania.

The centre of the Harghita is crossed by the DN13A road (with two roadside cabanas – Brădet and Chirui) running west from Miercurea Ciuc over the Vlăhiţa pass (987m, 3238ft) to Vlăhiţa and Odorheiu Secuiesc. Many of the placenames in this region testify to the presence of the Szeklers, a separate, Hungarian-speaking people, living well to the east of their fellow Hungarian-speaking Transylvanians. For a sample of Szekler culture, visit the Whitsun festival at Miercurea Ciuc.

Walking in the Harghita

The approach walk from Sicaz pass to Cabana Harghita-Mădăraş (about 20km, 12 miles; alt. gained to Harghita-Mădăraş summit 800m, 2642ft) goes south (blue stripe waymarks), over Fagul Roşu – 'Red Beech' summit (1330m, 4363ft) and on, south along the ridge, skirting Ostoroş crater to the west. It continues on the western side of the watershed, over Dealul Comşa (1391m, 4564ft) and skirts Muntele Mic (1589m, 5213ft) to the west. At Şaua Feratău you cross a forest road from Zetea in the west to Mădăraş in the east. Head south-west along the ridge towards Vf. Baia (1428m, 4685ft), the path keeping to the east of the summit, around the head of the Mădăraşu Mare valley. After Baia summit it climbs towards Harghita-Mădăraş summit and is joined by a path (blue triangle waymarks) from Mădăraş valley to the east. There is a choice of routes to the cabana, over the summit or skirting it to the west.

There is a path running north–south along the ridge (blue stripe waymarks) from Sicaz (or Sicaş) pass in the north to the spa town of Băile Tuşnad (see 'The Bodoc massif', below); maps are only available for the central section, west of Miercurea Ciuc. To start this you need to walk or get a lift from Gheorgheni 20km (12 miles) south-west to Sicaz pass (100m, 3281ft). Alternatively head south from Rastoliţa, on the southern edge of the Căliman, and walk south across the Gurghiului (pronounced 'Goor-gewloowee', like 'gurgle' – do not confuse with the Giurgeului, south of Borsec, pronounced like 'George'). The Gurghiu ridge runs north from Sicaz pass; north of Vf. Amza (1594m, 5230ft) it is crossed by the DN13B road from Gheorgheni to Sovata at Bucin pass, with a roadside cabana.

There is an exit route from **Cabana Harghita-Mădăraş to Vlăhiţa** (16km, 10 miles); head south-west, keeping left of the chair lift (blue cross waymarks) to Vf. Mare summit (1570m, 5153ft) and south, along the ridge, out of the forest at Piatra Altarului summit (1355m, 4447ft) and past Izvorul Urzicii spring then down the Homorodu Mic valley to Căpâlniţa

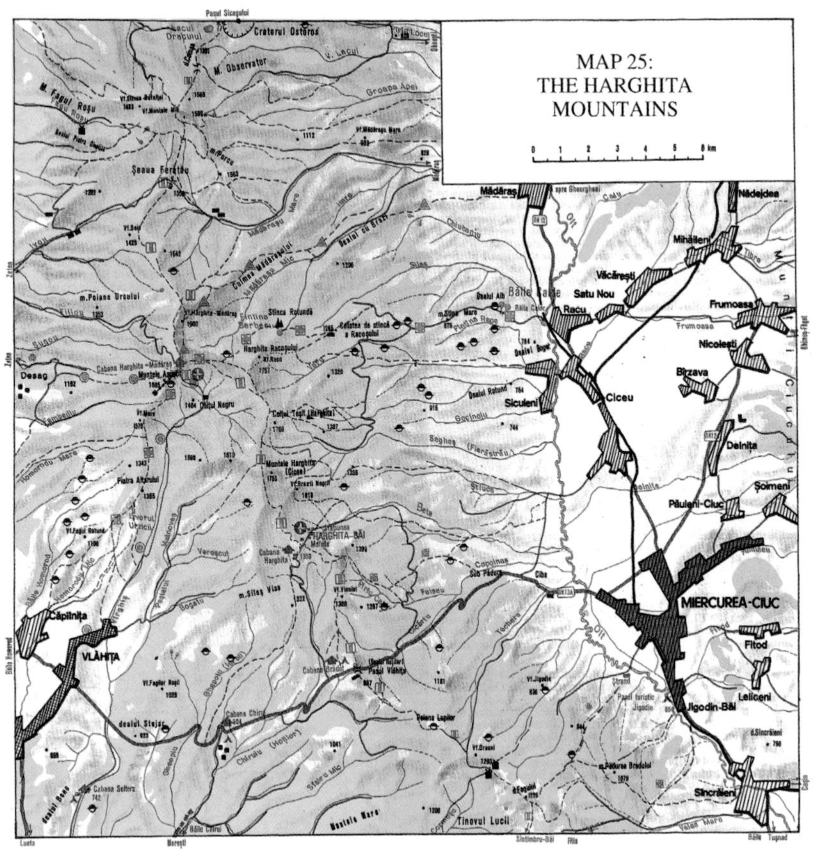

village on the DN13A road; there is an alternative route to the larger village of Vlăhița, 2km east of Căpâlnița.

An alternative route takes you to the roadside **Bradet cabana** (16km, 10 miles; alt. gained to Ciceu summit 1002m, 3346ft; lost to Bradet 620m, 2034ft) via the preferable Harghita-Băi resort. From Harghita-Mădăraș head east (blue stripe waymarks), up on to the ridge, then south-east, then south, skirting Colțul Teșit summit (1709m, 5607ft) to the west. The Harghita ridge is not clearly defined here. The path is difficult to follow, crossing several muddy loggers' tracks, keeping to the western side of the ridge heading south through the forest; several paths and tracks descend to the right, south-west to Vlăhița. You skirt Vf. Ciceu (1755m 5758ft) to the west, through a couple of marshy clearings before twisting down to Harghita-Băi. Crossing the road, head south, back into the forest (blue stripe waymarks) across the clearing towards Vf. Vinului (1380m, 4528ft), then steeply down to the road at Bradet cabana. It is possible to continue south, from Vlăhița pass to Băile Tușnad in the Bodoc massif (about 32km, 20 miles).

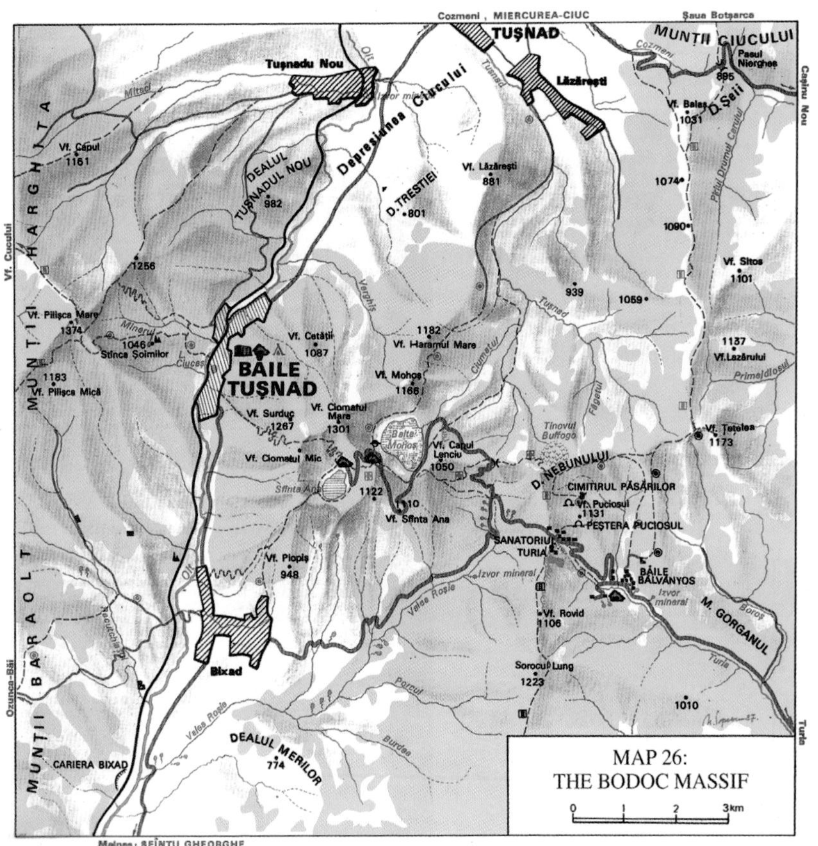

MAP 26:
THE BODOC MASSIF

0 1 2 3km

THE MUNȚII CIUCULUI

The Ciucului, lying east of the Harghita across the Olt valley, is a broad ridge of generally rounded grassy summits above the forest; another limestone area, it is well supplied with mineral springs. Waymarks are scarce and there are no cabanas. The Ciucului is crossed by two roads: the rough forest road along the Uz valley from Dărmănești in the east and the DN12A over the Ghimeș pass (1159m, 3802ft). It makes a useful continuation south from the Hășmaș.

It is possible to head south-east across the Ciucului in three days, finishing up at Cabana Sf. Ana, above Băile Tușnad. Space in the present edition prevents me from including detailed instructions. The three day stages are Piatra Singuratica cabana to Ghimeș pass (30km, 19 miles; alt. gained 390m, 1280ft), then Ghimes pass to Uz pass (28km, 18 miles; alt. gained 410m, 1345ft) and finally Uz pass to Cabana Sf. Ana (Appendix A).

THE BODOC MASSIF

The Bodoc massif is a southern continuation of the Ciuc ridge, running north–south between the valleys of the River Olt and the Râu Negru and its tributary, the

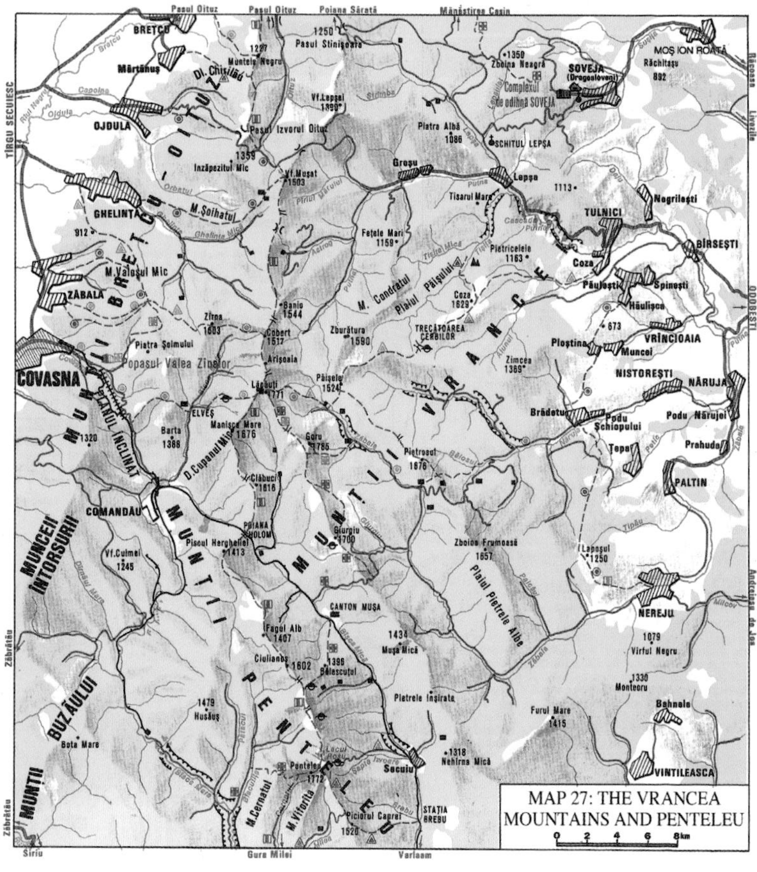

MAP 27: THE VRANCEA MOUNTAINS AND PENTELEU

Casin. In the north the ridge ends at the Niergheş pass (895m, 2936ft), carrying the DN11 road out of the Olt valley south-east towards Târgu-Secuiesc. North of here the forested ridge continues as the Ciucului massif. The Bodoc is almost entirely forested, with some evergreen oak and birch. Like the Harghita, a volcanic region, some of the mineral springs in this area issue forth naturally carbonated water. The highest point is Ciomatu (1301m, 4268ft), overlooking the spa town of Băile Tuşnad. Formerly there were two volcanic cones, one of these being Mohoş. The old crater of Ciomatul now shelters Lacul Sfânta Ana ('Saint Anna's Lake'), in a perfect forested bowl.

Heading south, the Bodoc represents something of a dead-end, for the lowlands of Covasna county have to be crossed before reaching the Ciucaş. There is small-scale walking, for example the steep 5km path east up through the forest from Băile Tuşnad up to Cabana Sf. Ana and the lakes.

THE VRANCEA MASSIF AND PENTELEU

The Vrancea massif lies is an extension of rounded hills, hiding a tangle of hidden forested valleys; the highest point is Vf. Gora (1785m, 5856ft). The Vrancea is possibly the range that best combines accessibility with remoteness. Many of the paths are seldom used and waymarking is sporadic; there are no cabanas. The geology is a complex blend of clays, marls, gritstone and various conglomerates. From this massif radiate a number of valleys: many of these have carved fine gorges, especially on the eastern side, such as the Tişiţa and Naruja. The Vrancea massif lies to the east of the town of Covasna, and is not reached by any major lines of communication.

Access

The Vrancei mountains are crossed in the north by the DN2D Târgu Secuiesc–Focşani road over the Izvorul Oituz pass (cf. Oituz pass on the DN11 to the north). The western flanks of the Vrancei (sometimes titled the Breţcu-Oituz mountains) dominate the territory of the Secui (Szekler) people, in the valley of the Râu Negru between Covasna and Târgu Secuiesc. A number of forest roads and tracks head up into the forested hills from the west, shown (but not particularly accurately) on the accompanying map. The easiest access is up the branch railway line from Sfântu Gheorghe to Covasna station, west of the town. East of here is the narrow-gauge railway planul inclinat. It is possible to get a lift up the line to its present terminus south of Vf. Lăcăuţi. Alternatively you can catch a bus from Covasna to the resort complex of Valea Zinelor and walk from there. If approaching the Vrancea from the Bodoc massif, you should walk in either from the station in Breţcu or from Oituz pass on the Breţcu–Oneşti road. Breţcu is the terminus of the branch line from Braşov, via Sfântu Gheorghe, with two trains a day. The two ranges offer a connecting route to the Ciucaş from the Eastern Carpathians; they do not merit a specific visit. Maps of the region are available.

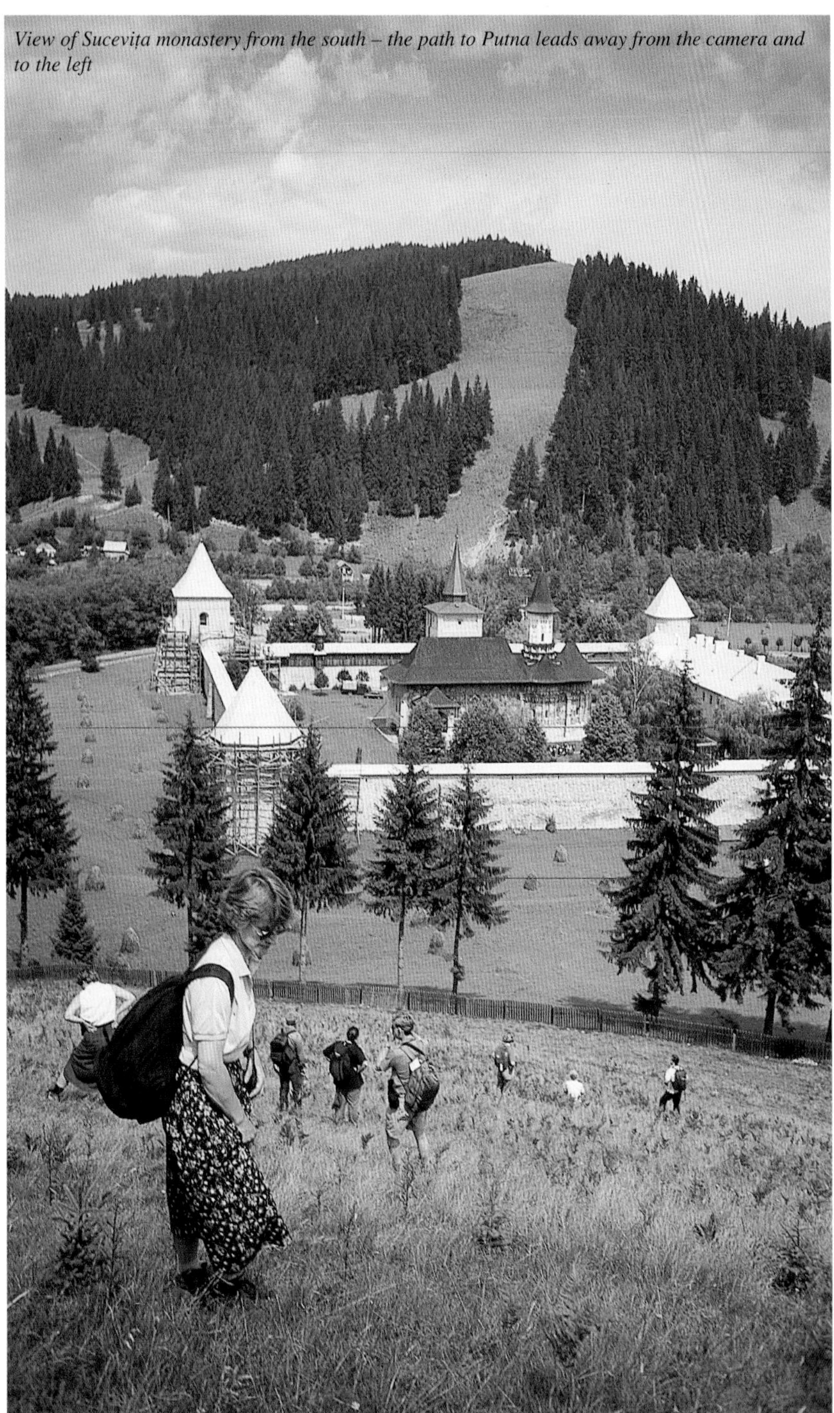

View of Sucevița monastery from the south – the path to Putna leads away from the camera and to the left

CHAPTER THIRTEEN

The Monasteries of Bucovina

Hidden away in the valleys among the forests near the border with Ukraine is one of Europe's most remarkable ecclesiastical treasures – the painted monasteries of Bucovina. Situated among forested hills they make enchanting punctuation in the text of a delightful walk. Mostly founded in the 1500s, these are still thriving religious communities. Whilst most churches in Romania have their interior walls entirely covered in paintings, what makes these remarkable are the frescoes painted on their outside walls, many of them as brilliant today as the day they were painted. The churches with external frescoes are Sucevița, Moldovița, Arbore, Humor and Voroneț. The fact that their surroundings of woods and fields have remained untouched gives them special charm – an inspired complement to the landscape of rolling wooded hills and hay meadows. Bucovina means 'the land of the beech trees' and the title is still justified today (although in fact spruce dominates; beech forests are commoner around the Neamț monasteries). The monasteries of Bucovina are not just monuments; their communities have maintained their way of life down to the present day; many of the monks and nuns are in their twenties. On warm summer evenings in early summer you can see the nuns in their habits, scything their hayfields, a scene lifted straight from a medieval book of hours.

Since the monasteries lie in the Sub-Carpathians, rather than in the Carpathians proper, they are, strictly speaking, outside the scope of this book. However they are ideally suited to visiting by walking between them, with the help of the odd bus-ride or lift, as likely as not on a horse and cart. The routes described are normally waymarked with the usual symbols. However the paint marks are not well maintained – a pity, because waymarkings are more necessary among the forests and sheep-pastures. There are hotels and the odd cabana scattered around the area. The area is wild enough and thinly populated enough to camp wild, if you are discreet. All the monasteries ask you not to visit in shorts; at Putna they even offer the loan of some rather nasty blue warehouse-coats. Take your own long trousers or skirt to don before entering.

If you are a cyclist or mountain biker you will find few more rewarding places to head for than Bucovina. The itinerary below (described as a walking itinerary) involves man-handling your bike for about one tenth of the time. If this is not for you, I recommend a road route – you will still have a superb time. The roads are rough enough to satisfy any mountain biker – and of course light enough in motor traffic to please any leg-powered road user.

Access

The node point for road and rail communications in the area is the town of Suceava. There are six trains a day from Bucharest to Suceava, the journey taking about six hours – a journey best done by sleeper since the scenery passed is unremarkable. Unfortunately overnight trains both to Vatra Dornei and Suceava (or

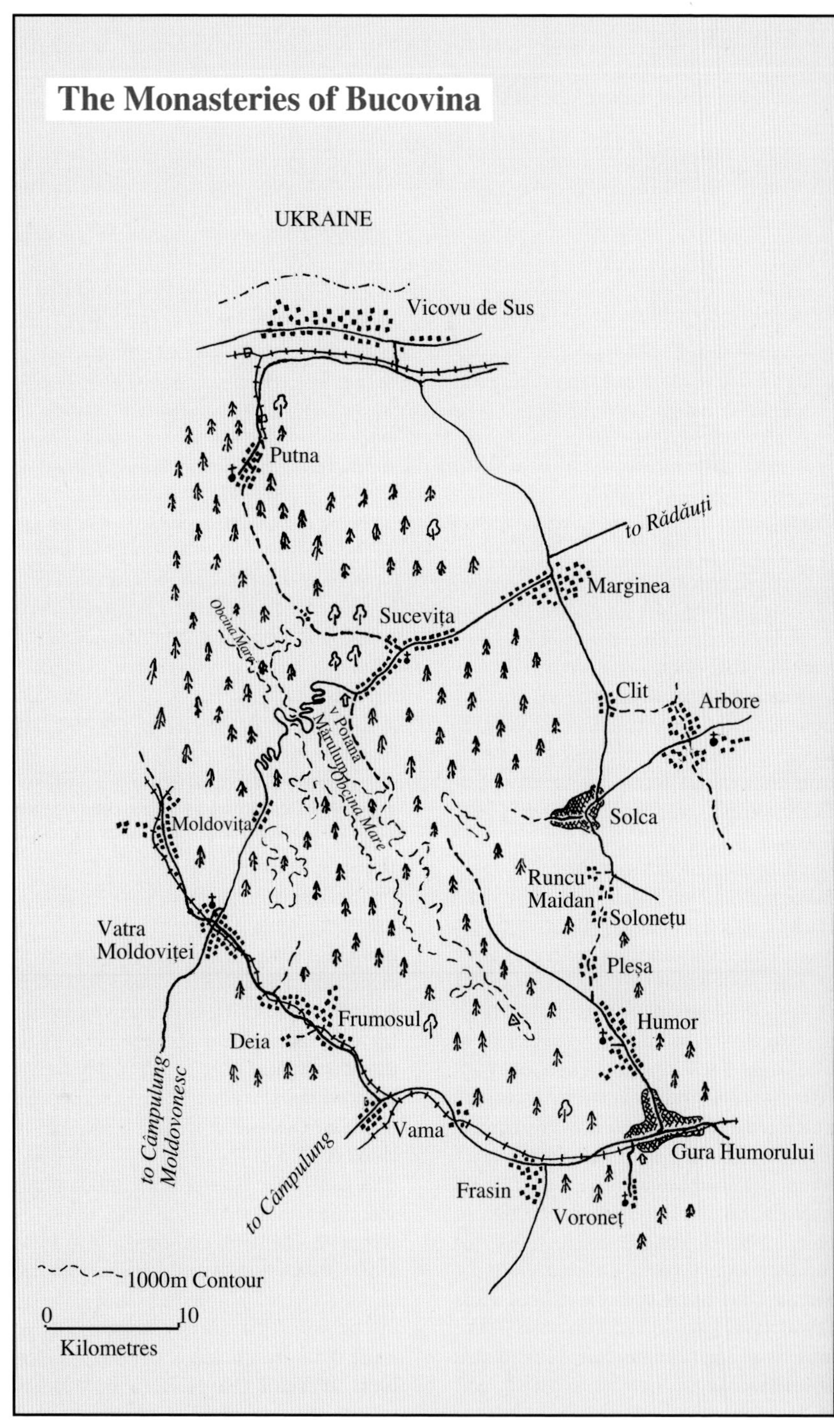
The Monasteries of Bucovina
UKRAINE
Vicovu de Sus
Putna
to Rădăuți
Marginea
Sucevița
Obcina Mare
v Poiana Mărului
Obcina Mare
Clit
Arbore
Solca
Moldovița
Runcu Maidan
Solonețu
Vatra Moldoviței
Pleșa
Humor
Frumosul
Deia
to Câmpulung Moldovonesc
Vama
Gura Humorului
to Câmpulung
Frasin
Voroneț
1000m Contour
0
10
Kilometres

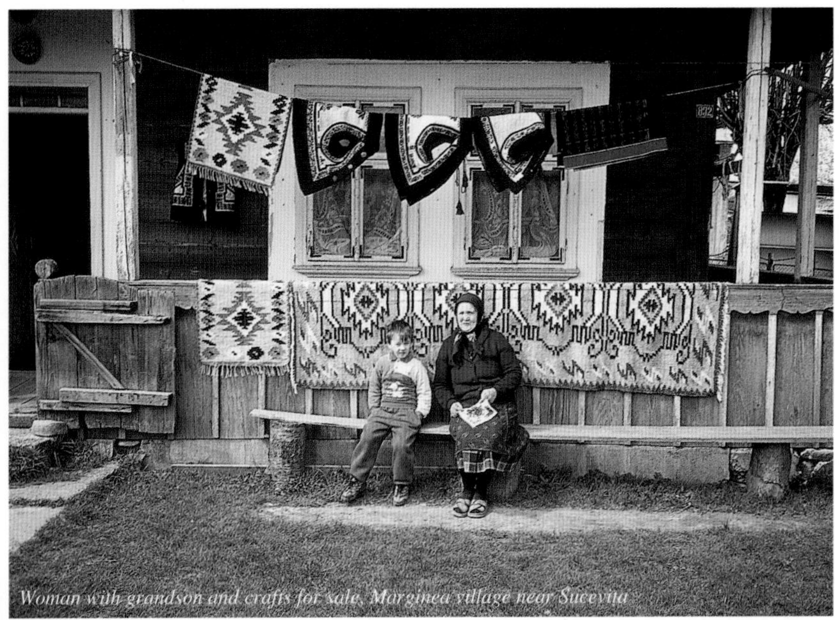

Woman with grandson and crafts for sale, Marginea village near Sucevita

Vereşti, just south of Suceava) arrive extremely early in the morning. The junction for the branch line to Putna is Dorneşti, but there are through trains from Suceava to Putna. There is a daily flight from Bucharest-Baneasa to Suceava, usually via Iaşi.

If heading in from the Rodna mountains and Maramureş to the west, you will need to get a lift or a bus over the Prislop pass, heading east to Câmpulung Moldovenesc along the DN18. The rail connection heads east from the junction at Salva (direct trains from Sighetu Marmaţiei and Vişeu in Maramureş) via a very scenic line twisting over the Bârgău massif and down to Vatra Dornei. If arriving this way, the best start point is Moldoviţa, reached by branch line from Vama junction, 11km (7 miles) north-east of Vatra Dornei. The itinerary would then be Moldoviţa, Suceviţa, out and back to Putna, then Arbore, Humor, and Voroneţ. I think the best way of discovering the area is to make your way through it, either by a combination of walking and hitching or on a bike. However, if you have the use of a car you may want to make a base in the region. In this case, the best central point would probably be Gura Humorului, Câmpulung Moldovenesc or Suceviţa. It is possible to walk out of Gura Humorului to Voroneţ and Humor monasteries.

The loose itinerary below is a point-to-point route, heading southwards through southern Bucovina. Unlike previous itineraries it does not depend solely on walking – you may well want to get the odd lift. An alternative would be to arrive at Putna by train, walk (easy to follow and delightful) to Suceviţa, or walk to Moldoviţa and take the train to Gura Humorului and base yourself there to visit Voroneţ, Humor and indeed Arbore.

ITINERARY

Putna to Suceviţa, 16km (10 miles)

This route is feasible for a mountain bike; leave Putna heading north-east

Moldoviţa monastery: the siege of Jerusalem, Persian army deploying. In fact the soldiers shown are contemporary Turks, almost certainly deploying against Suceava citadel

along the road through the village, past the wooden church and the parish church on the left. 400m from the monastery you come to Cabana Putna on the left; turn right down the tarred street opposite (signed to Chilia) and then first right after 200m. You are heading just west of due south along a rustic village street that turns to a rough surface; occasional concrete electricity poles are marked with red triangles and blue crosses. As you leave the village the street turns sharp right. Turn left here onto a concrete bridge over the Putna river and continue south-west along the lane.

After 2km along the nearly flat floor of the Putnişoara valley you reach the forest; a further 2km in the forest brings you to a junction of forest roads by some green foresters' buildings atop a bank on the right (Canton Silvic No. 13); keep left here, following the blue cross waymarks heading south-east (the right hand track is waymarked with blue triangles and offers a route up the Steja valley to Moldoviţa and Vatra Moldoviţei, a walk of some 27km, 17 miles, from Putna). 3km from the junction the road ends at a concrete bridge; take care here and turn left, steeply up a bank, then following a fairly well-used path (blue cross waymarks) up through the beech trees. 1km of gentle ascent is followed by a muddy path taking you steeply down to the Bercheza valley and a forest road to Suceviţa.

Suceviţa to Moldoviţa, 24km (15 miles)

It is possible to walk from Suceviţa to Moldoviţa in a day – but it is a long one with about 600m (2000ft) of climb to get over the Obcina Mare ridge. In fact the journey on to Moldoviţa monastery represents something of a detour off the relatively simple route from Suceviţa to Humor – although it is well worth it. Beware; a number of (otherwise dependable) maps show a continuous road from

1km west of Sucevița to Humor. There is a section of this route where there is no road, merely a path over a steep forested hill.

I recommend that you take the bus as far as Cabana Palma at Ciumârna pass (alt. 1100m, 3608ft) and pick up the walking directions below. If you want to walk all the way, follow the DN17 west from the monastery for 2km to the end of the village limits – the Drum Bun sign. If you cross a bridge and reach the Popas Turistic Bucovina, you have gone too far. Turn left here along the gravel track (the Poiana Mărului forest road) with a multitude of new holiday homes and turn right immediately after (ie beside, to the left of) the entrance to an alpine-style luxury home 600m after the road. You are heading west up a hidden, sunken log-slide marked with the occasional yellow triangle.

The path takes you steeply up and along the Dealul Plaiul Mare spur, heading west-south-west. You reach a hairpin bend on the main road 2km after leaving the track and see a prominent yellow triangle on the left hand side of the road immediately ahead. However I have found that this path soon dwindles away; good luck if you try – there should be a followable path all the way up on to the top of the Obcina Mare ridge, avoiding the main road, but I have been unable to find it and I recommend you follow the main road to the pass with its statue of an upturned hand.

At the top of the obvious pass a track heads south-east, turning left off the road and heading up to a stand of young conifers on the left, just off the road; you are making your way towards an obvious transmission mast. Immediately after leaving the road you go through a gate and make your way along the edge of the forest on your left, contouring along the top of the ridge. Below you to your right is a grassy bowl, the source of the Ciumârna stream. For the entire stretch, the path, not waymarked with symbols, is easy to follow. You go over a knoll with pines on your right and then return to walking along the forest edge with fields with barns on the right.

Descending, you enter the forest, the path wide and obvious along the ridge. Take care in the forest; 4km after leaving the road you come to two red stripe waymarks on the trunks of pine trees just 20m apart – having seen no more than a handful since leaving the road. Turn right here on an obvious path heading down, south through the deciduous forest. (The red stripe route continues along the Obcina Mare ridge all the way to Gura Humorului; supposedly there are waymarks all the way from Putna to Gura Humorului – altogether 60km, 37 miles). This is good easy walking, though without waymarks. The path, initially muddy, is well defined and becomes a sandy ledge on a steep slope down to your left among pinewoods. Around 1.5km after leaving the main red stripe route you reach a left hand turning, just before a clearing, where the main path swings right. Turn left here, descending and follow the path down to the ridge to the south of the scattered farms of Ciumârna village.

Above the village you pick up the first yellow triangle waymarks, prominently painted on a barn wall by an old windpump. You leave the fields of Ciumârna on your right, heading steeply down to a col in the woods where you cross a path. There is now a steep climb, up a well defined path, south-west up Vârful Lupoaia (1161m, 3809ft). The forest is dense on the climb; a well trodden path joins you from the right and you reach the top in a clearing among the pines. Approximately 1km after reaching the top, heading along the ridge, you reach a pile of mossy stones on your left, on the top of which is the usual square-section stone survey marker, this one marked 'KK'.

Now take care; follow the path on for about 100m to a clearing. You have now swung left off the ridge. As you reach the clearing, turn right, back on yourself to head west, contouring and descending gently through the forest with a steep slope down to your left. You come to a large grazed clearing about 400m after the 'KK' stone – this is Lupoaia clearing. Ahead is a fence on the skyline; look down to your left, along the straight edge of the clearing, south to the obvious entrance in the trees. This is the well defined, unmarked path which leads to the village of Dragoşa.

Head west across the clearing to meet a shepherds' hut and see a well defined track in the grass, heading south-west. This becomes more scant, with faint wheel tracks across the sheep-grazed turf; suddenly it becomes deeply gullied and obvious as it enters the young spruce trees. This leads steeply down, for much its length a log-slide, to reach the main DN17A road 4km north-east of the crossroads at Vatra Moldoviţei. It is not good walking. Take care as you leave Lupoaia clearing; about 40m after entering the forest you see a path turning left. It heads just west of due south and takes you perpendcularly down across the clearing made by clear felling, into the head of the Lupoaia valley. At the bottom of the clearing you reach the end of a forest road. Follow this (about 5km) all the way down the valley to Vatra Moldoviţei and turn right at the T-junction with the main road to walk through the village to the cross-roads and the monastery beyond.

Suceviţa to Arbore, 18km (11 miles)

A number of routes are available, none of them straightforward. Perhaps the one offering the least complication is the blue stripe route which leaves Suceviţa along the Obcina Trisciori ridge, heading south-east to Gura Humorului. Turn right out of the monastery gate and walk east along the pavement and turn right to head south-east along a track up into the forest (blue stripe waymarks) along the Obcina Trisciori ridge, past Pietrele Muierilor crags in the forest on the left. 3km after the crags you reach a path junction at Custura, a track turning right to head west, down to Poiana Micului. (At this point you can simply continue south-east – blue stripe waymarks – along the ridge to take you all the way to Humor monastery – see the directions below under 'Arbore to Humor', below). Turn left at Custura to head east-north-east, down to Solca and follow the road for 6km (3½ miles) north-east past the campsite to Arbore. Continue through Arbore village on the tarred road past the crossroads in the centre, in the direction of Rădăuţi; the church is at the far end of the village on the right. The visit to Arbore is a detour of altogether 30km (19 miles) on the way south to Humor and Voroneţ – but it is well worth it.

Moldoviţa to Arbore, about 35km (22 miles)

From the crossroads in Vatra Moldoviţei village head south-east along the DN176 towards Vama and Gura Humorului for 10km to Frumosu (buses and trains are available). From the halt at the road junction in Frumosu head north-east up the Fumosu valley on the rough road, continuing on the red triangle path to to the Obcina Mare ridge, briefly east along the main ridge route (for about 1km) before descending due east to the straggling village of Poiana Micului. A track leads east from the village, up onto the ridge to the path junction at Custura; follow the directions above from Suceviţa to Arbore from this point.

Other alternatives to continue from Moldoviţa might be to take the train

The south wall of the church, Voroneț monastery

(three per day) to Gura Humorului and base yourself there to visit Voroneț, Humor and Arbore. Vatra Moldoviței is the most delightfully railway halt imaginable; a path leads a few hundred metres across a small hay from the fortified monastery walls. The Vama–Moldovița branch line line runs for much of its length along the side of the road. Change at Vama to reach Gura Humorului. A more challenging alternative would be to walk to Humor (avoiding the detour to Arbore), the path marked with red stripe waymarks.

Arbore to Humor, about 27km (17 miles)

Turn left out of the monastery and retrace your steps westwards along the tarred road through Arbore village to Solca, retracing your steps due west, following the red triangle route up to its junction with the blue stripe route in the forest at Custura. Turn left to follow the blue stripe waymarks, taking you just east of due south, on the east side of the ridge. 1km south-east of the junction the path swings right to head south-west, around the head of the Solonet valley, still in the forest. Aproximately 7km (4½ miles) of walking along the ridge, very nearly all in forest, brings you to the strung-out village of Pleșa. Turn right to head south along the rough road for 1km and follow it 5km down the Humor valley to Humor monastery; it lies just west of the road, well signed.

Reaching Arbore from Gura Humorului, 15km (9 miles) by train and 12km (7½ miles) walking

This is a superb walk across the unenclosed medieval farming landscape of northern Moldova. There is a morning train (0900) from Gura Humorului to Suceava; buy a ticket to Pârtești and alight there (the station before it is Căcica). Turn right along the road out of the station and walk about 1km to the crossroads by a few shops. Turn right here and head north, along the unsurfaced road to Botoșana. Beyond Botoșana you reach a rural T-junction; turn left and after little more than 1km find yourself in Arbore. Turn right at the T-junction in the middle of the village to reach the church. The only return train to Gura Humorului from Pârtești is at 3pm, not allowing enough time to make the return walk to Arbore. However there are buses from Solca back to Gura Humorului.

Humor to Voroneţ, 12km (7½ miles)

From Humor it is 6km (3½ miles) by road south to Gura Humorului – there are a number of buses every day. If you want to avoid the town it is possible to bypass it and have a superb walk. Turn left out of the monastery; you arrive at a fork, with the main tarred road going south-east to Gura Humorului. Turn right, up the rough road heading south-west through the hamlet of Larga, following the valley of the same name (red cross waymarks). The markings give out; use your compass to turn left off the track once out of the houses to head south, up onto the Obcina Mare ridge (between the valleys of the Moldoviţa and Humor rivers). Vf. Toaca (alt. 834m, 2736ft) is the prominent hilltop; from the stone bench memorial on the summit there are superb views south across the Moldova valley and up the Voroneţ valley. There is a path descending the south side of Toaca inside the beech forest (red stripe waymarks). You exit from the woods on a rutted unmarked track and, 200m after the end of the trees, reach the first houses. Follow the track to the main road by a small new private restaurant. Turn left along the pavement for about 300m and then right, down the road signed to Voroneţ village and monastery.

Travelling on from Voroneţ and Gura Humorului

From Voroneţ it is 97km (60 miles) by road to Neamţ monastery; there is one bus a day, which follows a slow, twisting 65km (40 miles) from Gura Humorului to Târgu Neamţ. It is an awkward journey by train; you go from Gura Humorului to Suceava and change there to go down the main line to the junction at Pascani and change again there onto the branch line to its terminus at Târgu Neamţ.

If you are on a mountain bike (in my opinion the best way of travelling from the monastery area of southern Bucovina to the Neamţ area) you can reduce the distance slightly and avoid the busy stretch of the E85/DN2 south of Falticeni; to do this, turn right in the village of Cornu Luncii, 22km (14 miles) south-east from Gura Humorului, on the road signed to Slatina. Turn left after 1km to head south-east 7km (4½ miles) on the asphalt to Baia and keep straight on through the village, where the tarred road turns left to Falticeni. After 8km (5 miles) you reach a T-junction at Bogdaneşti; turn left and follow the DN15C road through Boroaia and Brusturi-Drăgăneşti to Târgu Neamţ.

If you are truly addicted to tackling the lonely forested Stânişoarei mountains, it should be possible to walk all the way to Neamţ, although there is no continuous path and I have not tried it. I would recommend the following route, having done some reconnaisance of it. Follow the Voroneţ valley up and head east 5km, to the summit of Dealul Mare (883m, 2900ft) and descend south-east 3km to the village of Slatina, taking the rough road south-east to the hamlet of Herla and continue south on the eastern edge of the forest 5km to Poiana Mărului. From there you need to make your way east-south-east through 6km (4 miles) as the crow flies, through the forest to Slătioara and follow the road 7km (4½ miles) east down the valley to Riscan and head due south 11km (7 miles) from there, over the summit of Dealul Cerdacului (911m, 3000ft) to Neamţ monastery. Good luck.

The monasteries of Neamţ

The county of Neamţ, with its county town of Târgu Neamţ, lies on the eastern flanks of the Stânişoarei mountains, part of the Eastern Carpathians. Whilst not embellished with the spectacular external frescoes of the monasteries near Suceava, these are still superbly located

The Carpathians may see few visitors in mid-winter, but local life goes on. This farmer is moving hay on a sled to the valley bottom, near Sucevița.

buildings and communities with great spiritual power and scenic beauty. The surroundings of the monasteries are the same as those to the west of Suceava – except that the forests have a higher proportion of beech. The whole area lends itself to the self-contained backpacker (or backpacking couple) who enjoy camping au sauvage. There is a good old state Popas Turistic (no rooms but accommodation in wooden 'Wendy-houses') serving food, at Braniște, 3km east of the road junction to Neamț monastery. There are small private hotels near Agapia and Văratec monasteries (see Appendix A). The locations of the monasteries make for an excellent small walking tour in itself, starting at Neamț and walking to, in order of visiting, Secu, Sihastria, Sihla Hermitage, Agapia and lastly Văratec.

Access

If travelling direct to Târgu Neamț station, access is by 31km (19 miles) of branch line from Pașcani, on the main line from Bucharest to Suceava and Ukraine. There are five trains per day up the line, taking 45mins. There are six fast trains (rapid or accelerat) from Bucharest to Pașcani, and many more from Brașov. There are three buses per day to Neamț monastery, departing from Târgu Neamț railway station.

Neamț monastery to Secu monastery, 10km (6 miles)

This is a pleasant, easy walk through forest and along a grassy valley with wooded sides. From Neamț monastery walk down the avenue and then the access road south-east along the Nemțișor valley and turn right up the access road to the zoo, then immediately left to walk across the small dam holding back a reservoir. From the end of the dam you should set south-south-west on your compass and head through the open beechwoods, following a path most of the way to bring you to the DN15B road in an area of parkland. Turn right along the road for a few hundred metres west to the turning left (south) to Secu monastery. This road gives access to the monasteries of Secu and Sihastria and also leads eventually to the Schitul (hermitage) at Sihla.

Sihastria to Agapia via Sihla, 10km (6 miles)

Sihastria monastery lies on the right as you approach from Secu; turn left immediately before the entrance to the monastery up a rutted track heading up the bank into the forest. The path to Sihla hermitage is well trodden with no junctions along the way. It takes you steeply up onto the ridge with the occasional crucifix cut into the bark of various trees. As you approach the monastery you cross and then join the recently made twisting road. For the final few hundred metres the road descends steeply; turn right off it to follow the beautiful path through the woods and then out of the trees to some rock outcrops and Saint Theodora's cave. You arrive at a tiny wooden chapel built against the side of a cliff like some of the Buddhist monasteries of the Himalaya. Head down the railed path to the courtyard of the hermitage extensively rebuilt in 1995.

The path to Agapia (also to Văratec) leads down from the far left corner of the hermitage complex as you look left from the church door. It is an obvious track heading down among the trees; there is a signpost for the path (blue disc waymarks) turning right immediately off it to Văratec. Head down the hill and join the forest road which takes you straight to Agapia – an easy and pleasant walk.

Agapia to Văratec, 6km (3½ miles)

Leave the monastery heading east along the road to Târgu Neamţ. Turn first right on the concrete road bridge over the Agapia river; the road swings immediately left and is easy to follow as it twists up along the eastern edge of the forests with occasional views east across the rolling farmland around the village of Baltăteşti. Turn right as you reach the village of Văratec to follow the road to the monastery entrance. Once inside the courtyard you are in an idyllic scene, shaded by trees and overlooked by balconies of the nuns' accommodation. On the left is a fine museum with icons and also an embroidery school founded by Queen Marie in the 1930s.

Travelling on from Văratec

From Văratec it is possible to walk west to the Ceahlău range. From Văratec a rough road heads south for 5km to the village of Magazia; turn right on the tarred road through the village and then right again in the village, off the dead-end road to Cracăul Negru. This is not passable by car all the way along its approximately 30km (18½ miles), but is certainly walkable and tacklable by mountain bike. The road takes you first to the remote foresters' settlement of Mitocu Balan, and a further 7km (4½ miles) up to the Doamnei (or Mitoc) pass (alt. 1130m, 3707ft). From here it descends the Hangu valley to the lake. From Hangu several buses per day make their way en route from Bicaz around the lakeshore to the resort of Durău, in the Ceahlău massif.

APPENDIX A:
Accommodation

This appendix has been divided into sections to correspond with chapter headings. Where the name of an establishment is given first (eg. Runc), it means that it is a cabana. Hotels, pensions, and so on, in towns are listed as 'Hotel ....'.

Hotels

The hotel lists for all the towns have been compiled with the most expensive usually at the top. It does not imply any recommendation by the author unless this is specified.

Mountain huts – cabanas

The old state-owned cabana network is steadily being privatised and facilities are altering. In general privatisation is good news; all services are still offered and in many cases much renovation has been done. I have tried to give information relevant at the time of going to press. Where access to a cabana is mentioned it is from the nearest road or habitation – there are generally many other paths from the cabanas, as is obvious from the maps and text. You may notice that several cabanas have the same telephone number listed; this is often the office in the town that controls several cabanas. In general where a 'refuge' is marked on the map, expect a rudimentary shelter only – a bothy; some more developed exceptions to this rule are listed below eg. Gențiana in the Retezat. All cabanas are open all year round unless stated otherwise and all have mains electricity and running water unless otherwise stated. If known, the altitude of the cabana is given in brackets, expressed in metres and feet.

In common with much of eastern Europe camping cabins (căsuțe) are popular; these are (almost always wooden) tiny bungalows usually with two beds and always with some form of communal plumbing. I have come to like them very much and have even cooked myself a meal in one, at Obârșia Lotrului when there was no other food.

Bucharest

Bucharest has lately become an expensive city to stay in. The mountain walker will want the briefest and cheapest of stays.

For an acceptable cost, I would tentatively suggest the **Hotel Batiștei** (Str. Dr. E Bacaloglu 2 – just east of the **Hotel Intercontinental** – Tel 021 314 9022, 021 314 0889, fax 314 0887) or the **Hotel Muntenia** (Str. Academiei 19-21, Tel 021 314 4824, fax 021 314 1782). You could also try **Hotel Helga** – but beware of thieves posing as agents for this – (Str. Salcâmilor 2, Tel and fax 021 610 2214) or **Hotel Banat** (Piata Rosetti 5, Tel 021 313 1056, Fax 021 312 6547).

Lastly I list some modest, cheap and shabby, but secure hotels near the Gara de Nord. The first can be found by turning right as you head out of the pillared portico exit of the station, the second by heading left from the same point. **Cerna** (Blvd Dinicu Golescu 29, Tel 021 311 0535, Fax 021 311 0721), **Marna** (Calea Buzești 3, Tel 021 650 6820, Fax 021 312 9455). Also in the vicinity of the railway station but smarter, more expensive and part of the international chain is **Hotel Ibis** (Calea Grivitei 143, Tel 021 222 2724, Fax 021 222 2723).

The Bucegi massif

The pleasantest place to stay in the Prahova valley is **Sinaia**. In descending order of price (and starting sky-high) there is the **Hotel Anda** (B-dul Carol I 30, Tel 0244 306 020, Fax 0244 306 025), the **Hotel Montana** (B-dul Carol I 24, Tel 0244 312 751, Fax 0244 312 754), the **Hotel International** (Str. Avram Iancu 1, Tel 0244 313 851, Fax 0244 313 855), the **Hotel Palace** (Str. Octavian Goga 4, Tel 0244 312 055, Fax 0244 310 625), the **Hotel Caraiman** on the busy main road (B-dul Carol I 4, Tel 0244 313 551, Fax 0244 310 625), the **Hotel Economat**, adjacent to Peleș Castle (Tel 0244 311 151, Fax 0244 310 353), the **Hotel Furnica** nearby (Str. Furnica 50, Tel 0244 311 151, Fax 0244 315 447), the **Hotel Sinaia** (B-dul Carol I 8, Tel 0244 311 551, Fax 0244 311 898), the **Hotel Stăvilar** (Aleea Peleșului, Tel 0244 313 719, Fax 0244 311 150), **Vila Mures** (Str. Furnica 73, Tel/Fax 0244 310 721) and **Cabana Schiorilor** (one dormitory room of 10 beds (980m, 3215ft), Tel 0244 314 751).

Bușteni has **Hotel Caraiman** (B-dul Libertății 89, Tel 0244 320 156, Fax 0244 320 121), the **Hotel Pârâul Rece** (Str. Libertății 155, Tel/Fax 0244 321 670), the **Hotel Silva** (large ski-type hotel by cable car, Str. Telecabinei, Tel 0244 321 412, Fax 0244 320 027). There are a large number of Vilas and Pensiuni available some smarter and more expensive than others. A number of Vilas like **Clabucet**, **Susai**, **Micsunica**, **Doina** can be booked at a central number Tel/Fax 0244 320 027. 5km north is **Cabana Gura Diham** (Tel 0244 321 108) often full of sports teams or school groups.

Predeal has the **Hotel Orizont** (large modern ski hotel Str. Trei Brazi 6, Tel 0268 455 150, Fax 0268 455 472), the **Hotel Speranta** (the road to Trei Brazi Tel/Fax 0268 455 255), **Hotel Carpați** (Str. Nicolae Bălcescu 1, Tel 0268 456 273, Fax 0268 455 411), the **Hotel Belvedere** (the former Cioplea – a large modern ski hotel east of the town, B-dul Libertății 102, Tel 0268 456 505, Fax 0268 456 871), the **Hotel Carmen** (B-dul Săulescu- the main road - 121, Tel 0268 456 517, Fax 0268 455 426), the **Hotel Predeal** (B-dul Muncii 6, Tel 0268 456 483, Fax 0286 455 433), the **Hotel Rozmarin** (B-dul Săulescu 139, Tel 0268 456 422, Fax 0268 455 683), the **Hotel Cirus** (Str. Avram Iancu 3, Tel 0268 456 035).

Trei Brazi Reached by dead-end tarred road 7km from Predeal, Tel 0788 315 321 (1128m, 3700ft). If you contact the **Antrec** organisation (Tel 0268 236 307) they can book for you accommodation in a number of Vilas and private agro-turistic places in Predeal and Bran area.

Pârâul Rece lies 6km west of Predeal on the DN73A to Râșnov. It has two hotels, the **Bucegi** (Str. Valea Rasnoavei 10, Tel 0268 456 491) and **Piatra Craiului** (Str. Valea Rasnoavei 10, Tel 0268 457 147). Just uphill is **Cabana Belvedere**, superb peaceful site with views of the Muchia Chei ridge, often full of school groups (about 1150m, 3800ft), Tel 0268 455 240. Just west, down the hill is **Cabana Cerbul** (6 beds in căsuțe and a café).

Cabanas

Babele At the top of the cable car from Bușteni and Peștera, bleak. 108 beds in rooms of 2, 3, 4, 5 and 8 beds; Caraiman or Omu are preferable (2206m, 7237ft).

Bolboci At the dam holding back Bolboci lake, on a gravel road past Zănoaga. 27 beds in rooms of 2, 3 and 4 beds (1460m, 4790ft).

Bradet Pleasant, on the twisting dead-end road winding up from Sinaia to Valea cu Brazi. 27 beds in rooms of 5 beds and fewer (1310m, 4298ft).

Caraiman A favourite, at the top of the Jepii gully, 1km directly above Bușteni – well managed by the Mazilu family, recommended. 24 beds in 2 dormitories, no running water – washing in a stream, earth toilet (2025m, 6644ft).

Cuibul Dorului Near the rough DJ121 road, leading off the DN71 from Sinaia. 94 beds in twin or four-bed rooms (1200m, 3937ft).

Diham Small, outside tap, in clearing on wooded spur (1320m, 4331ft).

Leaota Remote, on a gravel road from Pietroșița in the Ialomița valley. From the Bucegi a walking route takes you (red cross waymarks) west from the northern end of Zănoaga gorge, following the Zănoaga stream down to Cantonul Bratei where it continues due west up a ridge to Leaota summit (2133m, 7001ft). From the summit follow the red triangle and blue stripe waymarks due south for 12km to the cabana (1300m, 4265ft).

Mălăiești Superbly located at the foot of the craggy Padina Crucii ridge. 51 beds in rooms of 2, 4 and 8 beds, no electricity or running water – a spring nearby, not reliable in late summer. Burnt down in spring 1998, now rebuilt (1720m, 5643ft).

Miorița By the top of the cable car from Sinaia and often busy. 59 beds in twin and dormitory rooms (1970m, 6463ft).

Omu Spectacular location and wonderful staff serving good food and very welcome hot mulled wine – highly recommended. Its dormitory can become crowded in summer. No plumbing or electricity, 24 places (2505m, 8217ft). Usually closed Nov–May.

Padina A fine old wooden building, rough road access from Sinaia via Bolboci, often overcrowded in August, grim plumbing. 128 beds in various buildings, in twin and dormitory rooms. A further 44 beds in rather ugly huts in the meadow below (1525m, 5003ft), Tel 0244 314 331.

Peştera A large ski hotel at the base of the cable car up to Babele, connecting over to Buşteni, also reached by gravel road. 200+ beds in rooms of 2, 3, 5 and 8 beds, many with en suite bathrooms; it has been renovated so it is now comfortable (1610m, 5282ft), Tel 0244 311 094.

Piatra Arsă An eyesore on the eastern plateau of the Bucegi, accessible in summer by dirt road. Recently become a hotel, but still offering cabana accommodation (1950m, 6398ft). Also functions as a sports training establishment – excellent food and a well-stocked bar. Tel Hotel 0244 311 921, Tel Cabana 0244 314 414.

Valea cu Brazi Near the road up from Sinaia, close to the Hotel Alpin. 46 beds in rooms of 2, 4 and 8 beds (1885m, 6184ft), Tel 0244 314 751.

Vârful cu Dor Primarily a skiers' cabana at the head of the chairlift from near Valea cu Brazi, near to Mioriţa. 30 beds in rooms of 2, 4 and 8 beds (1885m, 6184ft).

Cheile Zănoagei (Zănoaga) on the rough road up to the head of the Ialomiţa valley, overlooking the now ruined Bolboci dam workers' camp, but still recommended. 97 beds in several dormitory buildings. Do not drink the water from the standpipe across the road (1400m, 4593ft), Tel 0245 772 176.

Cota 1000 'Level one thousand' (metres) on the DN71. 7km south-west of Sinaia. 5 beds in 2 rooms, 20 more in căsuţe.

Poiana Izvoarelor Fine location in a clearing, just accessible by 4WD. 90 beds in two buildings, in rooms of 2, 4, 5, and 8 beds, electricity and running water, occasional hot showers in the main building, not the annexes (1455m 4774ft). Book your bed ahead at the top of Omu for here.

Poiana Secuilor ('Szeklers' Clearing') adjacent to Trei Brazi. 54 beds in rooms of 2, 3, 4, 5, and 12 beds (1070m, 3510ft).

Scropoasă Decrepit; reached by a dirt road from Moroeni and Sinaia. 79 beds in rooms of 2, 3, 4, 5, and 8 beds (1205m, 3953ft).

Valea Dorului in a bowl on the Bucegi Plateau 1km west of Cota 2000. Dormitory rooms (1820m, 5971ft).

East of the Prahova

For hotels in Predeal, see the Bucegi above.

Baciu On the south of Săcele town near the path up into the Piatra Mare to Bonloc. 27 beds in small dormitories (680m, 2231ft).

Bunloc (Bonloc) A hilltop cabana above the forests south of Săcele, reached by a dirt road from Dâmbul Morii. No running water but electricity, 2 dormitory rooms (1000m, 3281ft).

Clăbucet Plecare at the top of the ski lift bove Predeal to the east. 78 beds in rooms of 2, 3 and 6 beds (1456m, 4777ft), Tel 068 25 63 12. NB Destroyed by a gas explosion in 1999; rebuilding is planned.

Gârbova South of Predeal on the Gârbova ridge. 54 beds, mainly in twin rooms. (1350m, 4430ft).

Piatra Mare Cabana in the massif of the same name was destroyed by fire in 1992. However all the signs in the area still point to it – do not be caught out.

Piscul Câinelui Half an hour's walk out of Sinaia, well signed up the blue disc path heading south and then east from Sinaia station. 17 beds in rooms of 2, 4, 5, and 12 beds (950m, 3116ft).

Susai Small, rustic in a hilltop clearing on the Gârbova ridge. Electricity, washing at a spring nearby. Just 8 beds in 3 rooms (1350m, 4429ft).

The Ciucaș

Babarunca Now more a truckers' halt, 22km south-east of Sacele on the DN1A road to Ploiești (680m, 2231ft).

Ciucaș 28 dormitory beds. No electricity or piped water (1550m, 5085ft).

Muntele Roșu Attractive, sited immediately above the tree line in a mountain bowl, reached by the tarred DJ22 road leading north from the main DN1A. 52 beds in rooms of 2, 4, 5 and 8 beds. Cabanier Bucurescu Vasile: a good map in the hall drawn by Emilian Cristescu from the Alpine Club in Ploiești (1260m, 4134ft).

Cheia Resort village, just off the main road, has a variety of accommodation.

Rusu Attractive privately-owned cabana, 200m west of the DN1A road on the south side of Cheia village; the entrance to it is adjacent to the 'end of village' Cheia sign. 2 wooden cabins; altogether accommodation for 18 (906m, 2972ft), Tel 0244 294 111.

The mountains of Brașov

Staying in the centre of **Brașov** can be expensive. The plushest hotel is the **Aro Palace** (Str Muresenilor 12, Tel 0268 477 664, Fax 0268 475 250), followed by the **Hotel Capitol** (B-dul Eroilor 19, Tel 0268 418 920, Fax 0268 472 999) and – my favourite as a city-centre hotel – the **Coroana** (B-dul Republicii 62, Tel 0268 544 330, Fax 0268 541 505); the cheaper rooms of this have been split off into the **Hotel Postăvarul** – still with the same telephone and fax; you can also try the **Hotel Silvania** (Str. Căprioarei 27, Tel/Fax 0268 471 979). The only cheap hotels in the centre are the **Hotel Aro Sport** (Str. St. Ioan 3, Tel 0268 478 800), the **Minihotel Viron** (Str. Traian Demetrescu 21, Tel 0268 552 095) and the **Hotel Tâmpa** (Str. Matei Basarab 68, Tel 0268 415 180); follow the street steeply uphill. Close to the station, in the modern part of the city, is **Hotel Codreanul** (Str. Albăstrelelor 29, Tel 0268 425 416). Outside the city on the left of the road to Bucharest, **Camping Dârste** also has rooms; 1km south along the DN1 is **Dâmbu Morii** (690m, 2264ft), a collection of cabanas and villas (Tel 0268 259 191). **Timiș** (en route to Predeal) has the **Hotel Geisser** (Șoseaua Nationala 5, Tel 0268 256 244), **Cabana Cotul Donului** (770m, 2526ft), 12 beds in 3 rooms (Tel 0268 256 116).

Poiana Brașov is a collection of identikit concrete ski-hotels. I list them in descending order of price. The **Alpin** (Tel 0268 262 343) has the highest pretensions, though it is little different from the nearby **Teleferic** (Tel 0268 262 253) and **Sport** (Tel 0268 262 313); also the **Ana Hotels** (Tel 0268 407 330), the **Condor** (Tel 0268 262 121), the **Caraiman** (Tel 0268 262 329), the **Ciucaș** and the **Șoimul** (Tel 0268 262 111 for both), the **Miruna** (Tel 0268 262 120, Fax 0268 262 035), the **Piatra Mare** (Tel 0268 262 226), and the **Ruia** (Tel 0268 262 046). Cheaper still is accommodation at **Cabana Junilor** or **Sat de Vacanța**. There are also a number of private Vilas of different levels of comfort and priced accordingly.

The village of **Bran** (770m, 2526ft) has the **Popasul Reginei** hotel, overlooking the central park opposite the castle, the long-established **Han Bran**, on the right of the main road to Râșnov and Brașov (Tel 0268 236 556) and **Cabana Bran Castel** (Tel 0268 236 404), 26 beds in rooms of 2, 3 and 4 beds; can be noisy with school parties staying and locals at the disco. There are a number of newer private places, such as the **Pensiunea Ana** near Bran castle (Str general Mosoiu 369, Tel 0268 236 463), the **Pensiunea Elena** (Str Bologa V. L. 318, Tel 0268 236 679), the **Pensiunea Andra** (Str Principala 104, Tel 0268 236 331). Bran and its neighbouring villages are well supplied with accommodation in private houses – 'agro-turism', all easily booked by **Bran Imex**, on the west side of the park (Str. Aurel Stoian 395, Tel 0268 236 642, Fax 0268 152 598), or the **Ovi-tours agency** in Poarta (Str. I Valeriu Bologa 16, Tel 0268 236 666). 12km north-east is the small town of **Râșnov**, with the pleasant **Hotel-Cabana Cetate** (also known by the locals as **Acapulco**, Tel 0268 230 266) on the road to Poiana Brașov (670m, 2198ft), 21 beds in rooms of 2, 3 and 4 beds.

Cheia In flat fields beside the DN73A Râșnov–Predeal road via Pârâul Rece – good food; note that it can be noisy during summer week-ends. 38 beds in rooms of 2, 3 and 4 beds (800m, 2625ft).

Cristianul Mare Near the summit of Postăvaru, superb views, popular with skiers at Poiana Brașov, close to the cable car top station (56 beds in rooms of 2, 3 and 4 beds) – recommended (1704m, 5590ft); also **Postăvarul** just below, 72 beds in rooms of 2, 3, 4, and 8 beds (1602m, 5256ft).

The Piatra Craiului and Iezer-Păpușa

Bătrâna 3km north-west up the valley of the same name (at its confluence with the Cătunu) from Cabana Voina, built by the 'Plaiuri Muscelene' club from Câmpulung. 22 beds in 3 rooms (1100m, 3608ft).

Brusturet on the road along the Seaca Pietrilor valley, 6 km north of Dâmbovicioara.

Cuca At the end of the road leading up the Cuca valley, 4km north of Voina, 52 beds in dormitory rooms (1175m, 3855ft).

Curmătura In a fine position in a clearing beneath the crags of the Piatra Craiului. There is a lovingly maintained Salvamont base 400m east. No electricity, water from a spring west of the cabana or a hosepipe outside the back door. 46 beds in dormitory rooms and a few twins (1470m, 4823ft).

Garofița Piatrei Craiului Private, off the western side of the Piatra Craiului, built and run by the România Pitorească club from Pitești. You may be able to find accommodation but probably no food.

Gura Râului On the edge of **Zărnești** village; often filled with school parties and noisy; 50 beds, mainly in twin rooms. Better to press on to Curmătura. If you ask nicely they serve good food (750m, 2460ft).

Refugiul Iezer Almost a cabana, 1km south-east of Vf. Iezer at the head of the Iezer valley; two rooms, sleeping about 60.

Plaiul Foii 12km west of Zărnești on a dirt road has been refurbished and is comfortable (849m, 2785ft). Try Roly's new private cabana on the other side of the river on the way back to Zărnești.

Voina A hotel-cabana, north of Râușor lake on the DJ734 road 12km north of Câmpulung (station) via Lerești. 158 beds in rooms of 2, 3 and 4 beds (950m, 3117ft), Tel (office in Câmpulung) 0248 821 573, 0248 822 634.

The Făgăraș and Cozia massifs

Făgăraș town has the wonderfully tiny, cheap and shabby **Hotel Piața** in the south-west corner of the market place (Tel 0268 216 257), the **Pensiunea Roata** (Str. Vasile Alecsandri 10, Tel 0268 212 415), the **Pensiunea Flora** (Str vasile Alecsandri 12, Tel 0268 236 307). At the western foot of the range, **Avrig** has the **Motel Fânânița Haiducului** (Tel 0269 550 464).

The **DJ7C Trans-Făgărașan road** has a number of cabana-type places along it that normally function when the road is open. From north to south these are **Vama Cucului**, 4km from Cârțișoara, 15 beds in rooms of 2, 3 and 4 beds, a further 18 beds in căsuțe (850m, 2789ft – not on the map), **Bâlea Cascada**, 63 beds in rooms of 2 and 3 beds (1234m, 4048ft), Tel 0269 524 255, **Bâlea Lac**, 71 beds in dormitory rooms, no electricity. Burnt down summer 1995, rebuilding is well underway (2034m, 6673ft). Adjacent is the simply wonderful **Vila Paltinu** (2034m, 6673ft) Tel 0269 524 277, 22 spaces. At the southern end of the tunnel is **Capra** (**Pârâul Capra**, **Valea Caprei**) burnt down 1992, and no sign of opening at the moment (1525m, 5003ft). On the south of the range, overlooking Vidraru Lare, are **Cumpăna**, reached by rough road round the western side of Vidraru Lake, 76 beds in rooms of 2 and 3 beds, 62 in căsuțe (920m, 3018ft), **Valea cu Pești** (really a hotel), 17km from Căpățâneni, 48 beds in rooms of 2 and 3 beds (850m, 2729ft) and **Izvorul Sec** (945m, 3100ft) in the Topolog Valley, 12km by forest road north of Sălătrucu de Sus. There is the **Casa Argeșană Posada SA**, in Curtea de Argeș (Str Basarabilor 27-29, Tel 0248 721 451, 0248 711 800, Fax 0248 721 109).

Road-accessible places on the northern side of the massif include, from west to east, **Valea Oltului**, on the main DN1-7 in the bottom of the Olt valley, not far from where the red stripe route heads due west from the western end of the Făgăraș range, 34 beds in twin rooms, a further 34 beds in căsuțe (350m, 1148ft), **Piscul Alb** (655m, 2149ft) 16 places, reached by forest road 5km above Sebeșu de Sus. The Avrig Valley, south of the town has **Ghiocelul** (520m, 17060ft, 15 beds), also the adjacent **Camping Zenove** with 5 two-bed camping huts; these lie 9km up the valley by forest road. 5km further is the pleasant and comfortable **Poiana Neamțului** (706m, 2316ft, 20 places). Accommodation accessible by heading up into the mountains from Victoria (or Arpașu de Sus) includes **Arpaș** (also known as **Fața Pădurii** – 600m, 1968ft, 7km south of Victoria), 42 beds in rooms of 5 beds and fewer, then **Complex Turistic Sâmbăta** (11km from Victoria, 690m, 2264ft), 47 beds in rooms of 2, 3 and 4 beds and some dormitory rooms, also 20 beds in căsuțe, then, 1km further, **Popasul Sâmbăta** (730m, 2395ft), 14 beds in dormitory rooms, electricity but no running water, 20 further beds in căsuțe, then, 2km further, the **Hotel Nitramonia** (800m, 2625ft), 32 beds.

Cabanas

Bârcaciu Remote and delightful, in a clearing on a spur, north-west of Scara summit, 80 minutes walk up from Poiana Neamț. 20 bunk spaces in a common dining and bed room, no electricity. Well run by Coana Mariana – recommended (1550m, 5085ft).

Negoiu Large, remote, well located among trees high in the western part of the Făgăraș. 170 beds in rooms of 2, 3, 4, 5 and 8 beds, no electricity – another notable cabanier – Sigi (1546m, 5072ft).

Podragu Large, near Podragu lake, in grassy bowl. 100 beds in dormitory rooms, running water but no mains electricity (formerly a small hydro generator) (2136m, 7008ft).

Prejba At the northern end of the Lotrulu, on a dirt road west from near Lăzarel village in the Olt valley, or by a 3hr walk up from Valea Sadului cabana. 44 beds in dormitory rooms. No running water or electricity (1630m, 5348ft).

Suru is now merely a refuge shelter in a former outhouse, the cabana having burnt down in December 1996 (1450m, 4757ft).

Turnuri In the Podragu valley, reached by following the red triangle route, first a dirt road then a path, southwards from Arpaș cabana. 20 beds in dormitory rooms. No electricity – washing at a spout outside (1520m, 4987ft), Tel 0269 438 405.

Urlea In a clearing on a steep spur, reached by heading up the Pojorta valley from the village of Breaza. 52 beds in dormitory rooms. No running water or electricity – washing at a spring nearby (1533m, 5029ft).

Valea Sâmbetei Just below the tree line, an hour's walk up the Sâmbata valley from cabanas at Sâmbata, initially on a dirt road up the valley of the same name. 55 beds in dormitory rooms, no electricity (1401m, 4596ft).

The Făgăraș is also well supplied with refuges, all located close to or on the main red stripe ridge route. From west to east these are: **Scara**, on Scara Pass (2146m, 7041ft), east of Vf. Scara summit, and **Călțun** (2135m, 7004ft) at Călțun Lake, just south of the watershed, 1.5km south-east of Vf. Negoiu. East of the TransFăgărașan road are **Fereastra Zmeilor**, in the glacial hollow of Fundul Caprei, just south of the watershed at Portița Arpașului pass, **Portița Viștei** (2310m, 7579ft), on the north side of the ridge at the head of the Viștea valley, **Berivoescu** (2190m, 7185ft), 800m south-south-west of Berevoescu Mare summit. **NB** that the former refuges of **Moldoveanu** and **Avrig**, still shown on some maps, no longer exist.

The Cozia massif

The Cozia is very well provided with hotels at its base in the little spa settlement of **Călimănești-Căciulata** along the busy corridor of the Olt valley. Stretching north up the DN7 road from Căciulata (250m, 820ft), these are the **Hotel Căciulata** (Calea lui Traian 790, Tel 0250 750 520, Fax 0250 751 137), the **Hotel Oltul** (Calea lui Traian 792, Tel 0250 750 401, Fax 0250 750 401), the **Hotel Cozia** (Calea lui Traian 791, Tel 0250 750 441, Fax 0250 750441), the **Hotel Central** (Tel 0250 750 990), the **Hotel Vâlcea** (Tel 0250 750 724), the **Motel Cozia** (Tel 0250 750 520, Fax 0250 750 270). 5km north is **Han Lotrișor**, now a truckers' roadhouse.

Cozia near the rocky summit of Cozia, reached by tarred, then gravel twisting road, 27km by road (much less on foot) from Călimanești (railway station). 25 beds in rooms of 2, 3 and 5 beds, washing facilities outside (1570m, 5150ft).

From the Olt to the Jiu

It may be that you have no choice other than to stay in **Petroșani** – actually not as grim as many would have you believe, for it lies in a fine valley. Here you do have a choice, of the **Hotel Parâng**, also known as the **Tulipan** (Str. 1 Decembrie 88, Tel 0254 543 582), the **Hotel Petroșani** (Str. 1 Decembrie 110, Tel 0254 544 425, Fax 0254 545 383) the **Hotel Cameleonul Internațional** (Str. 1 Decembrie 120, Tel 0254 542 122, Fax 0254 350 961) and the **Hotel Onix** (Str. 1 Decembrie 73, Tel 0254 544 613), also the **Hotel Intim** (Str. Brâncuși 17), **Cabana Argo Alpina** (Tel 0254 543 957) and the **Mini-Hotel** (Str. Bălcescu 17).

The Cindrel massif

Curmătura Stezii (cf. Curmătura in the Piatra Craiului) just outside Răsinari village. 10 beds in twin rooms, a further 14 in small huts (680m, 2231ft), Tel/Fax 0269 557 169.

Fântânele An isolated skiers' cabana north of the Cibin river, lying up the valley from the village of Fântânele, near Sibiel. No water or electricity. 52 beds in rooms of 2, 3, 5 and 8 beds (1257m, 4124ft) (cf. Fântânele in the Ceahlău).

Criuț A 'complex' of cabanas on the northern side of the Cindrel, reached by rough track 11km south-west from Săliște, 17km west of Sibiu on the DN1-7 (E68). 133 beds in different small cabanas (about 1250m, about 4100ft, cf. Criuț in the Șureanu).

Gâtul Berbecului Lakeside, in the Sadu valley on the road from Oasa Mică to Râu Sadului. 55 beds in rooms of 2, 3, 4 and 5 beds (1175m, 3855ft).

Oasa At the western end of the Cindrel ridge, by Oasa lake, on the DN67C road south from Sebeş to Novaci, 63km from Sebes, 53km from Petroşani. 38 beds in rooms of 2 and 4 beds (1280m, 4200ft).
Obârşia Lotrului At the junction of the DN7A east from Petroşani to Brezoi and the DN67C south from Sebeş to Novaci, buses direct to the cabana. 35 beds in 5 rooms, more in huts (1320m, 4330ft).

Păltiniş (1425m, 4675ft) A pleasant small resort reached by the DJ106A, 33km from Sibiu via Răşinari and Hotel Cindrel (Tel 0269 213 237). Better is **Vila Sinaia** (Tel c/o tourist office, 0269 223 860, 0269 574 035, Fax 0269 218 319, Str. Tribunei 3, Sibiu – near the station) or **Casa Turiştilor** (179 beds in mainly twin rooms, Tel 0269 216 001).

Peştera Bolii On the DN66 towards Haţeg, 3km from Petroşani; useful as a start point into the Retezat or Şureanu. 12 beds in 3 rooms.

Valea Aurie A roadside inn and campsite south-west of Sibiu on Calea Dumbravii, adjacent to the museum of popular technology. 18 beds in rooms of 2, 3 and 4 beds (470m, 1542ft).

The Parâng massif
Lainici A roadside cabana at the western end of the Parâng, in the Jiu valley between Târgu Jiu and Petroşani. 50 beds in rooms of 2 and 3 beds, 30 more in căsuţe (420m, 1378ft).

Petrimanu A lakeside cabana at the eastern end of the Parâng (1615m, 5298ft).

Rânca In the resort of the same name, on the south side of the Parâng, reached by the gravel DN67C road 19km north of Novaci, nearest station Târgu Jiu, 44km south-west. 58 beds in rooms of 2, 3, 4, 5 and 8 beds, running water, cabana's own generator (1600m, 5250ft).

Rusu 14km south-east of Petroşani, on the DN7A and side road via Slătinioara. Often full of school groups (1168m, 3832ft), Tel 0254 541 321. Try also **Cabana Start '93** (Tel 0254 542 833).

The Şureanu massif
Auşel Reached by rough road north from Petrila up the Bratcuş valley, about 5km south of Vf. Şureanu.

Lunca Florii In the Taia valley, reached by rough road 5km north of the town of Petrila, itself 5km east of the DN66 (E79) road north to Hunedoara from Petroşani (760m, 2493ft).

Cetatea Near the head of the Grădiștea valley, by the archaeological site of Sarmizegetusa Regia, reached by tarred, then rough road south from Orăștie.

Costești At the southern end of the village of the same name, 20km south of Oraștie town (itself on the DN7 27km east of Deva) on the DJ 705 road. 23 beds in rooms of 1, 2, 4 and 8 beds, 26 more in căsuțe (340m, 1115ft).

Groapa Seacă In the Jiet valley, 18km east of Petroșani on the DN7A road.

Prislop On the northern side of the range, reached by rough road south from Orăștie via the villages of Căstău and Sibișel, also south from Cugir. 50 beds in a total of 16 rooms (1100m, 3609ft).

Șureanu Reached by forest road west up the Cugir valley (no connection with the town of the same name) and west from Oasa cabana, over the Presaca pass, and through Poarta Raiului and just east of Vf. Șureanu. 46 beds in rooms of 4, 5 and 10 beds, no electricity, spring outside (1734m, 5348ft).

Voievodu In the Jiu de Est valley, between the Parâng and the Surean, as the crow flies 10km north-west of Obirsia Lotrului, reached by rough road 10km east from the eastern end of Petrila via Câmpa and Târlici. 78 beds in 17 rooms (810m, 2657ft).

The Căpățânii massif

Brazilor A spa cabana just to the north of Băile Olănești – useful as a base for exploring the monasteries and gorges around Horezu on the southern flanks of the Căpățânii; 69 beds in rooms of 2, 3 and 5 beds, a further 80 beds in căsuțe (450m, 1476ft).

Peștera Muierii At the south-west corner of the range, in the Cheile Galben gorge, reached by heading east from Novaci to Baia de Fier and heading north on a tarred road for 3km. 47 beds in various rooms, plus camping huts (585m, 1919ft).

The Lotru masssif

Valea Sadului A roadside cabana below the northern end of the massif, outside the village of Râu Sadului. 16 beds in rooms of 2, 3 and 4 beds, no running water (503m, 1650ft).

Prejba Reached by a dirt road heading west from near Lazarel village in the Olt valley, or by a slightly tricky 3hr walk up from Valea Sadului. 44 dormitory beds. No running water or electricity (1630m, 5348ft).

The Retezat massif

See **Petroșani** above; road-accessible accommodation on the south side of the range includes **Câmpu lui Neag** village, the cabana of the same name (80 beds); also ask at the shop in the village (or the bar behind it) for private accommodation (850m, 2789ft). The best bet is the new **private mini-hotel** at the entrance to Cheile Buta gorge, soon to be joined by another 2km east on the DN66A road to Uricani is **Motel Valea cu Pești** (Tel 0254 147 572). On the northern side there is only **Gura Zlata**, an attractive and well-kept (though often busy) cabana on the tarred road up the Râul Mare valley, 31km from **Cârnești** (railway station), 11km south-west of Hațeg. 47 beds in rooms of 2, 3, 4 and 5 beds – 12 more in căsuțe, washing block outside (775m, 2543ft).

Cabanas

Baleia At the eastern end of the Retezat, reached by dirt road south from the village of Pui (railway station), through Hobița. 68 beds in rooms of 2, 3 and 4 more beds, no running water or electricity (1410m, 4626ft). May be shut by the time of publication.

Buta Reached by forest road up from the Jiul de Vest valley at Câmpu lui Neag; outside toilets. 54 beds in 4 dormitories. Recommended (1580m, 5184ft).

Cascada On the roadside at Cârnic foresters' building, halfway between Nucșoara village and Pietrele cabana.

Gențiana In the Pietrele valley 2km south of Pietrele; no plumbing or electricity. 24 dorm. beds (1670m, 5479ft).

Pietrele Reached by rough (and latterly very steep) road up the Nucșoara valley from the Ohaba de Sub Piatra (station). 230 beds in rooms of 2, 3, 4, 5 and 8 beds, some with pleasant balconies, many căsuțe, water from stream outside, own generator for light only (1480m, 4856ft).

The Vâlcan massif

The only true mountain-hut cabanas are **Straja** and **Vulcan**, about 14km from Vulcan town by dirt road. 34 dorm. beds, spring outside (1419m, 4655ft). Apart from these there are only the road-accessible **Sohodol** (Bucium-Sohodol), 8km north of Runcu by DJ672C road. 28 beds in rooms of 2 and 3 beds, 22 more in căsuțe, washing facilities outside, own small hydro-electricity generator (410m, 1345ft), **Tismana** village, with the **Hotel Tismana** (Tel/Fax 0253 374 162) and **Motel Tismana** (or **Tismănița**) Tel 0253 374 265, also căsuțe.

The **Muntele Mic Massif** has the ski resort of the same name, with the **Hotel Sebeș** (Tel 0255 512 335, Fax 0255 511 769); ask here for cheaper rooms in villas adjacent.

The mountains of Banat

There are no remote mountain walkers' cabanas in the Semenic: instead they tend towards being larger tourist complexes, reached by car and public transport from Reşiţa.

Just east of **Reşiţa** is the little spa complex of **Staţiunea Secu** (280m, 919ft), along the southern shore of the lake of the same name, in forest. There is **Cabana Splendid**, 22 beds in twin rooms with rudimentary en suite facilities, only open in the summer (Tel 0255 413 463), **Cabana Constructorul**, 40 beds in twin rooms with rudimentary en suite facilities (Tel 0255 410 237), **Vila Petricica**, 18 beds in twin rooms (Tel 0255 413 463, Fax 0255 414 854) and **Hotel Turist** (Tel 0255 210 100, Fax 0255 216 900).

Staţiunea Crivaia (660m, 2165ft), 5km up the DJ582 road from the village of Văliug, on the DJ582 road from Reşiţa, has **Cabana Bârzava**, 130 beds in rooms of 2, 3 and 4 beds, many with rudimentary en suite facilities, and **Cabana Crivaia**, 53 beds in rooms of 6, 3, 2 and single beds, many with rudimentary en suite facilities).

Mărghitaş Isolated and run down, amidst deciduous forest, reached by bad tarred road 4km north of the town of Anina (station). 50 beds in rooms of 2 and 4 beds, many with rudimentary en suite facilities (565m, 1854ft).

Staţiunea Semenic (1410m, 4626ft), a modern complex on the skyline in the highest part of the massif, has **Hotel Gozna**, 116 beds in rooms of 2, 3 and 4 beds, many with rudimentary en suite facilities (Tel 0255 433 585), **Hotel Nedeea**, 230 beds (Tel 0255 433 039) and various villas and small cabins.

Trei Ape A small lakeside resort reached by buses from Reşiţa and Caransebes. 65 beds in rooms of 2 and 3 beds, many with rudimentary en suite facilities, 20 more beds in căsuţe (850m, 2789ft).

Băile Herculane, possibly the best centre in the country for day walks has a huge amount of accommodation available. The best is **Hotel Ferdinand** (Piata Hercules 1, Tel/Fax 0255 561 131) but very nice (and perfectly affordable) is the **Vila Belvedere** (Str. Nicolae Stoica Haţeg 6, Tel 0255 561 428, Fax 0255 561 439), uphill behind the grim central concrete block of the **Hotel Hercules** (Str Izvorului 7, Tel 0255 560 880) on the west bank of the river. Also good is **Hotel Claudia**, above the brick tower-block hotels just down the valley (Str Complexelor 9, Tel/Fax 0255 560 170). At the northern extremity of the town is the concrete **Hotel Roman** (Str. Romana 1, Tel 0255 560 390, Fax 0255 561 411). Of the communist-era blocks just down the hill in Pecinişca the best is the **Hotel Domogled**, adjacent to (and its reception handled by) the **Hotel Dacia** just above (Tel 0255 229 501, 0255 229 486, Fax 0255 229 504). The Dacia lookalikes, the **Minerva**,

Afrodita and **Diana** are pretty grim. The **Hotel Cerna** does not seem to cater for private visits.

The mountains of Maramureș

The Rodna Massif

Moisei Cabana Capra Neagra ('Chamois'), recently renovated in a slap-dash way, in the centre, on the main street. 10 beds (580m, 1900ft, Tel 0262 347 999). Across the road is a welcome ice-cream stall.

Vișeu de Sus has the very pleasant **Hotel Brădet**, run by the town's forestry company, right in the centre. There is also **Hanul Poarta** ('The Gates Inn'), a tiny roadside inn with a few beds at the extreme western end of town. There was the **Hotel Cerbul** ('the Stag', also known as Hotel Vișeul), an unattractive modern hotel by the river and railway at the western end of town; it shows no signs of re-opening.

Borșa has the old state **Hotel Iezer** (Str. Decebal 2, 72 beds, Tel 0262 343 430, Fax 0262 344 044) in the centre, on the south side of the main street. Almost opposite is the new, private, **Hotel Perla Maramureșului** (Str. Victoriei 27, Tel 0262 342 539, Fax 0262 344 161) – really the only place to eat. More upmarket is **Hotel Mia** (Str A. I. Cuza 237A, Tel 0262 342 347, Fax 0262 346 241).

Complex Turistic Borșa ('Stațiunea Borșa') is not as grimly Orwellian as its name implies, with its traditionally-built wooden church and delightful situation, right below the main Rodna ridge, reached by chairlift (running summer as well). By far the best place is the new (1998) **Hotel Cerbul** (Tel 0262 344 199 and ask for D-nul Stețcu, mentioning the author of this book). Three hotels, long overdue for restoration, are operated by Borșa Hospital; advance bookings can be made by fax (0262 433 916). The choice is between the **Hotel Stibina**, 170 beds, mainly in twin en suite rooms, and the similar **Hotel Cascada**, 120 beds, mainly in twin rooms with en suite bathrooms (Tel – both hotels – 0262 343 466). There is also **Vila Bradet**, just uphill (the least reliable hot water), 98 beds in twin en suite rooms, and **Hanul Butinarilor**, adjacent to the main road, opposite the school.

Cabana Prislop A scruffy roadside cabana (recently rebuilt after a fire) just west of Prislop pass. 3 rooms with a total of 10 beds. No running water or electricity – washing at a spring nearby (1413m, 4636ft). Site of a festival in August.

Cabana Puzdra (Puzdrele), 2hrs walk from Borșa. 30 dormitory beds. Washing at a spring nearby, no electricity (1540m, 5052ft). Burnt down – rebuilding under way.

Stațiunea Sângeorz-Bai is a run-down old spa resort to the south of the Rodna, not really catering for visiting mountain walkers but staff might take pity on you.

The options are **Hotel Somesul** (Str Trandafirilor 15, Tel 0263 370 079) or **Hotel Hebe** (Str. Trandafirilor 10, Tel 0263 370 228, Fax 0263 370 335) which has 902 beds (!), also 16 villas with a total of 676 beds among them and restaurants. Head north on the DN17D and turn left after 2km to **Cabana Farmecul Pădurii**, near Cormaia village at the confluence of the Cormaia and Vinului valleys (585m, 1919ft). Continue north-east on the DN17D a further 11km to the village of Rodna (in the railway timetable as 'Rodna Veche'), with the **Hotel Ineu**, 50 beds in various rooms, some with bathrooms (525m, 1722ft). 9km north of Rodna is **Stațiunea Valea Vinului**, with 2 villas (89 beds) and a restaurant – all under the auspices of the Romanian Writers' Union. They may be interested in helping a visiting walker.

The Gutâi massif

Stațiunea Izvoare Reached by tarred road north from Baia Mare and dirt road on to the DN18. 135 beds in total (916m, 3005ft), Tel 0262 437 676.

Cabana Mogoșa On the tarred side road east from the small mining town of Baia Sprie. 80 beds (731m, 2398ft), Tel 0262 460 800.

Cabana Baraj-Firiza On the tarred road north from Baia Mare to Izvoare, on the southern shore of Lake Firiza. 14 beds.

Hanul Pintea Viteazul On the DN18 from Baia Mare to Sighetu Marmației at the pass. 12 beds (987m, 3238ft).

The Apuseni

Arieșeni Roadside, in the Bihor, on the eastern end of the village of the same name, lying in the Arieșul Mare valley. 44 beds in rooms of 2, 3 and 4 beds, 20 more in căsuțe (950m, 3117ft).

Băișoara A large new hill-top building, reached by dead-end road from Băișoara village. 177 beds in rooms of 2 and 3 beds, most with en suite bathrooms (1385m, 4544ft).

Buru At the eastern end of Buru village, at the confluence of the Arieș and Iara valleys – at the eastern end of the Muntele Mare and the northern end of the Trascău massif.

Cheile Turzii (Cheia) Attractive, with a fancy turret, set among trees, at the end of Turda gorge, badly in need of refurbishment – 24 beds inside in rooms of 2, 3 and 4 beds, plus 20 more in căsuțe, unreliable running water, generally poor plumbing, more reliable electricity (950m, 3117ft).

Dezna (off the Bihor–Vlădeasa map, approximately 25km as the crow flies south-west of Ştei, also known as Dr Petru Groza) A small cabana outside the village of the same name in the Dezna valley, against the Codru-Moma massif, reached by tarred road from the little town of Sebis (see Dervla Murphy, Bibliography) in the Crişul Alb valley. There are footpath connections to Beiuş, via Moneasa and Vascău. 6 beds, 20 more in căsuţe (195m, 640ft). May be shut by the time of publication.

Făget Attractively located among pine trees on the outskirts of Cluj, overlooked by the Faget hills. 12 beds inside in several rooms plus 24 more in căsuţe (520m, 1706ft), Tel 0264 116 227.

Faget Pădure Close to Faget, near the village of Feleacu, 32 beds in rooms of 4 beds (536m, 1760ft), Tel 0264 162 991.

Întregalde Central to the Trascău massif, in Întregalde village, on the tarred road up the Galda valley, 24km from the Galda de Jos, itself 3km west of the DN1/E81 road, 13km north of Alba Iulia.

Leghia In the village of Leghia, just to the north of the DN1 Huedin-Cluj road. 22 dorm. beds (567m, 1860ft).

Leşu-Baraj Large, modern lakeside, reached by tarred road from the village of Remeţi, in the Pădurea-Craiului massif. 244 beds in rooms of 2 and 8 beds, most with en suite bathrooms (800m, 2625ft).

Meziad Just outside the village of Meziad, reached by the gravel DJ674C road 6km from the village of Beiuş (railway station). 46 beds in rooms of 2, 3 and 4 beds, mains but no running water (380m 1247ft).

Muntele Filii Pleasantly located among trees overlooking the Iara valley, reached by unsurfaced road from Băişoara. 25 beds in dormitory rooms, spring outside (550m, 1804ft).

Padiş Reached by gravel road, 17km east from the village of Pietroasa, south-east of Beiuş – often busy in summer with car-borne visitors; also a rough road heading 51km north to Huedin, on the main DN1 road and railway line Cluj–Oradea. 44 beds in rooms of 2, 4 and 5 beds, 14 more in căsuţe, washing block outside (1280m, 4200ft).

Râmeţi Large and modern, reached by tarred road 18km north-west up the Geoagiu valley from Teiuş, just north of Alba-Iulia. 38 beds in rooms of 3 and 4 beds, 16 more in căsuţe. More comfortable, attractive and welcoming accommodation can be found at the monastery (426m, 1398ft).

Sloboda Pleasantly located in woods on the road from the Aiud to Râmeţ. 24 beds in rooms of 4 and 5 beds, 20 more in căsuţe and camping available (550m, 1804ft), Tel 058 86 17 34.

Someşul Rece A roadside cabana 13km by road west of Cluj, on the way to the village of Măguri-Răcătău. 71 beds in rooms of 2, 3 and 4 beds, together with some dormitory rooms (426m, 1397ft).

Valea Drăganului A roadside cabana in the valley of the same name on the road to Drăgan lake. 84 beds in rooms of 2, 3, and 4 beds (550m, 1804ft).

Vlădeasa An attractively located cabana above Sacuieu village. 33 beds mainly in dormitory rooms. No running water or electricity (1430m, 4692ft).

The Eastern Carpathians

The Căliman, Rarău-Giumalău and Bârgău massifs

The heart of the Căliman massif has shelters rather than cabanas – see text.

Câmpulung Moldovenesc has the recommended **Pensiunea Minion** (Str. Dimitri Cantemir 26, Tel 0230 312 028, Fax 0230 311 581), the **Hotel Semeniuc** (Str. Nicolae Dracea 6, Tel 0230 314 549), the architecturally regrettable, but comfortable, welcoming and very central **Hotel Zimbrul** (Calea Bucovinei 1-3, Tel 0230 312 441, 0230 312 442, Fax 0230 314 358), the **Hotel Tineretului** (Str. Tineretului, Tel 0230 311 049), the **BTC Bucovina** (Str. Pinului 35-37, Tel/Fax 0230 314 163) and **Cabana Deia**, 51 beds in rooms of 2, 3, and 4 beds, just to the north of town (Tel 0230 811 060) – currently shut but may be open by the time of publication.

Vatra Dornei has several hotels: the **Hotel Idus** (Str Republicii 5, Tel 0230375 021, Fax 0230 375 020), the **Căliman-Bradul** (Str. Republicii 5, Tel/Fax 0230 371 150), the more modest **Rarău** (Tel 0230 371 306) a large number of Lodgings – 'Pensiune' in town and wooden cabins at **Cabana Runc**, a handsome building, above the town to the north-west, 62 beds in rooms of 2, 3, 4 and 5 beds (855m, 2805ft) Tel 0230 871 312.

Codrişor Small, now privatised as a hotel on the outskirts of Bistriţa to the west of the Căliman. 38 beds in rooms of 2, 3, and 4 beds (360m, 1181ft), Tel 0263 224 907.

Vila din Carpaţi Modern, set in pine trees on the DN17 road east of the Tihuţa pass.

Mestecăniș On the DN17, 20km from Câmpulung to Vatra Dornei, close to Mestecăniș railway halt. 7 beds inside, 20 in căsuțe, washing facilities outside (1100m, 3608ft).

Rarău An alpine ski-hotel, 14km south of Câmpulung Moldovenesc on the DJ175 to Chiril. 83 beds in rooms of 2, 3 and 4 beds, also dormitory rooms – some en suite rooms, Tel c/o Hotel Zimbrul in Câmpulung (1520m, 4987ft).

Zugreni (Vadu Bistriței) On the other side of the Bistrița river from the DN17B, 20km east of Vatra Dornei, in the Zugreni gorge nature reserve. 39 beds in rooms of 2, 4 and 6 beds (719m, 2359ft). A 3½ hour walk following the blue disc waymarks brings you 881m, 2890ft up to Giumalău cabana.

Piatra Fântânele, 5km south of the Tihuța pass on the DN17 to Bistrița, has a number of villas and also the **Hotel Dracula** (the former Motel Tihuța, Tel 0263 266 841, Fax 26 61 19). 320 beds in rooms of various sizes, shut in winter, also shops.

Gălăoia In the village of the same name on the DN15 road on the south side of the Căliman. 14 beds in rooms of 2–4 beds.

Șoimilor In Neagra village on the DN15 road on the south side of the Căliman. 26 beds in rooms of 1–3 beds.

Doi Brazi In Salard village, just west of the larger village of Lunca Bradului, on the DN15 road on the south side of the Căliman. 18 beds in twin rooms.

The Ceahlău massif

The little ski resort of Durău (800m, 2625ft) has the **Hotel Brândușa** (Tel 0233 678 273), **Casa Igor** (Tel 0233 678 288) and other private house accommodation – **Cabana Paulo**, the **Hotel Cascada** (Tel 0233 678 022), the **Hotel Bradul** (Tel 0233 678 078), the **Hotel Durău** (Tel 0233 678 254) at the top and, just above, **Cabana Fântânele** (70 beds in rooms of 2, 5 and 8 beds, washing facilities outside, 1220m, 4003ft). The nuns at the **monastery** can also accommodate walkers (Tel 0233 678 383).

Other road-accessible accommodation to the east of the massif is **Han Potoci** (Tel 0233 672 236) in the village of Potoci, on the eastern shore of Bicaz lake, 13km north of Bicaz, **Cabana Baraj-Bicaz** (530m, 1739ft) overlooking the dam, 206 beds in rooms of 2, 3, 4, 5 and 8 beds, Tel 0233 671 121, and **Izvorul Muntelui** (797m, 2615ft), 10km north-west of Bicaz town, 75 beds in rooms of 2, 3, 5 and 8 beds, water from nearby spring.

The only true mountain-hut is the lonely **Cabana Dochia**, 106 beds in rooms of 2, 4 and 8 beds (1828m, 5997ft).

The Hăşmaş massif

Lacu Roşu (1107m, 3632ft) has plenty of accommodation (ignore the hotels etc. named on Map 20a for in this respect it is out of date), including the late dictator's **Vila Borş**, also the **Hotel Bucur** (Tel 0266 162 949), **Hotel Făget** and several villas, including **Vila 14** and **Vila Vulturul**. Also rooms in private houses. 3km west, in **Bicaz Gorge** are **Cerbul**, 4 beds in two rooms, own small hydro-electric supply (740m, 2428ft) and the larger **Cheile Bicazului**, 90 beds in rooms of 4, 5 and 8 beds, 18 more in căsuţe (1828m, 5997ft). There is also **Ardeluţa**, in the Tarcău valley between the Tarcău and Goşman ridges. Access by tarred road (apart from last 2km) 30km south of Tarcău village, 2km east of Cicaz on the DN15 road, 50 beds (660m, 2165ft).

The only true mountain-hut is **Piatra Singuratică**, close to the top of the Hăşmaş ridge, 2 hours' walk up the red triangle path from Bălan. 30 beds in dormitory rooms of 8 beds, water from nearby spring, no mains (1430m, 4692ft).

The Harghita massif

Roadside places include **Cabana Brădet** (967m, 3172ft) on the DN13A 14km west of Miercurea-Ciuc, just east of **Vlăhiţa Pass**. 7km north is **Harghita-Bai**, on the rough DJ13A road from Brădet cabana 12km west of Miercurea-Ciuc. 45 beds in rooms of 2, 4 and 8 beds, natural hot spings (1350m, 4429ft). Further west along the road are, in order, **Cabana Chirui** and **Salteres**.

The only true mountain-hut is **Cabana Harghita-Mădăraş**, reached by a track 18km up from the village of Sub Cetate in the Târnava Mare valley to the west. 101 beds in rooms of 2, 3, 4 and 8 beds, running water, cabana's own generator, no mains; a Salvamont post and a few private cabanas adjacent (1801m, 5909ft).

The Bodoc and Ciucului massifs

There are no true mountain-huts here. The spa town of **Băile Tuşnad** (lying between the Bodoc and the Harghita massifs) has three hotels, the **Tuşnad** (Str. Olt 45, Tel/Fax 0266 115 074) attached to the spa treatment centre, the **Olt** (Str. Vointa 2, Tel 0266 111 676, Fax 0266 150 876) and the **Ciucaş** (Str. Voinicea 1, Tel 0266 122 184, Fax 0266 121 482). At **Băile Balvanyos** the former **Hotel Carpaţi** has now become the **Best Western Motel** (Tel/Fax 0267 361 449). **Lacul Sfânta Ana** has a single cabana, with 16 beds in rooms of 2, 4 and 5 beds, water from a well nearby, natural hot spings (1060m, 3478ft).

Bancu village (immediately south of Ciuc-Sângeorgiu) has a cabana, reached by heading east out of Miercurea-Ciuc on the DJ123 and turning right out the town of the DJ123B. Open June–September, 28 beds. **Brusturoasa**, 22km north-west of Comăneşti, on the DN12A towards Miercurea-Ciuc, has an old campsite with 24 beds in căsuţe.

The **Vrancea-Penteleu** region has no cabanas. **Covasna**, at the western foot of the massif, has a good supply of hotels.

The monasteries of Bucovina

Moldovița has the **Hotel Mărul de Aur** ('Golden Apple', Tel 0230 336 180, Fax 0230 336 201) at the crossroads and several houses that offer accommodation, showing 'Zimmer Frei' signs. Also ask at the monastery (ask for Sister Tatiana who speaks French and German) for a recommendation of where to stay in the village. **Sucevița** has the recently renovated and now very pleasant **Motel Sucevița** just east of the monastery on the south side of the road and the recommended **Popas Bucovina**, a Swiss-chalet hotel, with budget accommodation in camping-cabins (Tel 0230 417 000). It is at the western end of the village and has very good food. **Putna** has the **Cabana Turistică Putna** in the village opposite the turning to Chiril and Pensiunea Chitriuc Elena (Tel 0230 371 306). 10km east, in the village of **Vicov** is the **Motel Vicov** (Tel 0230 464 138). **Rădăuți** has the **Hotel Nordic** (Str. Unirii 67, Tel 0230 461 863, 0230 461 643) and **Pensiune Fast** (Str. Ștefan cel Mare 80, Tel 0230 462 698, Fax 0230 465 450). **Solca** has the **Motel Solca** (Tel 0230 477 182).

Gura Humorului has the **Hotel Carpați** (Str. 9 Mai 9, Tel 0230 231 103) and the **Hotel Best Western Bucovina** (Bd Bucovina 4, Tel 0230 207 000, Fax 0230 207 001), **Vila Ramona** (Str. Oborului 6, Tel/Fax 030 23 21 33) and my favourite, the recommended **Cabana Voroneț**, on the left of the side road to the monastery, on the bank of the River Moldova (Tel 0230 231 024, Fax 0230 522 866). 16km west is the village of **Vama**, with the **Pensiune Vila Lucuțar Lucreția** (Tel. 0230 520 160, 0744 555 837). **Voroneț** has accommodation with **Prof. Dorina Nistor** (Tel 0230 230 551, 0230 215 689).

Suceava is well supplied with hotels; I recommend the **Pension Bi-Com** (Bumbu Vichentie, proprietor; Str. Narciselor 20, Tel 0230 216 881, Fax 0230 520 007).

APPENDIX B:
Useful words/phrases in the Romanian language

Accommodation	**Cazare**
Where are the toilets, please?	Unde este toaleta vă rog?
Is there somewhere else nearby where I could stay?	Este un alt loc in apropiere unde aş putea sta?
Does anyone in the village rent out rooms for the night?	Este cineva aici care închiriază camere pentru noapte?
Can we have some sheets and blankets in our room, please?	Putem avea nişte cearceafuri şi pături în cameră vă rog?
Can we see the room, please?	Putem vedea camera vă rog?
Is there a (hot) shower?	Aveţi un duş (cu apă caldă)?
Where can we wash?	Unde ne putem spăla?
room, bed	cameră, pat

Food and drink	**Mâncare şi băutură**
A bottle of mineral water, please	O sticlă de apă minerală, vă rog
Tap water is fine, if it is good to drink!	Apă de la robinet, dacă este bună de băut!
I would like dinner/lunch/breakfast	Pot servi micul dejun/dejunul/cina vă rog.
I don't mind what I have – what is best?	Nu am preferinţe – ce este mai bun?
I just want a quick lunch, please – perhaps some salad, bread and salami	Vreau un prânz rapid – poate nişte salată, pâine si salam
Could you toast this bread/these rolls, please?	Puteţi să prăjiţii această pâine/aceste chifle vă rog?
What time is dinner tonight?	La ce oră este cina diseară?
Do you have anything apart from grilled meat?	Aveţi altceva în afară de friptură?
May I/we have a cup/two cups of tea?	Pot/putem avea o cană/două căni cu ceai, vă rog?
Can you let me have something to take with me/us for my/our lunch, please?	Puteţi să-mi/să ne daţi ceva la pachet pentru dejun?
I am a vegetarian: that means I don't eat meat at all	Sunt vegetarian: asta înseamnă că nu mănînc carne deloc
A bottle of champagne and one/two glasses, please	O sticlă de şampanie şi un pahar/două pahare vă rog
Do you have any Romanian beer – not imported?	Aveţi bere românească – nu de import ?

Do you have any beer/coffee/wine?	Aveți bere/cafea/vin?
What do you have to drink?	Ce aveți de băut?
May I buy you a drink?	Pot să vă ofer ceva de băut?
How much does the meal and drinks cost, please?	Cât costă masa și băuturile, vă rog?
How much does a bottle of wine cost?	Cât costă o sticlă de vin?
Have you any non-alcoholic drinks?	Aveți băuturi fără alcool?
Cheers – Good Health!	Noroc – Sănătate!
A bar of chocolate, please	O ciocolată vă rog
food, hot food, hot drinks	mâncare, mâncare caldă, băuturi calde
eggs, milk, peppers, beef, chicken	ouă, lapte, ardei grași, carne de vacă, pui,
breast of, leg of, cabbage, beef, liver,	piept de, pulpe de, varză, vacă, ficat,
kidney, tripe, fish, brains, trout	păstrăv, rinichi, burtă, pește, creier,
potato, soup, onion, garlic, rice,	cartofi, supă or ciorbă, ceapă, usturoi, orez
lovage, celery, carrot, parsley, chervil	leuștean, țelină, morcov, pătrunjel, asmățui
wheat, oats, rice, barley, rye, maize, millet	grâu, ovăz, orez, orz, secară, porumb, mei
fig, pepper, olive, orange, horseradish	smochin, piper, măslin, portocale, hrean

Mici ('meech')	a sausage of coarse meat, fried or grilled
Mămăligă	a savoury yellow porridge made of maize, tasty and filling
Sarmale ('sarrmahleh')	cabbage or vine leaves stuffed with spicy meat and rice
Ciorbă ('cheorba')	a tasty sour soup (cf. Arabic!)
Chiftele ('keef-tehleh')	a herby, meaty rissole or burger, served with vegetables
Ardei umpluți ('arrday umploots')	stuffed peppers – recommended
Cotlet de porc	pork chop
Friptură	chunk of grilled meat, usually pork,
Cartofi prăjiți	chips

On the path	**Pe traseu**
Which is the way to ....?	Care este drumul la ....?
How many kilometres to.....?	Câți kilometri sunt până la ....?
How many hours' walk is it to...?	Câte ore de mers sunt până la ....?
Is it possible to walk to....?	Este posibil să mergem până la ....?
descend, ascend, path	coborâre, urcare, potecă
high up, low down	sus (la înălțime), jos

in the valley, on a ridge, in the forest	in vale, pe creastă or pe culme, în pădure
dangerous path, muddy, rocky	cărare periculoasă, noroios, stâncos
cliff, steep, precipitous	stâncă, abrupt, precipitat
knoll, small hill, monastery, mill	dâmb, colină, mânăstire, moară
beech, oak, spruce, fir, grass, forest	fag, stejar, molid, brad, iarbâ, pâdure
dwarf pine, juniper, birch, alder	jnepen, ienupâr, mesteacân, ariniș
apple, pear, medlar, quince	măr, păr, moșmon, gutui
clearing, treeless, bare, shepherds' hut	poiană, fără copaci, gol, stână
stream, small river, confluence, bridge	izvor, pârâu, confluența, pod
village, house, wall, fence, signpost	sat, casă, zid, gard, indicator
gorge, field, plateau, plain	chei, câmp, platou, câmpie
hairpin bends, zigzags	serpentine, zig zag
pond, peat, tarn, pass, pool	baltă, turbă, tăul/lac glaciar, pas, iaz
opposite, on this side, on the other side	opus, pe partea asta, pe partea opusă
on the right/left, next to, behind	în drepta/stânga, lângă, în spatele
straight ahead/up/down	înainte/în sus/în jos
as far as, up to, near, far, towards	până, până la, lîngă, departe, spre
road, camp	drum, tabără

DN= Drum Național, equivalent to British A road

DJ= Drum Județean, county road or minor road

Weather	**Vremea**
clouds, rain, snow, frost, cold, hot	nori, ploaie, zăpadă, îngheț, frig, cald
sunny, storm, wind, heat	însorit, furtună, vânt, căldură
fog, lightning, thunder, drizzling	ceață, fulgere, vijelie, picură

Transport	**Transportul**
What time is the bus/train to ...?	La ce oră este autobuzul/trenul spre ....?
Where do I catch the bus to ...?	De unde pot să iau autobuzul spre ....?
Which platform does the ... train arrive at?	La ce peron vine trenul spre ....?
When does it reach ...?	Când ajunge la ....?
Can you take me to ...?	Puteți să mă luați până la ....?
train, car, bus, hitch hike	tren, mașină, autobuz, autostop

Time	**Timpul**
one hour, three hours, half an hour	o oră, trei ore, o jumătate de oră
at five o'clock, at quarter/half past/to six	la ora cinci, la şase şi un sfert/jumătate/fix
afternoon, evening, midday	după amiază, seara, amiază
morning, dusk, What time is last light?	dimineaţă, amurg, La ce oră se înserează?
tomorrow, today, yesterday	mâine, azi, ieri
last night, night, night-time, day, daytime	aseară, noapte, timpul nopţii, zi, timpul zilei

Getting what you need	
A loaf of bread, please	O pâine vă rog
A litre of petrol for my stove, please!	Puteţi vă rog să-mi vindeţi un litru de benzina pentru primus?
Does anyone speak English (in the office)?	Vorbeşte cineva Engleza (în birou)?

Making conversation	**Conversaţie**
Good morning/afternoon/evening	Bună dimineata/ziua/seara
How are you?	Ce mai faci?
I am/we are from Britain/ England/Scotland/ Wales/The United States	Eu sunt/noi suntem din MareaBritanie/ Anglia/Scoţia/ Ţara Galilor/Statele Unite
I live x kilometres north/south/west of....	Locuiesc la x kilometri nord/sud/vest de ...
I am a (profession).....	Sunt ..... .
I am/am not married	Sunt/nu sunt căsătorit
I am very/not tired	Sunt foarte/nu sunt obosit
beautiful, ugly	frumos, urât
friendly, yes, no, a little, a lot	prietenos, da, nu, puţin, mult
small/smaller/smallest	mic/mai mic/cel mai mic
big/bigger/biggest	mare/mai mare/cel mai mare
bad/worse/worst	rău/mai rău/foarte rău
good/better/best	bine/mai bine/cel mai bine

Numbers	**Numere**
one, two, three, four, five, six, seven	unu, doi, trei, patru, cince, şase, şapte
eight, nine, ten, eleven, twelve, thirteen	opt, nouă, zece, unsprezece, doisprezece, treisprezece

fourteen, fifteen, sixteen, seventeen	paisprezece, cincisprezece, şaisprezece, şaptisprezece
eighteen, nineteen, twenty, twenty-one	optisprezece, nouăsprezece, douăzeci,douăzeci şi unu
thirty, forty, fifty, sixty, seventy, eighty	treizeci, patruzeci, cincizeci, şaizeci,şaptezeci, optzeci
ninety, one hundred, one thousand	nouăzeci, o sută, o mie

Wildlife

Bear, Fox, Stoat, Wolf, Wild Boar	Urs, Vulpe, Hermelina, Lup, Mistreţ
Roe Deer, Red Deer, Squirrel, Chamoix	Căprior, Cerb, Veveriţă, Capra neagră
Hare, Frog, Toad, Stork, Eagle, Lizard	Iepure, Broasca, Barza, Acvila, Şopârla
Tortoise, Crow, Raven, Woodpecker	Testoasă, Cioară, Corb, Ciocănitoare
Oak, Beech, Larch, Birch, Rowan, Spruce	Stejar, Fag, Zada, Mesteacăn, Scoruşa, Molid
Fir, Firs, Grass, Dwarf Pine, Alder	Brad, Brazi, Iarbă, Jnepen, Arin

APPENDIX C: *Select Bibliography*

Guidebooks

Dan Richardson and Tim Burford, *The Rough Guide to Romania*, Rough Guides Ltd. ISBN 1-85828-0305-1. £10.99. In common with the other Rough Guides, this packs a lot of valid information between its covers and has a definite bias towards the traveller who wishes to discover the remoter regions as well as the cities – altogether recommended. The second edition is a notable improvement on the first. For the first time it is now illustrated; there is a very good bibliography. There are frequent mentions in the text of walks to be made.

Nicola Williams, *Romania and Moldova*, Lonely Planet. ISBN 0-86442-329-2. £10.99. Generally up to Lonely Planet's high standard – commendable in the amount of research that has been carried out, including ground-breaking work in Moldova. A few errors, but nonetheless recommended.

Caroline Juler, *Romania, The Blue Guide*, A&C Black ISBN 0-7136-4096-0 £15.99. This, the most recent of the current crop of guides, has an emphasis on history and culture. It packs a lot of information in; since it is scant on information about the mountains, it is an ideal complement to this book. Recommended. (In USA published by WW Norton and Co Inc., 500 Fifth Ave., NY 10110 ISBN 0-393-32015-4.)

James Roberts, *Romania – A Birdwatching and Wildlife Guide*, Burton Expeditions. ISBN 0-9513513-6-2 £22. Available from NHBS Ltd, 2–3 Wills Road, Totnes, Devon TQ9 5XN e-mail: nhbs@nhbs.co.uk Their website is www.nhbs.com Detailed information on the wildlife and ecology of the mountain areas is combined with a wealth of information on where to go birdwatching. Those interested in mountain flora will find a useful appendix, also on the large mammals. Discount, post-free copies are available from 4 Vineys Yard, Bruton, Somerset, BA10 0EU, Tel 01749 813704, e-mail jameselena@netgates.co.uk.

Lydle Brinkle, *Romania*, Hippocrene Books, New York. ISBN 0-902726-52-8. Available in the UK, £7.95. A depressingly poor book with much of its text seemingly reproducing communist-era tourist-office puff – explaining for example without any humour intended that at Poiana Brașov 'treatments exist for ... physical and intellectual overexertion'(!). Certainly none of the latter can have been suffered by Mr Brinkle in writing this book.

Travel autobiography

Sacheverell and Edith Sitwell, *Roumanian Journey*, Oxford University Press (orig. Batsford 1938). ISBN 0-19-282884. £5.99. An aristocratic foody's account of travels in the country in 1938. Delightfully entertaining and informative – very highly recommended.

Patrick Leigh Fermor, *Between the Woods and the Water*. Penguin. ISBN 0-14-009430-X. £4.95. This is his sequel to the brilliant *A Time of Gifts*. Starting in 1933 the author aged 19 set off from the Hook of Holland to walk to Istanbul. His accounts are superb. The writing has the unique quality of combining the enthusiasm and fire of his youthful experiences with an older man's knowledge of all aspects of the history of the regions he travelled through. It is a portrait of aristocratic, pre-war Romania, with a definite pro-Hungarian bias, as many of the families he stayed with in Transylvania were Hungarian. For this reason beware of enthusing about it too much to Romanians – nevertheless it is a superb account and very highly recommended, not only because his travels in Romania, in common with the research for this book, were on foot!

Leslie Gardiner, *Curtain Calls*, Duckworth. Now out of print but obtainable in libraries. An account of travels in Albania and Bulgaria, as well as Romania. A perceptive and readable account of the region – well worth searching for.

Georgina Harding, *In Another Europe*, Stoughton. An account of one woman's solo cycle ride across the region. She visited some unattractive regions of Romania at the nadir of conditions in the country under Ceaușescu – rather off-putting.

Dervla Murphy, *Transylvania and Beyond*, John Murray, 1992. ISBN 0-7195-5028-9. £16.95. An immensely perceptive account of travelling disasters at the time when the country was at its lowest possible ebb in fortunes. You will certainly find Romania a less tragic country than is portrayed; highly recommended as a read after a first visit. Some good insight into the behaviour of Ion Iliescu, the post-revolution president, re-elected to office in November 2000.

Anne Applebaum, *Between East and West*, Papermac/Macmillan, 1995. ISBN 0-333-64169-8. An account of post-revolutionary travels across areas of eastern Europe that have seen their borders change this century – regions inhabited by Poles, Germans, Lithuanians, Russians, Byelorussians, Ukrainians, Moldavians and Russians. A good account of contact with the locals in Cernauti, now in Ukraine, and in the republic of Moldova.

Sophie Thurnham, *Sophie's Journey*, Warner, 1994. ISBN 0-7515-1006-8. £6.99. The account of an MP's daughter and her involvement with a children's home and subsequently a home for adults with 'learning difficulties' in northern Moldavia. An account of encountering the worst of Romanian corruption and ignorance and sheer wrong-headedness and trying to succeed in improving patients' well-being despite them. No more a balanced view of Romania than if a Romanian had written a narrative of life in one of the worst of Britain's inner cities among a community of drug-addicts and criminals. Recommended nevertheless – but perhaps after a first visit to Romania.

Claudio Magris, *Danube – A Sentimental Journey from the Source to the Black Sea*, Collins Harvill (8 Grafton Street, London W1). ISBN 0-00-271155-9. Highly recommended. The author, a Germanophile Italian professor, manages to deliver central and eastern European culture in a highly readable way, using a journey along his beloved river as the means. What a pity that from the Yugoslavian border to Ruse he travels on the southern, Bulgarian bank, not the Romanian. One tenth of this book is about Romania – the value of the book lies in its placing of Romanian history in the context of the country's neighbours to the west.

Biography

Hannah Pakula, *Queen of Roumania*, Eland Books (53 Eland Road, London SW11 5JX) (Hippocrene in USA). ISBN 0-907871-91-7. £9.95. Originally published by Weidenfeld as *The Last Romantic*, this is a worthy biography of Queen Marie of Romania, the very popular British-born queen – a woman who changed the map of Europe. It is also useful in explaining Romanian history in the first half of the twentieth century, still relevant since Marie's grandson, the exiled King Mihai, is alive and well in Switzerland.

Wildlife

Richard Mabey, *Food for Free*, HarperCollins £9.99. ISBN 0-00-219865-7. In print since 1972; a ground-breaking work, laying out knowledge that all our ancestors had at their fingertips. Not entirely a red herring here; a read of this excellent pocket-sized book could make all the difference to your time in the Carpathians, by explaining what there is to eat growing wild. Highly recommended

Christopher Grey-Wilson and Marjorie Blamey, *The Alpine Flowers of Britain and Europe*, Collins. ISBN 0-00-220017-1. £12.99. This is quite excellent, and as far as I know the second edition (1995) is the only flower guide that covers Romania. Ignore its errors, such as a map of Europe's mountains without the Carpathians!

Guido Moggi, *The MacDonald Encyclopaedia of Alpine Flowers*. ISBN 0-356-10571-7. Originally in Italian, this covers alpine flowers of Asia as well as Europe. It is well illustrated with coloured photographs, just the right size for a daypack, but a little on the big side to be carried in the pocket.

For a more comprehensive list of books on wildlife covering the region, see the Bibliography of my book Romania – A Birdwatching and Wildlife. Guide.

Novels

Since Romania is such an unknown country, much can be learnt from novels set in the country, by local writers or foreigners.

Bram Stoker, *Dracula*, first published 1897, and in various imprints ever since. Notwithstanding the fact that the author never went near Transylvania, no one can visit Romania without reading this. A number of publishers periodically bring it out – make sure you buy a version that is complete and unabridged. An example is that published in 1993 by Wordsworth Classics (8B East Street, Ware, Herts SG12 9HU). ISBN 1-85236-086-X. £1.50.

Olivia Manning, *The Balkan Trilogy*, Penguin. ISBN 0-14-008296-4. The author lived in Bucharest during the early part of the Second World War and her experiences provide the background for her work. The first of the trilogy, *The Great Fortune*, is the one set in Bucharest – a portrayal of life in a well-defined social circle in the city at the time. The trilogy was filmed by the BBC.

Reference

Ilie Fratu, Andrei Beleaua, Octavian Fratu, *Pe Custurile Făgărașene*, Editura Pentru Turism, Bucharest, 1991. ISBN 973-48-0021-3. The definitive walker's guide to the Făgărăș, so good that it is useful even to the non Romanian-speaking walker, with its maps, diagrams and monotone photographs.

Nae Popescu, *Munții Retezat*, Editura Stadion, Bucharest 1973. Excellent (though now out-dated) guide, with one-colour sketch maps of the higher parts and monochrome photographs.

Walter Kargel, *Drumuri spre Culmi – Trasee alpine în Carpați*, Editura Sport Turism, Bucharest, 1988. The definitive guide to climbing routes in Romania.

Valeria Velcea, *Munții Nostri: Bucegi*, Editura Pentru Turism, Bucharest, 1974. A small staple-bound book with details of the geology and topography of the Bucegi, as well as walking routes. Useful diagrams and sketch maps.

Alexandru Brăduț Șerban, *Singurătatea Verticalelor*, Editura pentru Turism, Bucharest 1990. ISBN 973-48-0008-6. Autobiography of a climber who died young – useful climbing route diagrams.

Constantin Rusu, Ion Talaba, Gheorghe Lupascu, *Munttii Ciucului*, Ghid Turistic Abeona, 1992. ISBN 973-48-0082-5. Contains a passable map of the Ciucului – which are not the most spectacular of the Carpathians.

Ion Mac, Budai Csaba, *Munții Oas – Gutîi–Țibleș*, Abeona, 1992. ISBN 973-48-0000-0. Useful for the western end of the Maramureș area with a good map.

Mihial Gabriel Albota, *Munții Ceahlău*, Abeona, 1992. ISBN 973-48-0018-3. Contains a good map – a good guide.

Mention should be made of the *Munții Carpați* journal, published monthly by Concept Ltd. – a petrochemical company! This is aimed at hikers (less emphasis on climbing per se) and specialises in informative articles about the Romanian Carpathians, often grouping articles from several different writers on one mountain region. Well laid out and printed, in A5 format, every issue seems reproduce a good map of a particular area; there are occasional articles on Romanian expeditions overseas – eg. Caucasus, Himalayas, also on flora and fauna in the Carpathians. Well worth picking up a copy of the current issue, even if your ability to understand Romanian is limited. Usually on sale in gear shops in Bucharest – eg. Himalaya.

The Munții Noștrii Series

In the 1970s and 1980s the Editura Sport-Turism office in Bucharest produced a series of absolutely excellent small paperback guidebooks on every mountain and hill range in Romania – down to the modest Măcin ridge in Dobrogea. With walking instructions and information on geology, wildlife and more, each little book had its own map. My own collection is highly prized and has taken much effort and time to amass. Now long out of print, they are sadly missed by mountain walkers and what has appeared since the revolution is mostly nowhere near as good, though is printed on better paper.

Titles consulted during research (chiefly for their maps) were
Valentin Bălăceanu, Hedda Cristea, *Munții Făgărașului*, 1984
Nicolae Popescu, Dănuț Călin, *Masivul Cozia*, 1987
Iuliu Buta, Ana Aurelia Buta, *Munții Rodnei*, 1979
Rodica Maria Niculescu, *Masivul Ciucaș*, 1977
Florin Roman, *Munții Vrancei*, 1989
Nae Popescu, *Masivul Păring*, 1986
Mircea Buza, Simona Fesci, *Munții Cindrel*, 1983
Emilian Cristea, *Masivul Hășmaș*, 1978

One that has appeared since the revolution, in the same fine format is

Gheorghe Măhăra, Ion Popescu-Argeșel, *Munții Trăscău*, Editura Imprimeriei de Vest, Oradea, 1993, ISBN 973-96303-1-6

Maps

Sheet Maps of Romania

Three good sheet maps of the country are detailed below, in descending order of quality – though there is little to choose between the first three. The first two sheets cover Moldova in the same scale; the third does not.

1) the RV Verlag 1:800,000 sheet, published in Britain in the GeoCenter Euro-Map series, in a red cover, ISBN 3-575-33228-2, £4.99. This sheet has several key advantages; for example it shows the German names of the settlements in Transylvania (but not the Hungarian names) and nature reserves are well shown and highlighted. Now on sale in bookshops in Bucharest and other large cities for less than it costs in western Europe.

2) the Karpátia 1:700,000 map, published in UK by Freytag & Berndt, ISBN 3-85084-334-3, £6.95. This is the most comprehensive sheet map of the country, showing a good number of villages omitted by the RV Verlag sheet, but omitting nature reserves and noteworthy natural features such as caves and gorges (and see the advantages of the RV sheet above).

3) the Ravenstein Verlag 1:750,000 map, ISBN 90-6736-101-1, published in a red and blue cover in the Geocart World Travel Maps series. Similar to the RV Verlag in that it is very good in showing nature reserves and natural features.

4) the ADAC (German Automobile Club) 1:500,000 map, ISBN 3-87003-5374, £6.95, DM12.80. This is much the biggest sheet map, at a larger scale than the others – in fact it is cumbersome and impossible to re-fold in a vehicle. It has less information than the other two maps and cannot be recommended.

Romania – Atlas Turistic Rutier, ISBN 973-96135-1-9. The largest scale mapping available of Romania and extremely useful in that it shows woodland areas and a great number of villages omitted by the smaller-scale sheet maps. However many villages that sprawl over several kilometres are shown as mere dots and there are some areas where the roads are not accurately shown. If there is a discrepancy between any of the sheet maps above and this road atlas, place your reliance on the smaller-scale sheet map. It is usually available from Stanfords in London.

Walking Maps of the Mountain areas

Walking maps of Romania come in a variety of strange scales, though usually around 1:50,000.

Bucegi – you are usually assured of finding a map of the Bucegi on sale in Sinaia and often in Buşteni and Predeal as well. The best and newest is the Amco sheet, in a red cover. Another good sheet is the green-covereed CNTT Harta Ecotouristică sheet, issued in 1996.

Postăvarul and Piatra Mare – now out of print is the excellent pale green Editura Sport-Turism sheet, in the *hărţi turistice montae 'Carpaţi'* series.

Piatra Craiului – this small range is now covered by two sheets, north and south, from Editura Ecran in Braşov. The old Abeona sheet is preferable.

Apuseni – the limited area around Padiş is covered by the excellent 1:30,000 DiMAP sheet, which obviously has a Hungarian connection. Issued 1998, ISBN 963 03 5037 8. This is of Ordnance Survey quality – it even has a grid! Paths in gorges are shown in greater detail.

Research for this book was carried out using a large number of old map sheets bought second-hand, now long out of print. These were published by the old state-run Editure pentru Turism, taken over since the revolution by Abeona. New maps regularly appear, of varying quality.

The two best retail outlets for maps in Britain are:

Stanfords, 12–14 Long Acre, London WC2E 9LP, Tel 020 7836 1321, Fax 020 7836 0189. Their website is www.stanfords.co.uk

The Map Shop, 15 High Street, Upton upon Severn, Worcestershire WR8 0HJ Tel 01684 593146, Fax 01684 594559, E-mail themapshop@btinternet.com. Their website is www.themapshop.co.uk

APPENDIX D:
Ski Resorts – technical information

Local skiers maintain that their colour-coding is a degree less flattering than you will find in the Alps – that many runs that are classed as black runs in the Alps would be graded as being one stage easier in Romania.

Name of slope	length in metres	drop in metres	colour
Sinaia			
Carp *(Virful Furnica – Cota 1400)*	2500	585	black
Papagal *(Tirle – Telescaun)*	450	150	black
Vânturiș *(Virful cu Dor – Cota 1400)*	2350	560	red
Turistică *(Cota 1400 – Sinaia town)*	2800	450	black
Drumul Vechi – Cota 1300	300	60	white
Poiana Florilor	250	50	white
Piramida *(Virful cu Dor – Furnica)*	300	75	red
Dorului *(Virful cu Dor – Valea Dorului Cabana)*	600	150	red
Fața Dorului *(Furnica – Valea Dorului)*	1180	210	red
Babele	300	60	white
Predeal			
Subteleferic	1200	350	black
Subteleferic variant	600	110	black
Clăbucet	2400	400	red
Varianta Teleschi	600	90	red
Varianta Clăbucet	700	90	red
Clăbucet Plecare	200	50	red
Gârbova	900	180	red

Poiana Brașov

Lupului (The Wolf)	2860	775	black
Subteleferic	1000	280	black
Sulinar	2440	645	red
Kanzel	350	104	red
Ruia	540	194	red
Slalom-Poiana	450	170	red
Drumul Roșu (The red road)	3820	540	white

Păltiniș

Oncești	1660	240
Valea Dăneasa	500	140

Semenic

Semenic	350	42
Goznuța	300	54
Slalom	520	180

APPENDIX E
Mountain Rescue

Much as in Britain, mountain rescue ('Salvamont') is in the hands of local climbers and hikers who train regularly in rescue techniques. If you do need to reach them when up in the mountains, the nearest cabana is your best first point of contact. Most Salvamont teams in the more frequented areas now have mobile telephones; details of these are posted on the walls of many cabanas. General information about Salvamont services can be obtained from the town hall of towns in mountain areas.

The Bucegi
Salvamont Buşteni, Str. Mihai Eminescu, Tel 0244 32 06 71. Also can be contacted inside the town hall (primărie), adjacent to the post office on the main street (B-dul Libertății 91), Tel 0244 32 07 50, 32 00 48, 32 08 35.
Salvamont Sinaia, Platoul Bucegi, Sinaia, Tel 0244 32 10 05. Located adjacent to the middle cable-car station, Cota 1400. In town they can be contacted inside the town hall (primărie) on the main street opposite the Hotel Montana (Tel 0244 31 31 31).
See also Salvamont Predeal, below.

The Mountains around Braşov
Salvamont Braşov, Tel 0268 18 61 76
Salvamont Predeal, Str. Mihail Săulescu 2, Predeal, Tel 0268 45 62 69, 0268 45 63 32, 0268 45 62 37

The Piatra Craiului and Iezer-Păpuşa Massifs
Salvamont Zărneşti, adjacent Cabana Plaiul Foii (see Appendix A), Tel 0268 22 08 10

The Făgăraş Chain
Salvamont Sibiu, Str. Nicolae Bălcescu 9, Sibiu, Tel 0269 21 64 77

From the Olt to the Jiu
See Sibiu above

The Retezat
Salvamont Hunedoara, B-dul Libertății 17, Hunedoara, Tel/Fax 0254 71 25 43
Salvamont Petroşani, Str. 1 Decembrie 1918 nr. 93, Petroşani, Tel 0254 54 12 20, Fax 54 59 03
The base at Cabana Pietrele is usually manned in summer.

The Mountains of Banat
Salvamont Caransebeş, Str. Traian Doda 6, Caransebeş, Tel 0255 51 10 43, Fax 51 51 57

The Apuseni Mountains
Salvamont Alba Iulia, Str. Tudor Vladimirescu 32, Alba Iulia, Tel 0258 81 13 47

APPENDIX F:
Useful names and addresses

United Kingdom

The Romanian Embassy, Arundel House, 4 Palace Green, London W8 4QD, Tel 0207 937 9667, Fax 0207 937 8069. The e-mail address is visa@roemb.demon.co.uk. For visa information by telephone, call 09001 880 828 (60p per minute).The consular section is open 1000–1200, Monday to Friday.

The Romanian National Tourist Office, 17 Nottingham Street, London W1M 3RD. Tel. 020 7224 3692, Fax 020 7487 2913. (The office is closed on Wednesdays, and sometimes on other days as well.)

Eurolines in London, Tel. 0207 730 8235, or their Luton office, 01582 404 511, www.eurolines.co.uk

The British Trust for Conservation Volunteers, 36 St Mary's St, Wallingford, Oxon OX10 0EU. Tel 01491 39766. As well as organising 'Acorn Camp'-type volunteer working party holidays in Britain, their European programme extends to Romania.

The Long Distance Paths Advisory Service, 11 Cotswold Court, Sandy Lane, Chester CH3 5UZ supplies a map of European International 'E-route' footpaths. It is run by Peter Robins.

United States

Embassy of the Republic of Romania, 1697 Twenty-third St. NW, Washington DC 20008. Tel (202) 232 4747, Consular Section (202) 232 4748

The Romanian National Tourist Office, 573 Third Avenue, New York City, NY 10016. Tel (212) 697 6971

The Romanian Library, 200 E. 38th St., New York, NY 10016. Tel (212) 687 0180

Australia

Embassy of the Republic of Romania, 333 Old South Head Road, Bondi, Sydney. Tel (02) 365 015 or 305 718

Romania

The Romanian postal service has improved since the revolution. In 2000 post from Bucharest was taking between three and six days to reach Britain. Allow rather longer if in the provinces and about twice as long for mail sent into Romania to a Poste Restante address. If writing home to Britain from Romania, write 'Marea Britanie' (Great Britain), at the bottom of the address, or if you prefer, 'Anglia'. USA is 'SUA'; Australia is the same as in English.

Embassies in Bucharest

Office to obtain a visa extension: Strada Nicolae Iorga 7, Bucharest.

The following Bucharest numbers are correct if dialling from within Bucharest:

British Embassy and British Embassy Public Library, Str. Jules Michelet 24, 70154 Bucharest. Tel 312 03 05

American Embassy, Str Snagov 26, Bucharest. Tel 210 40 42

Canadian Embassy, Str. Nicolae Iorga 36, Bucharest. Tel 222 98 45

American Library in Romania, Str. Alexandru Sahia 5–7, Bucharest.

Airline offices in Bucharest

Tarom – information, reservations and sales
Str. Brezoianu 10, Tel 615 04 99, 613 42 95, 615 27 47
Str. Buzești, Tel 659 41 25, 659 41 85

Otopeni airport flight information. Tel 212 01 38, 212 01 42

Baneasa domestic airport flight information. Tel 633 00 30

British Airways, B-dul Regina Elisabeta 3 (Piața Universității), Tel 303 22 22, Fax 303 22 11. Office at Otopeni airport – Tel 204 20 01, 204 20 02

Lufthansa, Bulevard Magheru 18, Bucharest. Tel 312 95 59, Fax 312 02 11, lufthansa@softnet.ro

Air France, Bulevard Balcescu 35, Bucharest. Tel 312 00 86, Fax 312 23 95. Office at Otopeni airport – Tel 201 49 87

Austrian Airlines, Bulevard Bălcescu 7, Bucharest. Tel 614 12 21
in Timișoara: Hotel Internațional, Bulevard C. D. Loga 44. Tel 056 19 03 20

Swissair, Bulevard General Magheru 18. Tel 312 02 38, Fax 312 02 40

KLM, Bulevard General Magheru 41. Tel 312 01 49

Information in Bucharest

Librarie Dacia, Calea Victoriei (adjacent Cretzulescu Church), as above.

National Centre for the Guidance of Folk Creation, Str. Tache Ionescu 25, Sector 1, Cod 70166, Bucharest. Tel 659 70 17. For information on village festivals.

Clubul Alpin Român, Str. Gladiolelor 1 Ap 14B, Bucharest. Tel 614 82 17.

Tour operators who run mountain walking holidays in Romania

Kudu Travel, Woodford Mill, Middle Woodford, Salisbury, Wiltshire SP4 6NW. Tel/Fax 01722 782982, Email: kuduinfo@kudutravel.com, web: www.kudutravel.com

Explore Worldwide, 1 Frederick Street, Altershot, Hants G11 1LQ. Brochure request 01252 344161, dossiers and further information 01252 319448, Email: info@exploreworldwide.com, web: www. exploreworldwide.com (see Chapter One)

Exodus, 9 Weir Road, London SW12 0LT. Tel 020 8673 0859 (for brochure or dossier), 020 8675 5550, Fax 020 8673 0779, Email: sales@exodustravels.co.uk, website: www.exodustravels.co.uk. Exodus operate a tent-based walking tour across the Bucegi, Iezer and Făgăraş. I am bound to point out that, based in tents, isolated in the forest and even eating some food exported from UK, you are perhaps experiencing more an international Exodus package than sampling the Romanian scene. However, they have good leaders, though you may not get a Romanian specialist.

APPENDIX G:
Romania's 8000ft (2438m) summits

1. Moldoveanu 8346ft (2544m) ....Făgăraş
2. Negoiu 8316ft (2535m) ....Făgăraş
3. Vistea Mare 8290ft (2527m) ....Făgăraş
4. Lespezi 8274ft (2522m) ....Făgăraş
5. Parâng Mare 8264ft (2519m) ....Parâng
6. Peleaga 8232ft (2509m) ....Retezat
7. Păpuşa 8229ft (2508m) ....Retezat
8. Vânatoarea lui Buteanu 8225ft (2507m) ....Făgăraş
9. Omu 8217ft (2505m) ....Bucegi
10. Cornul Călţunului 8217ft (2505m) ....Făgăraş
11. Bucura 8212ft (2503m) ....Retezat
12. Dara 8202ft (2500m) ....Făgăraş
13. Coştila 8195ft (2498m) ....Bucegi
14. Scărişoară 8186ft (2495m) ....Făgăraş
15. Capra Neagră 8182ft (2494m) ....Făgăraş
16. Bucşoiu 8176ft (2492m) ....Bucegi
17. Scărişoara Mare 8166ft (2489m) ....Făgăraş
18. Retezat 8142ft (2482m) ....Retezat
19. Dintre Strungi 8123ft (2476m) ....Făgăraş
20. Urlea 8113ft (2473m) ....Făgăraş
21. Găvanele 8110ft (2472m) ....Bucegi
22. Scărişoara Mică 8110ft (2472m) ....Făgăraş
23. Gălăşescu Mare 8104ft (2470m) ....Făgăraş
24. Arpaşu Mare 8097ft (2468m) ....Făgăraş
25. Mircii 8093ft (2467m) ....Făgăraş
26. Podragu 8077ft (2462m) ....Făgăraş
27. Arpaşu Mic 8071ft (2460m) ....Făgăraş
28. Custura 8061ft (2457lm) ....Retezat
29. Gălbenele 8058ft (2456m) ....Făgăraş
30. Fundu Bândei 8038ft (2450m) ....Făgăraş
31. Muşeteica 8031ft (2448m) ....Făgăraş
32. Văiuga 8015ft (2443m) ....Făgăraş
33. Piculata 8002ft (2439m) ....Făgăraş

APPENDIX H:
Flowers and Wildlife of the Romanian Mountains

Romania's part of the Carpathian chain – the greater part of the whole range – represents a vast treasure-house of European wildlife whose value is little appreciated outside the country. The extent of the forests and the fact that they have been so little damaged has resulted in an extensive belt of habitat that has disappeared elsewhere in Europe. More complete information on the wildlife of the mountains is offered my book *Romania – A Birdwatching and Wildlife Guide* (see Bibliography).

Mammals

As valuable as other forms of wildlife are, it is the mammals of Romania's mountain forests that are its most remarkable treasure. A substantial fraction – between one third and two thirds of Europe's population of its three large carnivore species are in Romania; these are **Brown Bear** *Ursus arctos*, **Wolf** *Canis lupus* and **Lynx** *Lynx lynx*. Brown Bear is the only one of these that you have much chance of seeing, owing to its size, the large number of them (estimated as being between five and six thousand) and relatively bold habits, even occasionally appearing in daylight. Every party that I have promised to show bears to have duly seen them. At one site near Sinaia I counted twenty-eight with a spotlight at once, late one night in September 1999. Most cabanas that are in forests or adjacent to the them have visits have at least occasional from bears to their rubbish. Some individuals even enter the outskirts of the city of Braşov and can be seen under streetlights. I have once received a threat gesture from a female bear with cubs in Braşov, whilst working with a documentary film team in the dead of night. People are killed by bears in Romania, at a rate of a handful or less per year. I have heard of incidents of bears approaching tents for food but I have never heard of a camping hiker being killed by a bear and I believe this has never happened. Human deaths have been of locals defending their livestock. Almost all the research for this book has been done solo, sleeping in a tent, I continue to explore Romania's mountains in this way.

Whilst there is an extremely slim threat from bears, there is none at all from the population of wolves, which are shy in the extreme and largely confined to forest areas, though they do hunt and scavenge above the tree line. Principal prey species are Red and Roe Deer, also Chamoix; wolves also scavenge and are inveterate raiders of sheep-pens, just as bears are. Lynx are rare, even endangered, confined to high craggy areas and specialising in preying on chamois; they occur in the Făgăraş, Retezat, Piatra Craiului and Rodna massifs.

Apart from carnivores, the mammals that might be encountered when walking are **Chamoix** *Rupicapra rupicapra* in Alpine areas, though down in forests in winter. Chamoix are in the Rodna, Ciucaş, Apuseni, Făgăraş, Retezat, around Bicaz Gorge, in the Piatra Craiului and the Bucegi (a population here of 100+). The other quintessential high-mountain mammal is the Badger-sized **Alpine Marmot** *Marmota marmota*, found in the Făgăraş, Retezat and Rodna and usually first located by its yelping alarm call given by a sentinel to one of its colonies. **Brown Hare** *Lepus capensis* can occasionally be seen on high grassy areas, though they seem to be more nocturnal than in Britain; there is a remarkable population on the Bucegi plateau that has taken over the ecological niche of the Mountain Hare, sheltering in belts of dwarf pine for the winter. Grassy mountain moorland is of course home to a number of small rodent species – **Snow Vole** *Microtys* is widspread, **Tatra Vole** *Microtus tatricus* restricted to the Rodna, **Common Pine Vole** *Microtys subterraneus* is widespread up to about 2400m. **Bank Vole** *Clethrionomys glareolus* is very common in mountain forests, as are the two woodland mouse species – **Wood Mouse** *Apodemus sylvaticus* and **Yellow-necked Mouse** *Apodemus flavicollis*. **Red Squirrel** *Sciurus vulgaris* is fairly easily seen, especially around Sinaia; most have much darker fur than British Red Squirrels. **Wild Boar** *Sus scrofa* occur fairly commonly in hill forests though are very shy and are certainly not dangerous to walkers. Romania has two species of Polecat occuring in inland forest areas and a third near the coast, but these are shy indeed, as is **Pine Marten** *Martes martes*, whose droppings can fairly regularly be found on rocks on forest paths. **Fox** *Vulpes vulpes* is common in the mountains, up to the highest areas, though my sightings above 8000ft on Omu may simply be due to visitor pressure here, leaving rich pickings that are attractive to foxes.

Birds

Since the goal of many walkers is the high tops, above the tree line, I consider that it is worth giving brief introduction to the commonly-found birds there, especially for the non-specialist walker. The commonest bird of the high mountains is Water Pipit (cf Meadow Pipits on British mountains), with its parachuting song-flight. A clear second in terms of population in elevated areas of short grass, especially with odd stones, is Wheatear or Northern Wheatear. Around high crags Black Redstarts are common and White Wagtails regularly nest near shepherds' huts. Whilst on high craggy areas you may find parties of large pale swifts whipping past you at tremendous speed with a merry chattering call; you have just been buzzed by part of a colony of Alpine Swifts – a very exciting bird from any point of view. Belts of dwarf pine have populations of Dunnocks in spring, also Crossbills and Chiffchaffs, especially in late summer. In comparison to the Alps and Pyrenees, the Carpathians can be considered to be richer in mammals but poorer in birds of prey, effectively with no vultures and Golden Eagle now rare (for details see below); sadly the only really common bird of prey high up is the Kestrel. Crows and Ravens are easy to tell apart in Romania – in the mountains and lowlands alike, for Romania's crow is the grey-bodied Hooded Crow. The tame little fat bird, slightly bigger than a sparrow, found around some high cabanas (especially at Bâlea Lac in the Făgăraș) is the Alpine Accentor, a bird found only in high mountains in the breeding season. Linnet is surprisingly common high in the mountains.

Here goes with the species-by-species survey of birds that have any real likelihood of being seen in the mountains; they are dealt with in the following text in taxonomic order (the same as the field guides). **Honey Buzzard** *Pernis apivorus* is arelatively common bird of prey in areas of deciduous forest on the flanks of the Carpathians, especially in Transylvania, Bucovina and Maramureș. **Griffon Vulture** *Gyps fulvus* used to breed in the Carpathians (and occasionally wanders back for example, in the Bucegi for most of the summer of 1998) and may even return as a breeder. **Short-toed Eagle** *Circaetus gallicus* breeds near Pietroasa and in other areas of the Apuseni, favouring the warmer dryer mountains of western Romania and especially the mountains of Banat. **Goshawk** *Accipiter gentilis* is fairly common in Carpathian forests and **Sparrowhawk** *Accipiter nisus* can often be seen soaring above wooded areas. **Buzzard** *Buteo buteo* is quite common, though not as frequently seen as in western Britain. The western Apuseni and Semenic areas seem likely for this species. **Golden Eagle** *Aquila chrysaetos* is thinly distributed in the Carpathians; a pair regularly breed in Turda gorge in the Apuseni, around Domogled in the Banat and I have seen the species in the Cindrel, the Bucegi and Făgăraș. **Kestrel** *Falco tinnunculus* is quite common up to the highest parts of the mountains. **Hobby** *Falco subbuteo* can be found in the mountains eg. Cindrel, especially on passage. **Peregrine** *Falco peregrinus* is regularly seen in high, rocky areas.

Hazelhen *Tetrastes bonasia*, though shy, can be found. I have flushed coveys on two occasions in forests in Bucovina, once between Sucevița and Putna and also on the Obcina Mare ridge. **Black Grouse** *Lyrurus tetrix* has declined drastically this century; my sole encounter was a distraction display of hen with chicks in the Lotru massif. It also occurs in the Cindrel and Rodna. **Capercaillie** *Tetrao urogallus* is widespread though very elusive in Carpathian forests. **Quail** *Coturnix coturnix* is frequently heard in the many hay meadows of the mountain valleys – to a surprisingly high altitude such as in Bucovina and Maramureș. **Dotterel** *Eudromias morinellus* breeds at the Iezerului Cindrelului Reserve in the Cindrel massif. I did not locate it when exploring there in 1995. **Common Sandpiper** *Tringa hypoleucos* can be found fairly commonly alongside streams in the forests, breeding, for example on the banks of the Prahova near Sinaia and in Nera Gorge. **Eagle Owl** *Bubo bubo* is a truly mountain species, favouring open forest with high crags; I encountered it in scattered conifer forest in Zănoaga Gorge in August 1993. **Pygmy Owl** *Glaucidium passerinum* occurs. **Little Owl** *Athene noctua* is common in mountain valleys, breeding in Bran, for example. **Tawny Owl** *Strix aluco* is relatively common in all of Romania's forest areas. **Ural Owl** *Strix uralensis* is found in the Carpathians, such as forests in the Prahova Valley. **Long-eared Owl** *Asio otus* is quite as common in mountain forests as it is in the lowland; one investigated me sleeping out on the tree line in my bivvy bag at around 1600m in the Apuseni. **Tengmalm's Owl** *Aegolius funereus* is shy and scarce, occuring only in Transylvania.

Alpine Swift *Apus melba* is very much a mountain bird, favouring limestone cliff areas. **Hoopoe** *Upupa epops* is a popular bird in Romanian mythology and is widespread throughout, occuring in high villages in summer.

As you might expect, the vast upland forests of the Carpathians are very rich in a number of species of Woodpecker. **Wryneck** *Jynx torquila* is quite common on the edge of deciduous forest. **Grey-headed Woodpecker** *Picus canus* is quite tame in deciduous woodland near settlements. **Green Woodpecker** *Picus viridis* can occasionally be seen on sheep-grazed turf near deciduous trees at lower levels. **Black Woodpecker** *Dryocopus martius* is quite widespread in mountain (and lowland) forests and regularly feeds above the tree line on anthills or rotten tree stumps in the forest. If you hear a strange loud, almost electronic one-note call, look out for this dramatic bird. **Great Spotted Woodpecker** *Dendrocopos major* is the commonest Woodpecker in all forest areas, especially coniferous. **Middle Spotted Woodpecker** *Dendrocopos medius* is known as the 'oak woodpecker' in Romanian and is therefore not found in forests at higher levels; it is quite common in lowland forest. **White-backed Woodpecker** *Dendrocopos leucotos* can be found on south-facing mountain slopes with beech trees and much dead and rotten wood – such as the Prahova valley or Dealul Codlea in Transylvania. **Lesser Spotted Woodpecker** *Dendrocopos minor* is proverbially shy but occurs. **Three-toed Woodpecker** *Picoides tridactylys* is called the 'mountain woodpecker' in Romanian and can be found in areas of dead spruce in the mountains eg Piatra Mare, Bucegi.

Wood Lark *Lullula arborea* is a true mountain bird, and is frequently encountered in alpine meadows as well as on the edge of lowland forest areas. **Shore Lark** *Eremophila alpestris* is a bird of high mountain regions and breeds in a number of areas – such as Iezer Cindrelului reserve and elsewhere; it certainly occurs in the Bucegi on passage and may breedi as well. **Red-rumped Swallow** *Hirundo daurica* may occur in the Semenic and other mountain areas with a Mediterranean type of habitat. **Tree Pipit** *Anthus trivialis* is very common around the tree line in the mountians, especially where the pines give way to extensive grassland, rather than crags. **Meadow Pipit** *Anthus pratensis* is scarce and not really an upland bird as it is in Britain. By contrast **Water Pipit** *Anthus spinoletta* is the commonest bird above the tree line in Romania, especially near dwarf pine around 1800m altitude. **Grey Wagtail** *Motacilla cinerea* ('mountain wagtail' in Romanian) is confined almost exclusively to mountain areas in Romania, where it is a summer visitor. **White Wagtail** *Motacilla alba* is widespread and common, nesting in shepherds' huts and feeding up to the highest summits such as Omu. **Dipper** *Cinclus cinclus* is along hill streams and can be seen around the tree-line in summer; it has a pronounced altitude migration. **Wren** *Troglodytes troglodytes* is widespread in all forest areas, but not nearly common as in British woods, due no doubt to the fact that it overwinters and large numbers die off during the eastern European freeze-ups. **Dunnock** *Prunella modularis* is widespread in areas of bush among hayfields and forest margins with a few breeding in areas of Dwarf Pine. **Alpine Accentor** *Prunella collaris* is relatively common and tame in the highest parts of the Transylvanian Alps and regularly feeds near cabanas, including Bâlea Lac, Făgăraş, and Bucegi. **Black Redstart** *Phoenicurus ochruros* is a very common mountain bird, nesting among crags and also in villages. The sweet and scratchy song being delivered from a rooftops or boulder is one of the sweetest and most characteristic sounds of the high Carpathians. **Redstart** *Phoenicurus phoenicurus* is common around villages in Carpathian valleys. **Whinchat** *Saxicola rubetra* is not as common a summer visitor as, for example, among the farming villages of eastern Poland, but can be found in areas of scrub in mountain valleys – eg. the Bârsa Mare valley, below Piatra Craiului. **Stonechat** *Saxicola torquata* is purely a summer visitor and widespread though not abundant – for example, in the Vâlcan massif. **Northern Wheatear** *Oenanthe oenanthe* ('Mountain Wheatear' in Romanian) is very common above the tree line in summer. **Ring Ouzel** *Turdus torquatus* is very common around the tree line in hill forests; it breeds in Sinaia. **Fieldfare** *Turdus pilaris* is the commonest breeding thrush near settlements in the hill areas. **Mistle Thrush** *Turdus viscivorus* is the commonest thrush around the tree line, where it is a partial migrant, sharing much the same habitat as Ring Ouzel.

Lesser Whitethroat *Sylvia curuca* is common around clearings in spruce forest, also the margins of hay meadows and forest, also villages. **Blackcap** *Sylvia atricapilla* is common in deciduous and mixed forests. **Wood Warbler** *Phylloscopus sibilatrix* is especially common in beech forests. **Chiffchaff** *Phylloscopus collybita* is abundant in and on the edge of forests and isolated stands of trees, preferring deciduous or mixed woods. **Willow Warbler** *Phylloscopus trochilus* is not common as it is in Britain and is confined as a breeding bird to the north – eg. the Rodna. **Goldcrest** *Regulus regulus* is more often located by its thin tinkling song in conifer and mixed forests than by sight – it is common in all areas. **Firecrest** *Regulus ignicapillus* also occurs. **Spotted Flycatcher** *Muscicapa striata* is common. Often overlooked, **Red-breasted Flycatcher** *Ficedula parva* is, to my mind, one of Romania's star birds and breeds in most areas of hill beech forest. **Collared Flycatcher** *Ficedula albicollis* occurs in beech forest. **Pied Flycatche**r can be found on passage in April on passage in lowland areas and breeds widely in forest areas. **Willow Tit** *Parus montanus* is common in the spruce forests of the Carpathians. **Crested Tit** *Parus cristatus* is widespread but difficult to see. **Coal Tit** is abundant in forest areas; **Blue Tit** *Parus caeruleus* and **Long-tailed Tit** *Aegithalos caudatus* are common in all areas of deciduous trees and shrubs; both tend to avoid the higher areas; **Great Tit** *Parus major* is abundant in all mixed and deciduous forest areas, as is **Nuthatch** *Sitta europea*. **Wallcreeper** *Tichodroma muraria* is one of the notable birds of the high Carpathians, where it is an altitudinal migrant; widespread though not abundant, among other locations it breeds in the Tătarului gorge and Jepii gully in the Bucegi, Zărnești gorge in the Piatra Craiului and in 1991 nested in a wall of Valea Caprei cabana in the Făgăraș; look for it on sun-warmed cliff-faces. **Treecreeper** *Certhia familiaris* is usually encountered in forests in hill and mountain areas. **Red-backed Shrike** *Lanius collurio* is common in woodland margin areas of the Carpathians, and especially in areas of hay meadows with bushes. **Jay** *Garrulus glandarius* is common in forest areas, though less so in conifers. **Magpie** *Pica pica* is abundant in the country, though largely avoids the higher areas. **Nutcracker** *Nucifraga caryocatactes* ('Pine Jay' in Romanian) is common in mountain spruce forest. **Hooded Crow** *Corvus corone cornix* is the most common crow in Romania; in the high mountains it is less common and is to an extent replaced by **Raven** *Corvus corax*, which is also found in lowland forest. **Tree Sparrow** *Passer montanus* is common, though (notwithstanding its Latin name) it ventures no higher in the mountains than the level of human habitation. **Chaffinch** *Fringilla coelebs* is abundant in all the forests of the Carpathians; the song differs slightly from that heard in Britain. It generally ends with a 'tchick' that can make you think there is a woodpecker nearby. **Brambling** *Fringilla montifringilla* and **Redpoll** *Carduelis flammea* are winter visitors, when they haunt the forests of the sub-Carpathians. **Serin** *Serinus serinus* breeds commonly in the highest settlements and in areas of forest margin (eg. breeding in Sinaia, Râșnov, Bran etc.). **Siskin** *Carduelis spinus* is exclusively a bird of the mountain forests, although it moves into lowlands in winter. It is locally common in the vast areas of spruce forest, especially in and near stands of alders near springs or streams. **Linnet** *Carduelis cannabina* is a true mountain bird, found in summer well above tree line. The archetypal bird of the Carpathian pine forests is the **Crossbill** *Loxia curvirostra*. Family parties of this species move above the tree line in late summer, inhabiting the extensive belts of Dwarf Pine *Pinus mugo*. **Bullfinch** *Pyrrrhula pyrrhula* is frequently seen in mixed forests up to the tree line. **Hawfinch** *Coccothraustes coccothraustes* is elusive but widespread, especially in deciduous forests with Hornbeam ('Carpen'). **Rock Bunting** *Emberiza cia* is rare and local, favouring mountains with a Mediterranean aspect – for example lower parts of the Apuseni and the Semenic.

Reptiles and Amphibians

There are several kinds of amphibians that you are likely to come across that are not found in Britain. The first is **Yellow-bellied Toad** *Bombina variegata*, a tiny grey creature with a warty back but a vivid salamander-pattern yellow and grey underside. They occur in pools, puddles and water-filled cart ruts up to the tree line and are easy to catch in the hand. However wash you hands after touching one as their skin secretes an irritant which if you later touch your eyes having touched the toad, will give you some irritation and inflamation. **Alpine Newt** *Triturus alpestris*, also with an orange underside, is common; there is also **Montandon's Newt** *Triturus montandoni* in the Eastern Carpathians. **Smooth Newt** *Triturus vulgaris* also occurs in hill areas, as does **Warty** (or **Great Crested**) **New**t *Triturus cristatus*. The commonest frog in mountain areas is the same as in England – **Common Frog** *Rana temporaris*; **Moor Frog** *Rana arvalis* also occurs in isolated areas. **Fire Salamander** *Salamandra salamandra* can often be seen at night or in the day after rain, out plodding slowly in search of slugs; with its vivid red and orange colouring it can scarcely be missed. The attractively-patterned **Green Toad** *Bufo viridis* has been found up to 1700m.

There are only three species of snake in the mountains. The first is **Common Vipe**r or **Adder** *Vipera berus*, found in hill forests below the beech areas. You have to be extremely careless or foolhardy to be in any danger of being bitten. **Grass Snake**s *Natrix natrix* are found higher up, but tend to be tied more to water. Around the Semenic area, and especially near Băile Herculane and Vârful Domogled is a population of **Nose-horned Viper** *Vipera ammodytes*, Europe's fastest-moving, most aggressive and most poisonous snake.

Flowers

The Carpathians of Romania offer one the best possible destinations for a mountain walking holiday for the lover of mountain flowers, with dense populations of a great number of species. In fact the blossoming of Romania's mountains can start as early as March, with crocuses spearing their way through the retreating snows of the alpine pastures below the forests. Colstfoot and snowdrops can be found, and relatively elevated sites in for example the Piatra Craiului, Hăşmaş and Postăvaru have *Daphne blagayana* and *Daphne mezerum* in bloom. May and June are the best time to combine good weather for walking and to see many of the flowers in bloom. With some of the Alpine flowers above the tree line blooms follow the springtime upwards retreat of the snow level by a matter of days.

Every bit as remarkable as the Alpine flowers are the flowers of the hay meadows in May and June; this is also the best time for forest flowers such as lungwort *Cardamine glanduligera* and *Waldsteinia ternata*. As you descend out of the woods, the path often takes you through the pasture where you trail your fingers through the delicate blooms, soon to be felled by the swish of the scythe. High summer is notable for great belts of Alpenrose or Dwarf Rhododendron *Rhododendron kotschyi* in bloom in many Alpine areas. Autumn, too is rich, with some fine displays of autumn crocuses. The bibliography at Appendix C lists two flower guides which should cover most species seen.

As one might expect from their location, the Romanian Carpathians have a number of species found in the Alps and others typical of the Balkans. Species typical of the latter range include *Bruckenthalia spiculifolia, Veronica baumgarteni, Silene lerchenfeldiana* and *Potentilla haynaldiana*. There are a number of endemics to the area, such as the Piatra Craiului Pink *Dianthus Callizonus, Saxifraga demissa, Aquilegia transsilvanica, Campanula carpatica, Lichnis nivalis*.

NOTES

NOTES

LISTING OF CICERONE GUIDES

BRITISH ISLES CHALLENGES, COLLECTIONS AND ACTIVITIES

The End to End Trail
The Mountains of England and Wales
1 Wales & 2 England
The National Trails
The Relative Hills of Britain
The Ridges of England, Wales and Ireland
The UK Trailwalker's Handbook
The UK's County Tops
Three Peaks, Ten Tors

MOUNTAIN LITERATURE

Unjustifiable Risk?

UK CYCLING

Border Country Cycle Routes
Cycling in the Hebrides
Cycling in the Peak District
Cycling the Pennine Bridleway
Mountain Biking in the Lake District
Mountain Biking in the Yorkshire Dales
Mountain Biking on the South Downs
The C2C Cycle Route
The End to End Cycle Route
The Lancashire Cycleway

SCOTLAND

Backpacker's Britain
Central and Southern Scottish Highlands
Northern Scotland
Ben Nevis and Glen Coe
Great Mountain Days in Scotland
North to the Cape
Not the West Highland Way
Scotland's Best Small Mountains
Scotland's Far West
Scotland's Mountain Ridges
Scrambles in Lochaber
The Ayrshire and Arran Coastal Paths
The Border Country
The Cape Wrath Trail
The Great Glen Way
The Isle of Mull
The Isle of Skye
The Pentland Hills
The Southern Upland Way
The Speyside Way
The West Highland Way
Walking Highland Perthshire
Walking in Scotland's Far North
Walking in the Angus Glens
Walking in the Cairngorms
Walking in the Ochils, Campsie Fells and Lomond Hills
Walking in Torridon
Walking Loch Lomond and the Trossachs
Walking on Harris and Lewis
Walking on Jura, Islay and Colonsay
Walking on Rum and the Small Isles
Walking on the Isle of Arran
Walking on the Orkney and Shetland Isles
Walking on Uist and Barra
Walking the Corbetts
1 South of the Great Glen
2 North of the Great Glen
Walking the Galloway Hills
Walking the Lowther Hills
Walking the Munros
1 Southern, Central and Western Highlands
2 Northern Highlands and the Cairngorms
Winter Climbs Ben Nevis and Glen Coe
Winter Climbs in the Cairngorms
World Mountain Ranges: Scotland

NORTHERN ENGLAND TRAILS

A Northern Coast to Coast Walk
Backpacker's Britain
Northern England
Hadrian's Wall Path
The Dales Way
The Pennine Way
The Spirit of Hadrian's Wall

NORTH EAST ENGLAND, YORKSHIRE DALES AND PENNINES

Great Mountain Days in the Pennines
Historic Walks in North Yorkshire
South Pennine Walks
St Oswald's Way and St Cuthbert's Way
The Cleveland Way and the Yorkshire Wolds Way
The North York Moors
The Reivers Way
The Teesdale Way
The Yorkshire Dales
North and East
South and West
Walking in County Durham
Walking in Northumberland
Walking in the North Pennines
Walks in Dales Country
Walks in the Yorkshire Dales
Walks on the North York Moors – Books 1 & 2

NORTH WEST ENGLAND AND THE ISLE OF MAN

Historic Walks in Cheshire
Isle of Man Coastal Path
The Isle of Man
The Lune Valley and Howgills
The Ribble Way
Walking in Cumbria's Eden Valley
Walking in Lancashire
Walking in the Forest of Bowland and Pendle
Walking on the West Pennine Moors
Walks in Lancashire Witch Country
Walks in Ribble Country
Walks in Silverdale and Arnside
Walks in the Forest of Bowland

LAKE DISTRICT

Coniston Copper Mines
Great Mountain Days in the Lake District
Lake District Winter Climbs
Lakeland Fellranger
The Central Fells
The Far-Eastern Fells
The Mid-Western Fells
The Near Eastern Fells
The Northern Fells
The North-Western Fells
The Southern Fells
The Western Fells
Roads and Tracks of the Lake District
Rocky Rambler's Wild Walks
Scrambles in the Lake District
North & South
Short Walks in Lakeland
1 South Lakeland
2 North Lakeland
3 West Lakeland
The Cumbria Coastal Way
The Cumbria Way and the Allerdale Ramble
Tour of the Lake District

DERBYSHIRE, PEAK DISTRICT AND MIDLANDS

High Peak Walks
Scrambles in the Dark Peak
The Star Family Walks
Walking in Derbyshire
White Peak Walks
The Northern Dales
The Southern Dales

SOUTHERN ENGLAND

A Walker's Guide to the Isle of Wight
Suffolk Coast & Heaths Walks
The Cotswold Way
The North Downs Way
The Peddars Way and Norfolk Coast Path
The Ridgeway National Trail
The South Downs Way
The South West Coast Path
The Thames Path
Walking in Berkshire
Walking in Kent
Walking in Sussex
Walking in the Isles of Scilly
Walking in the New Forest
Walking in the Thames Valley
Walking on Dartmoor
Walking on Guernsey
Walking on Jersey
Walking on the Isle of Wight
Walks in the South Downs National Park

WALES AND WELSH BORDERS

Backpacker's Britain – Wales
Glyndwr's Way
Great Mountain Days in Snowdonia
Hillwalking in Snowdonia
Hillwalking in Wales
Vols 1 & 2
Offa's Dyke Path
Ridges of Snowdonia
Scrambles in Snowdonia
The Ascent of Snowdon
Lleyn Peninsula Coastal Path
Pembrokeshire Coastal Path
The Shropshire Hills
The Wye Valley Walk
Walking in Pembrokeshire
Walking in the Forest of Dean
Walking in the South Wales Valleys
Walking on Gower
Walking on the Brecon Beacons
Welsh Winter Climbs

INTERNATIONAL CHALLENGES, COLLECTIONS AND ACTIVITIES

Canyoning
Europe's High Points
The Via Francigena (Canterbury to Rome): Part 1

EUROPEAN CYCLING
Cycle Touring in France
Cycle Touring in Ireland
Cycle Touring in Spain
Cycle Touring in Switzerland
Cycling in the French Alps
Cycling the Canal du Midi
Cycling the River Loire
The Danube Cycleway
The Grand Traverse of the Massif Central
The Rhine Cycle Route
The Way of St James

AFRICA
Climbing in the Moroccan Anti-Atlas
Kilimanjaro
Mountaineering in the Moroccan High Atlas
The High Atlas
Trekking in the Atlas Mountains
Walking in the Drakensberg

ALPS – CROSS-BORDER ROUTES
100 Hut Walks in the Alps
Across the Eastern Alps: E5
Alpine Points of VIew
Alpine Ski Mountaineering
1 Western Alps
2 Central and Eastern Alps
Chamonix to Zermatt
Snowshoeing
Tour of Mont Blanc
Tour of Monte Rosa
Tour of the Matterhorn
Trekking in the Alps
Walking in the Alps
Walks and Treks in the Maritime Alps

PYRENEES AND FRANCE/SPAIN CROSS-BORDER ROUTES
Rock Climbs in The Pyrenees
The GR10 Trail
The Mountains of Andorra
The Pyrenean Haute Route
The Pyrenees
The Way of St James
France & Spain
Through the Spanish Pyrenees: GR11
Walks and Climbs in the Pyrenees

AUSTRIA
The Adlerweg
Trekking in Austria's Hohe Tauern
Trekking in the Stubai Alps
Trekking in the Zillertal Alps
Walking in Austria

EASTERN EUROPE
The High Tatras
The Mountains of Romania
Walking in Bulgaria's National Parks
Walking in Hungary

FRANCE
Chamonix Mountain Adventures
Ecrins National Park
GR20: Corsica
Mont Blanc Walks
Mountain Adventures in the Maurienne
The Cathar Way
The GR5 Trail
The Robert Louis Stevenson Trail
Tour of the Oisans: The GR54
Tour of the Queyras
Tour of the Vanoise
Trekking in the Vosges and Jura
Vanoise Ski Touring
Walking in the Auvergne
Walking in the Cathar Region
Walking in the Cevennes
Walking in the Dordogne
Walking in the Haute Savoie North & South
Walking in the Languedoc
Walking in the Tarentaise and Beaufortain Alps
Walking on Corsica

GERMANY
Germany's Romantic Road
Walking in the Bavarian Alps
Walking in the Harz Mountains
Walking the River Rhine Trail

HIMALAYA
Annapurna
Bhutan: A Trekker's Guide
Everest: A Trekker's Guide
Garhwal and Kumaon: A Trekker's and Visitor's Guide
Kangchenjunga: A Trekker's Guide
Langtang with Gosainkund and Helambu: A Trekker's Guide
Manaslu: A Trekker's Guide
The Mount Kailash Trek
Trekking in Ladakh

ICELAND & GREENLAND
Trekking in Greenland
Walking and Trekking in Iceland

IRELAND
Irish Coastal Walks
The Irish Coast to Coast Walk
The Mountains of Ireland

ITALY
Gran Paradiso
Sibillini National Park
Stelvio National Park
Shorter Walks in the Dolomites
Through the Italian Alps
Trekking in the Apennines
Trekking in the Dolomites
Via Ferratas of the Italian Dolomites: Vols 1 & 2
Walking in Abruzzo
Walking in Sardinia
Walking in Sicily
Walking in the Central Italian Alps
Walking in the Dolomites
Walking in Tuscany
Walking on the Amalfi Coast
Walking the Italian Lakes

MEDITERRANEAN
Jordan – Walks, Treks, Caves, Climbs and Canyons
The Ala Dag
The High Mountains of Crete
The Mountains of Greece
Treks and Climbs in Wadi Rum, Jordan
Walking in Malta
Western Crete

NORTH AMERICA
British Columbia
The Grand Canyon
The John Muir Trail
The Pacific Crest Trail

SOUTH AMERICA
Aconcagua and the Southern Andes
Hiking and Biking Peru's Inca Trails
Torres del Paine

SCANDINAVIA
Walking in Norway

SLOVENIA, CROATIA AND MONTENEGRO
The Julian Alps of Slovenia
The Mountains of Montenegro
Trekking in Slovenia
Walking in Croatia
Walking in Slovenia: The Karavanke

SPAIN AND PORTUGAL
Costa Blanca: West
Mountain Walking in Southern Catalunya
The Mountains of Central Spain
The Northern Caminos
Trekking through Mallorca
Walking in Madeira
Walking in Mallorca
Walking in the Algarve
Walking in the Cordillera Cantabrica
Walking in the Sierra Nevada
Walking on La Gomera and El Hierro
Walking on La Palma
Walking on Tenerife
Walking the GR7 in Andalucia
Walks and Climbs in the Picos de Europa

SWITZERLAND
Alpine Pass Route
Canyoning in the Alps
Central Switzerland
The Bernese Alps
The Swiss Alps
Tour of the Jungfrau Region
Walking in the Valais
Walking in Ticino
Walks in the Engadine

TECHNIQUES
Geocaching in the UK
Indoor Climbing
Lightweight Camping
Map and Compass
Mountain Weather
Outdoor Photography
Polar Exploration
Rock Climbing
Sport Climbing
The Book of the Bivvy
The Hillwalker's Guide to Mountaineering
The Hillwalker's Manual

MINI GUIDES
Avalanche!
Navigating with a GPS
Navigation
Pocket First Aid and Wilderness Medicine
Snow